Study Guide to Accompany

BUSINESS
LAW
TODAY

Roger LeRoy Miller
Gaylord A. Jentz

Prepared by
Nancy L. Hart
Midland College, Texas

West Publishing Company
St. Paul   New York   Los Angeles   San Francisco

COPYRIGHT © 1988 by   WEST PUBLISHING CO.
50 W. Kellogg Boulevard
P.O. Box 64526
St. Paul, MN 55164-1003

ISBN 0-314-79308-9

Contents

iii

Introduction

This study guide is designed to serve as a supplement, not a
replacement for the main text. The outlines are drawn from my
teaching notes and will serve to highlight the main principles
in the text. There are three types of study questions at the
end of each chapter: fill-in the blank, true-false, and
multiple-choice. Some questions test your knowledge of facts;
others ask you to apply the rules you have learned.

ACKNOWLEDGMENTS

I wish to thank my students for their inspiration and
patience, and my family and friends for their support.

UNIT I
THE LEGAL ENVIRONMENT OF BUSINESS

Chapter 1   Law as a Contemporary Social Force

General Principles

Law is a set of rules which can be enforced by the government. These rules govern the relationships between individuals (private law) and between individuals and their government (public law). The rules come from cases, statutes, constitutions and administrative agencies. The government enforces the rules through court decisions.

Business law is the set of rules which governs commercial transactions. The Commerce Clause of the United States Constitution governs some aspects of business law but state law is the primary source. Because state laws may differ, the Uniform Commercial Code attempts to create a set of business rules which apply in every state.

Chapter Summary

I.   The Law and Social Forces--Law can be seen as a reaction to social forces; law changes when society changes. Others argue that law is the initiator of change and that it guides society. Business law is reactive; it responds to changes in society.

II.   Sources of Law

    A.   English Law--The law of the United States originated in England. The first set of laws was established by the king's court in 1066. Before that time, suits were settled by local custom. The king's court was an attempt to standardize the rules.

B.   <u>General</u>--Our law originates from four sources.

   (1)   <u>Common Law</u>--May also be called case law or judge-made law. Law is created when a judge makes a decision in a lawsuit. In a common law system, the judge looks for earlier cases or <u>precedent</u> (from the word "precede") which have similar facts and follows the rule of the earlier cases. This process is <u>stare decisis</u>. Stare decisis promotes fair decisions because people in similar circumstances will receive similar decisions. It is also faster and easier for the judge if he or she has guidelines to follow. The law is also more stable and predictable because of this adherence to past rules.

   (2)   <u>Constitutional Law</u>--The U.S. Constitution is the highest law in the country. Any other law which conflicts with its principles will be declared unconstitutional. State constitutions are the highest law within each state but are inferior to the U.S. Constitution.

   (3)   <u>Statutory Law (Legislation)</u>--Created by the U.S. Congress and state legislatures.

   (4)   <u>Administrative Law</u>--Created by administrative agencies. These agencies are created by the legislative or executive branches of government and usually deal with very specific subjects.

C.   <u>Commercial Law</u>--The four sources listed above are also sources of business or commercial law. However, because business tends to cross state lines, uniform or model laws are created by experts in the field. The model laws are proposed as legislation in each state and a state can adopt all, some, or none of the model law. The Uniform Commercial Code is an example of a uniform law.

III. <u>Classifications of Law</u>

A.   <u>Civil v. Criminal Law</u>--Criminal law regulates the relationships between an individual and society as a whole. The government is always involved in a criminal law case. Civil law regulates the rights between individuals and between individuals and the government.

B.   Private v. Public Law--Public law deals with the relationships between individuals and their government. Private law, such as contracts, deals with the relationships between private persons or organizations.

IV.   Constitutional Law and Business

A.   The Commerce Clause--The federal government has the power to regulate business dealings if such actions "affect" interstate commerce. The business dealings do not have to cross state borders. Each state has police powers which give it the right to regulate the health, safety and public welfare. However, if a state law based on police power interferes with interstate commerce, the necessity of the law will be weighted against burden placed on commerce.

B.   Freedom of Speech--Not all speech is protected. Slander, obscenity and words likely to incite fights or riots are not protected at all. Advertising and other forms of commercial speech are less protected than non-commercial speech.

C.   Freedom of Religion--Involves both an individual's right to practice religion and a ban on a government religion (Establishment Clause). An employer must make reasonable accommodations to an employee's religion. Sunday closing laws have been challenged but upheld on non-religious or secular grounds as a day of rest.

Study Questions

Fill-in-the-Blank Questions

A law passed by the U.S. Congress is an example of *statutory*
_____ law.
                                                    (common/
statutory)

A regulation adopted by the Internal Revenue Service is an
example of _____ *adm.* _____ law.
            (common/administrative)

The Commerce Clause is an example of _____ *const.* _____
law.
                                    (constitutional/statutory)

True-False Questions

1.   Criminal law is private law. __F__

2.   "Stare decisis" is process of using earlier cases as guidelines in resolving current disputes. __T__

3.   The Uniform Commercial Code was passed by the United States Congress. __F__ F T

4.   Administrative agencies are created by the executive or legislative branches of government. __T__

5.   An employer must make whatever changes are necessary to accommodate a worker's religion. __F__

6.   Commercial speech is absolutely protected by the United States Constitution. __F__

7.   A law passed by the Oregon legislature which conflicts with the provisions of the United States Constitution will be held unconstitutional. __T__

8.   A state's police powers are its powers to regulate the health and safety of its citizens. __T__

9.   Case law is a synonym for statutory law. __F__

10.   The "affectation" doctrine is used in freedom of religion cases. __F__

Multiple-Choice Questions

1.   The right to regulate commerce between the several states is found in:

      a.   a law passed by Congress.
      b.   the Uniform Commercial Code.
      (c.)   the United States Constitution.
      d.   common law.

2.   Jones v. Smith is a contract case decided in 1965. Johns v. Teller is a similar case being decided today. The Jones case is __a__ for the Teller case.

      a.   precedent.
      b.   stare decisis.
      c.   preface.
      d.   premise.

3.   American common law is based on law in:

    a.   France.
    b.   Germany.
    (c.) England.
    d.   Canada.

4.   The Commerce Clause regulates:

    a.   intrastate commerce only.
    b.   interstate commerce only.
    c.   foreign commerce only.
    (d.) all of the above is interstate commerce is burdened.

5.   The supreme or highest law of the land is:

    a.   legislation passed by Congress.
    (b.) the United States Constitution
    c.   common law.
    d.   administrative law.

Answers to Study Questions

Fill-in-the-Blank Questions

A law passed by the U.S. Congress is an example of statutory law or legislation; common law is case law. A regulation adopted by the Internal Revenue Service is an example of administrative law. The Commerce Clause is part of the United States Constitution.

True-False Questions

1. F. It is public law.

2. T.

3. F. The UCC is a uniform law which is proposed and passed or rejected by the legislature of each state.

4. T.

5. F. An employer need only make reasonable accommodations.

6. F. It is protected but to a lesser extent than other forms of speech.

7. T.

8. T.

9. F.   Case law is a synonym for common law.

10. F.   It is used in cases involving the Interstate Commerce Clause.

Multiple-Choice Questions

1. c
2. a
3. c
4. d
5. b

Chapter 2   Courts and Procedures

The American judicial system is composed of two sets of courts: state and federal. The federal courts hear only certain types of cases; most disputes are settled in state courts. Each system has three levels: a trial court, a middle-level or court of appeals, and a supreme court.

The formal process of litigation is similar in each state. Modern procedure attempts to settle disputes quickly and fairly. Note that a case can end before the parties have reached the courtroom.

I.   <u>Court Systems</u>--The federal judicial system and most state systems have a three-tiered system: a trial court, a middle level court of appeals, and a supreme court. There are fifty-two systems in all; one for each state and for the District of Columbia and a federal system.

II.   <u>Jurisdiction</u>--Jurisdiction is technically the power of a court to hear a case. As a practical matter, it tells a lawyer in which court to file a case.

     A.   <u>Personal Jurisdiction</u>--The defendant has a right to be sued in his or her home state. Long-arm statutes are exceptions to this rule. Typical long-arm statutes involve a corporation may be sued in the state in which it is incorporated, where it has its main plant, and any state where it does business. Non-residents who are involved in an auto accident may be sued where the accident occurred.

B. <u>Subject Matter Jurisdiction</u>--A court's power to hear a case may be limited by the type of case or the money amount involved. A court with restricted powers has <u>limited</u> jurisdiction; a court which hears most cases has <u>general</u> jurisdiction. Federal courts have limited jurisdiction and hear only the types of cases listed below.

    (1) <u>Diversity of Citizenship</u>--Plaintiff and defendant are from different states and the amount in dispute is more than $10,000.

    (2) <u>Federal Question</u>--A case involving the interpretation of a federal statute or the United States Constitution.

    (3) The United States government is a party to the suit.

    (4) <u>Exclusive v. Concurrent Jurisdiction</u>--Some cases can only be brought in federal court; the federal court has <u>exclusive</u> jurisdiction. If the case can be heard in either state or federal court, the courts have <u>concurrent</u> jurisdiction.

C. <u>Original v. Appellate Jurisdiction</u>--Trial courts which hear the case for the first time have <u>original</u> jurisdiction. Courts of appeal and supreme courts, which hear the case only after it has been tried, have <u>appellate</u> jurisdiction.

    (1) <u>Standard of Appellate Review</u>--An appellate court consists of a panel of judges who review the testimony of witnesses, the documents, and the written arguments or briefs of the attorneys. The appellate court will only change or reverse a trial court decision if a serious mistake of law has been made. The appellate courts will not change a decision if the facts of the case could support its original outcome.

    (2) <u>Right to Appeal v. Certiorari</u>--In the federal system and in most states, the party who loses at trial has the right to take the case to a middle-level court of appeals for review. After a decision by that court to hear the

case by filing an application for a <u>writ of certiorari</u>. In most cases, the court can decide whether or not to hear the case; it is a matter of discretion.

D. <u>Jurisdiction v. Venue</u>--Jurisdiction over the person tells the lawyer in which state a suit may be brought. Jurisdiction over the subject matter determines which kind of court will hear the case. Venue determines the geographic location of a suit. All three requirements must be satisfied.

<u>Example</u>: A resident of Houston, Texas receives a traffic ticket. Jurisdiction over the person is in Texas, jurisdiction over the subject matter is in the municipal court, and the venue is Houston.

E. <u>Jurisdiction of the United States Supreme Court</u>-- The jurisdiction of the U.S. Supreme Court is determined by the U.S. Constitution and by Congress. The Constitution sets the outside limits; but Congress can set other limits.

(1) <u>Original Jurisdiction</u>--Case involving ambassadors, consuls, disputes between two states and disputes between a state and a citizen of another state.

(2) <u>Right to Appeal</u>--Four categories of cases which usually involve the constitutionality or validity of a federal law. Remember that judicial review gives the courts the power to determine the validity of constitutionality of a law.

(a) A federal court invalidates a state law which conflicts with federal law.

(b) A state court invalidates a federal law or upholds a state law which is claimed to violate federal law.

(c) A federal court invalidates a federal law and a member of the federal government is a party.

(d) A civil injunction, which requires the decision of federal judges, is granted or denied.

(3) Certiorari--Usually only cases involving important constitutional issues. Heard only if the justices agree to hear it.

III. Civil Trial Procedure--Note the points at which a case can be decided at the trial level; these points are marked with a *.

A. The Pleadings--The initial documents filed by a plaintiff and a defendant.

(1) Petition (Complaint)--Filed by the plaintiff. Must state the facts, the rule of law violated by the defendant and the remedy sought.

(2) Summons--Notice of the suit and a copy of the petition is given to the defendant. Usually served in person. If the defendant does not answer, the plaintiff wins automatically by default.

(3) Answer, Counterclaim or Motion to Dismiss-- Possible responses by the defendant.

(a) Motion to Dismiss (or Demurrer)*--Asks the judge to dismiss the case because of plaintiff's petition does not show a legal wrong. If it is granted, the case ends and the loser may appeal.

(b) Answer--May deny what the plaintiff claims or admit that the facts of the petition are true but there is another reason the defendant should not be liable (affirmative defense). Examples of affirmative defenses are statute of limitations, contributory negligence, and fraud.

(c) Counterclaim--The defendant not only denies liability but claims that the plaintiff is liable.

B. Judgment on the Pleadings and Summary Judgment*--A judgment on the pleadings asks the judge to look at the initial documents filed by both parties and to decide the case. A motion for summary judgment is similar, however the judge may look at other evidence such as sworn statements or affidavits. A motion for summary judgment will be granted only if the facts are not in dispute.

C.   Discovery--The attorneys trade information about
the case. It is designed to make trials shorter
and equitable. Methods of discovery include
depositions (questions answered oath by witnesses
or parties) and interrogatories (written questions
answered by parties and their attorneys only).

D.   Pretrial Hearing--If a case has not been settled,
the judge and the attorneys meet to plan the trial
and resolve disputes over evidence and other
matters.

E.   Trial--In almost all cases, the parties are
entitled to a jury trial. The case can be decided
by a judge if neither party requests a jury.

(1)   Voir Dire--The lawyers select the jury from a
panel by asking questions. The questions are
designed to show if a juror is biased in favor
of one side or the other.

(2)   Plaintiff's Case--Because the plaintiff
initiated the lawsuit, he or she has the
burden of proof and must proceed first. The
procedure is the same for all witnesses; the
plaintiff's attorney asks questions on direct
examination and the defendant's attorney
cross-examines the witnesses. The plaintiff's
attorney may then ask questions of the same
witness or redirect examination and the
defendant's attorney may ask questions on
re-cross examination. At this time, the
plaintiff also introduces exhibits or relevant
items.

(3)   Motion for Directed Verdict*--At the end of
the plaintiff's evidence, the defendant may
claim that the plaintiff has failed to make
out a case. If the judge agrees and grants to
motion, the case ends.

(4)   Defendant's Evidence--If a directed verdict is
not granted, the defendant must present his or
her evidence. At this stage, the defendant
conducts direct exmaination of his or her
witnesses and the plaintiff conducts
cross-examination.

(5)   Rebuttal and Rejoinder--The plaintiff is given
a chance to refute the defendant's evidence on
rebuttal. The defendant is then entitled to
do the same on rejoinder.

    (6) <u>Closing and Arguments</u>--Each side is given opportunity to summarize the evidence and persuade the jury.

    (7) <u>Instructions (Court's Charge)</u>--The judge tells the jury the rules of law to be used in deciding the case, and the definitions of legal terms.

    (8) <u>Jury's Verdict</u>*

    (9) <u>Motion for New Trial of J.N.O.V.</u>*--After the jury has decided the case, the loser may ask the judge to grant a new trial or to reverse the jury's verdict (J.N.O.V.) If the motion for J.N.O.V. is granted, the loser becomes the winner.

IV. <u>Appellate Procedure</u>--The loser has the right to ask a middle-level appeals court to hear the case. The loser's attorney submits the record on appeal which consists of the documents in the case, the testimony of the witnesses and the attorneys' written agruments or briefs. The attorneys may also choose to appear before the appellate court for oral argument.

The appellate court can reach three possible decisions:

    (1) <u>Affirm</u>--The trial court decision stands because the appellate court agrees with the verdict reached at trial.

    (2) <u>Reverse</u>--The trial court decision is overturned or reversed if a mistake was made at trial. The loser at trial court becomes the winner.

    (3) <u>Remand</u>--The appellate court sends the case back for a new trial.

V. <u>Alternative Dispute Resolution (ADR)</u>--Less formal, non-judicial resolution of legal disputes. A disinterested third party listens to both parties.

A. <u>Mediation</u>--The parties reach the decision by working with a third party.

B. <u>Arbitration</u>--A more formal hearing in which the third party or arbitrator makes the decision or award. Many contracts specify that any disputes will be settled by arbitration.

Study Questions

Fill-in-the-Blank Questions

Mary claims that John owes her money and John refuses to pay. Mary decides to sue.

The document that Mary's lawyer will file to start the suit is a _____*petition*_____ .
(petition/demurrer)

John's lawyer claims that Mary has no case and asks the judge to bar Mary's claim and end the suit. The document that John's lawyer will file is a(n)_____*motion to dismiss*_____ .
(answer/motion to dismiss/counterclaim)

If the case goes to trial and Mary wins, John's lawyer may file a document asking the court to reverse the jury's verdict. This document is a motion for a _____*J.N.O.V.*_____ .
(directed verdict/J.N.O.V.)

True-False Questions

1. The United States Supreme Court has no original jurisdiction. _*F*_

2. When a plaintiff's attorney questions a witness for the defendant, he or she is conducting rebuttal. _*F*_

3. A synonym for the instructions given to the jury is the court's charge. _*T*_

4. The federal courts have limited jurisdiction. _*T*_

5. A long-arm statute is used by lawyers is selecting a jury. _*F*_

6. When two or more courts could hear the same case, the courts have appellate jurisdiction. _*F*_

7. If a party makes a motion for summary judgment and the judge grants the motion, the case will be decided by a jury. _*F*_

8. Most states have a two-tiered court system. _*F*_

9. An application for a writ certiorari is filed in trial court. _*F*_

10. In an arbitration proceeding, a third party decides who will win the case. _*T*_

Multiple-Choice Questions

1. Which of the following are correct chronological order?

    a. voir dire, motion for summary judgment, summons, motion for j.n.o.v.
    b. voir dire, summons, motion for summary judgment, motion for j.n.o.v.
    c. summons, motion for summary judgment, voir dire, motion for j.n.o.v.
    d. summons, motion for j.n.o.v., voir dire, motion for summary judgment

2. When a case can only be brought in one court, that court has _____ of the case.

    a. original jurisdiction
    b. concurrent jurisdiction
    c. limited jurisdiction
    d. exclusive jurisdiction

3. If the defendant's lawyer asks the judge to decide the case immediately after the plaintiff has presented evidence at trial, he or she will ask for a:

    a. counterclaim.
    b. directed verdict.
    c. new trial.
    d. voir dire.

4. The decision made by an arbitrator is called a(n):

    a. verdict.
    b. award.
    c. motion.
    d. none of the above.

5. Mary bought a microwave oven from AAA Applicance, a company which is incorporated in Delaware, has its main office in Atlanta, Georgia and does business in Milwaukee, Wisconsin, where Mary purchased her oven. If the oven malfunctions and Mary decides to sue, in which states can she sue AAA?

    a. Delaware only
    b. Delaware or Georgia only
    c. Wisconsin only
    d. Delaware, Georgia or Wisconsin

6.   Written questions are answered by a party and his or her
      lawyer as a part of discovery are called:

      a. interrogatories.
      b. interrogations.
      c. depositions.
      d. dispositions.

7.   Which of the following documents would not be filed by a
      defendant to a lawsuit:

      a. Counterclaim
      b. Motion to dismiss
      c. Answer
      d. Petition

8.   Bob owns a video rental store in Santa Fe, New Mexico.
      He recently agreed to purchase $5,000 of video equipment
      from a supplier in New York City. If the supplier
      breaches the contract, Bob:

      a. can sue in federal court because of diversity of
          citizenship.
      b. can sue in federal court because a federal question
          is involved.
      c. can in federal court because federal courts have
          general jurisdiction.
      d. cannot sue in federal court.

9.   Which of the following are in correct chronological
      order?

      a. summons, motion for directed verdict, pre-trial
          hearing, counterclaim
      b. summons, pre-trial hearing, counterclaim, motion for
          directed verdict
      c. summons, counterclaim, motion for directed verdict,
          pre-trial hearing
      d. summons, counterclaim, pre-trial hearing, motion for
          directed verdict

10.   The United States Supreme Court has original
      jurisdiction over which of the following types of cases:

      a. A dispute between residents of different states
      b. A dispute between two states
      c. A federal question
      d. A case involving the constitutionality of a state
          law

11.   Peter sued Cynthia in trial court and Peter won the case. Cynthia has decided to appeal. If the court of appeals agrees with the decision of the trial court, the case will be:

        a. affirmed.
        b. remanded.
        c. reversed.
        d. none of the above.

12.   If the court of appeals disagrees with the decision of the trial court and decides that Cynthia should win, the case will be:

        a. affirmed.
        b. remanded.
        c. reversed.
        d. none of the above.

13.   If the defendant in a lawsuit fails to respond to a summons, the plaintiff will receive:

        a. an award from an arbitrator.
        b. a new trial.
        c. a default judgment.
        d. a directed verdict.

14.   The prisoners in a county jail want to file suit against the county because they are not allowed to drink coffee in jail. The prisoners claim that the ban on coffee is in violation of the Eighth Amendment of the United States Constitution. The prisoners:

        a. can sue in federal court because of diversity of citizenship.
        b. cannot sue in federal court because there is no diversity of citizenship.
        c. can sue in federal court because a federal question is at issue.
        d. cannot sue in federal court because a federal question is at issue.

15.   The power of a court to hold a statute or law unconstitutional is:

        a. judicial review.
        b. judicial arbitration.
        c. exclusive jurisdiction.
        d. writ of certiorari.

16.   The geographic region within a judicial district where a case can be brought is:

       a.   jurisdiction over the person.
       b.   jurisdiction over the subject matter.
       c.   venue.
       d.   federal question.

17.   If a party loses a case at trial and on the first appeal and wants a supreme court to hear the case, he or she:

       a.   can file an appeal and the court must hear the case.
       b.   can file an application for a writ of certiorari which the court may or may not grant.
       c.   cannot file another appeal.
       d.   can file an application for a writ of certiorari and the court must hear the case.

18.   A trial court which can hear most types of cases has:

       a.   appellate jurisdiction.
       b.   exclusive jurisdiction.
       c.   limited jurisdition.
       d.   general jurisdiction.

19.   When the plaintiff's attorney questions a witness for the defense for the first time, he or she is conducting:

       a.   cross-examination.
       b.   direct examination.
       c.   recross examination.
       d.   redirect examination.

20.   There are several points during a case when it can end at the trial stage. Which of the following, if granted by the judge, will not end the trial?

       a.   Motion for directed verdict
       b.   Counterclaim
       c.   Motion for summary judgment
       d.   Motion to dismiss

21.   The number of court systems in the United States is:

       a.   fifty.
       b.   fifty-one.
       c.   fifty-two.
       d.   none of the above.

22.   Which of the following is in chronological order?

      a.   Instructions to the jury, motion for new trial, appeal to the court of appeals, application for a writ of certiorari
      b.   Motion for new trial, appeal to the court of appeals, instructions to the jury, application for a writ of certiorari
      c.   Application for a writ of certiorari, motion for new trial, instructions to the jury, appeal to the court of appeals
      d.   Instructions to the jury, motion for a new trial, application for a writ of certiorari, appeal to the court of appeals

23.   Which of the following are pleadings in a civil trial?

      a.   Petition and motion for summary judgment
      b.   Petition and motion to dismiss
      c.   Petition and motion for j.n.o.v.
      d.   Motion to dismiss and motion for summary judgment

24.   Madeline sues Patsy for negligence. Patsy's lawyer files a motion for judgment on the pleadings. If the judge grants the motion, who will win the case?

      a.   Patsy
      b.   Madeline
      c.   No one, the jury must still hear the case
      d.   No one, the judge must still hear the case

25.   Which of the following facts about arbitration is not true?

      a.   The parties cannot appeal the decision reached in arbitration.
      b.   Arbitration is a form of alternative dispute resolution.
      c.   Arbitration must follow the court rules of evidence and procedure.
      d.   The arbitrator, not the parties, decides the case.

Answers to Study Questions

Fill-in-the-Blank Questions

Mary's lawyer will file a petition. A demurrer or motion to dismiss would be filed by the defendant if he or she thought that there was no basis for the suit.

John's lawyers will file a motion to dismiss. An answer denies the facts in the plaintiff's petition but does not ask the judge to dismiss the case. A counterclaim is filed by a defendant if he or she not only denies responsibility but sues the plaintiff.

John's lawyer will file a motion for a j.n.o.v. A j.n.o.v asks the court to disregard the jury's verdict and to reverse the jury's decision. A motion for directed verdict is filed at the conclusion of the plaintiff's evidence, in the middle of the lawsuit.

True-False Questions

1.   F.   Although the original or trial jurisdiction of the United States Supreme Court is limited, it can hear cases involving ambassadors, consuls, and disputes between states.

2.   F.   This is a description of cross-examination. Rebuttal is the plaintiff's chance to present more evidence after the defendant has presented his or her case.

3.   T.

4.   T.

5.   F.   A long-arm statute allows a non-resident defendant to be sued in the plaintiff's home state.

6.   F.   They have concurrent jurisdiction. Appellate jurisdiction is the power of a court to hear a case on appeal.

7.   F.   Summary judgment occurs before a jury is picked and is used when the facts of the case are not in dispute. If the facts are not in dispute, there is no need for a jury.

8.   F.   Most states have a three-tiered system: trial court, court of appeals, and supreme court.

9.   F.   It is filed in a supreme court.

10.   T.

Multiple-Choice Questions

1.	c	11.	a	21.	c
2.	d	12.	c	22.	a
3.	b	13.	c	23.	b
4.	b	14.	c	24.	a
5.	d	15.	a	25.	c
6.	a	16.	c		
7.	d	17.	b		
8.	d	18.	d		
9.	d	19.	a		
10.	b	20.	b		

Chapter 3   Torts

General Principles

A tort is a personal injury committed by one private party against another. Distinguish a tort from a crime; a crime is a wrong committed against society as a whole. Personal injury may include physical injury, emotional distress, injury to property, and injury to a person's reputation.

There are three kinds of torts: intentional, negligence, and strict liability. The difference depends on the state of mind of the person committing the tort. An intentional tort requires a conscious, deliberate action, although not necessarily the intent to do the harm which results. Negligence is based on carelessness; strict liability is no-fault liability.

A plaintiff will not be successful in a tort suit unless he or she can provide the elements of the tort. Each tort has separate elements and each element must be met. If one or more element is missing, that tort has not occurred.

Chapter Summary

I.   Intentional Torts against Persons

    A.   Assault--The elements are:

        (1)   An intentional act

        (2)   The act causes fear or apprehension

        (3)   The fear of immediate bodily contact

(4) The contact would be harmful or offensive to a reasonable person

B. Battery--The elements are:

(1) An intentional act

(2) The act is unexcused

(3) Bodily contact (includes items closely connected with a person)

(4) The contact would be harmful or offensive to a reasonable person

The defenses to assault and battery include:

(a) Consent by the plaintiff to the touching (e.g. in football games or other contact sports)

(b) Self-defense or defense of another if reasonable force is used to repel an attack; the defense is good even if there is no real danger if a reasonable person would have thought that the danger existed.

(c) Defense of property if reasonable force is used, but never force which would cause serious bodily injury or death.

C. False Imprisonment--The elements are:

(1) Intentional

(2) Unjustified

(3) Confinement or restraint of another

In most states, a merchant protection statute allows store owners to detain suspected shoplifters if there is probable cause to stop the customer and if the detention is reasonable.

D. Infliction of Emotional Distress--The elements are:

(1) An intentional act

(2) The act is outrageous or extreme

(3) The act causes serious emotional distress

(4)   Physical symptoms of distress (some states)

E.   Defamation--Protects injury to reputation. Slander is oral; libel is written. The elements are:

(1)   An intentional statement

(2)   Made to a third party (publication)

(3)   The statement holds the plaintiff up to ridicule or hatred

Some statements are presumed to satisfy element (3) They are categorized as defamation per se.

(a)   Plaintiff has a loathsome communicable disease.

(b)   Plaintiff has committed business indiscretions.

(c)   Plaintiff has been imprisoned for a serious crime.

(d)   Plaintiff is an unmarried woman and is unchaste.

Defenses:

(1)   Truth

(2)   Absolute privilege-Statement made on the floor of Congress by members of Congress or statements made by judges or attorneys during trial

(3)   Conditional privilege--Publication to an instrument of publication (e.g. a secretary)

(4)   Public figure--If the plaintiff is a public figure, malice or reckless disregard of the truth must be shown.

F.   Invasion of Privacy (4 types)

(1)   Unpermitted use of a person's picture or likeness

(2)   Intrusion on a person's affairs

(3)   Public disclosure of private and objectionable facts (not necessarily false)

(4)   Disclosure of information which misleads the public about a person

G.   <u>Misrepresentation</u>--The elements are:

(1)   Misrepresentation of material facts--Puffing and opinions will not suffice; the fact misrepresented must have been important

(2)   Misrepresentation is in order made to induce reliance

(3)   Justifiable reliance by the plaintiff (Would a reasonable person have relied?)

(4)   Damages

(5)   The damages were caused by or related to the misrepresentation. If damages were suffered because of some other reason, there may be a case for negligence or strict liability but not for misrepresentation.

II.   <u>Intentional Torts against Property</u>--Property is either real estate (land or items permanently attached to it such as a carport or fence) or personal (everything else).

A.   <u>Trespass to Land</u>--The elements are:

(1)   Unpermitted (owner does not consent)
(2)   Instrusion above, on, or under land
(3)   The land belongs to another
(4)   Injury is <u>not</u> required

Defenses are few but the defendant's conduct may be excused if he or she entered the property in an emergency or if he or she can prove that the plaintiff does not own the land.

B.   <u>Trespass to Personal Property</u>--The elements are:

(1)   Unjustified and intentional

(2)   Interference

(3)   With the personal property of another

The defenses are the same as for trespass to land. Note that the property does not have to be moved and <u>distinguish</u>:

C.   Conversion--The civil wrong which corresponds to the criminal wrong of theft. The elements are:

   (1)   Unjustified and intentional

   (2)   Taking--removal

   (3)   The property belongs to another

III.   Negligence--The actions of the defendant do not have to be deliberate; carelessness is the standard. Most auto accidents are caused by negligence. The elements are:

A.   Duty owed by the Plaintiff to the Defendant--May be extremely broad such as the duty one driver owes another to drive safely. Certain persons, such as parents and children, owe a duty of care to each other as a consequence of their relationship.

B.   Breach of Duty--Ask yourself if the defendant acted carelessly. The standard is a reasonable man in the defendant's position. E.g. a lawyer must act as a reasonable lawyer would act.

C.   Injury--The plaintiff must have suffered some (although not necessarily physical) injury.

D.   Cause in Fact--The defendant's action must have been the physical cause of the injury. The "but for" test is used to see if this element has been met. Ask yourself: "If the defendant had not acted, would the injury have occurred?" (But for the defendant's conduct; the injury would not have occurred.)

E.   Proximate or Legal Cause--Based on the idea that a defendant should only be responsible for injuries that can be foreseen by his or her careless conduct. Distinguish intentional torts where the defendant is liable whether the injuries are foreseeable or not. Determine the breach committed by the defendant then ask yourself what type of injuries are foreseeable from this type of conduct. If the injury suffered is foreseeable, there is proximate cause; if not, there is no proximate cause.

F.   Defenses to Negligence

(1) <u>Superseding or Intervening Cause</u>--An unforeseeable event such as an act of God or nature
breaks the casual connection between the
defendant's breach and the injury. This
defense cancels the cause in fact element.

(2) <u>Assumption of Risk</u>--The plaintiff knows that
his or her conduct involves risk but
voluntarily decides to act.

(3) <u>Contributory Negligence</u>--If the plaintiff is
also negligent, contributory negligence bars
any suit by the plaintiff regardless of which
party was more at fault. Because of possible
harsh results, the courts developed the <u>last
clear chance</u> test, which states that even if
both parties were negligent, if the defendent
had the last clear change to avoid the injury,
he or she will still be responsible to the
plaintiff.

(4) <u>Comparative Negligence</u>--Because of the
difficult and circular reasoning in
contributory negligence cases, most states
have adopted a comparative negligence
standard. The negligence of the plaintiff and
the defendant are compared. In the <u>pure</u> form
of comparative negligence, the plaintiff may
sue regardless of the amount of fault. In
other states, if the plaintiff is more than
50% at fault, the suit is barred.

IV.   <u>Strict Liability</u>--No-fault liability. It is not
necessary to find that the defendant breached a duty. It
is used with high-risk activities such as blasting and
keeping wild animals and is a cost of that type of
business. Assumption of risk is a defense; comparative
and contributory negligence are not.

V.   <u>Business Torts</u>

A.   <u>Defamation</u>--Slander of title occurs when someone
makes a false statement about the ownership of the
plaintiff's property. Disparagement of goods takes
place when a false statement is made about the
quality of goods. Defamation by computer occurs
when a plaintiff's reputation is injured as a
result of computerized statements (e.g. a false
credit report).

B.   Wrongful Interference with a Contractual Relation-ship--The elements are:

(1)   A valid contract between A & B.
(2)   C knows that the contract exists.
(3)   C intentionally causes A or B to break the contract. The plaintiff must show that the contract would not have been broken without the interference of C.

Note that the outsider is sued for this tort. The party to the contract that acted wrongfully may be sued for breach of contract.

C.   Wrongful Interference with a Business Relationship --Same elements as above but a business relation-ship instead of a contract exists between A & B. Usually occurs when the defendant harasses the plaintiff's customers.

D.   Wrongfully Entering the Business--The defendant enters into business with the sole intention of ruining the plaintiff's business.

E.   Infringement of Copyright, Trademark and Patents-- Occurs with unauthorized and unjustified use of the owner's rights.

(1)   Trademark--A mark or motto that identifies the goods. Protects the consumer from similar products by others. If a word is used, it must be fanciful and not generic. A service mark is used to distinguish services rather than products. A trade name relates to a business name.

(2)   Patent--A device, design or process.

(3)   Copyright--Applies only to literary or artistic creations. The "fair use" defense allows a person to reproduce copyrighted materials without infringement if used for purposes of commentary, news reporting, or teaching.

Study Questions

Fill-in-the-Blank Questions

Thomas Tortfeasor is shopping in the grocery store. He becomes impatient with two ladies blocking the aisle. He bumps one lady with his cart. She falls down and breaks her hip. He swings his fist at the other lady but misses.

When Thomas bumped the woman with his cart, he committed _____.
      (assault/battery/neither)

When Thomas attempted to hit the second woman, he committed _____.
      (assault/battery/both)

Thomas _____ responsible for the woman's broken hip.
          (is/is not)

True-False Questions

1.   Trespass to land is an intentional tort. ____

2.   A teacher asks a student into her office, closes the door and calls him a "cheat". Assuming that the statement is false and only the student heard the remark, the teacher has committed slander. ____

3.   Assumption of risk is a defense to negligence. ____

4.   Strict liability is a synonym for no-fault liability.____

5.   Paul and Susan have a contract. Raul knows of the contract and induces Susan to break it. Susan can be sued for wrongful interference with a contractual relationship. ____

6.   "The Whopper" is a trade name. ____

7.   Necessity is a defense to trespass to land. ____

8.   The difference between trespass to personal property and conversion is that in conversion, the property must be moved. ____

9.   False light is a form of invasion of privacy. ____

10.   The "fair use doctrine" is a defense to defamation. ____

Multiple-Choice Questions

1. Mrs. Harris buys a new toaster. The first time she uses it, she notices that sparks are flying from the toaster. She continues to use the toaster and is severely burned. If Mrs. Harris sues the toaster manufacturer in negligence, it can use which of the following defenses to defeat her claim?

    a. Contributory negligence only
    b. Assumption of risk only
    c. Both contributory negligence and assumption of risk
    d. Neither contributory negligence or assumption of risk

2. Which of the following is <u>not</u> a defense to assault?

    a. Consent
    b. Necessity
    c. Self-defense
    d. Defense of property

3. Nancy is walking her dog without a leash. The dog sees a cat, chases it, and tramples a rose bush. The neighbor witnesses the chase and suffers a heart attack. Nancy is responsible for:

    a. the damage to the rose bush.
    b. the neighbor's medical bills.
    c. the damage to the rose bush and the neighbor's medical bills.
    d. neither the damage to the rose bush nor the neighbor's medical expenses.

4. Susan is shopping for a new car. A car salesman tells her that the car she has selected is the best car in the price range. After Susan buys the car, she discovers that another car in the price range gets better gas mileage and has more safety features. If Susan sues the salesman for misrepresentation:

    a. she will succeed because the second car was better.
    b. she will succeed because she was induced to buy the first car.
    c. she will not succeed because she was not induced to buy the car.
    d. she will not succeed because the salesman did not misrepresent a fact.

5.   Molly's ex-husband tells his drinking buddies that she
        had a baby out of wedlock. Assuming that the statement
        is true; Molly can sue her ex-husband for:

        a. defamation.
        b. false light.
        c. public disclosure of private facts.
        d. defamation and public disclosure of private facts.

6.   Judith owns a grocery store. One of her employees tells
        her that he saw Mr. Jones put a steak under his shirt.
        As Mr. Jones is leaving the store, Judith stops him,
        takes him to store office, locks the door and calls the
        police. The police arrive 10 minutes later and discover
        that Mr. Jones is not guilty. If Mr. Jones sues Judith
        for false imprisonment, he will:

        a. succeed because he was confined intentionally.
        b. succeed because Judith lacked probable cause to
            detain him.
        c. not succeed because the confinement was reasonable.
        d. not succeed because Judith did not intend to confine
            him for a long period of time.

7.   Tony's Pizza sends out a false press release which
        states that several people who ate at a competitor's
        restaurant have contracted food poisoning. The
        competitor can sue Tony's for:

        a. slander of title.
        b. disparagement of goods.
        c. negligence.
        d. public disclosure of private facts.

8.   Two students find their teacher's business law book.
        They pour ink on the torts chapter. The students have
        committed:

        a. trespass to personal property.
        b. conversion.
        c. trespass to personal property and conversion
        d. neither trespass to personal property nor
            conversion.

9.   Paul owns a construction company. He carelessly sets
        out dynamite. When the blast occurs, the windows in a
        nearby house shatter. The owner of the house can sue
        Paul for:

a. negligence only.
b. strict liability only.
c. negligence and strict liability.
d. trespass to personal property, negligence and strict liability.

10. Mr. Smith sees a man collapse on the sidewalk. Mr. Smith rushes past without stopping. The man suffers serious injuries because he remained on the sidewalk until someone took him to the hospital two hours later. If the man sues Mr. Smith, he will not succeed because one of the following elements is missing. Which one?

a. Duty of care from Mr. Smith to the injured man
b. Cause in fact
c. Contributory negligence
d. Injury

11. Bill sees Sandra's new bicycle in the driveway. He takes the bicycle and rides to the store. Sandra can sue Bill for:

a. theft only.
b. conversion only.
c. theft and conversion.
d. trespass to personal property and conversation.

12. Linda carelessly parks her car on a hill and forgets to set the parking brake. While Linda is gone, a flood occurs and her car is swept through a store window. Linda's best defense to a negligence suit by the store owner is:

a. contributory negligence.
b. assumption of risk.
c. last clear chance.
d. superseding cause.

13. Robert is shopping with his 3 year-old son. Robert allows the boy to wander through the store. A stockboy sees the child approaching a meat grinder but does nothing. The child is seriously injured when he sticks his hand in the meat grinder. If Robert sues the store for negligence, the store's best defense is:

a. contributory negligence.
b. assumption of risk.
c. last clear change.
d. intervening cause.

14. Alice is involved in an auto accident and sues the other driver, Carl. The jury finds that the accident was 30% Alice's fault. If Alice lives in a state that recognizes contributory negligence, Alice will recover:

    a. 100% of her damages.
    b. 70% of her damages.
    c. 30% of her damages.
    d. nothing.

15. If Alice lives in a state that recognizes comparative negligence, Alice will recover:

    a. 100% of her damages.
    b. 70% of her damages.
    c. 30% of her damages.
    d. nothing.

16. The mayor of Cantonville, who is running for re-election, is suing the local paper for a story leaked to the paper by members of the opposing political party. Assuming that the story is false, the mayor will win the suit if he can show that:

    a. the reporter who wrote the story was negligent in checking her sources.
    b. the reporter who wrote the story knew that the story was false when she wrote it.
    c. the paper printed the story and the intentions of the reporter do not matter.
    d. the story was false and the intentions of the reporter do not matter.

17. Ron is riding his horse when he sees Dave, an old enemy. Ron deliberately gallops toward Dave and stops just 1 foot away. As a result of Ron's actions, Dave's ulcer flares up and he is hospitalized. If Dave sues Ron for intentional infliction of emotional distress:

    a. Dave will win the suit but cannot recover damages for his hospitalization because the ulcer flare-up was unforeseeable.
    b. Dave will win the suit and can recover damages including his medical expenses.
    c. Dave will not win the suit because Ron did not intend to cause physical injury.
    d. Dave will not win the suit because the horse did not touch him.

18.   Which of the following is a defense to strict liability?

      a.   Comparative negligence
      b.   Assumption of risk
      c.   Necessity
      d.   None of the above; there are no defenses to strict
           liability

19.   Sam, a salesman for a best Computer Company, is upset
      over the new sales route to which he has been assigned.
      Oscar, the owner of a rival computer company, sees Sam
      in a restaurant and tells Sam, "If you ever decide to
      leave Best, come see me". Sam quits working for Best
      two days later and goes to work for Oscar. If Best sues
      Oscar for wrongful interference with a contractual
      relationship, Best will:

      a.   win if Sam had a contract with Best because Oscar
           know that Sam worked for Best.
      b.   win even if Sam had no contract because Oscar knew
           that Sam worked for Best.
      c.   lose even if Sam had a contract with Best because
           Oscar did not induce Sam to quit.
      d.   lose even if Sam had a contract because Oscar was
           negligent in speaking with Sam.

20.   Skaggs Alpha Beta is a well-established supermarket
      chain in the southwestern United States. A competitor
      opens a new chain of stores called "Skaggs Alpha Zeta".
      Skaggs Alpha Beta should sue the newcomer for:

      a.   infringement of a trade name.
      b.   infringement of a trademark.
      c.   infringement of a service mark.
      d.   infringement of a copyright.

21.   Louise purchases a new food processor from Gourmet
      Emporium. The salesman tells her that the food
      processor will grind anything, including nuts in the
      shell. Louise tries the food processor, discovers that
      it will not grind shelled nuts and the shells ruin the
      food processor. If Louise sues Gourmet Emporium for
      misrepresentation, the store's best defense will be:

      a.   the salesman did not misrepresent a fact but merely
           expressed an opinion
      b.   Louise has not suffered any damages.
      c.   the salesman did not intend for Louise to rely on
           his statement.
      d.   Louise's reliance was unjustifiable, because a
           reasonable person would not believe that a food
           processor could grind nuts in the shell.

22.   Betty is a book reviewer for a magazine. In the last
       issue, she criticized a new novel by Larry Lucas and
       emphasized her point by quoting from the second chapter.
       If Larry sues Betty for copyright infringement, her best
       defense will be:

       a. absolute privilege.
       b. the fair use doctrine.
       c. truth, because she really believed that the book was
           poorly written.
       d. conditional privilege, because Larry is a public
           figure.

23.   Texas Tamales, Inc. is a manufacturer of Mexican food.
       Barbara purchased a can of the company's Coahuila Chili.
       When she opened the can, she discovered a dead fly in
       the chili. When Barbara sued for negligence, a Texas
       Tamale supervisor proved that the company took
       reasonable measures to ensure that foreign objects were
       removed from the chili. Barbara lost the case. Which
       element is missing?

       a. Texas Tamales did not owe a duty to Barbara.
       b. It is unforeseeable that a fly would be found in a
           can of chili.
       c. Texas Tamales did not breach its duty to Barbara.
       d. None, Barbara should not have lost the case.

24.   There have been several robberies in Sidney's neighbor-
       hood. When Sidney goes on vacation, he leaves a loaded
       rifle attached to a trip wire. A burglar opens the door
       and is seriously injured. The burglar sues Sidney for
       battery.

       a. The burglar will win because the use of a deadly
           weapon is not permitted to protect property.
       b. The burglar will lose because a battery did not
           occur.
       c. The burglar will lose because Sidney acted in self-
           defense
       d. The burglar will lose because Sidney did not intend
           to injure the burglar but only to frighten him.

25.   Amy owns a small airplane and as a practical joke she
       flies over Rose's house at a low altitude. After two
       weeks, Rose threatens to sue Amy for trespass to land if
       she does not stop. If Rose decides to sue, she will:

       a. lose because she has not suffered any monetary loss.
       b. lose because Amy flies over Rose's house and does
           not touch it.
       c. lose because Amy only intended to play a joke.
       d. win because all the elements are satisfied.

Answers to Study Questions

Fill-in-the-Blank Questions

When Thomas bumped the woman with his cart, he committed battery. Battery is an unexcused, intentional harmful or offensive touching. If the woman saw Thomas threatening to bump her with the cart, he may also have committed assault.

When Thomas attempted to hit the second woman, he committed assault. Assault differs from battery in that no touching is required, but the victim must be aware of the defendant's act.

Thomas is responsible for the broken hip. This is true even though he did not intend serious injury. It is also irrelevant that the broken hip may or may not have been foreseeable. Proximate cause is an element of negligence but not intentional torts.

True-False Questions

1.   T.

2.   F.   The publication requirement has not been met.

3.   T.

4.   T.

5.   F.   Raul can be sued for wrongful interference with a contractual relationship. He is the outsider who induced Susan to breach the contract. Susan can be sued for breach of contract.

6.   F.   It is a trademark. A trade name refers to the name of a company.

7.   T.

8.   T

9.   T.

10.   F.   The "fair use doctrine" is a defense to copyright infringement.

Multiple-Choice Questions

1.	c	11.	d	21.	d
2.	b	12.	d	22.	b
3.	a	13.	a	23.	c
4.	d	14.	d	24.	a
5.	c	15.	b	25.	d
6.	c	16.	b		
7.	b	17.	b		
8.	a	18.	b		
9.	c	19.	c		
10.	a	20.	a		

Chapter 4   Criminal Law

Some actions may be the basis for a tort in a civil action and for a crime in a criminal prosecution. Crimes, however, are committed against society and it is the government which sues to enforce the criminal laws.

The defendant in a criminal case is afforded several safeguards against wrongful prosecution. Some forms of protection are procedural (probable cause is required for an arrest); some are substantive (defenses and guilt beyond a reasonable doubt).

Chapter Summary

I.   Crimes v. Torts

Crimes	Torts
1. Committed against society as a whole.	1. Committed against an individual.
2. The plaintiff is the government.	2. The plaintiff is a private individual.
3. Punishment is a fine, imprisonment or both.	3. No punishment, but the plaintiff may recover money damages.
4. Primarily statutory law.	4. Primarily common law.

II.   Classification of Crimes--The classification of crimes is established by the legislature or Congress and is defined by statute.

    A.   Felonies--The most serious crimes. Usually punishable by imprisonment in a penitentiary.

    B.   Misdemeanors--Less serious crimes. Usually punishable by confinement in the country or city jail for a short period of time (less than one year).

    C.   Violations (Petty Offenses)--Usually not considered a crime although the offenses are defined in the criminal statutes. Includes parking and traffic violations.

III.   Elements of Criminal Liability--Requires an act which is prohibited by statute and the required mental state. The required mental state is defined as part of the crime. The range of mental states is intentional, reckless, or negligent. An act may include an attempt or conspiracy to commit an act.

IV.   Defenses to Criminal Liability--Most negate the required state of mind.

    A.   Infancy--Children under seven are exempt from criminal prosecution because it is assumed that they lack the required mental intent. Between seven and fourteen, children are presumed to lack the mental intent, but the prosecution may prove otherwise. At age fourteen, children may be prosecuted but may prove they lacked the mental intent.

    B.   Intoxication--Involuntary intoxication, including unknowingly taking liquor or drugs, acts as a complete defense, if the defendant was so intoxicated that he or she did not know that a crime had been committed. Voluntary intoxication is not a complete defense, but the defendant may be able to lessen the degree of the crime by showing that he or she did not act intentionally.

    C.   Insanity

        (1)   M'Naghten Test--Most strict. Defendant must prove that he or she lacked the understanding to know what occurred or that he or she did not know that it was wrong.

      (2) **Irresistible Impulse**--Because of disease, the defendant was unable to conform his or her conduct to the norm.

      (3) **Model Penal Code**--Most liberal. Combines the M'Naghten and irresistible impulse tests. Behavior can be excused if the result of mental disease _or_ defect. Defendant need not lack total understanding of the circumstances but only the substantial capacity to understand.

D. **Mistake**--Mistake of fact is a defense if the defendant lacked the required mental state. Mistake of law is excused only if the law has not been widely published or if the individual relies on the advice of a government official.

E. **Consent**--Available as a defense only if one element of the crime is "against the will of the victim".

F. **Duress**--The defendant is forced to commit a crime against his or her will because of threats by another. The harm threatened must be more serious than the crime that the defendant is forced to commit.

G. **Self-Defense/Defense of Others/Defense of Property**--As with torts, force is justifiable if used to repel an attack by another. Deadly force is only justifiable if the defendant is threatened with immediate death or serious bodily injury.

H. **Entrapment**--A government official, such as a policeman, suggests to the defendant that a crime be committed **and** persuades the defendant to commit the crime. The test is whether the defendant would have committed the crime anyway (predisposition). If so, the entrapment defense fails.

I. **Immunity**--Part of the plea bargaining process. One defendant is protected from prosecution or given a reduced sentence in return for testimony against other wrongdoers.

V. **Criminal Procedure**--Note the safeguards of independent decisionmakers.

A. **Arrest**--A warrant will be issued only if an independent judge or magistrate is convinced that there is probable cause or a considerable possibility that the defendant has committed a crime. A police officer can act without a warrant if there is not time to get one and his or her belief meets the probable cause test.

B.   <u>Indictment/Information</u>--The defendant is formally charged with a crime. A grand jury made up of impartial citizens issues an indictment for felony crimes. A magistrate issues an information for misdemeanor crimes.

C.   <u>Trial</u>--The prosecution must prove that the defendant is guilty beyond a reasonable doubt. Compare the burden of proof in civil cases where the plaintiff must prove his or her case by a preponderance of the evidence (more likely than not). The defendant in a criminal action has the burden of proving a defense if the government meets its burden.

VI.   <u>Business Crimes</u>

A.   <u>Forgery</u>--The defendant must make a false writing or alter a legal writing. Forgery also includes passing forged writing to another if the defendant knows it has been forged.

B.   <u>Theft</u>--Encompasses several crimes; the elements of each are distinct.

(1)   <u>Larceny</u>--The wrongful or fraudulent taking of the property of another. "Property" is defined by statute and may or may not include intangible (non-touchable) items such as computer time or software programs.

(2)   <u>False Pretenses</u>--The defendant receives goods based on a false or fraudulent representation.

(3)   <u>Receiving Stolen Goods</u>--The defendant must know or have reason to know that the goods have been stolen.

(4)   <u>Embezzlement</u> --The defendant must be an agent of the victim or otherwise entrusted with the stolen property. Embezzlement was created to fill in gaps left by theft statutes. Assume that a teller jimmies the books or receives money from a customer but does not turn the money over to the bank. Who owns the money at that point in time?

C. Robbery--Robbery is theft accomplished through the use of force or fear.

D. Burglary--The defendant must enter property owned by another with the intent to commit a crime. Note that the crime does not have to be completed. Most states have eliminated the requirement of breaking and entering.

E. Bribery

   (1) Public Officials--The recipient of the bribe must be a public officeholder and the defendant must intend to gain some private advantage.

   (2) Foreign Officials--Same standard as above. Covered by federal law.

   (3) Commercial--Wrongful business practices accomplished by payoffs to the defendant.

   Note that in all cases, the offer of the bribe is sufficient; the intended recipient does not have to accept the bribe.

F. Bankruptcy Fraud

   (1) False Claims of Creditors--A creditor who realizes that he or she may only receive a portion of the money owed by the debtor increases his claim in order to gain more money when the debtor's assets are distributed.

   (2) Fraudulent Transfer of Property--Shortly before bankruptcy, the debtor conveys property to a relative or friend. When the debtor declares bankruptcy, the property would not be considered part of the debtor's estate which is used to pay creditors. Therefore, the creditors are deprived of an asset to the estate.

   (3) Scam Bankruptcy--Planned by debtor in advance. The debtor establishes a business with a high turnover rate and a good credit rating with suppliers. At some point when the creditors have advanced inventory or supplies, the defendant sells the inventory, closes the business, and leaves town with the only assets that cold be used to satisfy the creditors.

G.   RICO (Racketeer Influenced and Corrupt Organization Act)--Designed to curb organized crime by providing civil and criminal penalties. The civil action usually involves business fraud as part of a continuing enterprise. The defendant may lose property and the victim may be awarded treble (triple) damages. The criminal action requires racketeering activity or the conspiracy to commit a crime via racketeering. Can be used in mail or securities fraud cases.

Study Questions

Fill-in-the-Blank Questions

The following events took place over the course of a year at Walt's Drug Store. Mr. Jones wrote a check to Walt's on an account he knew he had closed the month before. Mr. Jones' nine year-old son took a comic book from the rack without paying for it. Daniel, the night manager, and Frieda, the bookkepper, deliberately failed to record payments by several customers. Robert entered the store with a knife and demanded that Walt give him a free soda.

Mr. Jones has committed _____.
                              (larceny/robbery/theft
                               by false pretenses)

Daniel and Freida have committed _____.
                                 (larceny/embezzlement/robbery)

Mr. Jones' son has committed _____.
                              (larceny/robbery/embezzlement)

Robert has committed _____.
                     (theft by false pretenses/robbery/burglary)

True-False Questions

1.   In a criminal trial, the defendant has burden of proof with regard to a defense. ____

2.   Voluntary intoxication is a complete defense to a crime. ____

3.   The duty of a grand jury is to decide if the defendant is guilty or not guilty. ____

4.   In order to convict a defendant, the prosecution must prove only that the defendant performed a prohibited act. ____

5.   In most states, an element of burglary is breaking and entering. ____

6.   Children between the ages of seven and fourteen are presumed capable of committing a crime. ____

7.   The judge decides whether a crime is a felony or a misdemeanor. ____

8.   In a civil case, the victim is the plaintiff; in a criminal case, the government is the plaintiff. ____

9.   A speeding ticket is an example of a felony. ____

10.   Mistake of law is never a defense to a crime. ____

Multiple-Choice Questions

1.   Cindy has a $45,000 debt. Her only asset is a condominium in Colorado. Cindy sells the condo to her brother Ralph for a price of $50 and she declares bankruptcy. Cindy has committed which of the following bankruptcy crimes?

      a.   Scam bankruptcy
      b.   Fraudulent transfer of property
      c.   False claims of creditors
      d.   Embezzlement

2.   Which of the following statements is _false_?

      a.   In civil law, a fine may be imposed against the defendant.
      b.   Criminal law is primarily statutory law.
      c.   In criminal law, a wrong is committed against society as a whole.
      d.   In civil law, the burden of proof is by a preponderance of the evidence.

3.   Sammy enters Mrs. Smith's house planning to steal her television set. Mrs. Smith's large dog meets Sammy in the living room and he runs away without taking anything. Sammy has committed:

      a.   robbery.
      b.   burglary.
      c.   larceny.
      d.   no crime, because he didn't take the television set.

4.   The formal charge issued by a grand jury in a felony
      case is an:

      a. information.
      b. incrimination.
      c. indisposition.
      d. indictment.

5.   In order for a magistrate to issue an arrest warrant, he
      must believe:

      a. beyond a reasonable doubt that the accused committed
          the crime.
      b. by a preponderance of the evidence that the accused
          committed the crime.
      c. that there is probable cause to arrest the accused.
      d. that it is more likely than not that the accused
          committed the crime.

6.   Mary attends a Christmas party where a fellow guest had
      "spiked" the punch. Mary did not know that liquor had
      been added to the punch. She drank several glasses and
      then committed a misdemeanor on the way home from the
      party. Mary's best defense would be:

      a. voluntary intoxication.
      b. involuntary intoxication.
      c. mistake of law.
      d. immunity.

7.   Which of the following defenses is usually connected
      with plea bargaining?

      a. Mistake of law
      b. Mistake of fact
      c. Immunity
      d. Entrapment

8.   Which of the following "legal" definitions of insanity
      is hardest for the defendant to meet?

      a. The M'Naghten test
      b. Irresistible impulse
      c. Model Penal Code
      d. None of the above

9.   Which of the following facts constitute forgery?

    a.   Lucy deliberately alters her age on her marriage license.
    b.   Robert steals Allen's checkbook and writes a check to his accountant.
    c.   Sidney knows that his wife has "doctored" the amounts on an insurance claim form, but he submits it to his insurance company for payment.
    d.   All of the above constitute forgery.

10.   Pete enters Bill's backyard, grabs Bill's new power drill and is jumping over the fence into the alley when Bill sees him and shoots him. If **Bill** if prosecuted, he:

    a.   will be found not guilty if he pleads self-defense.
    b.   will be found not guilty if he pleads defense of property.
    c.   will not be found guilty because he did not commit a crime.
    d.   will be found guilty.

11.   In Question 10, Pete has committed:

    a.   larceny.
    b.   robbery.
    c.   burglary.
    d.   theft by false pretenses.

12.   As Robert is leaving a restaurant, he picks up a hat from the rack in the front of the restaurant. Later in the day, he discovers that he has taken someone else's hat although his hat looks exactly like the one he took. Robert has committed:

    a.   theft but he has a good defense if he pleads mistake of fact.
    b.   theft but he has a good defense if he pleads mistake of law.
    c.   theft and he has no defense.
    d.   robbery and he has no defense.

13.   RICO stands for:

    a.   Robbery and Intentional Corruption by Organized Crime Act.
    b.   Racketeering and Intentional Corruption by Organized Crime Act.
    c.   Racketeering Influenced and Corrupt Organization Act.
    d.   Racketeering Influenced by Corruption and Organized Crime Act.

14.   RICO has:

        a. criminal remedies only.
        b. civil remedies only.
        c. civil and criminal remedies.

15.   In a scam bankruptcy, the crime is committed by:

        a. debtors only.
        b. creditors only.
        c. debtors and creditors.
        d. debtors, creditors and government officials.

16.   Roger enters a bank, pulls out a gun, and forces the
        teller to fill a bag with money and to steal the bank
        president's car. The teller's best defense to a charge
        of theft would be:

        a. self-defense.
        b. duress.
        c. entrapment.
        d. duress to a charge of stealing of money but she has
            no defense to stealing the bank president's car.

17.   Roger, a building contractor, submits a bid to the City
        of Midville for construction of a new jail. He offers
        two city councilmen 5 percent of the profits if he is
        awarded the contract. The city councilmen refuse the
        money and vote to give the contract to Dennis. Roger
        has committed:

        a. commercial bribery.
        b. bribery of a public official.
        c. no crime because the councilmen did not take the
            money.
        d. no crime because he was not awarded the contract.

18.   If a defendant tries to plead entrapment as a defense to
        a crime, he or she must show:

        a. that a private person suggested that the crime be
            committed and that the private person persuaded him
            or her to commit the crime.
        b. that a public officer suggested that the crime be
            committed and that the public officer persuaded him
            or her to commit the crime.
        c. that a public official told the defendant that his
            actions were not a crime.
        d. that another person forced him or her to commit the
            crime.

19. The following crimes are listed in order from most to least serious. Which is correct?

   a. Misdemeanors, violations, felonies
   b. Felonies, misdemeanors, violations
   c. Misdemeanors, felonies, violations
   d. Felonies, violations, misdemeanors

20. Consent, if proven, would be a proper defense to which of the following crimes?

   a. Bribery
   b. Forgery
   c. Theft
   d. Bankruptcy fraud.

21. Allen has supplied credit for several years to Ace Drilling Co. When the price of oil drops, Allen learns that Ace is about to declare bankruptcy. Although Ace owes Allen $20,000, Allen files a claim form in bankruptcy court showing that $40,000 is owed. Which crime has been committed?

   a. Scam bankruptcy
   b. Fraudulent claims of creditors
   c. Theft
   d. Embezzlement

22. Plasma Labs, Inc. offers Dr. Schlock a 4% return on any blood test or X-ray ordered by Dr. Schlock and performed by Plasma. Plamsa's offer is an example of:

   a. embezzlement.
   b. receipt of stolen property.
   c. commercial bribery.
   d. forgery.

23. Which of the following persons determines if a particular crime is a felony or a misdemeanor?

   a. The judge
   b. The prosecuting attorney
   c. The jury
   d. The legislature

24.   Tort law differs from criminal law because in tort law, the defendant:

   a. may pay a fine but will not receive a prison sentence.
   b. may pay compensation to the victim but will not receive a prison sentence.
   c. may pay a fine and may receive a prison sentence.
   d. may pay compensation to the victim and may receive a prison sentence.

25.   When a police officer arrests a suspect, he must:

   a. have probable cause to believe that the suspect committed the crime.
   b. believe beyond a reasonable doubt that the suspect committed the crime.
   c. neither of the above, an arrest warrant must be issued before a police officer can arrest a suspect.
   d. none of the above, the grand jury must issue an indictment before a police officer can arrest a suspect.

Answers to Study Questions

Fill-in-the-Blank Questions

Mr. Jones has committed theft by false pretenses; by writing a check, he represented to Walt that he had a current bank account. Daniel and Frieda have committed embezzlement. Mr. Jones' son has committed larceny; he has not committed robbery because he did not use force or fear when he took the comic book. Robert has committed robbery and larceny; a robbery always includes larceny.

True-False Questions

1.   T.

2.   F.   Voluntary intoxication may lessen the degree of the charge; involuntary intoxication is a complete defense.

3.   F.   The duty of the grand jury is to decide if there is enough evidence to hold the defendant for trial.

4.   F.   The prosecution must also prove that the defendant possessed the required state of mind.

5.   F.   Most states have eliminated this requirement.

6.   F.   They are presumed incapable but the prosecution can rebut that proof.

7.   F.   The legislature decides when it passes a statute.

8.   T.

9.   F.   It is an example of a violation.

10.   F.   It is a mistake if the law has not been published or widely circulated or if the defendant relies on the advice of a government official such as an attorney general.

Multiple-Choice Questions

1.	b	8.	a	14.	c	20.	c
2.	a	9	d	15.	a	21.	b
3.	b	10.	d	16.	b	22.	c
4.	d	11.	a	17.	b	23.	d
5.	c	12.	a	18.	b	24.	b
6.	b	13.	c	19.	b	25.	b
7.	c						

Chapter 5 Contracts— Nature, Classification, and Form

General

A contract is a legal obligation to perform an act or to refrain from performing an act. When a person sues for breach of contract he or she must prove the following facts:

1. A valid contract was formed. The requirements are listed below.

2. The defendant has no legal excuse. The most common defenses are listed below.

3. The contract was breached. The defendant failed to perform as promised.

4. The plaintiff has suffered injury. Even if a contract was made and breached, the plaintiff cannot recover unless he or she can prove injury.

Chapter Summary

I. Requirements for Formation of a Contract

    A. Agreement--One party must make a valid offer to perform and the other party must accept the offer.

    B. Consideration--Each party must be willing to do an act or to refrain from doing an act.

C.   Contractual Capacity--Each party must have the
      legal ability to make a contract. Minors, insane
      persons, and intoxicated persons are protected by
      law.

D.   Legality--The subject matter of the contract must
      be lawful. A court will not enforce an illegal
      contract.

In addition, the plaintiff must show that the defendant
has no defense against payment. The most common
defenses include:

E.   Reality of Assent--The defendant must consent to
      the agreement. No mistake, fraud, duress, or undue
      influence.

F.   Form--Some contracts must be in writing.

II.   Types of Contracts

A.   Bilateral v. Unilateral

      (1) Bilateral--Promise in exchange for another
           promise. Most common.

      (2) Unilateral--Promise in exchange for an act.
           The best example is a contest.

It is often difficult to distinguish between the
two. Ask yourself if the person making the first
promise (the offeror) will be satisfied with a
promise to perform from the other party (offeree).
If a promise is insufficient, then the contract is
unilateral.

EX: A disk jockey promises a free album to the 9th
caller. The disk jockey would not be satisfied
with your promise to be the 9th caller. You must
be the 9th caller. The contract is unilateral.

In a unilateral contract, the offeror cannot revoke
the offer if the offeree has started performing.
It would be unfair for the disk jockey to take back
his promise once you have begun dialing.

B.   Express v. Implied Contract

      (1) Express--Terms are stated; need not be
           written.

(2) Implied--Contract is implied from the conduct
     of the parties. It is an objective test. Ask
     yourself how a reasonable person would have
     interpreted the conduct.

     Proof of an implied-in-fact contract:

     1. The plaintiff furnished some service or
         property.
     2. The plaintiff expected to be paid for his
         trouble and a reasonable person would have
         realized that payment was expected.
     3. The defendant had a chance to reject the
         plaintiff's offer but did not do so.

C.   Contract Implied in Fact v. Contract Implied in Law

     (1) Implied in Fact--Contract implied from conduct
          of the parties.

     (2) Implied in Law (Quasi-Contract)--Not a true
          contract because one or more elements are
          missing but one party (plaintiff) has
          performed and it would be unfair to let the
          defendant receive something for nothing.

          Proof of a Contract Implied in Law:

          1. The plaintiff did an act that benefited
              the defendant.
          2. The defendant was unjustly enriched. (The
              defendant got something for nothing.)
          3. The plaintiff was not negligent or
              dishonest.

D.   Formal v. Informal Contracts

     (1) Formal--Requires a special format or a special
          procedure to execute them. A contract under
          seal requires a special seal to be placed on
          the document. A recognizance (surety bond), a
          negotiable instrument, and a letter of credit
          require certain formalities.

     (2) Informal--All other contracts.

E.   Executed v. Executory

     (1) Executed--Has been performed by both parties.

(2) Executory--An agreement has been reached but neither party has performed. A contract can be executory on one side and executed on the other.

F.   Valid, Void, Voidable and Unenforceable Contracts

(1) Valid--Meets all the requirements for formation listed above and no defense to performance exists.

(2) Unenforceable--Meets the requirements of formation but a defense exists and the plaintiff cannot sue the defendant for failure to perform.

(3) Voidable--One or both parties can legally cancel the contract. Usually occurs with a minor or insane person.

(4) Void--No contract and neither side can enforce its terms. Illegal contracts are usually void.

Study Questions

Fill-in-the-Blank Questions

Tom offers in writing to sell his TV to Bridget for $50. Bridget accepts the offer in writing and promises to pay Tom on Tuesday. On Tuesday, Tom hands Bridget the TV set but Bridget refuses to pay.

The contract between Tom and Bridget is *bilateral*.
                                    (bilateral/unilateral)

The contract is *informal*.
                (formal/informal)

The contract is *express*.
                (express/implied in fact)

True-False Questions

1.   Quasi-contract is another name for a contract implied in fact. __F__

2.   A bilateral contract consists of a promise given in exchange for another promise. __T__

3.   A voidable contract may be cancelled by one or both of the parties. __F__ T

4.   An express contract must be written. __F__

5.   Fraud is a defense to enforcement of a contract. __F__ T

6.   Consideration is required for formation of a contract. __T__

7.   An implied-in-fact contract is formed by the conduct of the parties. __T__

8.   A letter of credit is an example of a formal contract. __T__

9.   The defendant in a suit for quasi-contract is the party who received the goods or services. __F__ T

10.   Contractual capacity is one requirement for formation of a contract. __T__

Multiple-Choice Questions

1.   Nancy enters Lucy's cafeteria and places an order of fried chicken and a salad on her tray. The cashier hands Nancy a ticket showing the cost of the meal. The contract between Nancy and Lucy's is:

      a. implied in law and Nancy must pay for the meal.
      c. implied in fact and Nancy must pay for the meal.
      c. express and Nancy must pay for the meal.
      d. unenforceable because Nancy did not agree to pay.

2.   Burger Queen restaurant is sponsoring a promotion to introduce its new "Topper" hamburger. Burger Queen promises to give a T-shirt to the first 20 customers who order a "Topper". Ned is the 15th customer. Burger Queen:

      a. is the offeror and the contract is bilateral.
      b. is the offeror and the contract is unilateral.
      c. is the offeree and the contract is bilateral.
      d. is the offeree and the contract is unilateral.

3.   The contract between Ned and Burger Queen is:

      a. implied in law and unenforceable.
      b. implied in fact and unenforceable.
      c. express and unenforceable.
      d. express and enforceable.

4. Sol hires Benjy to rake his lawn and burn the dry grass
    and leaves. A city ordinance prohibits burning trash,
    leaves and grass. The contract between Benjy and Sol is:

    a. valid.
    b. voidable.
    c. void.
    d. unenforceable.

5. Beverly takes her silk blouse to the dry cleaners and
    asks them to clean it. Anne leaves an identical blouse
    at the same store. She asks the owner to clean it and
    to replace the buttons. The owner scrambles the order
    and replaces the buttons on Beverly's blouse. Although
    Beverly likes the new buttons, she refuses to pay for
    them. The owner sues Beverly on which of the following
    theories?

    a. Implied-in-fact contract
    b. Implied-in law contract
    c. Express contract
    d. Informal contract

6. The owner will be:

    a. successful because Beverly was unjustly enriched.
    b. successful because the owner furnished the buttons.
    c. unsuccessful because the owner was negligent.
    d. successful because a reasonable person would have
        paid for the buttons.

7. Bill offers to walk Cindy's dogs every day next week at
    a rate of $2 per day. Cindy agrees to pay him $10 after
    the Friday walk. The contract between Bill and Cindy is:

    a. unilateral and implied in fact.
    b. unilateral and express.
    c. bilateral and express.
    d. bilateral and implied in law.

8. On Tuesday, the contract is:

    a. executed on Bill's side and executory on Cindy's
        side.
    b. executed on Cindy's side and executory on Bill's
        side.
    c. executed on both sides.
    d. executory on both sides.

9. Which of the following is not required for formation of a contract but is defense to enforcement of the contract?

    a. Agreement
    b. Form
    c. Consideration
    d. Legality

10. Which of the following is not a formal contract?

    a. A sales contract
    b. A negotiable instrument
    c. A surety bond
    d. A letter of credit

11. Mary, age ten, buys a yo-yo from the toy store. Because Mary is a minor, she can cancel the contract at any time. The contract between Mary and the store is:

    a. void.
    b. voidable.
    c. valid.
    d. invalid.

12. Linda is shopping at Al's Grocery. She fills her cart and gets in line at the cash register. After the cashier has rung up the purchases, Mary writes a check to pay for the goods. The next day Mary stops payment on the check, returns the groceries and tells Al that she was only kidding. She would never buy groceries from him. The contract between Linda and Al:

    a. is enforceable because of the objective theory of contracts.
    b. is unenforceable because Mary didn't really intend to make a contract.
    c. is unenforceable because the contract is implied and not express.
    d. is unenforceable because it is unilateral and not bilateral.

13. Alice rents an apartment from Oscar. State law requires that all leases be in writing. The contract between Alice and Oscar is:

    a. void.
    b. voidable.
    c. valid.
    d. unenforceable.

14.   Andrew tells Ted that he will pay Ted $100 if Ted will
       find Andrew's lost dog. The contract between Ted and
       Andrew is:

       a. bilateral and formal.
       b. bilateral and informal.
       c. unilateral and formal.
       (c.) unilateral and informal.

15.   Aunt Becky tells Tom that she will pay him $4 if he will
       paint her fence. After Tom has painted part of the
       fence, Aunt Becky tells Tom that she has decided to hire
       a professional painter. Aunt Becky:

       a. can revoke her offer because Tom has not accepted.
       b. can revoke her offer because the contract is
           informal.
       (c.) cannot revoke her offer because Tom has begun
           performance.
       d. cannot revoke her offer because the contract is
           bilateral

Answers to Study Questions

Fill-in-the-Blank Questions

The contract is bilateral. Tom promised to sell and Bridget
promised to buy. The contract is informal. It does not matter
that the contract is written; it is not a letter of credit,
recognizance, and does not require a seal. The contract is
express; the terms are stated.

True-False Questions

1.   F. Quasi-contract is a synonym for a contract implied
      in law.

2.   T.

3.   T.

4.   F. An express contract is one whose terms have been
      stated; it may be oral.

5.   T. Remember genuineness of assent.

6.   T.

7.   T.

8.   T.

9.   T.

10.   T.

Multiple-Choice Questions

1.	b	8.	d
2.	b	9.	b
3.	d	10.	a
4.	c	11.	b
5.	b	12.	a
6.	c	13.	d
7.	c	14.	d
		15.	c

Chapter 6   Agreement and Consideration

The first requirement for a valid contract is agreement between the parties: an offer by one party that is accepted by the other party. The offeror is the "master" of the offer; he or she establishes the terms of the agreement. The offeree can accept these terms or propose new ones. When the offeree accepts, there is agreement, and the first condition for a contract is satisfied.

Consideration is another requirement for an enforceable contract. Each party to a contract must make a commitment or give up a legal right. In most contracts, one party promises to pay money and the other promises to provide goods or services but consideration need not be money. If only one party provides consideration, a gift, not a contract, exists.

Chapter Summary

I.   Agreement--The Offer--An offer expresses a serious intent to be bound to a contract. It must be reasonably definite so that the court could order a remedy if one party should breach. The offer must be communicated to the offeree.

  A.   Seriousness Intent to Be Bound Immediately--An offer creates the power in the offeree to accept and conclude a binding agreement, the offeror must be willing to perform. Do not confuse performance with intention to be bound. A legal contract is formed when the parties agree although performance may not take place immediately.

(1) <u>Seriousness</u>--A statement made in anger, <u>frustration</u>, or as a joke is not an offer. The effect of the statement is measured by what a reasonable person would think if he or she heard it. This is the <u>objective</u> theory of contracts.

(2) <u>Present Intent to Be Bound</u>

    (a) Distinguish an invitation for offers from a genuine offer. Ads, auctions, price lists, and solicitation for bids are <u>not</u> true offers. Remember that a true offer would allow everyone who saw the ad or submitted a bid to accept and the offeror would be obligated to fill numerous contracts. An invitation to offer requires three steps to agreement instead of the usual offer and acceptance: 1) invitation to offer; 2) offer; 3) acceptance.

        <u>Example</u>:   Auctioneer asks for bids (invitation for offers); bidders propose prices (offers); the auctioneer drops the hammer and says "Sold" (acceptance).

        <u>Exception</u>: Occasionally an advertisement can be considered an offer. If the contract is unilateral and the ad is very specific, the courts may rule that it is an offer.

    (b) Distinguish an expression of intention from a true offer. Equivocal language such as, "I plan to" or "I intend to" are insufficient.

(3) <u>Statements of Opinion</u>--Distinguish a pre-diction from a promise.

B.   <u>Definiteness</u>--Also an indication of intent to be bound. If many terms are left blank, it is reasonable to assume that the parties are still negotiating. In a contract for the sale of goods, the UCC will allow the courts to fill in several blanks using reasonable terms or industry customs. Ask yourself if one party breached, would a court be able to determine the obligations of each party. If so, the contract is sufficiently definite.

C. Communication--Only the intended offeree has the power to accept; a bystander cannot. An offeree cannot accept an offer if he has not receive it.

II. Agreement--Termination of the Offer

A. Acts of the Parties

(1) Revocation--As a general rule, the offeror can revoke the offer at any time prior to acceptance. The revocation is effective when it is received by the offeree.

There are three exceptions to this rule: 1) an option contract where the offeree pays the offeror to hold the option open; 2) action by the offeree due to reliance on the offer; 3) a signed, written offer by a merchant for a sale of goods (time limit no more than ninety days).

(2) Rejection--If the offeree expressly indicates that he or she will not accept the terms proposed, the offer is terminated.

(3) Counteroffer--If the offeree makes a new proposal, a counteroffer is created. It is treated as a new offer and the offeree becomes the offeror. In non-sales contracts, any variance from the original offer becomes a counteroffer.

In sales contracts, if the important terms are agreed on by the parties, a contract may exist even though the details are not settled. This situation usually occurs when the offeree uses a different form to respond (battle of the forms). The new terms may become a part of the contract depending on the sophistication of the parties.

(a) Non-Merchants--The new terms proposed by the offeree do not become a part of the contract.

(b) Merchants--Because merchants deal with contracts routinely, new terms may become a part of the contract unless the new terms include important or material changes, the offeror insisted on a "take it or leave it" acceptance, or the offeror refuses the new terms within a reasonable time.

B.   Operation of Law

(1) Lapse of Time--If the offer is not accepted within a reasonable time, it expires. Reasonableness may depend on the subject matter of the contract.

(2) Destruction of the Subject Matter

(3) Death or Incompetency of a Party--Notice is not required. Some option contracts may be binding on the heirs of a party.

(4) Supervening Illegality--The offer was legal when made but the laws changed and it is now illegal.

III.   Agreement--Acceptance--The acceptance requires the same commitment as the offer; the offeree must intend to make a contract. Silence is generally not acceptance unless the offeree's actions show a willingness to go through with the contract. Distinguish prior dealings between the parties and the continuation of performance of a contract.

Example: Many book and record clubs will send a member a monthly selection unless notice is received. Remember that the contract was formed when the member joined the club. The monthly offerings are performance of the contract.

A.   Communication--Unless specified by the offeror, communication is not necessary. However, if the offeror does not receive an answer, the offer may lapse.

B.   Mode--Unless specified by the offeror, any reasonable method of acceptance is acceptable. Mail is normally adequate.

C.   Time of Effect--An acceptance is effective when it is sent (mailbox rule). An offeror should not make an offer unless he or she is willing for another party to accept. If the acceptance is lost in the mail due to the negligence of the offeree, it is not effective until it is received. An offer can expressly require receipt of acceptance.

D.   Acceptance and Rejection--If the offeree sends both an acceptance and a rejection, the first communication to be received is effective. It is immaterial which was sent first. Examine the rule from the offeror's point of view; he or she does not know that a second communication has been sent and should be able to rely on a response when it is received.

IV.   Consideration--A bargained-for exchange of value between the parties.

    A.   Bargain--The parties must agree to the exchange at the time the contract is formed. An act performed in the past before the promise is made is not valid consideration.

    B.   Legal Value--Each party must promise to do something that he or she is not legally obligated to do or each party must give up a legal right (forbearance).

    C.   Adequacy of Consideration--The monetary value exchanged need not be equal or equivalent. If the contract is extremely one-sided, it may be an indication that one party was forced or tricked into agreeing and the contract may be cancelled for that reason.

    D.   Problem Areas--A suggested approach is to write each party's name and the consideration provided. If only one party has provided real value, then consideration fails.

        (1)   Pre-Existing Duty Rule--Occurs with modification of contracts. If a contract is modified, then each party must provide new consideration. The rule was created to prevent blackmail.

            EX: Paul's Plumbing agrees to install a new shower at a cost of $600. When Paul is halfway done, he informs the homeowner that he will walk off the job if the owner does not pay an extra $400. The owner reluctantly agrees. There is no consideration for the owner's promise to pay $400.

            It is unenforceable even though he has agreed.

Paul	Homeowner
install shower	$600
+	+
_____	$400

Exceptions:

(a) <u>Unforeseen Difficulties</u>--If Paul had experienced difficulties which a reasonable plumber would not have predicted, his extra work is consideration for the extra money.

(b) <u>Rescission and New Contract</u>--If both parties willingly agree to give up rights under the old contract, they have given up legal rights and the new contract is enforceable.

(c) <u>Sales of Goods</u>--No consideration is necessary to modify a sales contract but the change must have been made in good faith.

(2) <u>Illusory Promises</u>--Ask if one party has given up something of value or if it only appears so.

(a) <u>Requirements Contracts</u>--Usualy made between a large seller and a small buyer. The buyer promises to buy all the seller's goods that he or she <u>needs</u>. The buyer gives up the right to buy from anyone else; the seller promises to fulfill the buyer's needs before selling to others. Must be expressed in terms of needs and not desires.

(b) <u>Output Contracts</u>--The opposite of a requirements contract and involves a large buyer and small seller. The seller promises to sell all his production to the buyer and gives up the right to sell to others. The buyer agrees to buy all the seller's goods before purchasing from another.

(3) <u>Settlement of Claims</u>

(a) <u>Accord and Satisfaction</u>--A debtor offers to pay a creditor less than the total amount due. The accord is the new agreement; the satisfaction is the performance of the new agreement. A settlement will be enforceable if the amount is genuinely in dispute (unliquidated). If the amount is predetermined and the only quarrel is a refusal to pay, then settlement for less than the full amount is not adequate consideration.

EX: Mary purchases a washing machine from AAA Applicances. She agrees to pay $400 a month for 2 months. The washer breaks down and Mary sends AAA a check for $1 marked paid in full.

Creditor	Debtor
gives up $799	_____

If Mary had given up the right to sue for breach of contract, then the accord and satisfaction would be enforceable.

(b) Release--Usually occurs as settlement of a lawsuit or other unliquidated claim. Each party gives up the right to prove the actual damages and the release is enforceable.

(c) Covenant Not to Sue--Resembles an accord and satisfaction. A promise not to sue by one party is based on another's promise to pay for damages. If payment is not forthcoming, the substituted performance fails and the injured party may sue for breach of contract.

D. Promissory Estoppel (Detrimental Reliance)--An equitable remedy which may be used to enforce a contract if all the following elements are present:

(1) D made a promise to P.

(2) P justifiably (reasonably) relied on the promise.

(3) P suffered substantial detriment as a result of the reliance.

(4) Injustice cannot otherwise be avoided.

Study Questions

Fill-in-the-Blank Questions

John puts an ad in the paper, "1968 Cadillac for sale. Vintage condition. $2000." Rob reads the ad, calls John and says, "I'll take it".

John has made a(n) _____ *invitation to offer* _____.
(offer/invitation to offer)

Rob has made a(n) _____ *acceptance* _____.
(offer/acceptance)

There ___ *is not* ___ a valid agreement between Rob and John.
(is/is not)

True-False Questions

1. If the offeree makes a counteroffer, the original offer is terminated. __T

2. A covenant not to sue is another term for a release. __F

3. In an auction contract, acceptance is made when the auctioneer says "Sold". __T

4. A requirements contract is an exception to the pre-existing duty rule. __F

5. In non-sales contracts, an acceptance must agree to the offer as stated and any change will be considered a counteroffer. __T

6. A properly executed accord and satisfaction will discharge a liquidated debt. __F

7. An option contract is an irrevocable offer. __T

8. If the price is omitted from a sales contract, the contract cannot be enforced. __F

9. An offer may be terminated if the subject matter of the contract is destroyed. __T

10. The seriousness of an offer is measured by the subjective intent of the offeror. __F

Multiple-Choice Questions

1. Sandra writes to Paula and offers to sell her 10-speed bicycle for $200. Sandra mails the offer on Monday and it is received on Wednesday. Paula calls Sandra on Thursday and tells Sandra she will buy the bicycle. She mails a check to Sandra on Friday. Sandra receives the check on Saturday. Paula's acceptance is effective on:

    a. Wednesday.
    b. Thursday.
    c. Friday.
    d. Saturday.

2. Sandra could have revoked the offer legally on:

    a. Monday.
    b. Thursday after Sandra's call.
    c. Friday.
    d. none of the above; Sandra has no right to revoke an offer.

3. Bobby sees a dog wandering on the street. He reads the dog's tags and returns the dog to its owner, Susan. When Bobby returns home, he reads the evening paper and discovers that Susan is offering a reward for the return of her dog.

    a. Bobby can collect the reward because he provided consideration by returning the dog.
    b. Bobby can collect the reward because Susan's ad in the newspaper was an offer and Bobby accepted when he returned the dog.
    c. Bobby cannot collect the reward because Susan has not provided consideration.
    d. Bobby cannot collect the reward because he has not provided any consideration.

4. Mrs. Evans worked as a secretary for Big M Corporation for 25 years. When she retired, the board of directors of Big M passed a resolution which promised to pay Mrs. Evans $200 per month for the rest of her life "in consideration of her loyalty to Big M Corporation". Mrs. Evans received the money for 2 years but when a new board was elected, it refused to pay. Mrs. Evans sued the board and Big M.

a. Mrs. Evans will win because she provided consideration to the company by working for 25 years.
b. Mrs. Evans will win because she accepted the payments.
c. Mrs. Evans will win because she relied on the promise made by Big M's board.
d. Mrs. Evans will lose because the board's declaration was not an offer.

5. Phineas Pharmaceuticals offers to sell Dr. Smock a case of its newest creation, "Mega-Multi Vitamin". The offer is received by Dr. Smock but before he can respond, the Food and Drug Administration bans the sale of the vitamin. Dr. Smock is unaware of the ban.

a. Phineas must revoke the offer before Dr. Smock accepts.
b. The offer will terminate only if Dr. Smock does not accept.
c. The offer terminated automatically when the vitamin was banned and Phineas does not have to revoke the offer.
d. The offer has not been terminated.

6. Vern's Wholesale Vegetables offers to sell Sizemore Supermarkets 20 cartons of frozen peas for $100 per carton. The president of Sizemore writes to Vern and states, "Please send 20 cartons of peas and include 2 boxes of your new Gourmet Carrots". Sizemore's president:

a. has rejected Vern's offer.
b. has accepted Vern's offer.
c. has made a counteroffer.

7. E-Z Auto Finance sells a used car to Mrs. Smith for $4,000. Mrs. Smith soon discovers that the car has engine trouble and is only worth $400.

a. The contract between Mrs. Smith and E-Z is invalid because she provided more consideration than E-Z.
b. The contract is invalid because Mrs. Smith did not accept E-Z's offer.
c. The contract is invalid because E-Z has provided no consideration.
d. Both parties have provided consideration and a valid contract has been formed.

8. Rose belongs to the Bargain Book Club. The club agreement states that Rose will receive a book each month unless she notifies the club in writing. Rose received a book in the mail last week but refuses to pay.

    a. Rose does not have to pay because silence is never acceptance.
    b. Rose does not have to pay because the book club did not make an offer.
    c. Rose must pay for the book because she accepted the terms of the agreement when she joined the club.
    d. Rose does not have to pay for the book because she has not accepted it.

9. Linda buys a stereo from AAA Appliances. She pays $50 down and agrees to pay $50 per month for 6 months. The stereo quits working after the first month. Linda sends AAA a check for $1 with the notation "payment in full". AAA cashes the check.

    a. AAA can sue Linda for the remaining amount due because the debt is liquidated.
    b. AAA can sue Linda for the remaining amount because the debt is unliquidated.
    c. AAA cannot sue Linda because there has been an accord and satisfaction and the debt is liquidated.
    d. AAA cannot sue Linda because there has been an accord and satisfaction and the debt is unliquidated.

10. Paul writes to Pete and offers to sell his bicycle to him for $30. Pete does not want the bicycle but Pete's roommate Tony sees the letter and writes Paul and promises to pay him $30.

    a. There is a contract between Paul and Tony because Tony accepted Paul's offer.
    b. There is a contract between Paul and Tony because Tony provided consideration by sending $30.
    c. There is no contract between Paul and Tony because Tony did not receive an offer.
    d. There is no contract between Paul and Tony because a promise to pay $30 is not valid consideration.

11. Oliver writes to Sidney and offers to sell him his house. Sidney receives the offer on Monday. He mails an acceptance on Tuesday but has second thoughts and sends a telegram on Thursday rejecting the offer. The rejection is received on Thursday; the acceptance is received on Friday.

a. There is a contract because the acceptance was sent before the rejection.
b. There is a contract because the acceptance was effective on Tuesday and Sidney cannot change his mind.
c. There is not a contract because Sidney sent the rejection after the acceptance.
d. There is not a contract because the rejection arrived before the acceptance.

12. Paul's Painting offers to paint Sally's house for $500. Sally agrees. After beginning work, Paul refuses to complete the job unless Sally pays an additional $200. Sally reluctantly agrees but later refuses to pay.

a. Sally is within her rights because she accepted Paul's original offer.
b. Sally is within her rights because of the pre-existing duty rule.
c. Sally must pay the extra $200 because she promised Paul that she would.
d. Sally must pay the extra $200 because the modification of a service contract needs no consideration to be binding.

13. Mrs. Foster's dog escapes from her backyard and tramples the neighbor's garden. Mrs. Foster offers to pay the neighbor $50 for the damage and the neighbor accepts. Mrs. Foster writes him a check for $50. He signs a statement that the $50 is accepted for all damages. Three days later, the neighbor tells Mrs. Foster that his actual damages were $150 and he intends to sue her for the difference.

a. The neighbor will not succeed because he has signed a valid release.
b. The neighbor will not succeed because he has signed a valid convenant not to sue.
c. The neighbor will not succeed because he has signed a valid accord and satisfaction.
d. The neighbor will succeed.

14. Which of the following is <u>not</u> an exception to the pre-existing duty rule?

a. Modification of a sales contract
b. Price change due to inflation
c. Unforeseeable difficulties
d. Rescission and new contract

15. McRonald's restaurant contracts with Farmer Brown to buy all the eggs Brown's chickens can produce for $.60 per dozen. The agreement between McRonald and Farmer Brown:

 a. is invalid because it is indefinite.
 b. is invalid because Farmer Brown has not provided consideration.
 c. is a valid requirements contract.
 d. is a valid output contract.

16. Which of the following is <u>not</u> a requirement for promissory estoppel?

 a. Justifiable reliance by the promisor
 b. A promise by the promisor
 c. Substantial action or forbearance by the promisee
 d. A promise by the promisee

17. Bill writes to Sandy and offers to mow her lawn for $25 per week. Sandy calls Bill on the phone and accepts.

 a. There is no contract because Sandy did not accept by using the same mode used by Bill to send the offer.
 b. There is no contract because an oral acceptance is never effective.
 c. There is no contract because Bill did not make an offer.
 d. There is a contract between Sandy and Bill.

18. Marge sees a chair she likes at a garage sale. She does not promise to buy the chair but tells the owner she will come back later in the day with the money for the chair. When Marge returns, she discovers that the chair has been sold. If Marge sues the seller, she will:

 a. succeed because she accepted an offer to buy the chair.
 b. succeed because the seller had no right to revoke the offer.
 c. succeed because the seller accepted her offer to buy.
 d. not succeed.

19. Fine China, Inc. places an ad in the local paper which states that Rosebud silver pattern is on sale for $50 per setting. Bob reads the ad and drives to Fine China's store. When he arrives, he offers to buy 10 settings but the manager tells him that they have sold all the Rosebud settings.

a. Bob can sue Fine China for breach of contract because he accepted their offer to buy the silverware.
b. Bob cannot sue Fine China because his promise to buy 10 settings is not valid consideration.
c. Bob cannot sue Fine China because its ad was not an offer.
d. Bob can sue Fine China for breach of contract because Fine China revoked its offer to sell.

20. Which of the following is <u>not</u> an irrevocable offer:

a. A signed, written offer by a boat salesman to sell a sailboat for $4000.
b. A signed, written offer by an attorney to sell a sailboat for $4000.
c. An option contract offering to sell a house for $40,000.
d. An option contract offering to build a house for $40,000.

21. Susan tells her friend Dave that she is planning to sell her TV. She tells him, "I should get about $200." Dave says, "I'll take it".

a. Susan's statement was an offer.
b. Susan's statement was not an offer.
c. Dave's statement was an acceptance.
d. Dave's statement was a counteroffer.

22. George tells Louise he will paint her house for $1500. Louise says, "OK but only if you also paint the shed in the backyard."

a. Louise has accepted George's offer.
b. Louise has rejected George's offer and has not made a counteroffer.
c. Louise has made a counteroffer.
d. George did not make an offer.

23. George tells Louise he will paint her house for $1500 using AAA paint. Louise tells George that the price is right but that she wants him to use Coverall brand paint.

a. Louise's statement is a counteroffer.
b. Louise's statement is an acceptance, but George can use AAA paint.
c. Louise's statement is an acceptance, but George must use Coverall paint.
d. Louise's statement is a revocable.

24.   Which of the following is <u>not</u> an example of termination of an offer by operation of law.

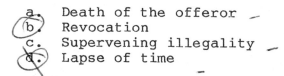

    a.   Death of the offeror
    b.   Revocation
    c.   Supervening illegality
    d.   Lapse of time

25.   Jimmy accidentally drives his car through his cousin's garage door. Jimmy promises to pay for the door if the cousin will not sue. The cousin agrees but Jimmy's check bounces and he refuses to pay.

    a.   The agreement between Jimmy and his cousin was a covenant not to sue and the cousin cannot sue because he agreed not to do so.
    b.   The agreement between Jimmy and his cousin was a covenant not to sue and the cousin can sue because Jimmy breached the covenant.
    c.   The agreement between Jimmy and his cousin was a valid release and the cousin cannot sue.
    d.   The agreement between Jimmy and his cousin was an accord and satisfaction and Jimmy did not complete the satisfaction and the cousin can sue.

Answers to Study Questions

Fill-in-the-Blank Questions

John has made an invitation to offer. An ad is an invitation to offer unless it is very specific and is unilateral. Rob has made the offer. Because thee has been no acceptance, there is not a valid agreement between Rob and John.

True-False Questions

1.   T.

2.   F. A covenant not to sue is a promise not to sue made in exchange for another party's promise to pay damages. If payment is not made, suit is possible. In a release, each party gives up the opportunity to prove the actual amount of damages.

3.   T.

4.   F. A requirement contract exists when a buyer promises to purchase all the goods he or she needs from one seller.

5.   T.

6.   F. It will discharge an unliquidated debt.

7.   T.

8.   F.

9.   T.

10.   F. It is measured by what a reasonable person would have thought. This is an objective test.

Multiple-Choice Questions

1.	b	10.	c	19.	c
2.	a	11.	d	20.	b
3.	d	12.	b	21.	b
4.	c	13.	a	22.	c
5.	c	14.	b	23.	a
6.	b	15.	d	24.	b
7.	d	16.	d	25.	b
8.	c	17.	d		
9.	a	18.	d		

Chapter 7   Capacity and Legality

The public welfare sometimes overrides the legal obligation to complete a contract. The law protects certain types of people from the legal obligations of a contract. The law also prohibits illegal contracts and prevents them from being enforced. The law tries to balance the need for protection with the general duty to fulfill contracts.

Minors and insane or intoxicated persons are given the option of completing or cancelling a contract. If they choose to cancel the contract, they must return any benefits they have received from the contract. Nevertheless, these people may be responsible for basic necessities or if they have deceived the other party to the contract.

Contracts to perform illegal acts are unenforceable. The law may also prohibit contracts which threaten public safety or free enterprise. A court may choose to enforce part of the contract or it may regard the whole contract as unenforceable. People will be discouraged from making illegal contracts if they cannot enforce them.

Chapter Summary

I.   <u>Contractual Capacity</u>--Minors, insane persons, or intoxicated persons are under a "legal disability". They also have the option to cancel or <u>disaffirm</u> the contract.

A.   Protected Persons

    (1)   Minors--Usually age eighteen. Not necessarily the same as the legal drinking age. Some states permit underage persons to be declared adults if they marry before age eighteen or if they petition the court to act as adults.

    (2)   Intoxicated Persons--May be voluntary or involuntary. The test is whether the intoxicated party could understand the legal consequences of his or her actions.

    (3)   Insane Persons--A person who has been officially declared insane by a court of law cannot make a contract. Any attempt to make the contract is void. A guardian appointed by the court makes all legal decisions for the incompetent. A person who is insane but has not been declared insane is treated in the same matter as an intoxicated person.

B.   Dissaffirmance--Right to cancel a contract. The contract is voidable.

    (1)   Who can disaffirm?--Only the person under the disability (the minor, insane, or intoxicated person). The other party is bound.

    (2)   The entire contract must be disaffirmed; no partial cancellation.

    (3)   Duty of Restoration--The disaffirming party must return the goods he or she has received. A few states require that the goods be returned in the same condition as they were received (duty of restitution).

    (4)   Time Limit--A minor must disaffirm while he or she is underage or within a reasonable time after becoming an adult. An insane or intoxicated person must disaffirm within a reasonable time after sanity or sobriety is restored.

    (5)   Liability for Tort--A minor who misrepresents his or her age has the ability to cancel the contract. Some states allow the minor to be sued in tort for deceit.

C. Ratification--Opposite of disaffirmance. The party who is under a disability can agree to complete the contract.

    (1) Time Limits--Can occur only after the disabled party regains contractual capacity. A minor can ratify at age eighteen. An insane or intoxicated person may ratify as soon as he or she understands the consequences of the contract.

    (2) Methods--Can be express or can be implied from conduct. Can be assumed if a contract is not disaffirmed within a reasonable time after the party gains contractual capacity.

D. Liability for Necessaries--A disabled party is liable for contracts involving basic necessities.

    (1) Definition--Any item or service which is essential such as clothing, food, and shelter. Insurance is not usually a necessary but some states allow enforcement of contracts for health or life insurance. Loans are not necessaries unless the lender controls the funds and food, clothing, or shelter is purchased.

    (2) The contract is enforceable only for the reasonable value of the goods or services. The law encourages merchants to sell to minors by allowing the merchants to collect a fair price.

E. Approach--The following set of questions is suggested to determine if the contract is enforceable.

    (1) Is the party under a disability? If no, the contract is enforceable.

    (2) Has the party ratified the contract? If yes, the contract is enforceable.

    (3) Has the party misrepresented his status? If yes, some states will allow a suit for deceit.

    (4) Is the subject of the contract a necessary? If yes, the party is responsible for the reasonable value of the goods or services.

II.   <u>Illegality</u>--State or federal statutes may determine the legality of some contracts. Other contracts are detrimental to the public welfare and are outlawed even though no specific rule states that they are illegal.

A.   <u>Contracts Contrary to Statute</u>

(1)   <u>Usury</u>--Loans made above the maximum rate of interest. Exceptions for small loans or loans to corporations. In some states revolving credit card charges, which allow monthly payments, are exempt from usury laws.

<u>Legal</u> rate of interest is the rate established by the state and is used in contracts where the interest rate is not stated.

<u>Judgment</u> rate of interest is the amount accruing on an award of money at the conclusion of a lawsuit. If the loser doesn't pay immediately, the money earns interest.

If a loan is usurious, the court may void the entire contract, but this is rare. Most states allow the lender to collect the principal of the loan or the principal plus the maximum rate of interest.

(2)   <u>Gambling Contracts</u>--Prohibited in most states. Includes any situation where a person pays money or other consideration for a chance to receive property. The element of chance is the crucial factor. For this reason, lotteries are illegal in some states.

An insurance contract can be considered a gambling contract if the purchaser has no legitimate interest in the subject matter of the contract. You cannot purchase a life insurance contract on the life of another person. A person to whom money is owed and who has a lien on property to secure payment of the loan does have a legitimate (insurable) interest in the property and may purchase insurance. Commodity futures contracts are also exempt from gambling laws.

(3)   <u>Sabbath Laws</u>--Prohibits contracts made on Sunday. The most commom type is the "blue law" which prohibits the sale of certain goods on Sunday. These laws have been declared unconstitutional in some states.

(4)   Licensing Statutes--May or may not be enforceable depending on the purpose of the statute.
If the purpose of the statute is to protect
the public from fraudulent experts and a
competency test is required to obtain the
license, then the contract will be unenforceable. Contracts with doctors, lawyers,
dentists, and realtors fall into this
category. If the purpose of the statute is
merely to raise revenue, then the contract
will be enforceable.

B.   Contracts Contrary to Public Policy--These
contracts may or may not be the subject of a
specific statute. If not, a court may decide that
they are illegal according to common law.

(1)   Contracts to Commit an Immoral Act--Contracts
prohibiting marriage or contracts for the sale
of children.

(2)   Contracts in Restraint of Trade--Illegal only
if they unreasonably restrain trade.
Exclusive distributorships and franchises may
be reasonable if they are not too restrictive.

Covenants Not to Compete--Legal only if the
following requirements are met:

(a)   part of an employment contract or sale of
a business
(b)   reasonable in time
(c)   reasonable in geographic scope (depends
on type of business)

(3)   Unconscionability--Must shock the conscience
of the court (outrageous terms). May include
fine print, legalese or lack of opportunity to
read the contract. Usually occurs in one-
sided contracts where a consumer is presented
with a take-it-or-leave-it situation.

(4)   Exculpatory Clauses--Excuses one party from
liability even if he or she is negligent. Not
enforceable if the party is grossly negligent
or careless. Some courts may enforce a
contract disclaiming liability negligence
unless the injured party is in a protected
class (e.g. employee).

C.   Effect of Illegality--The court may enforce the entire contract, part of the contract or it may void the whole contract. The general rule is that neither party can enforce the contract and therefore, such contracts are discouraged.

If one party is relatively innocent or is induced to enter a contract by fraud or duress, that party only may sue. Some statutes are designed to protect people. If the protected party wants to enforce the contracts, the court will usually do so. Otherwise, the contract is unenforceable.

STUDY QUESTIONS

Fill-in-the-Blank Questions

Tom, age seventeen, rents a garage apartment from Mrs. Murphy. He signs a six-month lease and agrees to pay $250 per month. Mrs. Murphy is aware of Tom's age but thinks that he is a responsible young man. After two months, Tom finds a cheaper apartment and moves. He refuses to pay the remainder of the rent. Similar apartments rent for $200-300 per month.

Tom _____*is*_____ under a disability.
         (is/is not)

The apartment _____*is*_____ a necessary.
                  (is/is not)

Tom has _____*disaffirmed*_____ the lease.
         (ratified/disaffirmed)

The contract _____*is*_____ enforceable.
              (is/is not)

True-False Questions

1.   A minor may ratify a contract while he or she is still underage. __*F*__

2.   Loans to corporations are usually exempt from usury laws. __*T*__

3.   A party may ratify a contract by words or by conduct. __*T*__

4.   A covenent not to compete is illegal unless it is part of a sale of a business or an employment contract. __*T*__

5.   Sporting equipment is considered a necessary. _F_

6.   An exculpatory clause gives a minor the right to disaffirm a contract. _F_

7.   A person who becomes intoxicated voluntarily cannot disaffirm a contract. _F_

8.   A person who has been declared insane in a court of law can make a valid contract. _F_

9.   A contract which contains fine print is an example of a contract which may be unconscionable. _T_

10.   A lottery is an example of a gambling contract. _T_

Multiple-Choice Questions

1.   Barry attends a party and drinks too much. He offers to sell his mixed-breed dog to Sam for $25. The next day when Sam comes to collect the dog, Barry claims he doesn't remember making the offer.

      a.   Sam can enforce the contract if a reasonable person would have believed that the offer was genuine.
      b.   Sam cannot enforce the contract even if a reasonable person would have realized that Barry was intoxicated when he made the offer.
      c.   Sam cannot enforce the contract because Barry cannot remember making the offer.
      d.   Sam can enforce the contract even if he knew Barry was too drunk to know what he was saying.

Use the following facts to answer questions 2-5. John, seventeen, and Sandy, fifteen, purchase stereos from AAA Appliances. Both pay one-third down and agree to pay $35 per month for twelve months. John told the salesman that he was nineteen. Sandy said nothing. Two months later, when John and Sandy's mother discovers the stereos, she orders them to return the stereos and collect the money they have paid.

2.   a.   The contract is enforceable against John because he lied about his age.
      b.   The contract is not enforceable against John but he may be liable in tort because he lied about his age.
      c.   The contract is enforceable against Sandy.
      d.   John can return the stereo but AAA can keep his down payment.

3.   a.   Sandy cannot return the stereo because he kept the
            stereo for two months.
      b.   Sandy can return the stereo but he cannot recover
            his down payment.
      c.   Sandy can recover his down payment but he does not
            have to return the stereo.
     (d.)   Sandy can recover his down payment but he must
            return the stereo.

4.   a.   Sandy and John have ratified the contracts.
      b.   John has ratified the contract but Sandy has not.
      c.   Sandy has disaffirmed the contract, but John has
            not.
     (d.)   Sandy and John have disaffirmed the contracts.

5.   a.   The contracts with AAA are void.
      b.   The contracts with AAA are valid.
     (c.)   The contracts with AAA are voidable at the option of
            John and Sandy.
      d.   The contracts with AAA are voidable at the option of
            AAA.

6.   Melinda, an aspiring fashion model, contracts with
      Orville, an orthodontist, to straighten her teeth.
      Orville straightens Melinda's teeth and sends her a bill
      for $4,000. Melinda then discovers that Orville has
      never been licensed to practice by the state.

      a.   Melinda must pay the bill but if she is not
            satisfied with Orville's work, she can sue him.
      b.   Milinda must pay Orville only if she is satisfied
            with his work.
     (c.)   Melinda does not have to pay regardless of Orville's
            work.
      d.   Melinda does not have to pay because $4,000 is an
            unreasonable charge for Orville's services.

7.   A "blue law" is:

      a.   a contract in restraint of trade.
     (b.)   an example of a Sabbath law.
      c.   an example of a law contrary to public policy.
      d.   an example of a gambling contract.

8.   Which of the following types of contracts may be exempt
      from usury laws?

      a.   Lotteries
     (b.)   Loans to corporations
      c.   Licensing statutes
      d.   Covenants not to compete

9.   Mary sues John for injuries she received in an
      automobile accident. The court awards Mary $15,000 in
      damages. If John does not pay immediately, the $15,000:

      a. will earn interest at the legal rate.
      b. will earn interest at the judgment rate.
      c. will earn interest at the maximum rate of interest
          allowed in Mary's state.
      d. will not earn interest.

10.   Sid is celebrating his new promotion and has too much to
      drink. While he is in this state, a magazine salesman
      sells him a 10-year subscription to Today's Executive.
      Sid receives the magazine for 6 months and then decides
      to disaffirm the contract. Today's Executive refuses to
      cancel.

      a. Sid can disaffirm because he was intoxicated when he
          made the contract.
      b. Sid cannot disaffirm because he drank voluntarily.
      c. Sid cannot disaffirm because he has ratified the
          contract.
      d. Sid has not ratified the contract.

11.   Jerry has been declared insane by a court of law and
      Bill is appointed as his guardian. Jerry orders a set
      of golf clubs from the pro shop. The guardian discovers
      the clubs and tries to return them. The contract
      between Jerry and the pro shop:

      a. is valid.
      b. is voidable at the option of Jerry.
      c. is voidable at the option of the pro shop.
      d. is void.

12.   When the guardian attempts to return the clubs, he will
      be:

      a. successful because Jerry had no contractual
          capacity.
      b. successful only if Jerry appeared insane to a
          reasonable person.
      c. unsuccessful because Jerry ratified the contract
          when he kept the clubs.
      d. unsuccessful because the contract is voidable at the
          pro shop's option.

13.   Mary, age sixteen, buys a car from Paul's Pontiac. The
      next day Mary wrecks the car and attempts to return it.
      In Mary's state, Mary can return the car but she must
      pay for the damage. Mary's obligation is the:

a. the duty of restoration.
b. the duty of ratification.
c. the duty of restitution.
d. the duty of cancellation.

14.   Cindy and Joe purchase a house and sign a mortgage with
      First Bank. Which of the following parties can purchase
      fire insurance on the house?

      a. Cindy only
      b. Joe only
      c. Cindy and Joe only
      d. Cindy, Joe and First Bank

15.   Allen is in desperate need of money and borrows $10,000
      from Don Corleone. Corleone charges 35% interest. The
      maximum legal rate is 21%. When Allen refuses to pay,
      Corleone sues. The court:

      a. may cancel the entire contract.
      b. may allow Corleone to collect the principal only.
      c. may allow Corleone to collect the principal and 21%
          interest.
      d. may choose any of the above.

16.   Which of the following is least likely to be considered
      a necessary?

      a. A winter coat
      b. An apartment lease
      c. A can of tomato soup
      d. Auto insurance

17.   Which of the following is an example of an exculpatory
      clause?

      a. Seller reserves the right to cancel at any time.
      b. Seller is not responsible for personal injury or
          property damage regardless of the cause of the
          injury.
      c. Buyer agrees to pay any costs of collection.
      d. Buyer agrees to notify seller of any change in
          address.

18.   Abel Attorney signs an employment contract with Crook &
      Low, Attorneys at Law. The contract contains the
      following clause, "Employee promises not to practice law
      in this state for 8 months following termination of
      employment". The clause:

a. is unenforceable because it is unreasonable in time.
b. is unenforcealbe because it is unreasonable in geographic scope.
c. is unenforceable because the contract is not for the sale of a business.
d. is enforceable.

19. Jim, age seventeen, purchases a computer from Harold's Hardware. Jim pays $1,000 down and promises to pay $50 per month for twenty-four months. Jim pays for eighteen months then the computer breaks down. Jim attempts to disaffirm the contract and collect the payments he has made. Harold claims that Jim has ratified the contract.

a. Jim will be successful because he did not expressly agree to ratify the contract when he turned 18.
b. Jim will be successful because he made the contract when he was a minor and he retains the right to disaffirm.
c. Jim will be unsuccessful because he should have disaffirmed before he turned 18.
d. Jim will be unsuccessful because he made several payments on the computer after he turned 18.

20. A state law makes it illegal to sell a car without a written statement from the seller that the odometer has not been turned back. Ed buys a car from Susan but no statement is signed.

a. The contract is voidable at Susan's option.
b. The contract is voidable at Ed's option.
c. The contract is voidable at the option of Ed or Susan.
d. The contract is valid.

21. Patti suffers from manic-depressive illness. She takes medication for her illness and acts rationally most of the time. She purchases a $40 pair of tennis shoes from Sneaker Emporium.

a. Patti can disaffirm the contract and collect her $40.
b. Patti can disaffirm the contract but will be liable in quasi-contract for the sneakers.
c. Patti can disaffirm the contract but she will be liable for any damage to the sneakers.
d. Patti cannot disaffirm the contract because she understood that she was buying sneakers.

22.   The city of Woodside collects an annual license fee from all restaurants which serve alcohol. Bob, a patron of the Too Far Bar, learns that the bar has not paid the fee for several years. Bob orders $25 worth of drinks and then refuses to pay the bill.

   a.   Bob can refuse to pay the bill because the contract for the drinks was illegal.
   b.   Bob can refuse to pay the bill because the bar was not licensed to sell alcohol.
   c.   Bob can refuse to pay the bill because the drinks were sold in violation of the licensing statute.
   (d.) Bob cannot refuse to pay the bill.

23.   A contract most likely will be declared unconscionable if:

   a.   it is unfair to one party.
   b.   it contains a cancellation clause.
   (c.) it shocks a court's sense of right and wrong.
   d.   it is signed by a minor.

24.   Which of the following is an exception to the general rule that illegal contracts cannot be enforced by either party?

   a.   One party is a minor
   b.   One party is insane
   c.   One party is induced to enter the contract through fraud
   (d.) One party is in violation of a licensing statute

25.   Randy is the owner of the only dry cleaners in Midtown. He learns that Howard is planning to open a dry cleaning shop in the next block. Randy offers to pay Howard $5,000 if Howard will not open a shop within 2 miles of Randy's shop. Howard agrees. The contract between Howard and Randy:

   a.   is legal because it is reasonable in geographic scope.
   b.   is legal because it contains no time limit.
   c.   is illegal because it contains no time limit.
   (d.) is illegal becuase it is not part of a sale of Randy's business.

ANSWERS TO STUDY QUESTIONS

Fill-in-the-Blank Questions

Tom is under a disability; he is a minor. The apartment is a necessary. Tom has disaffirmed the lease. The contract is enforceable because the apartment is a necessary and because it was rented at a reasonable rate.

True-False Questions

1.   F. A minor must have reached the age of majority before he or she can ratify.

2.   T.

3.   T.

4.   T.

5.   F. Food, clothing, and shelter are necessaries.

6.   F. An exculpatory clause relieves one party from suit caused by negligence.

7.   F.

8.   F. A person who is judged insane cannot make contracts; only his or her guardian can.

9.   T.

10.   T.

Multiple-Choice Questions

1. c	11. d	21. d
2. b	12. a	22. d
3. d	13. c	23. c
4. d	14. d	24. d
5. c	15. d	25. d
6. c	16. d	
7. b	17. b	
8. b	18. b	
9. b	19. d	
10. c	20. b	

Chapter 8   Genuineness of Assent and Form

General Principles

Chapters 6 & 7 explained the necessary elements of a contract: agreement, consideration, legality, and contractual capacity. This chapter discusses two defenses to enforcement of a contract. The contract may have been validly formed but it may not be enforceable.

Genuineness of assent relates directly to agreement. If a party is mistaken as to the nature of the contract or is fraudulently induced to enter a contract, then he or she has not agreed to the true terms of the contract, he or she has not consented willingly. These defenses are simple in theory but difficult to prove.

Most laymen think that all contracts need to be written, but only a few categories of contracts require a writing. A written contract is the best proof of an agreement. The formality of a writing serves another purpose; it gives the parties a chance to reflect on the legal commitments they are about to undertake. Most contracts which require a writing involve significant expenditures of time or money.

If a writing is necessary, then the next question is how much of a writing is required? A contract need not be several pages long. If a writing shows the basic terms of the agreement, it is sufficient. If there is a written contract, it should reflect the entire agreement of the parties. If it does not, and a dispute arises, a court may hear testimony to explain or supplement the writing.

Chapter Summary

I.   Genuineness of Assent

A.   Bilateral (Mutual) Mistake--Both parties must be mistaken about an important (material) fact; either party can rescind or cancel the contract. If the mistake concerns value, then the contract stands. It is sometimes difficult to tell the difference but ask yourself if both parties knew that they were taking a risk. If so, the mistake is probably one of value and the contract is enforceable.

B.   Unilateral Mistake--Error is made by only one party. The contract is usually enforceable. The only exceptions reinforce obligations of good faith. If the non-mistaken party should have known that a mistake has been made, he or she is not allowed to take advantage of it. Similarly, if a mathematical error has been made, the mistaken party may be entitled to relief, but only if he or she has not been careless or grossly negligent.

C.   Fraudulent Misrepresentation--All of the elements below must be proven. The deceived party has the choice of rescinding the contract or suing for the damages he or she has suffered.

   (1)   Misrepresentation of a Fact--Opinion is not fact. Adjectives such as "fine, best or wonderful" are opinion; facts must be capable of proof. The fact must have been an important part of the contract. Occasionally, if an expert takes advantage of a layman, the court will allow rescission. Positive action is required; silence is not misrepresentation unless there is a serious problem and the other party had no reason to be suspicious.

   (2)   Intent to deceive (Scienter)--May be proven by showing that the guilty party had knowledge of a fact and lied about it.

   (3)   Justifiable Reliance--The defrauded party must show that it was reasonable to rely on the facts as presented by the other.

   (4)   Injury--If the innocent party chooses to sue for damages, he or she must prove injury.

D. <u>Undue Influence</u>--Occurs when someone in a position of trust influences a weaker party to agree to a contract with a 3rd party. Some relationships automatically fall into this category (fiduciary): doctor-patient, attorney-client, guardian-ward, trustee-beneficiary, and husband-wife.

E. <u>Duress</u>--A party is forced into a contract by threats or blackmail. A threat to sue on an unrelated matter constitutes duress; a threat to sue for breach of contract does not. Economic pressure is also insufficient to prove duress.

II. <u>Form--The Statute of Frauds--Contracts Which Must be In Writing</u>--Certain contracts must be in writing. A contract "within" the Statute must be written; a contract "outside" the statute may be oral.

A. <u>An Interest in Land</u>--Includes sale of real estate or mineral interests, mortgages, and leases over one year.

It may also include life estates and easements (the right to use another's land) unless the easement is obviously necessary, e.g. a house situated on a land-locked piece of property.

<u>Exception</u>: Buyer has moved onto the land, begun substantial improvements and has paid part of the purchase price. The actions are evidence of a contract.

B. <u>One-Year Rule</u>--Must not be physicaly capable of being performed in a year or less. If a non-sales contract is made on a project basis, it need never be in writing. The formula below should help in "close cases". List:

(a) Date contract is formed.

(b) Day after (a), which is the date the time begins to run.

(c) Date performance starts.

(d) Date performance ends.

Compare (b) and (d), if more than one year, the contract must be in writing.

C.   Collateral Promises--A third party (surety) promises to pay the debt of another if the original party cannot pay (not a co-signer). Requirements:

(a) Promise between debtor and creditor

(b) Promise between 3rd party and creditor

(c) Third party promises to pay if debtor doesn't

Rule applies only to the promise made in (b). The main purpose rule is an exception. If the surety is making the promise for his own benefit, the promise can be oral.

D.   Promises Made in Consideration of Marriage--Includes pre-nuptial agreements and situations where one party is paid to marry another.

E.   Sale of Goods--Price (not value) of $500 or more. 3 exceptions (all show proof of a contract):

(a) Custom-made goods when performance by the seller has begun

(b) Admission under oath that a contract existed

(c) Partial performance--Buyer has paid for or received some of the goods. Contract is enforceable only to extent the buyer has performed.

III. Statute of Frauds--Sufficiency of the Writing--Need show only the essence of the contract. Different rules for sales contracts.

A.   Sales Contracts--Quantity and signature of the party to be charged (defendant).

B.   Non-Sales Contracts--Parties, subject matter, consideration, and quantity. Land contracts usually must have a description of the land so that it can be identified.

IV.   The Parol Evidence Rule--Applies only if there is a written contract. Oral evidence given in court cannot contradict the writing. Ask yourself whether the parties would have included the term in the writing. If so, oral evidence on that subject will not be allowed. The exceptions listed below concern situations where the parties might not have thought to include the disputed term.

(1) <u>Subsequent Modification</u>--Change after signing would not have been included in the contract so evidence is allowed.

(2) <u>Void/Voidable</u>--Can introduce evidence to show a contract was never formed.

(3) <u>Ambiguous</u>--Oral evidence is allowed to explain unclear terms.

(4) <u>Incomplete</u>--If contract is obviously incomplete, oral evidence is allowed to fill in blanks. No totally new provisions.

(5) <u>Prior Transactions/Trade Usage</u>--Applies to sales contracts only. Can show prior dealings between the same parties or general customs of the trade if the contract doesn't address the problem specifically.

(6) <u>Conditional Contract</u>--Agreement based on a condition that never comes about. Only proof of the condition is allowed.

(7) <u>Clerical Error</u>--Must be obvious from the face of the contract. Evidence is allowed to show correct terms.

STUDY QUESTIONS

Fill-in-the-Blank Questions

Abel Attorney orders two electric typewriters from Office Products, Inc. The salesman fills out a receipt for the typewriters which shows that Abel ordered two Model Z typewriters at a price of $400 each on January 3, 1988. The salesman places his initials on the receipt.

The contract between Abel and Office Products _____*does*_____ require a written contract.
(does/does not)

The receipt _____*is*_____ sufficient to prove a contract.
(is/is not)

The contract _____*is*_____ enforceable against Office Products.
(is/is not)

At trial, Abel wants to testify that the price of the typewriters was $350 each. Abel _____*will not*_____ be allowed to testify about the price.
(will/will not)

True-False Questions

1.   "Surety" is another word for co-signer. ~~T~~ F

2.   A change made after a contract has been signed is an exception to the parol evidence rule. ~~F~~ T

3.   A mutual mistake in the value of the contract allows either party to cancel the contract. F

4.   An attorney-client relationship is an example of a fiduciary relationship. T

5.   In order for a plaintiff to recover damages in a misrepresentation suit, he or she must prove injury. T

6.   In order to be enforceable, a sales contract must show the price of the goods. F

7.   Unilateral mistake is never a defense to enforcement of a contract. F

8.   A party who is forced to sign a contract under threat of blackmail, will be allowed to rescind the contract. T

9.   All leases of real property must be in writing. ~~T~~ F

10.   The main purpose rule is an exception to the requirement that sales contracts must be in writing. F

Multiple-Choice Questions

Use the following facts to answer questions 1-3.

1.   Sally is shopping for a new car. A salesman at Midland Motors shows her the new Delight model. He describes it as very dependable and tells Sally that it will get 35 miles to the gallon in town. Sally and the salesman sign a sales contract for $12,000, payable in 36 installments. The car breaks down after 2 weeks. Sally:

      a.   can sue the salesman for misrepresentation because he told her the car was very dependable.
      b.   can rescind the contract on the basis of mutual mistake because neither the salesman nor Sally knew that the car would break down.
      c.   cannot sue for misrepresentation because she signed a written contract.
      d.   cannot sue for misrepresentation because "very dependable" is not a factual description of the car.

2.   If Sally discovers that the car gets only 18 miles to the
      gallon in town, she:

      a. can sue because a material fact was misrepresented.
      b. cannot sue because it is unreasonable to believe that
          a car could get 35 miles to the gallon.
      c. cannot sue because she signed a written contract.
      d. cannot sue because the average miles per gallon is
          statement of opinion, not fact.

3.   If the case goes to trial, which of the following will
      not be barred by the parol evidence rule:

      a. testimony that the price of the car was really
          $10,000.
      b. testimony that the salesman misrepresented the gas
          mileage.
      c. testimony that Sally agreed to buy a different model.
      d. testimony that she agreed to make 48 monthly
          payments.

4.   Allen finds a shiny blue rock while he is walking in the
      woods. He shows the rock to Herman, who agrees to buy it
      for $30. Herman shows the rock to a geologist friend who
      tells him that the rock is worth $700. When Herman tells
      Allen, Allen claims that he never would have sold the
      rock if he had known its true worth.

      a. Allen can rescind the contract on the ground of
          unilateral mistake.
      b. Allen can rescind the contract on the grounds of
          bilateral mistake.
      c. Allen can rescind the contract on the grounds of
          misrepresentation.
      d. Allen cannot rescind the contract.

5.   Herman:

      a. cannot enforce the contract because there was no
          written contract and the value of the rock is $700.
      b. cannot enforce the contract because there was no
          written contract and the price of the rock is $30.
      c. can enforce the contract because the price of the
          rock is $30.
      d. can enforce the contract because Allen is claiming
          unilateral mistake.

6.   Best Publishing orally hires Peter to write a textbook on the law of contracts. They agree that Peter will have 15 months to complete the book. After Pete begins work on the book, Best tells him that they have hired another author for less money. The contract between Best and Peter:

    a.   is unenforceable because it is oral and cannot be completed within one year.
    b.   is unenforceable now but will be enforceable if Peter can complete the book in less than one year.
    c.   is enforceable because Peter could complete the book in one year.
    d.   is enforceable but Peter can collect only for the work which he has performed and Best can cancel the rest of the contract.

7.   Which of the following is not a fiduciary relationship?

    a.   Lawyer-client
    b.   Husband-wife
    c.   Buyer-seller
    d.   Doctor-patient

8.   Sandra realizes that she has charged too many purchases on her credit card. She visits E-Z Finance Co. where a loan officer proposes a bill consolidation loan of $7500 at the legal rate of 19% interest. Sandra feels that she will have to declare bankruptcy and reluctantly agrees to E-Z's terms.

    a.   The contract is voidable at Sandra's option.
    b.   The contract is voidable at E-Z's option.
    c.   The contract is void.
    d.   The contract is valid.

9.   Sandra:

    a.   can rescind the contract on the basis of duress.
    b.   can rescind the contract on the basis of unilateral mistake.
    c.   can rescind the contract on the basis of undue influence.
    d.   cannot rescind the contract.

10.   Which of the following is not an exception to the rule that a contract for the sale of goods over $500 must be in writing:

   a. The seller has shipped the goods.
   b. The buyer has paid for the goods.
   c. The buyer has ordered custom-made goods and the seller has begun performance.
   d. The seller has admitted in court that a contract exists.

11. Jerry orders a shipment of plywood from Larry's Lumberyard. The written order form, which is initialed by Larry, states that Jerry will pay $850 for the lumber which is to be delivered on June 1. When the lumber arrives, Larry refuses to deliver until Jerry pays cash. Jerry refuses and Larry sues. At trial, which of the following oral evidence will be admitted as an exception to the parol evidence rule?

   a. Jerry's testimony that he has always charged on account.
   b. Larry's testimony that the shipment was not due until July 1.
   c. Jerry's testimony that a 10% discount was accidentally omitted from the contract.
   d. Larry's testimony that the price of the lumber was $1850.

12. The order form is:

   a. sufficient to prove a contract if Larry is the defendant.
   b. sufficient to prove a contract if Jerry is the defendant.
   c. sufficent to prove a contract if either Jerry or Larry is defendant.
   d. insufficient to prove a contract.

13. Sally, a newly licensed beautician, orders $300 worth of beauty supplies from Pretty Hair, Inc. The manager of the beauty supply store does not know Sally and asks Ron, an established hair dresser, to guarantee payment and Ron agrees.

   a. Ron's promise to pay if Sally doesn't is a primary promise.
   b. Ron's promise to pay if Sally doesn't is a secondary promise.
   c. Sally's order is a collateral promise.
   d. Ron is a co-signer.

14.   Which of the promises in problem 13 must be in writing?

a.   Sally's order
b.   Ron's promise to the manager of Pretty Hair
c.   Both Sally and Ron's promises
d.   Neither Sally's nor Ron's promise

15.   Which of the following real estate contracts must be in writing?

a.   A 10-year lease
b.   A sale of a house
c.   A mortgage
d.   All of the above

16.   Bob places a telephone order for 2000 widgets from Widget World; the widgets are priced at $1 each. Bob sends a check for $400 as a down payment. When the widgets arrive, Bob refuses to pay for them and asks Widget World to refund his down payment. The contract between Widget World and Bob is:

a.   unenforceable because the contract is oral and Widget World must refund the down payment.
b.   enforceable and Bob must pay $1600.
c.   enforceable to the extent of 400 widgets.
d.   unenforceable because of the parol evidence rule.

17.   Bettina is contemplating plastic surgery. Her doctor, Paul tells her that acupuncture is much less expensive and that he will refer her to Abe, a specialist. Abe and Paul tell Bettina that she will "look twenty again". Bettina agrees to a series of ten treatments but has second thoughts. Bettina:

a.   can rescind the contract on the grounds of duress.
b.   can rescind the contract on the grounds of undue influence.
c.   can rescind the contract on the grounds of fraudulent misrepresentation.
d.   cannot rescind the contract.

18.   A written contract for a non-sales transaction is sufficient if it shows:

a.   the parties and the consideration.
b.   the parties and the subject matter.
c.   the parties, the subject matter, and the consideration.
d.   the consideration and the subject matter.

19.   On May 1, 1988, Nancy, a college professor, orally agrees to teach a business law class during the 1988-9 academic year. Classes begin on August 25, 1988 and end on June 2, 1989. On August 1, 1988, the college notifies Nancy that it will no longer require her servies. Nancy sues to enforce the contract. Nancy:

   a.   will win because she will teach for less than 10 months.
   b.   will win because the college waited until August to cancel the contract.
   c.   will lose because the contract cannot be performed in less than one year.
   d.   will lose but only if the college agreed to pay her more than $500.

20.   The dates used to measure the length of the contract in problem 19 are:

   a.   June 1, 1988 to June 2, 1989.
   b.   August 25, 1988 to June 2, 1989.
   c.   August 1, 1988 to June 2, 1989.
   d.   June 1, 1988 to August 25, 1988.

21.   U.S. Bus Lines is badly in need of qualified drivers. Ron, the personnel director, hires Al to drive the Phoenix to Dallas route. U.S. Bus Lines requires all employees to pay for their uniforms. Al orders $200 worth of uniforms from a local store. The store telphones Ron and asks him to pay if Al cannot. U.S. Lines agrees. Al quits after two weeks and leaves town. The uniform supplier sues Ron for the cost of the uniforms. Ron claims that the contract must be in writing:

   a.   Ron is incorrect because the cost of the uniforms is less than $500.
   b.   Ron is incorrect because he is the primary debtor.
   c.   Ron is incorrect because the main purpose rule applies.
   d.   Ron is correct.

22.   Peggy agrees to sell her prize German Shepard to Tammy. Peggy draws up a written contract for $300 but mistakenly omits a zero. She sends the contract to Tammy who accepts immediately. When Tammy comes to collect the dog, she shows Peggy the contract and refuses to pay more than $30. Peggy:

a. can rescind the contract because Tammy should have known that the price was incorrect.
b. can rescind the contract because of mutual mistake.
b. cannot rescind the contract because it is written.
d. cannot rescind the contract because unilateral mistake is never a defense to enforcement of a contract.

23. Paul orally agrees to represent Dora in a divorce case. He tells Dora that his fee will be $5000. Paul makes several threats and Dora reluctanly signs the contract. Which of the following is <u>not</u> an example of duress sufficient to allow rescission of the fee agreement?

a. Threatening to publish false and damaging rumors
b. Threatening to publish true and damaging facts
c. Threat of criminal prosecution for adultery
d. All of the above are sufficient to allow rescission

24. In a case of misrepresentation, a plaintiff must prove all of the following except:

a. a material fact was misrepresented
b. justifiable reliance on the misrepresentation
c. intent to deceive
d. a fiduciary relationship

25. The parol evidence rule states that:

a. a surety agreement must be in writing.
b. intent to deceive can be proven by the action of the parties.
c. oral evidence will not be admitted to contradict terms of a written contract.
d. an oral contract for the sale of land is valid if it is shown that the buyer has moved on the land, has made a down payment, and has made improvements to the property.

ANSWERS TO STUDY QUESTIONS

Fill-in-the-Blank Questions

The contract must be in writing because the price of the type-writers is $800 and a contract for the sale of goods for $500 or more must be in writing. The receipt is sufficient to prove a contract against Office Products only. A sales contract requires only the quantity and the signature of the party to be charged (defendant). Abel will not be allowed to testify about the price of the typewriters because the $350 price contradicts the receipt and Abel's testimony would be violation of the parol evidence rule.

True-False Questions

1.   F. A surety is secondarily liable; a co-signer is primarily liable.

2.   T.

3.   F. A mutual mistake as to the <u>identity or subject matter</u> allows rescission.

4.   T.

5.   T.

6.   F. The court will supply a reasonable price. The sales contract need show only the quantity and the signature of the party to be charged.

7.   F. It is a defense if the non-mistaken party should have known that a mistake had been made. Also, if an arithmetic error has been made and gross negligence is not shown, the mistaken party can rescind.

8.   T.

9.   F. Only leases in excess of one year must be in writing.

10.   F. It is an exception to the collateral promise or surety rule.

Multiple-Choice Questions

1.	d	11.	a	21.	c
2.	a	12.	a	22.	a
3.	b	13.	b	23.	d
4.	d	14.	b	24.	d
5.	c	15.	d	25.	c
6.	c	16.	c		
7.	c	17.	b		
8.	d	18.	c		
9.	d	19.	c		
10.	a	20.	a		

Chapter 9   Third–Party Rights and Discharge

General Principles

Each party to a contract receives a benefit and is obligated to perform a duty. As a general rule, the benefit and the duty can be transferred to a third party. They can be transferred separately or together. If the transfer would cause hardship to one party, it may be prohibited.

A contract between two parties may affect a third party. If the contract was made with the intent to benefit the third party, then he or she acquires rights in the contract and may sue to enforce these rights. If the effect on the third party is coincidental, then no rights are acquired and the third party cannot sue.

The last half of this chapter deals with performance of the contract. The level of performance may vary greatly; it may be perfect, contain minor or major flaws, or be absent altogether. The seriousness of the error or breach determines the rights of the other party. As a general rule, the law favors the enforcement of contracts and a minor flaw may not allow cancellation of the contract but it may allow money damages to correct the error. Cancellation is permitted only in the most serious cases.

Chapter Summary

I.   Assignment of Rights and Delegation of Duties--A transfer of rights or benefits under a contract is an assignment. A transfer of obligations or duties is a delegation.

A.   Assignment--The transferor is the assignor; the transferee (third party) is the assignee. The obligor is the party who contracted originally with the assignor. After the assignment and notice, the obligor will perform for the assignee. All contracts can be assigned except those listed below.

    (1)   Exceptions

        (a)   A statute prohibits transfer. The most common examples are laws which forbid the assignment of wages, employee benefits or child support payments.

        (b)   The contract states that the rights cannot be assigned.

        (c)   The rights acquired are personal. An obligation to pay money is not personal.

        (d)   The obligor's duty is substantially changed or enlarged. This exception often goes hand-in-hand with (3); if the right is personal, it is likely that the obligor's duty will have changed.

    (2)   Notice--An assignment is effective without notice. However, if the obligor has begun performance, it would be unfair to allow transfer. Until the obligor receives notice, he or she can fulfill the contractual obligation by giving performance to the assignor, the original party to the contract.

B.   Delegation--The opposite of assignment; a party's duty under a contract is transferred. The transferor is the delegator; the transferee is the delegatee. The obligee is the person entitled to performance who originally contracted with the delegator. As with assignments, almost all duties can be delegated. The exceptions are similar to those noted above.

    (1)   Exceptions

        (a)   The contract requires the personal talents of the delegator, the original party. An artistic project, design, or professional service usually requires individual performance.

   (b) There is a trust relationship between the
        original parties to the contract.

   (c) Performance by a third party would differ
        greatly from the original service.
        Usually occurs with (a).

   (d) Contract prohibits transfer.

(2) Liability of Parties--If the delegation is
     legal, the obligor must accept substitute
     performance. If the delegatee fails to
     perform, most states hold that both the
     delegatee and the delegator can both be sued.

II. Third-Party Beneficiary Contracts--A party may sue to
have an agreement enforced if he or she has rights under
the contract (standing to sue). The original parties
who have reached an agreement with each other have
privity of contract; they are bound together by the
agreement and have the right to sue if something goes
wrong. A third party may acquire similar rights if he
or she was intended to benefit from the contract.

   A. Intended Beneficiaries--Can enforce the contract.
       Ask if the contract between the original parties
       was made with the third party in mind. There are
       two basic categories of intended beneficiaries:

       (1) Creditor Beneficiary--Owed a duty (usually
            money) by one of the parties to the contract.
            The most common example is the sale of an item
            on which the seller owes money to a creditor.
            If the buyer agrees to take over the payments,
            the creditor of the seller is a third party
            beneficiary.

       (2) Donee Beneficiary--Receives a gift or free
            benefit as a result of the contract between
            the original parties.

   B. Incidental Beneficiary--Happens to benefit from the
       contract between the original parties. Cannot sue
       to have the contract enforced. Ask if the contract
       was made with the 3rd party in mind. If not, he or
       she is incidental.

   C. Vesting of Rights--A third-party has standing to
       sue if he or she is an intended beneficiary and the
       contract is finalized. The contract normally
       becomes final when the third party consents to the

contractors or when he or she makes committments relying on the benefits to be received. If the original contract specifies that the parties have the right to cancel or alter the agreement, the third party rights may never vest.

III.   <u>Conditional Contracts</u>--Most contracts contain the implied condition that one party will perform only if the other also performs. Some contracts are more explicit and a stated condition must be satisfed before performance is due. Remember to separate the validity of a contract from its performance. A contract may be valid but a condition may cancel the duty to perform.

    A.   <u>Conditions Precedent</u>--The duty to perform does not occur until a condition is satisfied. If the condition is not met, there is no duty to perform and neither party can sue for breach of contract. Fulfillment of the condition <u>precedes</u> the duty to perform.

    B.   <u>Conditions Subsequent</u>--The duty to perform is absolute unless a condition relieves a party of this obligation. The condition <u>follows</u> the duty to perform.

    C.   <u>Concurrent Conditions</u>--The parties are obligated to perform at the same time. The only difference between concurrent conditions and implied conditions is that the former is expressly stated in the contract. Before a party can sue, he or she must show that he or she is ready to act (tender of performance).

IV.   <u>Discharge</u>--Most contracts are terminated when both sides perform. However, the parties may agree to cancel the contract, to transfer the contract to others, or performance may become impossible.

    A.   <u>Performance</u>--When performance is incomplete or unsatisfactory, the non-breaching party acquires certain rights. These rights depend on the severity of the mistake and the specifity of the contract.

        (1)   <u>Strict (Complete) Performance</u>--Requires absolute compliance with the terms of agreement or the non-breaching party can cancel. Because this rule can be abused, the agreement must specifically state that only perfect execution will do <u>and</u> the

non-breaching party must prove the nature of the contract requires conformity to exact specifications.

(2) <u>Substantial Performance</u>--Requires satisfaction of the major provisions of the contracts. The non-breaching party must carry out his or her side of the bargain but may sue for any damages as a result of incomplete or unsatisfactory performance.

(3) <u>Material Breach</u>--Serious errors. The non-breaching loses the benefits of the contract and is excused from performance.

(4) <u>Personal Satisfaction</u>--If expressly stated, performance must meet the standards of a designated person. May be seen as a condition precedent to payment or as a promise which could be satisfied by substantial compliance. If the non-breaching party is being picky only to avoid payment, the contract will be enforceable.

(5) <u>Anticipatory Repudiation</u>--Performance is not due until the time stated in the contract and no right to sue accrues until that time. However, if one party tells the other that he or she intends to breach, the innocent party can sue immediately or can make plans for substitute performance.

B. <u>Discharge by Agreement</u>--The parties can agree to cancel the contract or to change the terms.

(1) <u>Rescission</u>--An agreement to cancel the contract. Requires offer, acceptance, and consideration on both sides. The consideration is satisfied if each party agrees to give up rights under the contact. If one party has performed, he or she must receive some consideration, usually payment or a refund of money. Rescission need not be in writing unless the contract or other law so specifies.

(2) <u>Novation</u>--Similar to assignment or delegation but all three parties agree to a new contract. When a proper novation is executed, the original contract is cancelled and a new one is formed. The original obligor is no longer liable in contrast to the rule outlined above with respect to delegation of duties.

(3) <u>Accord and Satisfaction</u>--Parties agree to
substitute performance. The accord is the new
agreement and the satisfaction is the
performance of the new agreement.

NOTE: Can occur when one party is paying for
a faulty performance or bad service and
tries to cancel the debt by sending
payment for less than the full amount.
If the creditor accepts the partial
payment, he may be accused of agreeing
to the accord. The test is whether the
amount of the debt is liquidated or in
genuine dispute. If the debt is
liquidated, partial payment will not be
considered an accord and satisfaction.
A second way to understand this problem
is to examine the consideration
required to support the accord or new
contract. If the creditor accepts less
than full payment, he is giving up his
right to full payment. The debtor is
providing no consideration, therefore
the accord is invalid.

(4) <u>Discharge by Impossibility of Performance</u>--An
<u>unforeseeable</u> event occurs between the time
the contract is formed and the time for
performance. The courts will cancel the
contract if performance becomes <u>objectively</u>
impossible (no one could do it).

Automatic discharge when a party to a personal
service contract dies or a change in law would
make performance illegal. If the subject
matter of the contract is destroyed, the
contract may be cancelled if the subject
matter was specifically stated and is not
available from other sources. However, if the
subject matter is described generally,
discharge may not be allowed.

<u>Commercial impracticability</u> is a new
application of the impossibility rule. Courts
may excuse a party from contractual
obligations if a change in conditions makes
performance more difficult <u>and</u> the change was
unforeseeable. If the change was brought
about by a normal risk of doing business (e.g.
inflation) the court will enforce the
contract.

STUDY QUESTIONS

Fill-in-the-Blank Questions

Penny purchases a 1986 VW on the installment plan. She owes twenty-four installments of $200 each when she decides to sell the car to Tom. Tom agrees to apy $500 cash and assume the payments.

With regard to the loan agreement between Penny and Tom, Penny is the _____*assignor*_____.
(assignor/assignee)

The bank is the _____*obligee*_____.
(delegatee/obligee)

Tom is the _____*obligor*_____.
(delegator/obligor)

The bank is an _____*intended*_____ beneficiary.
(intended/incidental)

True-False Questions

1. A duty cannot be delegated if the original contract called for the personal skill of the obligor. __T__

2. A condition precendent excuses one party from performance until the condition is satisfied. __X__ T

3. If one party complies substantially with the terms of the contract, the other party does not have to perform. __X F__

4. A novation usually requires three parties. __T__

5. Impossibility of performance is a method of discharging a contract. __T__

6. Rescission occurs when two parties agree to substitute a new contract for the original contract. __F__

7. A creditor beneficiary is an intended beneficiary. __T__

8. An assignor is a 3rd party to whom contract rights are transferred. __F__

9. If a delegatee fails to perform a contractual duty, the party to whom performance is due, can sue the delegatee and the delegator. __X__ T

10.   The beneficiary of a life insurance policy is an example
       of an incidental beneficiary. __F__

Multiple-Choice Questions

1.   Joe is re-roofing Alice's house. Joe and Alice agree
      that instead of paying Joe, Alice will send the payment
      to Joe's banker, Sid. Sid is:

      a. the assignee of Joe's right.
      b. the assignor of Joe's right.
      c. the delegator of Joe's right.
      d. the delegatee of Joe's duty.

2.   Alice is:

      a. the delegator.
      b. the assignor.
      c. the assignee.
      d. the obligator.

3.   Bobby agrees to mow Terry's lawn for ten weeks at $25
      per week. Terry decides that her lawn needs to be mowed
      only five times, and she assigns her rights to Mary.
      She tells Joe that he should mow Mary's lawn every other
      week. The assignment is:

      a. invalid because Terry has not notified Mary.
      b. invalid because Mary is not paying Joe.
      c. valid only if Joe agrees.
      d. valid only if Joe's duty is not increased
          significantly.

4.   Farmer Brown has ten apple orchards. He contracts with
      Paul's Produce to deliver three bushels of apples per
      week. Two of Farmer Brown's orchards are destroyed by
      fire. The contract between Farmer Brown and Paul's is:

      a. discharged due to impossibility of performance.
      b. discharged due to accord and satisfaction.
      c. not discharged because Farmer Brown can deliver
          apples from the remaining eight orchards.
      d. not discharged because the contract was conditioned
          on good weather.

5.   Which of the following duties cannot be delegated:

      a. Designing a wedding gown.
      b. Paying money to a bank.
      c. Delivering televisions sets.
      d. Selling television sets.

6.   Allen agrees to sell ten typewriter's to Sally at a 10%
     discount if he can buy them at the wholesale price from
     Tim. The contract between Allen and Sally has:

     a. a condition precedent.
     b. a condition subsequent.
     c. concurrent conditions.
     d. no conditions.

7.   If Tim refuses to sell the typewriters to Allen:

     a. Sally can sue Allen for material breach.
     b. Sally cannot sue Allen because the contract was
         discharged due to accord and satisfaction.
     c. Sally cannot sue Allen, because Allen has
         substantially performed.
     d. Sally cannot sue Allen, because Allen's promise was
         conditional.

8.   Bob hires Susan the Snake Charmer to dance at Dave's
     birthday party. Susan refuses to perform at the last
     minute. Bob, Dave, and the guests are upset and threaten
     to sue. Which of the following parties can sue Susan?

     a. Bob only
     b. Bob or Dave.
     c. Bob, Dave, or the guests.
     d. Dave only.

9.   Dave is:

     a. an incidental beneficiary.
     b. a creditor beneficiary.
     c. a donee beneficiary.
     d. as assignor.

10. The guests are:

     a. incidental beneficiaries.
     b. intended beneficiaries.
     c. obligors.
     d. assignors.

11. Ross agrees to sell Kathleen a Model X washer for $450.
     Ross then discovers that Model X is out of stock and he
     offers to sell Kathleen a Model Y for $400. Kathleen
     agrees. The agreement between Ross and Kathleen is:

     a. a novation.
     b. an accord and satisfaction.
     c. rescission.
     d. an assignment.

12.   Paul borrows money from First Bank to build an apartment complex. He tells his tenants to send their rent to First Bank. Paul is:

    a.   the assignee.
    b.   the delgator.
    c.   the incidental beneficiary.
    (d.)   the assignor.

13.   Larry, a new tenant, is not told about the payment arrangements and sends his rent to Paul. Larry:

    (a.)   has discharged his duty to pay the rent by sending the money to Paul, because he did not receive notice of the assignment.
    b.   has not discharged his duty to pay the rent, because the assignment states that he must pay First Bank.
    c.   has discharged his duty to pay rent, because he did not agree to the assignment.
    d.   has discharged his duty to pay rent because the assignment was invalid.

14.   The bank is:

    (a.)   a creditor beneficiary of the lease agreement between Larry and Paul.
    b.   an incidental benenficiary of the lease agreement between Larry and Paul.
    c.   a delegatee.
    d.   a delegator.

15.   Margaret is building a new house. She requests that her contractor use a bathroom tile made by the Trane Co. The contractor is unable to obtain the tile from Trane and uses similar tile made by Tilex Co. Margaret:

    a.   does not have to pay the contractor because he used the wrong tile.
    (b.)   must pay the contractor but can recover damages for the difference in the two brands.
    c.   does not have to pay the contractor because of anticipatory breach by the contractor.
    d.   must accept the new tile and cannot sue for damages.

16.   Failure to give strict or complete performance by one party will discharge the other party only if:

    a.   the contract expressly requires strict performance.
    (b.)   the contract expressly requires strict performance and only strict performance can discharge the promise.
    c.   only strict performance can discharge the promise.
    d.   the contract is substantially performed.

17. Glenda hires Will to build a monument to her great-grand-father Thomas Jefferson Lee, a Civil War hero. The contract specifically states that Glenda has approval of all details and that she must be satisfied before payment is due. When the statue is complete, Glenda refuses to pay on the grounds that she is dissatisfied with the project. Will sues for breach of contract. Which of the following statements is true?

   a. Glenda must pay if a reasonable person would be satisfied with the statue.
   b. Glenda must pay if a court determines that Glenda is acting in bad faith and trying to avoid payment.
   c. Glenda must pay because Will has substantially performed.
   d. Glenda will not have to pay under any circumstances.

18. Mrs. Richards has worked for XYZ company for 25 years. As a retirement gift, the president of the company has his stock dividends assigned to her. Mrs. Richards thanks him for the present and tells him that she can now afford an expensive 4-bedroom condo. Mrs. Richards' rights to the dividends:

   a. vested when the president assigned the stock.
   b. vested when she retired.
   c. vested when she signed the agreement to buy the condo.
   d. can never vest because she is a donee beneficiary.

19. Regan's department store contracts with Narrow Shirts for an order of 200 white T-shirts to be delivered March 1. In February, Narrow tells Regan that it will be unable to deliver the shirts.

   a. Regan can sue immediately because of anticipatory breach.
   b. Regan cannot sue until March 1 because Narrow has until that date to perform.
   c. Regan cannot sue because the contract was discharged by accord and satisfaction.
   d. Regan cannot sue because the contract was discharged by rescission.

20. Peter agrees to paint Art's house. Pete is overworked and asks Art if John can complete the work. Art agrees and a new contract is drawn up. If John does not paint Art's house, Art can sue:

   a. Peter only.
   b. Peter or John, but not both.
   c. John only.
   d. Peter and John.

21.   Perry orders fifteen rolls of film from Photon
       Photography. The contract states that Perry will pay
       when the film is delivered and Photon will deliver the
       film when Perry pays. This contract is an example of:

       a. a condition precedent.
       b. a condition subsequent.
       c. concurrent conditions.
       d. strict compliance.

22.   If Photon refuses to deliver the film:

       a. Perry can sue immediately without further action.
       b. Perry can sue only if he pays first.
       c. Perry can sue only if he pays or shows that he is
           willing to pay for the film.
       d. Perry can sue because Photon is excused from
           performance.

23.   Melinda makes an appointment with Dr. Spock. When
       Melinda arrives, she discovers that Dr. Spock has been
       called out on an emergency and that Dr. Cure is taking
       his calls. Melinda:

       a. must see Dr. Cure or she will be in breach of
           contract.
       b. has no duty to see Dr. Cure, because she was given
           no notice of the delegation.
       c. has no duty to see Dr. Cure, because a doctor's
           services are personal and cannot be assigned.
       d. must see Dr. Cure because Dr. Spock is excused from
           performance.

24.   Bob's Barbeque agrees to cater the refreshments for the
       Pecos rodeo. As he is driving to the rodeo, he learns
       that the rodeo has been cancelled due to a stampede of
       Brahma Bulls. Bob:

       a. can sue the rodeo officials for material breach.
       b. can sue the rodeo officials for anticipatory breach.
       c. cannot sue the rodeo officials because the contract
           was discharged by impossibility of performance.
       d. cannot sue the rodeo officials because the contract
           was discharged by rescission.

25.   Which of the following is least likely to result in
       discharge of a contract by commercial impracticability?

       a. A war between the U.S. and Mexico
       b. Inflation
       c. A computer failure
       d. A trucker's strike

ANSWERS TO STUDY QUESTIONS

Fill-in-the-Blank Questions

Penny is the assignor. The bank if the obligee. Tom is the obligor. The bank is an intended (creditor) beneficiary.

True-False Questions

1. T.

2. T.

3. F. The other party must perform but may receive damages for any injuries received.

4. T.

5. T.

6. F. This is the definition of accord and satisfaction.

7. T.

8. F. An assignor is the person who transfers the rights.

9. T.

10. F. It is an example of an intended beneficiary.

Multiple-Choice Questions

1. a	11. b	21. c
2. d	12. d	22. c
3. d	13. a	23. c
4. c	14. a	24. c
5. a	15. b	25. b
6. a	16. b	
7. d	17. b	
8. b	18. c	
9. c	19. a	
10. a	20. c	

Chapter 10 Breaches and Remedies

General Principles

Once it has been determined that a valid contract exists and that one party has breached the agreement, the next step is to determine the remedy of the non-breaching party. There are two general types of remedies: legal and equitable.

Legal remedies are monetary awards or damages. Contract law will award the non-breaching party money only for injuries that can be proven. The non-breaching can recover funds equal to the benefit of the bargain so that he or she is in the same position as if the contract has been performed.

Equitable remedies usually do not involve money and are only awarded when money is an inadequate remedy. The plaintiff must show not only that substitute performance cannot be obtained elsewhere but also that he or she has acted in good faith and is entitled to this special remedy.

Chapter Summary

I.   Damages

    A.   Types of Damages

        (1)   Compensatory Damages--The non-breaching party receives money lost due to the breach but any money saved must be subtracted to determine the final amount.

(a) Service Contracts--The extra cost, if any, of replacement services less money saved.

(b) Sale of Land--If the buyer breaches, the seller receives the difference between the contract price and the market price. If the seller breaches, the buyer can sue for the equitable remedy of specific performance or is entitled to the refund of any down payment. A few states also award the buyers money spent in performing the contract, e.g. title searches, appraisers' and attorneys' fees.

(c) Sale of Goods--The difference between the contract price and the market price. If the goods are custom-made, the seller can sue for lost profits and costs incurred in manufacture.

(d) Construction Contracts--If the homeowner breaches, the contractor is entitled to lost profits + labor used + material used. If the contractor breaches, the homeowner is entitled to the difference between the value if the contract had not been breached and the value as performed or the cost of repair, whichever is less. If the breach occurs during construction, the homeowner is entitled to the cost of finishing. The homeowner also may be able to sue for expenses incurred in delay.

(2) Consequential Damages--Occur as a result of the breach, usually lost profits. Must be foreseeable or the breaching party must have reason to know that additional damages would be incurred. Can be eliminated if stated in the contract.

(3) Punitive Damages--Designed to punish the breaching party and are not available in a contract suit. May be available in some contract suits which also involve a tort, such as misrepresentation. Awarded on a showing of bad faith or intentional wrongdoing.

(4) Nominal Damages--A small monetary amount, usually one dollar. Occurs when there is a breach but the non-breaching party suffers no financial loss.

B.   Mitigation of Damages--Because contract law only awards damages for actual losses, the non-breaching party has a duty to lessen or mitigate damages. He or she cannot allow the damages to accumulate maliciously.

C.   Liquidated Damages--A pre-set amount of damages agreed on by the parties. Must be distinguished from an illegal penalty which punishes the breaching party. Ask yourself if damages would be difficult to estimate (e.g. loss of time) and if so, are the liquidated damages a reasonable estimate of the loss to be suffered. If the answer to both questions is yes, the liquidated damages are enforceable.

II. Equitable Remedies--Although an equitable remedy may involve the transfer of money, it is usually not granted if money damages would compensate the plaintiff. A plaintiff seeking equity must act timely and in good faith.

A.   Specific Performance--Breaching party is ordered by the court to perform the contract. Rarely granted because this remedy must be supervised and enforced by the court. Usually occurs in cases involving the sale of land or unique items. Never allowed for enforcement of personal service contracts.

B.   Rescission and Restitution--Rescission is can- cellation of the contract. Restitution returns the parties to the position they were in before the contract. (Compare damages which tries to put the parties in the same positions as if the contract had been performed.) If money has changed hands, it must be returned. The exact goods must be returned if possible (in specie) or the money equivalent. Usually granted if the plaintiff has decided to cancel the contract and does not want substitute performance.

C.   Reformation--Correction of a contract. Occurs when an error has been made in drafting the final contract. The parties do not want to cancel the agreement.

D.   Quasi-Contract (Contract Implied in Law)--Used when the contract between the parties is unenforceable and one party has already performed. The other party would get a free ride, so equity will pay the performing party for the work he or she has done (not the contract price). A plaintiff must show:

(1) The defendant received a benefit.
(2) The defendant should have known that he or she was expected to pay.
(3) The plaintiff was not negligent or malicious in performing.
(4) The defendant is receiving something without paying for it (unjust enrichment).

III. Common Contractual Provisions

A. Election of Remedies--The non-breaching party may choose between available remedies but cannot choose more than one. If damages are granted, then specific performance is unavailable because the non-breaching party would be getting twice the benefits.

B. Waiver of Breach--The innocent party may intentionally or accidentally overlook a breach. He or she can still sue for consequential damages. If a breach is overlooked several times, the innocent party may give up the right to complain about a similar breach in the future.

C. Limitation of Remedies--Most will be allowed if the court determines that the parties willingly agreed to the terms.

(1) Limit on Amount Recoverable--Permissible to set liquidated damages.

(2) Limit on Types of Damages--Permissible to deny consequential damages if not unconscionable. Damages due to negligence may also be denied if parties are on equal footing. Cannot restrict damages for personal injury or intentional wrongs.

(3) Limit on Type of Remedy--In sales contracts, recovery can be limited to repair or replacement. If a remedy fails, then the limitation clause does not apply.

Study Questions

Fill-in-the-Blank Questions

Yum-Yum Bakery orders 4 dozen jars of cinnamon-flavored heart-shaped candy from Sweet Nothings Confectioners. The candy is to be delivered on January 25, in time for Yum-Yum to use them for Valentine Day's specials. The jars cost $25 per dozen. On January 26, Sweet Nothings informs Yum-Yum that it will be unable to deliver the hearts and offers no explanation. Yum-Yum buys replacement candy from Ken's Kandy Shoppe at a price of $29 per dozen and has to pay freight charges of $50. Sweet Nothings' delivery charge was $10.

Yum-Yum should sue for _____*compensatory*_____ damages.
(compensatory/punitive)

Excluding freight and shipping costs, Yum-Yum's damages are _____*16*_____ .
$16/$4/$116

Yum-Yum should _____*add*_____ the freight charges to the total above.   (add/subtract)

Yum-Yum should _____*subtract*_____ the delivery charges from Sweet Nothings.   (add/subtract/ignore)

Yum-Yum's total damges are _____*56*_____ .
($16/$56/$66/$156)

True-False Questions

1. Specific performance is usually granted if a personal service contract is breached. __*F*__

2. Nominal damages may be awarded if the plaintiff has not suffered economic loss. __*T*__

3. Liquidated damages are always illegal. __*F*__

4. An exculpatory clause which denies recovery for personal injury is illegal. __*F*__

5. Specific performance would be an appropriate remedy if a seller breached a contract for the sale of a Picasso painting. __*T*__

6. Consequential damages are awarded to punish the defendant. __*F*__

7. Mitigation of damages is the duty of breaching party to lessen damages. __*F*__

8. Reformation would be appropriate remedy if a party wants to correct a description of land in a real estate sales contract. __*T*__

9. Quasi-contract is an equitable remedy. __*T*__

10.   In a suit based on quasi-contract, the plaintiff must show that he or she was not negligent. _F_

Multiple-Choice Questions

1.   Sally buys a used car from Midville Motors. The salesman tells Sally that the car has never been involved in an accident. Sally then discovers that the salesman is lying. Sally can:

a. sue for misrepresentation and collect damages.
b. sue for breach of contract and collect damages.
c. sue for rescission and recover her payments.
d. sue for breach of contract, rescission or misrepresentation.

2.   If Sally sues for breach of contract, she can collect:

a. compensatory damages.
b. punitive damages.
c. nominal damages.
d. compensatory and punitive damages.

3.   Ron buys a watch from Clockex Inc. The contract states, "Buyer's remedy is limited to repair or replacement." The clause is:

a. illegal because it limits damage and Ron can cancel the contract.
b. enforceable if the watch can be repaired or replaced.
c. unenforceable and Ron can sue for damages.
d. enforceable even if the watch cannot be repaired or replaced.

4.   Cecil Cosgrove, a famous conductor, agrees to speak to the advanced music class at State University for a fee of $2000. He also agrees to sell a rare copy of "Brahms Lullaby" to the university library for $10,000. Cecil is a tempermental artist and refuses to honor any part of the contract. With regard to the speech, the univeristy:

a. can sue Cecil for specific performance.
b. cannot sue Cecil for specific performance, but may sue for damages.
c. can sue Cecil for specific performance, but cannot sue for damages.
d. can sue Cecil for specific performance or for damages.

5.   With regard to the sheet music, the university:

      a.   can sue Cecil for specific performance.
      b.   cannot sue Cecil for specific performance, but may
           sue for damages.
      c.   can sue Cecil for specific performance, but cannot
           sue for damages.
      d.   can sue Cecil for specific performance or for
           damages.

6.   Cindy purchases an automobile insurance policy from AAA
      Liability Co. After Cindy has paid the first premium,
      she discovers that the policy describes her automobile
      as a Suburban when in fact she owns a Subaru. The
      premiums for a Suburban are substantially higher than
      those for a Subaru. Cindy does not want to cancel the
      policy but she does want to correct the contract. She
      should sue for:

      a.   rescission.
      b.   reformation.
      c.   quasi-contract.
      d.   punitive damages.

7.   Mrs. O'Leary faints while shopping in the supermarket.
      Dr. Jones administers first aid and calls an ambulance.
      When Mrs. O'Leary regains consciousness, she refuses to
      pay the ambulance bill. The ambulance company should
      sue for:

      a.   breach of contract and compensatory damages.
      b.   reformation.
      c.   rescission.
      d.   quasi-contract.

8.   Bob agrees to buy a house from Sid and signs an earnest-
      money contract. Sid agrees to take his house off the
      market for 30 days. The contract states that if Bob
      decides not to buy the house, he must pay damages of
      $500. The damages clause is:

      a.   an illegal penalty and is unenforceable.
      b.   a legal liquidated damages clause because Sid
           suffers damages when he removes his house from the
           market and the damages are difficult to estimate.
      c.   a legal liquidated damages clause because Bob agreed
           to its terms.
      d.   a legal penalty and is enforceable.

9.   Halloween Heaven, a costume and novelty store, orders twenty vampire costumes from Count Dracula Supplies. The costumes cost $30 each and are scheduled to arrive by October 15. Count Dracula informs Halloween Heaven that it will be unable to ship the costumes in time for Halloween. The costume shop immediately orders from another supplier but is only able to buy fifteen costumes at a price of $50 each. As a result, the costume shop must turn away five customers. The costume shop sues for the extra price of the costumes and for the loss of business. The lost profits are:

a.   compensatory damages.
b.   nominal damages.
c.   consequential damages.
d.   punitive damages.

10.   The extra price of the costumes would be classified as:

a.   compensatory damages.
b.   nominal damages.
c.   consequential damages.
d.   punitive damages.

11.   Assuming that Count Dracula had not been paid, Halloween Heaven's damages are:

a. $750 + lost profits.
b. $600 + lost profits.
c. $150 + lost profits.
d.   lost profits only.

12.   Millie takes her pet poodle to Doggie Do's for grooming services. She asks the groomer to shampoo and clip her dog. On the same day, Connie brings her dog to the shop and requests the deluxe treatment including toenail painting and matching bows. The groomer scrambles the orders and Millie's dog is given the deluxe treatment. When Millie collects her dog, she refuses to pay the higher amount. The groomer sues in quasi-contract. The groomer:

a.   will be successful because Millie was unjustly enriched.
b.   will be successful because he did the work and should be paid.
c.   will be unsuccessful because Millie was not unjustly enriched.
d.   will be unsuccessful because he was negligent.

13. Ollie's Orange Juice has a long-standing contract with Farmer Brown to deliver three carloads of oranges on the first day of every month. In January, the truckers go on strike and the oranges are not delivered until January 10th. Ollie is grateful for any deliveries during the strike and accepts the late oranges. Ollie:

a. has waived the right to complain about the January shipment but has not waived his right to complain about other late shipments.
b. has waived his right to complain about the January shipment and also has waived his right to complain about future late shipments.
c. has not waived his right to complain about the late January shipment because he must notify Farmer Brown that he does not intend to sue.
d. has not waived his right to complain about the late January shipment because he must sign a written waiver.

14. Bright Lights disco purchases a stereo system from Sound Sensations. The contract states that Sound will not be responsible for any property damage resulting from malfunction of the stereo or lost profits. Sound has tried to disclaim:

a. compensatory damages.
b. nominal damages.
c. consequential damages.
d. compensatory and consequential damages.

15. The stereo breaks down immediately and Bright Lights is forced to close for 3 days while it is being repaired. According to the contract between the parties, Bright Lights can sue for:

a. the cost of repairing the stereo and profits lost during closing.
b. the cost of repairing the stereo only.
c. the lost profits only.
d. neither the lost profits nor the repair costs.

16. Mr. Jones contracts with Top-Notch Housing for the construction of a five bedroom house. Before Top-Notch begins work, Jones suffers financial setbacks and cancels the contract. Top-Notch's damages will equal:

a. the cost of the house.
b. Top-Notch's profits + labor + materials used.
c. Top-Notch's profits + labor only.
d. Top-Notch's profits only.

17.   Assume that Jones had breached after Top-Notch had
       started construction, Top-Notch's damages will equal:

       a.   the cost of the house.
       b.   Top-Notch's profits + labor used + materials used.
       c.   Labor used + materials used.
       d.   Top-Notch's profits only.

18.   Aaron agrees to sell his land to Sid.   After the
       contract is signed, Aaron finds someone who is willing
       to pay more and tells Sid that he will not sell.   If Sid
       sues, he:

       a.   can seek specific performance, refund of the
             purchase price, and expenses.
       b.   can seek specific performance or the refund of the
             purchase price.
       c.   can seek refund of the purchase price only because
             specific performance is not available.
       d.   can seek specific performance only because damages
             are not available.

19.   Mobile Home Manufacturing orders 3,000 custom-made fiber
       glass showers from Glassworks, Inc.   Glassworks has
       completed one-third of the order when the manufacturing
       company cancels.   Glassworks can recover:

       a.   lost profits only.
       b.   the cost of the doors completed only.
       c.   lost profits and the cost of the completed doors.
       d.   the entire contract price.

20.   McBurger Restaurant orders 400,000 bushels of potatoes
       from Wholesale Vegetables, Inc.   At the time of the
       order, the potatoes are selling for $15 per bushel. Due
       to falling crop prices, at the time of the contract,
       potatoes are selling at $10 per bushel.   If Wholesale
       breaches and McBurger sues, it will be entitled to:

       a.   nominal damages only.
       b.   nominal damage and compensatory damages.
       c.   compensatory damages.
       d.   punitive damages.

21.   Ron's Car Wash has posted the following sign at the
       entrance to the car wash: Not responsible for loose
       chrome, antennas, property damage caused by accidental,
       negligent, or intentional acts of the owner or its
       employees.   Damages for personal injury are limited to
       $5,000 per person.   Which of the clauses, if any, are
       unenforceable?

a.   The entire disclaimer is enforceable.
b.   The disclaimer is enforceable with the exception of
     the limit on personal injury damages.
c.   The disclaimer is enforceable with the exception of
     the limits on personal injury damages and damages
     suffered by intentional acts of Ron's employees.
d.   The entire disclaimer is unenforceable.

22.   Dr. Denton contracts with Home Nursing Services to
      provide car for his patients for one year at a cost of
      $200 per month per patient. After two months, Home
      cancels. Dr. Denton waits ten months and sues. He did
      not hire a replacement nursing service. Dr. Denton:

      a.   can sue for the cost of 10 months nursing care.
      b.   can sue for the cost of 10 months nursing care less
           the cost of a replacement service because he had the
           duty to mitigate damages.
      c.   cannot sue because he had the duty to mitigate
           damages.
      d.   can sue for punitive damages.

23.   Susan contracts with Home Builders, Inc. to build a new
      office for her silk-flower business. After the building
      is completed, Susan discovers that the workroom is two
      feet shorter than the contract specifications. Susan:

      a.   can refuse to pay until Home Builders rebuilds the
           workroom.
      b.   can sue Home Builders for the cost of enlarging the
           workroom regardless of the cost.
      c.   can sue for the difference between the value of the
           building as specified or the cost of repair, which-
           ever is less.
      d.   cannot sue because the breach is minor.

24.   Merlin the Magnificent, a magician, performs at birthday
      parties. Sarah hires him to perform at her son's
      birthday party. The contract price is $60. The day
      before the party, Sarah cancels. Merlin is lucky enough
      to find other work at a bar mitzvah but it pays only
      $45. Merlin:

      a.   can recover $60 from Sarah.
      b.   can recover $15 from Sarah.
      c.   can recover $15 and punitive damages from Sarah.
      d.   cannot recover from Sarah because he found other
           work.

25.   Assuming that Merlin was unable to find other work on
       such short notice, he:

       a. can recover $60 from Sarah.
       b. can recover $60 and punitive damages from Sarah.
       c. can recover in specific performance.
       d. can recover punitive damages.

Answers to Study Questions

Fill-in-the-Blank Questions

Yum-Yum can only sue for compensatory damages. Punitive
damages are not allowed for breach of contract. Excluding
freight and shipping (incidental) damages, Yum-Yum's damages
are the difference in the price between Sweet Nothings and
Ken's. $4 per jar ($29 - $25) multiplied by the number of jars
ordered (4) or $16. Ken's freight charges should be added.
Yum-Yum should subtract Sweet Nothings' delivery charge because
it saved that amount. Yum-Yum's total damages are the cost of
the replacement candy ($16) + the cost of extra freight ($50)
less any savings ($10) or $56.

True-False Questions

1.   F.   The court will not force a person to perform a
           service contract.

2.   T.

3.   F.   Liquidated damages are legal; a penalty is illegal.

4.   T.

5.   T.

6.   F.   They are awarded to compensate the plaintiff for
           loss which occurs as a result of the breach.

7.   F.   It is the duty of the non-breaching party.

8.   T.

9.   T.

10.   T.

Multiple-Choice Questions

1.	d	10.	a	19.	c
2.	a	11.	c	20.	a
3.	b	12.	d	21.	c
4.	b	13.	a	22.	b
5.	d	14.	c	23.	c
6.	b	15.	b	24.	b
7.	d	16.	d	25.	a
8.	b	17.	b		
9.	c	18.	b		

Chapter 11   Introduction to Sales Contracts and Their Formation

General Principles

The UCC (Uniform Commercial Code) establishes the rules for contracts involving the sales of goods. In Chapter 6, you learned that sales contracts sometimes followed different guidelines than those of non-sales contracts. In general, the UCC has fewer formal requirements. This chapter reviews the essential elements for formation of a contract but addresses only sales contracts.

You should also keep in mind that if one or both parties to a contract are merchants, the rules change yet again. It is assumed that merchants are familiar with the business world; their contracts are less rigid.

Chapter Summary

I.   What Is a Sale of Goods?

A.   Sale--Passage of title or formal ownership in exchange for consideration. A gift does not involve an exchange of consideration. Although the UCC may apply to leases, a lease does not normally involve a transfer of ownership.

B.   Goods--Goods are tangible (can be touched) and movable.

(1) <u>Tangible</u>--Money, stock certificates, accounts receivables, and checks represent a legal right but they are not tangible. For example, a stock certificate represents ownership in a corporation.

(2) <u>Movable</u>--Real estate is not movable and sales of land are not covered by the UCC. <u>Fixtures</u> are personal property which has become attached to the land. The test for a fixture is whether its removal will cause material damage to the real estate. If so, the item is a fixture. Note that a fixture was a good before it became attached to the land.

Crops and timber, which are grown in order to be sold, are always goods, even before they are removed from the ground. Oil, gas, and other minerals are goods if the seller removes them and fixtures if the buyer removes them.

(3) <u>Goods v. Services</u>--Some transactions such as a permanent given by a beautician or a blood transfusion combine goods and services. The UCC does not specify and leaves the decision to the courts with one exception: the sale of food by a restaurant, regardless of whether is it eaten on the premises, delivered, or carried out <u>is</u> a sale of goods.

II. <u>Who is a Merchant?</u>--Although the UCC offers three different definitions of a merchant, he or she is someone who has experience or expertise in a particular area. A person is a merchant of one product is not necessarily a merchant for another type of product. A person who hires a broker or a specialist to conduct the sale is also a merchant. As the text indicates, the courts have split on whether a farmer is a merchant.

III. <u>Contract Formation--Relaxed Rules for Sales Contracts</u>

A. <u>Offer and Acceptance</u>

(1) <u>Firm Offer</u>--A merchant who makes a <u>written, signed</u> offer and promises to hold it open cannot revoke it for the period stated in the offer or if no time perid is stated, for a reasonable time. Three months is the maximum length of time. An option contract, with a down payment, is not required.

(2) <u>Means of Acceptance</u>--Any reasonable means is satisfactory. If the offer specifies a particular form of acceptance and that form is not used by the offeree, the acceptance is still effective if it reaches the offeror by the time set out in the offer.

<u>Acceptance by Shipment</u>--An offer to buy can be accepted by a promise or by shipment. No notice of shipment is necessary unless the shipment will be delayed. If the seller ships goods that do not meet contract specifications (nonconforming), the acceptance is still valid, but the seller has breached the contract. If the seller ships non-conforming goods, but specifies that they are shipped only as an accommodation, the accommodation is a counteroffer and the buyer can either reject or accept the goods. An accommodation may occur if the seller is out of stock of the goods requested but ships more expensive goods at the same price or ships similar goods at a discounted price.

(3) <u>Acceptance or Counteroffer</u>--The mirror-image rule does <u>not</u> apply. If the offeree accepts but includes minor different or additional terms, there is a contract. If the offeree conditions acceptance on the new terms, he or she has made a counteroffer.

If the offeree has accepted, the next question is which terms control: the offeror's or the offeree's. If <u>either</u> of the parties is a non-merchant, the original terms control. If both of the parties are merchants, the new terms proposed by the offeree control unless:

(1) the original offer was a "take it or leave it" proposition, or:

(2) the new terms materially (greatly) alter the original offer, or;

(3) the offeror objects within a reasonable time.

This rule allows merchants to include new terms in the contract without additional communication. Note that the new terms cannot be forced on the offeror; he or she need only object.

B. <u>Open Terms</u>--If other evidence shows that the parties intended to make a contract; the following terms can be left open. Keep in mind that the more open terms, the less likely a court is to find that the parties did intend to make a contract. The contract must always specify the <u>quantity</u> of goods.

    (1) <u>Price</u>--Reasonable price at the time of delivery.

    (2) <u>Payment terms</u>--Payment on delivery is presumed.

    (3) <u>Delivery terms</u>--Buyer takes delivery at seller's unless a third location is indicated. If the contract indicates that the goods are to be shipped, the seller can make reasonable arrangements.

    (4) <u>Cancellation of ongoing contract</u>--Each party has the right to cancel within the bounds of good faith and commercial practice.

    (5) <u>Assortment</u>--Buyer specifies within reason.

C. <u>Consideration</u>--An exception to the pre-existing duty rule. (See Chapter 6.) A modification, proposed in good faith, is binding without additional consideration.

D. <u>Writing (Statute of Frauds)</u>--Required if price of goods is $500 or more; must be signed by the party who is being held to the contract. The exceptions listed below provide evidence that a contract does exist.

    (1) Admissions by a party in court documents.

    (2) Custom-made goods, if they cannot be sold elsewhere and the seller has made a significant start.

    (3) Partial performance to the extent that the buyer has accepted or paid for the goods.

    (4) <u>Merchant's memo</u>--If one merchant sends a signed copy of the contract to the other party, who must also be a merchant, the writing is treated as being signed by both of them unless the recipient objects within 10 days of receipt. This rule applies only if the recipient had reason to know that the memo contains the terms of the contract.

E.   The Parol Evidence Rule--Remember that the written parol evidence rule is designed to prevent parties from testifying in court that the written contract conflicts with the terms of an earlier oral agreement. However, if the testimony explains the contract, it will be allowed. The following types of evidence, as long as it does not contradict the written contract, are admissible:

(1)   Explanation of ambiguous terms

(2)   Additional terms that do not differ from the written contract

(3)   Commercial practices between the parties, including the course of performance under the present contract, the course of dealing under several contracts, trade usage in the industry

If there is a conflict between the commercial practices, the most specific controls: express terms, course of performance, course of dealing and finally, trade usage.

F.   Unconscionability--Blatantly unfair contracts may be cancelled in whole or in part by the court, which also has the option to restrict the enforcement of harsh terms.

Study Questions

Fill-in-the-Blank Questions

Leather Loafers, Inc., a shoe manufacturer, offers to manufacture 5,000 pairs of custom-made tennis shoes for Walkin' Tall, a nation-wide retailer. Leather Loafers, Inc. proposes a price of $20 per pair, delivery in 6 months, with a WT logo on the toe of every pair. The manager of Walkin' Tall sends the following oral reply: "We will gladly accept your offer, please place logo on the heel of each pair". Leather has begun production when it learns Walkin' Tall will breach.

Walkin' Tall's reply is a(n) _____.
                              (counteroffer/acceptance)

The logo must be placed on the _____.
                                 (heel/toe)

The contract _____ unenforceable because it is oral.
             (is/is not)

The contract does not specify a delivery or shipment terms. It
is _____.
   (enforceable/unenforceable)

True-False Questions

1.   The parol evidence rule states that no consideration is
    necessary to modify a contract for the sale of goods. ____

2.   An offer to sell can be accepted by a promise to ship
    goods or by a shipment of goods. ____

3.   The time limit for a merchant's firm offer is two months.
    ____

4.   The mirror-image rule of offer and acceptance applies to
    service contracts but it does not apply to a contract for
    a sale of goods. ____

5.   Trade usage is a synonym for industry custom. ____

6.   A contract for the sale of goods which specifies more than
    500 items must be in writing. ____

7.   Food purchased in a restaurant and eaten in the restaurant
    is a sale, not a service. ____

8.   A business law teacher, who raises hamsters for sale in
    her spare time, is a merchant with regard to hamsters.____

9.   If an offer for the sale of goods specifies a particular
    means of acceptance, a reply received within the time
    limits of the offer will be an acceptance, even if the
    offeree used a different means of acceptance. ____

10.   If a court determines that a contract is unconscionable,
    it can eliminate the unconscionable terms but it cannot
    prevent enforcement of the contract. ____

Multiple-Choice Questions

1.   Which of the following is least likely to be considered a
    fixture?

    a.   A built-in bookcase
    b.   A 40 year-old oak tree
    c.   A microware oven sitting on a counter
    d.   A central air conditioning system

2.   Susan's Sewing Supply offers to buy 300 spools of "Royal Blue" thread from Martin's Mills at a price of $.02 per spool. Martin ships "Peasant Blue" thread instead at the same price. Martin gives no notice of the change.

   a.   There is no contract between Martin and Susan because Martin sent the wrong color of thread.
   b.   There is no contract between Martin and Susan because Martin never promised to ship the thread.
   c.   There is a contract between Martin and Susan but Martin has breached the contract.
   d.   There is a contract between Martin and Susan and Martin has not breached the contract if he reasonably believed that Susan would accept the substitution.

3.   Same facts as above, except that Martin sends a notice to Susan telling her that his stock of "Royal Blue" is temporarily depleted and he hopes that she will accept the substitution.

   a.   There is no contract between Martin and Susan because Martin sent the wrong color of thread.
   b.   There is no contract between Martin and Susan because Martin never promises to ship the thread.
   c.   There is a contract between Martin and Susan but Martin has breached the contract.
   d.   There is a contract between Martin and Susan and Martin has not breached the contract if he reasonably believed that Susan would accept the substitution.

4.   Ozzie's Office Machines writes to Crook & Low, Attorneys at Law, and offers to sell them a used personal computer for $1000. The letter states that the offer will remain open for five days. On the fourth day, Crook & Low try to accept but Ozzie tells them that he has sold the computer to someone else.

   a.   Ozzie has breached the contract, because he promised to keep the offer open.
   b.   Ozzie has not breached the contract, because Crook and Low should have made a down payment.
   c.   Ozzie has not breached the contract, because Crook and Low are not merchants with regard to computers.
   d.   Ozzie has not breached the contract, because he revoked before Crook & Law tried to accept the offer.

5.   Bennie orders four books from Literary Times, a used book dealer for a total of $50. The order blank says nothing about payment terms.

a. Bennie will have to pay for the books when he receives them.
b. Bennie will have a reasonable time to pay for the books.
c. There is no contract because payment terms were not specified.
d. Bennie will have thirty days to pay for the books.

6. Farmer Brown, who owns an orchard, offers to sell thirty truckloads of oranges to Sweet Juice, Inc. for $1,000 per carload. A trucker's strike makes delivery by truck impossible so Brown telephones Sweet Juice and proposes to send the oranges by train, even though Sweet will have to pay $50 more per truckload. Sweet Juice agrees but later refuses to pay the extra money.

a. Sweet Juice is within its rights because of the pre-existing duty rule.
b. Sweet Juice is not within its rights of Farmer Brown is not considered a merchant.
c. Sweet Juice is not within its rights because the change in shipping terms was made in good faith.
d. Sweet Juice is within its rights because Farmer Brown has provided no consideration for the extra shipping costs charged to Sweet.

7. Which of the following is not a sale of goods?

a. Sale of lumber to be cut by the seller
b. Sale of lumber to be cut by the buyer
c. Sale of a "hamburger to go" by McDonald's
d. Sale of stock in a corporation

8. Sylvia is negoitating a sale of her dogs, three golden retrievers, to Brad. Brad and Sylvia have lunch and agree on a price of $200 per dog and that Sylvia will deliver them to Brad's house next week. Sylvia scribbles the following items on a paper napkin, "3 goldens, $200 each, send to Brad next week". Sylvia asks Brad to sign the "contract". Brad feels silly but does so; Sylvia does not sign the contract.

a. The contract is enforceable against Brad only.
b. The contract is enforceable against Sylvia only.
c. The contract is enforceable against Brad and Sylvia.
d. The contract is enforceable; the napkin is not a writing.

9.   Using the same facts in Question 8, answer the following question. Assume that Brad refuses to buy the dogs. The napkin is admitted as evidence at trial when Sylvia sues him for breach of contract. Which of the following testimony would <u>not</u> be allowed by the parol evidence rule?

     a.   Testimony that "goldens" refers to golden retrievers
     b.   Testimony that the price was $200 total
     c.   Testimony that the sale of a dog usually includes a copy of the animal's vaccination record
     d.   Testimony that Sylvia promised to groom the dogs before she sold them to Brad

10. Mary, an insurance saleswoman and Pete, a doctor, are neighbors. Mary offers to sell her car to Pete for $1500. Pete says, "That's a great price. I accept at $1500 for the car and the fuzzy dice hanging from the rear-view mirror.

     a.   Mary and Pete do not have a contract, because Pete made a counteroffer.
     b.   Mary and Pete have a contract, but it does not include the fuzzy dice.
     c.   Mary and Pete have a contract and it does include the fuzzy dice.
     d.   Mary and Pete do not have a contract, because the mirror-image rule applies.

11. Same facts as above, but Mary sells used cars for a living.

     a.   Mary and Pete do not have a contract, because Pete made a counteroffer.
     b.   Mary and Pete have a contract, but it does not include the fuzzy dice.
     c.   Mary and Pete have a contract and it does include the fuzzy dice.
     d.   Mary and Pete do not have a contract because the mirror-image rule applies.

12. Which of the following is (are) merchants?

     a.   Betty, a lawyer, who hires Donald, a horse breeder to sell her Appaloosa mare
     b.   Boy Scouts selling candy as a one-time fundraiser
     c.   Both Betty and the Boy Scouts are merchants
     d.   Neither Betty nor the Boy Scouts are merchants

13.   Karen's Cosmetics places a telephone order for five cartons of eyeshadow, twenty cartons of lipstick and eighteen cartons of mascara from Color Me, Inc., a wholesaler of cosmetics. The cost of the order is $800. Color Me's shipping department sends Karen a copy of the order which contains the following information: Karen's name and address, the quantity of each item, the price per item and the initials of the clerk who took the order. Karen receives the copy of the order but decides to cancel the contract.

a.   Karen is within her rights because the order does not contain enough information to show a contract.
b.   Karen is within her rights because she never signed a written contract.
c.   Karen is not within her rights because the contract did not have to be in writing.
d.   Karen is not within her rights because a representative of Color Me signed the order and Karen failed to object.

14.   If a contract for the sale of goods fails to state a price:

a.   the contract will be unenforceable unless both parties are merhcants.
b.   the contract will be unenforceable regardless of whether parties are merchants.
c.   the contract will be enforceable and the court will use a reasonable price at the time of delivery.
d.   the contract will be enforceable and the court will use a reasonable price at the time the contract was formed.

15.   Merlin's Party Shop telephones Nancy and tells her that it has a set of reindeer antlers in stock for $15, if Nancy can pick them up by the end of the week. Nancy comes in that afternoon and discovers that the reindeer antlers have been sold to someone else. Nancy tells the manager of Merlin's that it was obligated to sell the antlers to her.

a.   Nancy is correct because Merlin is a merchant.
b.   Nancy is correct because Merlin promised.
c.   Nancy is incorrect because both parties must be merchants.
d.   Nancy is incorrect because Merlin did not make its promise in writing.

16.   If a contract for the sale of goods fails to specifiy a place for delivery and shipment is <u>not</u> expected, delivery takes place:

    a.   at the seller's place of business.
    b.   at the buyer's place of business.
    c.   at neither location; the contract is too indefinite to be enforced.

17.   Strong Brothers Department Store orders 500 pairs of assorted gloves to be delivered in ten installments. The price of the entire contract is $1000.

    a.   The contract must be in writing because 500 pairs of gloves were ordered.
    b.   The contract need not be in writing because each shipment of gloves contains only 100 pairs.
    c.   The contract must be in writing, but if it is not, Strong is responsible for any gloves it accepts.
    d.   The contract must be in writing, and if it is not, Strong can cancel the contract and send back any gloves it ha delivered.

18.   Which of the following terms cannot be omitted from a contract for the sale of goods?

    a.   The price
    b.   The quantity
    c.   The shipment terms
    d.   None of the above, all must be included

19.   The customary practice of parties in an installment contract is:

    a.   trade usage.
    b.   course of performance.
    c.   course of dealing.
    d.   admission

20.   Rod's Sporting Goods offers to sell Herman a stationary bicycle for $400. Herman tells the salesman, "It sounds good. I'll take it if you can deliver it by tonight".

    a.   Herman and Rod's have a contract, but Rod's is not obligated to deliver the bike tonight.
    b.   Herman and Rod's have a contract and Rod's is obligated to deliver the bike tonight.
    c.   Herman and Rod no not have a contract because Herman changed the terms of Rod's offer.
    d.   Herman and Rod do not have a contract because Herman's response was conditional and was a counteroffer.

21.   Which of the following is most likely to be considered a merchant?

   a.   A mother having a garage sale
   b.   A university bookstore selling spiral notebooks
   c.   A car salesman selling his boat
   d.   A farmer selling a used fishing rod

22.   Gardenscape Nursery orally offers to sell Mrs. Jones fifteen tomato plants at a price of $1.50 per plant. She accepts and tells Gardenscape that she will pick them up this afternoon. When Mrs. Jones arrives, the plants have been sold to someone else. Mrs. Jones threatens to sue for breach of contract.

   a.   Mrs. Jones will win because the contract did not need to be in writing.
   b.   Mrs. Jones will lose because Gardenscape's offer was not in writing.
   c.   Mrs. Jones will lose because although there was an offer and an acceptance, the contract should have been in writing.
   d.   Mrs. Jones will lose because she is not a merchant.

23.   General Motors offers to sell AAA Auto Parts five clutches for $50 each. General Motors' offer specifies that all acceptances must be sent by mail and postmarked no later than January 15, 1988. AAA sends a telegram, which arrives on January 2.

   a.   There is no contract because AAA did not accept by mail as specified in the offer and the contract needed to be in writing.
   b.   There is no contract because it needed to be in writing.
   c.   There is a contract because AAA accepted by the deadline and the contract did not need to be in writing.
   d.   There is no contract because even though the contract did not need to be in writing, AAA's acceptance by telegram was ineffective.

24.   Mr. Brown buys a lawnmower from Draper Hardware. The terms of the contract state, "Draper is not responsible for personal injury received as a result of use, regardless of the negligence of Draper and/or its retailers". If a court finds that the clause is unconscionable, which of the following modifications could be enforced by the court?

a. The court could cancel the contract.
b. The court could extend Draper's liability and hold it responsible for person injury damages caused by Draper's negligence.
c. Either of the above.
d. Neither of the above; a contract cannot change the terms of a contract.

25. If a court agrees to hear parol evidence to help interpret a contract, if all of the following testimony is offered and is in conflict, which will control?

a. Course of dealing
b. Course of performance
c. Trade usage
d. Industry custom

Answers to Study Questions

Fill-in-the Blank Questions

Walkin's Tall's reply is an acceptance. Its response clearly expressed an intent to make a contract, was not conditional, and did not contain a material difference from the offer. Because both parties are merchants and because Leather Loafers did not object, the new terms control. The logo must be placed on the heel of each shoe. The contract is enforceable if Leather Loafers has made a substantial commitment towards the manufacturer. This is true because the goods are custom-made. Delivery and shipment terms may be left open; the contract is enforceable without them.

True-False Questions

1. F. The parol evidence rule states that oral testimony cannot contradict a written contract.

2. T.

3. F. It is three months or a date specified in the offer, whichever is less.

4. T.

5. T.

6. F. It must be in writing if the price is $500 or more.

7. T.

8.   T.   She has expertise in raising hamsters and holds herself out as having that knowledge.

9.   T.

10.   F.   A court can do either if it determines that a contract is unconscionable.

Multiple-Choice Questions

1. a	11. b	21. b
2. c	12. a	22. a
3. a	13. d	23. c
4. a	14. c	24. c
5. a	15. d	25. b
6. c	16. a	
7. d	17. c	
8. a	18. b	
9. b	19. b	
10. b	20. d	

Chapter 12   Title, Risk, and Insurable Interest

General Principles

This chapter focuses on a common problem in sales contracts: destruction or damage to goods after they have been completed but before the buyer has received actual delivery of the goods. The problem can arise while the goods are being stored at the seller's warehouse or at an intermediate destination or while the goods are in transit. Obviously, one party to the contract must bear the loss. If the seller bears the loss, then the buyer has the right to cancel unless the seller provides replacement goods. If the buyer bears the loss, he or she must pay regardless of whether the goods have been delivered as promised.

Pre-UCC law allocated loss based on which party had title or technical ownership of the goods. Title did not depend on the location of the goods or the actions of the parties. It was also difficult to determine the exact moment when title passed and the court decisions were confusing. The UCC separates risk of loss from title. Generally, if a party has breached the contract, he or she will bear the risk of loss. If neither party has breached, then the party with control over the goods is more likely to bear the risk of loss. Insurance coverage may also affect the distribution of loss.

Chapter Summary

I.   Identification of the Goods--Identification is the designation of the goods. The goods then "belong" to a particular contract between buyer and seller and cannot be sold to another. Goods must be identified before title or risk of loss can pass.

A. Sale or Contract to Sell--Title and risk of loss cannot pass until a sale has taken place. A sale occurs when the goods contracted for are in existence and the goods have been identified to the contract between the buyer and the seller. Before this time, there is only a contract to sell the goods (future goods) and a sale has not occurred.

B. Process of Identification--May depend on the type of goods to be sold.

   (1) Agreement of the Parties--Always controls if there is a specific provision in the contract.

   (2) General Rule--Marked or otherwise noted by the seller. This can include a notation on an invoice or physical separation of the goods. Separation must take place if the goods are part of a larger group. If the goods are separated at the time the contract is made, then identification occurs when the contract is formed.

   (3) Fungible Goods--Usually commodities stored in a silo or other container and impossible to distinguish except by separation (e.g. grains, liquids). In most cases, several sellers that share storage containers are called "tenants in common". Identification takes place when the buyer replaces the seller as the tenant in common.

   (4) Farm Products--Contract for animals to be born or crops to be harvested within twelve months of the contract date are identified when the animals are conceived or when the crops begin to grow.

II. Passage of Title--Formal passage of ownership. Identification must have occurred.

A. General Rule--Parties can agree on time of passage. If the buyer picks up the goods, title passes when the goods are identified to the contract.

B. Carrier Cases--Applies when the goods are moved. Under a shipment contract, title passes when the seller delivers the goods to the carrier and arranges for transportation. Under a destination contract, title passes when the seller tenders or tries to deliver the goods at a location designated in the contract. Note that physical delivery is not required.

C. <u>Bailee Cases</u>--When the goods are held by a third party (bailee), title passes when the buyer receives any documents necessary to pick up the goods, regardless of whether the goods are picked up at that time.

D. <u>Sales by Non-Owners</u>--This is not so much a question of when title passes as if title passes. Usually causes problems when the seller has title problems, but sells to the buyer and the buyer sells to a third party.

(1) <u>Void Title</u>--No title at all. Occurs when the goods have been stolen. The thief and anyone who obtains the goods after him has no title and the true owner can reclaim them.

(2) <u>Voidable Title</u>--Although the seller's title may be rescinded by the true owner, the seller has the power to pass good title to others who pay for them and do not know of the seller's title problems. (The person who buys the goods from the seller must act in good faith and pay value for the goods.) Occurs when the seller obtained the goods from a minor or by fraud or payment with a bad check. Can also occur if the seller was insolvent when he or she bought them.

(3) <u>Entrustment</u>--Occurs with bailments when the true owner delivers the goods to a merchant for repair. The merchant can pass good title to a third party who buys the goods from him or her. The true owner can then sue the merchant-seller.

(4) <u>Bulk Transfers</u>--Sale of a major part of equipment or inventory used in a seller's business. Does not cover usual sales made by seller. Designed to protect the seller's creditors. Unless the buyer and seller follow the rules listed below, the seller's creditors have claim on the goods for six months after the sale. In order for the buyer to obtain clear title:

(1) the seller must furnish under oath a list of his creditors;

(2) the buyer and seller must list property to be transferred;

(3)   the buyer must keep the list for 6 months and make it available to the seller's creditors;

(4)   the buyer must send notice of the transfer to the seller's creditors at least 10 days before payment or possession by the buyer.

III.   <u>Risk of Loss</u>--The UCC attempts to distribute loss between buyer and seller only. In most cases, a carrier or an insurance company may be liable in the end. May or may not coincide with the time that title passes. Determine first if the contract distributes risk of loss or if one party has breached the contract.

A.   <u>Breached Contracts</u>--Risk of loss usually rests on the breaching party.

(1)   <u>Seller Breaches</u>--Risk stays on seller if he or she ships goods which do not conform to the contract and would give the buyer a right to reject them. (This rule refers to a buyer's right to reject discussed in Chapter 13). If the buyer accepts the goods, in spite of defects, risk of loss passes on acceptance. If the buyer discovers a hidden defect, acceptance can be revoked and the risk shifts back to the seller but only to the extent that the buyer's insurance does not cover the loss.

(2)   <u>Buyer Breaches</u>--If the buyer breaches, he or she immediately becomes responsible for any damage to the goods if they have been identified to the contract. Because the seller will probably want to reclaim the goods if the buyer breaches, the following limits apply. The buyer bears the risk only for a commercially reasonable time after the seller learns of the breach and only to the extent that the seller's insurance does not cover the loss.

B.   <u>No Breach</u>--Depends on the type of contract, although as a general rule, the party with possession of the goods and who is more likely to have insurance will bear the loss.

(1)   <u>Contract Terms</u>--Some affect price only; for risk of loss purposes, the question remains whether the contract is shipment or destination contract.

(a) <u>F.O.B. (free on board)</u>--A destination contract which requires the seller to ship the goods at his or her cost to a specific location. Note that the location may be in the seller's city. "Destination" does not necessarily mean the buyer's city or place of business.

(b) <u>F.A.S. (free alongside)</u>--Usually a shipment contract where the seller is required to deliver the goods to the vessel and make arrangements for shipment.

(c) <u>CIF or C&F (cost, insurance, freight or cost and freight)</u>--A shipment contract. These terms relate to the cost of the goods, not the seller's duty to deliver.

(d) <u>Delivery ex-ship (from the carrying vessel)</u>--A destination contract. The seller bears the risk until the goods are properly unloaded.

(2) <u>Carrier Cases</u>--The rules are the same as for passage of title. Under a <u>shipment</u> contract, the risk passes when the seller delivers the goods to a carrier. Under a <u>destination</u> contract, the risk passes when the seller tenders or tries to deliver the goods at a specified location. In the absence of shipping terms, the UCC presumes a <u>shipment</u> contract.

(3) <u>Bailee Cases</u>--When the goods are held by a third party, risk of loss passes when the bailee acknowledges the right of the buyer to the goods or when one of the following events occurs. If documents of title (documents showing ownership) are involved, the answer depends on the type of document. If the document is negotiable, the risk passes when the buyer receives the document. If the document is non-negotiable, the risk passes when the buyer receives the document and has had a reasonable time to present it to the bailee and take possession of the goods.

(4) <u>Goods Held by Seller</u>--If the seller is a merchant, the risk passes when the buyer physically picks up the goods. If the seller is not a merchant, the risk passes when the seller tenders the goods. Note that a merchant seller is much more likely to have insurance covering the goods than is a non-merchant seller.

(5) <u>Sale on Approval</u>--Seller makes only an offer to sell the goods and allows the buyer to take possession on a trial basis. Because no sale has occurred, the risk stays on the seller. If the buyer keeps the goods beyond the trial period or acts as owner, the risk shifts. A sale on approval, as opposed to a sale or return, is presumed if the buyer is to use the goods in his business (equipment).

(6) <u>Sale or Return</u>--Seller delivers goods to buyer but the buyer can return or keep all or part of the goods. The risk shifts to the buyer when the buyer receives possession. If the buyer chooses to return some goods, the risk shifts back to the seller when the goods are returned. A sale or return is presumed if the buyer intends to sell the goods (inventory).

IV. <u>Insurable Interest</u>--A buyer or seller can purchase insurance on goods only if he or she has an interest in the goods. It is possible for both the buyer and the seller to have an interest in the goods. If this concept is difficult to understand, think of buying a car on time. The buyer has insurance but so does the bank or the seller until the final payment is made.

A. <u>Buyer</u>--Acquires an insurable interest when the goods are identified to the contract.

B. <u>Seller</u>--Has an insurable interest until title passes. Can have an insurable interest until payment is received to secure payment (security interest).

Study Questions

Fill-in-the-Blank Questions

Video Visions, a New York manufacturer of television sets, receives an order for 300 Model XX television sets from Shopper's Universe, a retailer. The contract calls for delivery F.O.B. Shopper's warehouse in Chicago. Video's foreman prepares the order, places the 300 sets on the loading dock and marks them for shipment. Before the sets can be loaded onto the dock, a fire destroys all of the television sets.

At the time of the fire, _____ has title to the television sets.   (Video Visions/Shopper's
                                                                            Universe

At the time of the fire, the risk of loss is on _____.
(Video Visions/Shopper's Universe)

At the time of the fire, Video _____ have an insurable interest in the sets.   (does/does not)

Video Visions and Shopper's Universe have a _____
contract.   (destination/
                                                        shipment)

True-False Questions

1. It is possible for a buyer and seller of goods to have an insurable interest in the same property at the same time. ____

2. If goods are to be shipped delivery ex-ship, the buyer is responsible for the goods when the seller leaves them with the carrier. ____

3. If the seller breaches the contract, the risk of loss does not shift to the buyer until the buyer rejects or accepts the goods. ____

4. Goods must be identified to the contract before risk of loss can pass from the seller to the buyer. ____

5. Identification of fungible goods can take place only after the goods have been separated. ____

6. The purpose of the bulk transfer rules is to protect the seller from revocation by the buyer. ____

7. Transfer of title to goods and risk of loss always pass to the buyer at the same time. ____

8. A contract which calls for delivery CIF is a destination contract. ____

9. When a contract calls for the sale of crops to be harvested, identification takes place when the crops are harvested. ____

10. The parties can agree to change point at which the risk of loss passes from seller to buyer. ____

Multiple-Choice Questions

1. Under the law existing before the Uniform Commercial Code, risk of loss passed from seller to buyer when:

    a. the goods were identified to the contract.
    b. the buyer acquired title the goods.
    c. the goods were delivered to the buyer's business.
    d. the seller transferred the goods to a carrier.

2. REV, an automobile manufacturer, receives an order from the Texas State Police for fifty patrol cars. REV records the serial numbers of the cars for shipment to Texas. At this time:

    a. the cars have been identified to the contract because the serial numbers have been recorded.
    b. the cars have been identified to the contract because REV has filled the order.
    c. the cars have not been identified to the contract, because they have not been separated from other cars.
    d. the cars have not been identified to the contract, because they have not been shipped to Texas.

3. Needlepoint Notions, a manufacturer, ships fifty needle-point kits to the Yarn Barn, a retailer. Needlepoint and Yarn have agreed that Yarn may select any or all of the kits for resale to its customers. Any unsold kits are to be returned to Needlepoint within six weeks. The contract between Needlepoint and Yarn Barn is:

    a. a sale or return.
    b. a sale on approval.
    c. a contract to sell, no sale has taken place.
    d. a final sale.

4.   If a fire destroys the kits two weeks after they are
      received and while they are stored at the Yarn Barn, who
      will bear the risk of loss?

      a.   Needlepoint, because the sale to Yarn Barn is not
           final.
      b.   Needlepoint, because Yarn Barn has not accepted the
           kits.
      c.   Yarn Barn, because it has accepted the kits.
      d.   Yarn Barn, because title and risk of loss have
           passed to it.

5.   Future Electronics, a retailer, orders fifty transistor
      radios from Audiotronics. Payment is due within sixty
      days. The day after the goods are received, but before
      Future pays Audiotronics, Future sells one of the radios
      to Mrs. Murphy. One week later, Future sends a check to
      Audiotronics, but the check bounces. Who has title to
      the radio purchased by Mrs. Murphy?

      a.   Audiotronics, because Future did not pay for the
           radio which was sold to Mrs. Murphy.
      b.   Mrs. Murphy, because she paid for the radio in good
           faith.
      c.   Audiotronics, because Mrs. Murphy received voidable
           title.
      d.   Future, because Mrs. Murphy received voidable title.

6.   Mr. Smith is having a garage sale. Susan sees a desk
      that she likes and asks Mr. Smith to hold the desk for
      her until she can arrange for transportation. Mr. Smith
      puts a "sold" sign on the desk. Before Susan can
      return, another shopper at the garage sale carelessly
      backs over the desk with her car. Between Susan and Mr.
      Smith, who will bear the loss?

      a.   Mr. Smith, because he had possession of the desk
           when it was destroyed.
      b.   Mr. Smith, because the risk does not pass until the
           desk is received by Susan.
      c.   Susan, because the risk shifted when the contract
           was made.
      d.   Susan, because the risk shifted when Mr. Smith
           tendered delivery.

7.   At the time the desk was destroyed, who had title to the
      desk?

      a.   Mr. Smith, because he had possession of the desk.
      b.   Mr. Smith, because Susan had not paid for the desk.
      c.   Susan, because title passed when the contract was
           made.
      d.   Susan, because Mr. Smith is not a merchant.

8.   Printed Word, a publishing company, contracts with
      Mystery Bookstore for the sale of fifty copies of the
      latest best seller. The books are to be shipped F.O.B.
      Mystery Bookstore. The seller marks the books for ship-
      ment and then receives a phone call from the manager of
      Mystery Bookstore. The manager informs Printed Wood that
      he will not honor the contract. The next day, the books
      are destroyed when the seller's warehouse is demolished
      by a storm. Who bears the risk of loss to the books?

      a.   Mystery Bookstore must bear the total loss because
           it breached the contract.
      b.   Mystery Bookstore must bear the loss but only if
           Printed Word had insufficient insurance.
      c.   Printed Word must bear the total loss because the
           books had not been shipped.
      d.   Printed Word must bear the total loss only if
           Mystery Bookstore's insurance will not cover the
           loss.

9.   In a bulk transfer of assets, the seller must:

      a.   swear to his or her creditors that either the seller
           or the buyer will pay existing debts.
      b.   notify each creditor of the sale.
      c.   give the buyer a list of creditors.
      d.   file the list of creditors in a designated public
           office.

10.   The entrustment rule:

      a.   applies to risk of loss in breached contracts.
      b.   applies to passage of title.
      c.   applies to bulk transfers of goods.
      d.   applies to identification of goods.

11.   If goods are to be shipped "F.A.S.":

      a.   a shipment contract exists and the seller will bear
           the cost of shipping to the buyer's place of
           business.
      b.   a shipment contract exists and the buyer will bear
           the cost of shipping.
      c.   a destination contract exists and the seller will
           bear the cost of shipping to the buyer's place of
           business.
      d.   a destination contract and the buyer will bear the
           cost of shipping.

12.   Farmer Jones has stored his wheat crop in a silo in the
      Midwest. He is a tenant in common with other farmers
      who also store their wheat crops in the silo. He
      contracts with Breakfast Foods, a cereal manufacturer,
      for the sale of the wheat. Identification of the wheat
      to the cotnract will occur when:

      a. the contract is made between Farmer Jones and
          Breakfast Foods.
      b. the wheat is removed from the silo.
      c. Breakfast pays for the wheat.
      d. the wheat is removed from the silo and shipped to
          Breakfast Foods.

13.   Assuming a negotiable document of title is required,
      title to the wheat will pass when:

      a. the document of title is sent by the seller.
      b. the document of title is received by the buyer.
      c. the document of title is presented to the owner of
          the silo.
      d. the contract is made between Farmer Jones and
          Breakfast Foods.

14.   Assuming a negotiable document of title is required,
      risk of loss to the wheat will pass when:

      a. the document of title is sent by the seller.
      b. the document of title is received by the buyer.
      c. the document of title is presented to the owner of
          the silo.
      d. the contract is made between Farmer Jones and
          Breakfast Foods.

15.   Computer Country delivers a personal computer to L.
      Eagle, Attorney at Law. Eagle has agreed to try the
      computer for one week. Two days after the computer is
      delivered, a fire destroys Eagle's office. Who will be
      responsible for the loss of the computer?

      a. Eagle, because this contract is a sale or return and
          the risk of loss is on the buyer.
      b. Computer Country, because this contract is a sale on
          approval and the risk of loss is on the seller.
      c. Computer Country, because this contract is a sale or
          return and the risk of loss is on the buyer.
      d. Computer Country, because this contract is a sale or
          return and the risk of loss is on the buyer.

16.   Martin's Mills, a shirt manufacturer, receives an order from Carter Clothing, a retailer. The contract calls for shipment of 200 cotton shirts F.O.B. Martin's Mills. The shirts are destroyed in transit. The contract between Martin's Mills and Carter Clothering is:

    a.   a destination contract and Martin is responsible for the loss.
    b.   a shipment contract and Martin is responsible for the loss.
    c.   a destination contract and Carter is responsible for the loss.
    d.   a shipment contract and Carter is responsible for the loss.

17.   Cindy buys a prom dress from Fine Fashions and leaves the dress for alteration. The dress is accidentally sold to Matilda, another promgoer. To whom does the dress belong?

    a.   Cindy, because Fine Fashions had no title to the dress.
    b.   Cindy, because Matilda has voidable title.
    c.   Matilda, because Fine Fashions has void title.
    d.   Matilda, because Fine Fashions was entrusted with Cindy's dress.

18.   Walter purchases a new couch from Fred's Furniture. Walter makes arrangements to pick up the couch on Wednesday. Fred's warehouse and Walter's couch are destroyed by flood on Tuesday. Who will bear the loss of the couch?

    a.   Walter, because he has paid for the goods and Fred tendered delivery.
    b.   Walter, but only to the extent that Fred's insurance won't cover the loss.
    c.   Fred, because Walter has not taken delivery of the couch.
    d.   Fred, but only if Walter's insurance doesn't cover the loss.

19.   Verdant Veggies, a wholesale distributor of canned foods, contracts to sell Sunshine Market six cases of green beans. The manager of Verdant Veggies tells his shipping foreman to reserve six cases for Sunshine. The foreman forgets to fill Verdant's order. Before the goods can be shipped, a fire destroys Verdant's warehouse. Who will bear the loss of the green beans?

a. Verdant, because the goods have not been identified to the contract.

b. Verdant, because although the goods have been identified to the contract, they have not been shipped.

c. Sunshine, because the goods have been identified to the contract.

d. Sunshine, because the goods have been identified to the contract and it has an insurable interest in the goods.

20. "Delivery ex-ship" means:

a. the seller must deliver the goods alongside the vessel or carrier.

b. the seller must deliver the good to the carrier and the seller will pay the freight costs.

c. the seller must deliver the goods to a particular destination and the seller will pay the freight.

d. the seller bears the risk of loss until the goods leave the carrier and are unloaded properly.

21. Lawn and Garden Supply orders 200 leaf rakes from Green Thumb Manufacturer's. The contract calls for the goods to be shipped F.O.B. Lawn and Garden Supply. When the goods arrive, the manager of Lawn and Garden Supply discovers that grass rakes have been sent by mistake. Lawn stores the rakes in its storeroom until it can arrange for shipment to the manufacturer. The rakes are destroyed accidentally. Who will bear the risk of loss?

a. Lawn and Garden, because the rakes were in its possession.

b. Lawn and Garden, because the rakes were identified to the contract.

c. Green Thumb, because this is a destination contract.

d. Green Thumb, because it is in breach.

22. Dr. Burns orders an X-ray machine from Orton's Medical Equipment. A shipping charge appears on the bill and Dr. Burns' address appears on the box but no other shippng terms are noted in the contract or on the merchandise. If the goods are destroyed in transit, who will be responsible for the loss?

a. Dr. Burns, because in the absence of express terms, a destination contract is presumed.

b. Dr. Burns, because in the absence of express terms, a shipment contract is presumed.

c. Orton, because in the absence of express terms, a destination contract is presumed.

d. Orton, because in the absence of express terms, a shipment contract is presumed.

23.   Which of the following would not be subject to the bulk
        transfer rules?

        a. Sale by a computer manufacturer of its entire stock
            of computers
        b. Sale by a doctor of his practice to another doctor
        c. Sale by a clothing store of all its inventory except
            accessories
        d. Going out of business sale by a univeristy bookstore

24.   Dyer's Drugstore purchases an insurance policy which
        covers all goods in which Dyer has an interest or title.
        Dyer orders forty cases of aspirin from Cure-All
        Pharmaceuticals. The aspirins are destroyed on the
        manufacturer's loading dock and Dyer files a claim with
        his insurance.

        a. Dyer's claim will be denied because the goods had
            not been identified to the contract.
        b. Dyer's claim will be denied because he did not have
            an insurable interest in the aspirin.
        c. Dyer's claim will be denied because he did not have
            title to the aspirin.
        d. Dyer's claim will be allowed because he had an
            insurable interest in the aspirin.

25.   Texas Wines, Inc., a bottler in Dallas, agrees to buy
        2,000 gallons of wine from Vicon Vineyards, which is
        located in Lubbock. The wine is stored in a vat in
        Lubbock. The storage facilities are owned by Commodity
        Storage, Inc. In order to take possession of the wine,
        a party must present a receipt of ownership to
        Commodity's manager. Texas Wines receives a non-
        negotiable receipt from Vicon and plans to withdraw 200
        gallons. Between Texas Wines and Vicon, who will bear
        the loss of the wine?

        a. Vicon, because Texas had not withdrawn any wine.
        b. Vicon, but only if Texas had not had a reasonable
            time to withdraw the wine.
        c. Texas Wines, because it had title to the wine.
        d. Texas Wines, because it had an insurable interest in
            the wine.

Answers to Study Questions

Fill-in-the-Blank Questions

At the time of the fire, the goods have been identified to the contract, because Video Visions's foreman segregated them. Because the goods are to be moved, the rules involving carriers apply. Title passes when the goods are moved, therefore title remains in Video Visions. The risk of loss is also on Video Visions. Shopper's Universe does have an insurable interest in the goods; an insurable interest arises when the goods are identified to the contract. This is a destination contract; Video Visions has the responsibility for shipping the goods to Shopper's warehouse.

True-False Questions

1.   T.

2.   F. The seller bears the risk until the goods are properly unloaded at their destination.

3.   T.

4.   T.

5.   F. If the goods are stored in a silo or other facility, the buyer can replace the seller as a tenant in common of the fungible goods.

6.   F. The purpose of the bulk transfer rules is to protect the creditors of the seller by giving them notice of the proposed sale of assets.

7.   F. The rules are different.

8.   F. It is a shipment contract. CIF relates to cost of shipment only.

9.   F. Identification takes places when the crops begin to grow.

10.   T.

Multiple-Choice Questions

1. b	6. d	11. b	16. c	21. d
2. a	7. c	12. a	17. d	22. b
3. a	8. b	13. b	18. c	23. b
4. b	9. c	14. b	19. a	24. d
5. b	10. b	15. b	20. d	25. b

Chapter 13 Performance and Breach

As you learned in Chapter 10, if one party fails to complete a contractual duty, breach results. The first part of this chapter defines the duties of parties to a sales contract. In general, the seller has the duty to provide the exact goods promised at the time and place set out in the contract. The buyer has the duty to pay for the goods according to the terms of the agreement. The UCC also imposes a duty on the buyer to inform the seller of any defect in the goods, so that if possible, the seller can correct the error.

The second half of this chapter deals with the remedies available to the parties once a breach has been established. Although a buyer or seller may have several options, some choices are available only in specific cases. Note also that some remedies involve monetary compensation while others provide for possession of the goods.

Chapter Summary

I.   Obligations of the Buyer and the Seller--Both the buyer and the seller have the duty to comply with the following standards.

    A.   Good Faith--This is an obligation to act fairly and honestly. Consumers and non-merchants are held to a <u>subjective</u> standard of innocence; honesty, not stupidity, is the standard.

B. <u>Commercial Reasonableness</u>--Merchants are held to a higher standard. They must not only act honestly but their conduct must comform to reasonable business standards. Note the many places in this chapter where "reasonableness" is the test for performance.

II. <u>Duties of the Seller</u>

A. <u>Tender of Delivery</u>--Tender is the duty to be ready, willing, and able to perform the contract. The seller has the duty to provide conforming goods at the time specified in the contract. If the buyer is to take delivery, the seller must notify the buyer and give the buyer a reasonable time to collect the goods.

B. <u>Place of delivery</u>--Usually specified in the contract.

   (1) <u>Presumption</u>--Buyer picks up the goods at the seller's place of business or at the seller's home if the seller has no established place of business.

   (2) <u>Carrier Cases</u>--Under a shipment contract, the seller has the duty to deliver the goods to a carrier, to make the contract for delivery, and to notify the buyer of the shipment. If a document such as a bill of lading is required to obtain the goods, the seller must forward it to the buyer.

   Under a destination contract, the seller has the responsibility of transporting the goods to an agreed location and to notify the buyer of their arrival. Notice must be given at a reasonable hour and the buyer must have a reasonable time to collect the goods.

   (3) <u>Agreed Location</u>--If identified goods are stored at a warehouse or grain elevator, delivery takes place at that location.

C. <u>The Perfect Tender Rule</u>--States that the goods tendered by the seller must conform to the contract in every detail; they must be perfect. If the goods are not perfect, the buyer has the right to reject; there is no substantial performance. Because a buyer who wishes to get out of a contract might be able to do so by seizing on trivial errors; the UCC lists several exceptions to the perfect tender rule. The exceptions include:

(1) <u>Agreement of Parties</u>--If the contract makes allowances for imperfect tender, the buyer must adhere to the provisions of the contract.

(2) <u>Cure</u>--This is the seller's right to correct mistakes. The buyer has the duty to inform the seller of problems (mitgiation of damages). If the buyer does not do so, he or she loses the right to reject the goods, <u>if</u> the mistake could have been remedied.

The seller has the right to cure if the time for performance has not passed. Even if the deadline has passed, the seller can cure if there is reason to believe that the goods shipped would have been an acceptable substitute. (e.g. a more expensive model at the same price).

(3) <u>Substitution of Carriers</u>--When the goods cannot be shipped in the manner specified in the contract, and the seller is not at fault, he or she can make other reasonable arrangements for transport.

(4) <u>Installment Contracts</u>--Basically a substantial performance requirement. The buyer may reject an installment only if the value of that installment is substantially impaired and cannot be remedied. The buyer can cancel the <u>entire</u> contract (all installments) only if the value of the whole contract is seriously damaged.

(5) <u>Commercial Impracticability</u>--Same rule as non-sales contracts. The seller is relieved of contractual duties if an unforeseeable event beyond his or her control makes performance impracticable. If only part of the contract is affected, the seller must apportion the remaining goods among the buyers and each buyer has the right to accept or reject.

(6) <u>Destruction of Identified Goods</u>--Same rule as non-sales contracts, if the seller still bears the risk of loss. If the buyer bears the risk when the goods are destroyed; then the seller has performed and the buyer must pay. The buyer has the option to accept damaged goods at a reduced price.

III.   <u>Duties of the Buyer</u>

    A.   Furnish a place for the goods to be stored.

    B.   Pay for the goods at the time at the place the goods are delivered. Note that delivery occurs when the seller has completed his or her responsibility and may have nothing to do with the physical location of the goods.

    C.   The buyer accepts goods by words or conduct. Failure to complain after a reasonable opportunity to inspect is acceptance. If the buyer uses the goods or in any way acts as the owner of the goods, acceptance has occurred. Partial acceptance is proper if made in commercial lots.

    D.   The buyer has a right and duty of inspection if he or she is obligated to pick up the goods. Payment constitutes acceptance. Therefore, if the goods are to be delivered C.O.D. or before the buyer has a chance to inspect them, the buyer retains a right to revoke acceptance of nonconforming goods.

    E.   <u>Revocation of Acceptance</u>--Because the buyer has the duty to inspect the goods, the right to revoke acceptance is limited. It is available only if the buyer had reason to believe that the seller was performing as agreed. The value of the goods must be damaged seriously <u>and</u> one of the following events occurs.

        (1)   The buyer notified the seller of the problem; the buyer reasonably expects the seller to cure and the seller has not done so.

        (2)   The defect is hidden.

        (3)   The seller assured the buyer that the goods were acceptable and the buyer, relying on the seller's promise, did not inspect the goods.

IV.   <u>Anticipatory Repudiation</u>--If either party has notice of breach before the delivery date, the non-breaching party can (1) pursue any of the remedies available when a contract is breached; (2) wait for a reasonable time to see if the breaching party will perform (note that if the waiting period is unreasonable, the non-breaching party has not mitigated damages); (3) stop performance.

V.   Remedies of the Seller

A.   Possession of the Goods

(1) Withhold delivery

(2) Stop goods on their way to the buyer. Must notify the carrier in time to stop delivery and give substitute instructions. The seller is responsible for any additional cost. Must be at least a carload or larger.

(3) If the buyer is insolvent, the seller can demand cash for the goods or withhold delivery. The seller may also reclaim goods in possession of a bankrupt buyer if the seller acts within ten days of delivery. This time limit does not apply if the buyer misrepresented his or her financial condition in writing within three months before delivery.

B.   Monetary Remedies

(1) Resell the goods at a commercially reasonable sale (not necessarily public). The seller must inform the buyer of the sale unless the goods are perishable and losing value and the delay would result in further decline. The seller can then sue the buyer for any deficiency including the expense of the sale.

The seller can use this remedy even if at the time of the contract, the goods have not been identified to the contract (set aside for the buyer). The seller can identify the goods before sale. In the case of partially manufactured goods, the seller can cease production and sell the goods for scrap or complete the goods and sell them. The decision must be reasonable.

(2) The seller can sue for the entire purchase price and expenses only under extaordinary circumstances (usually when the goods are not available for resale).

(a) When the buyer has accepted the goods and has not paid.

(b) When conforming goods have been lost or damaged and the risk of loss is on the buyer.

(c) When the goods have been identified to the contract and the seller cannot resell (custom-made goods).

(3) If the seller can show that the traditional damages outlined above do not compensate for the loss which has occurred, he or she may sue for wrongful repudiation of the contract. The damages include lost profits and incidental expenses. Usually available with high-price, low-volume items such as airplanes.

VI.   Remedies of the Buyer

A.   Non-Monetary Remedies

(1) The buyer can always reject noncomforming goods but remember that the buyer must notify the seller of the problem. A merchant buyer must make adequate provisions for storing the goods or reshipping them to the seller. If the goods are perishable, the buyer can sell them and send the proceeds to the seller less the expenses of the sale.

(2) Specific performance if unique goods are involved.

(3) If the buyer can show that substitute goods are not available, he or she may also be able to replevy the goods or to recover the goods if the goods have been identified to the contract. The buyer cannot force the seller to manufacture or to identify the goods.

(4) If the seller is insolvent at the time of payment or becomes insolvent within ten days, the buyer has the right to possession of any identified goods.

(5) Cancel the contract in whole or in part. Notice must be sent to the seller.

B.   Monetary Remedies

(1) A buyer who has paid for the goods or incurs expenses with regard to them, receives a security interest to enforce payment. If the goods remain in the buyer's possession after rejection, the buyer can use any of the seller's options including resale of the goods to other buyers. Excess monies must be remitted to the seller.

(2) The most popular remedy is cover or the buyer's right to buy substitute goods. Cover corresponds to the seller's right of resale. The buyer can sue the seller for the extra cost of the goods and expenses. The buyer may also sue for losses which are foreseeable as a result of the breach (consequential damages).

(3) If the buyer decides not to purchase substitute goods, the seller may be sued for breach of contract. The damages are the difference between the contract price and the time the buyer learned of the breach. The buyer may also recover incidental and consequential damages.

(4) If the buyer decides to keep the damaged goods, the seller may be sued for the difference between the value of the goods promised and the value of the goods received if the suit is for breach of warranty. In other cases, the buyer can sue for foreseeable losses. The buyer can deduct the losses from the purchase price owed to the seller.

Study Questions

Fill-in-the-Blank Questions

Holiday Cards, Inc., a manufacturer of greeting cards, contracted with Sam's Stationery Shoppe to deliver 100 boxes of Christmas cards at a price of $2 per box. Sam specified delivery by November 15. The cards arrived on November 7th but due to a mix-up on the loading dock, Hanukkah cards were sent. Sam opened the cards when they arrived but chose not to notify Holiday. Instead, he purchased substitute cards from Creative Cards at $2.15 per box. Sam shipped Holiday's cards back to them after the first of the year.

At the time of breach, November 7th, Holiday _____ have a right to cure.   (did/did not)

If the cards had arrived on November 15th, Holiday _____ _____ a right to cure.   (would have had/would not have had)

Sam's purchase of substitute cards is _____.
                                             (cover/reclamation)

True-False Questions

1. A merchant must always act in a commerically reasonable manner, regardless of whether he or she breached the contract. ____

2. Anticipatory repudiation is the buyer's right to purchase substitute goods. ____

3. If no place of delivery is stated in the contract, delivery takes place at the buyer's place of business. ____

4. Replevin is the right of the buyer to take possession of specific goods in the seller's possession. ____

5. The perfect tender rule cannot be altered by an agreement between the parties. ____

6. If a buyer receives damaged goods, he or she may keep them and sue for breach of warranty. ____

7. If the buyer breaches the contract after the seller has begun production of the goods, the seller has the option of finishing the goods or ceasing manufacture and selling the partially finished goods for scrap. ____

8. A seller may sue for the entire contract price if the goods have been identified to the contract. ____

9. Commercial impracticability is an exception to the perfect tender rule. ____

10. If the goods are destroyed while the buyer bears the risk of loss, the contract is cancelled. ____

Multiple-Choice Questions

1. Sleep-Easy Mattress Co. delivers fifty mattresses to the Good Night Sleep Shop. When Good Night receives the mattresses, it sends Sleep-Easy notice that it is filing for bankruptcy and it cannot pay. Sleep-Easy:

   a. can reclaim the goods within ten days of delivery.
   b. can reclaim the goods within three months of delivery.
   c. cannot reclaim the goods but can sue for damages.
   d. cannot reclaim the goods and cannot sue for damages.

2.   Tender of delivery occurs when:

     a.   the goods are placed in the hands of buyer.
     b.   the seller notifies the buyer that the goods are
          ready.
     c.   the buyer pays for the goods.
     d.   the buyer accepts the goods.

3.   Houndog Pet Food and Herman's Feed Store have a shipment
     contract for the sale of fifty bags of dog food at $7
     per bag. Houndog's duty with regard to transportation
     of the dog food is:

     a.   placement with a carrier.
     b.   notice to Herman.
     c.   neither of the above.
     d.   both of the above.

4.   If the goods are destroyed in transit, after the risk
     has passed to Herman, Houndog:

     a.   cannot sue Herman for the price of the goods because
          Herman never received them, but Houndog is not
          obligated to replace the destroyed goods.
     b.   cannot sue Herman for the price of the goods because
          Herman never received them and Houndog must replace
          the goods.
     c.   can sue Herman for the price of the goods.
     d.   can sue Herman for the cost of the goods.

5.   Bernard's Grocery orders 500 cases of liquid diswasher
     soap from Kleen Products, Inc. Delivery is to take
     place in ten installments of fifty cases on the
     fifteenth of each month. In the fourth month, Bernard
     opens the shipments and discovers that all the bottles
     of soap have leaked.

     a.   Bernard can cancel the remaining portions of the
          contract and sue for breach of contract.
     b.   Bernard can reject the fourth shipment and cancel
          the rest of the contract.
     c.   Bernard can reject the fourth shipment only.
     d.   Bernard cannot reject the fourth shipment but he can
          sue for damages.

6.   Parsons Manufacturing orders a widget-maker from Miscel-
     laneous Parts, Inc. Parsons inspects the machine and
     pays for it. Two days later, when the machine has been
     in use for twenty-four hours, Parson discovers a defect.
     Parsons:

a. has not accepted the machine.
b. cannot revoke his acceptance because he paid for the machine.
c. cannot revoke his acceptance because he inspected the machine.
d. can revoke his acceptance of the machine because the defect was not apparent.

7. Initially Yours, a monogram shop, contracts with Central University, for the sale of thirty-five sweaters with the college's logo. A week before the date of delivery, Central informs Initially Yours that due to budget cuts, it will not pay for the sweaters. Initially Yours:

a. can wait for Central to perform or sue immediately.
b. must wait for the delivery date and sue.
c. must sue immediately.
d. must cancel the contract.

8. In which of the following cases, can the seller sue for the purchase price of the goods?

a. The buyer refuses payment and the goods can be resold at a loss.
b. The buyer refuses payment and the goods cannot be resold.
c. The buyer refuses payment and revokes acceptance.
d. The buyer refuses payment and the goods are destroyed at the seller's warehouse.

9. Unless otherwise specified in the contract, the buyer must pay for the goods:

a. when the goods are physically in the buyer's hands.
b. when the goods are delivered to the buyer under the terms of the contract, regardless of the physical location of the goods.
c. within ten days of delivery.
d. within twenty-four hours of delivery.

10. The buyer's right of inspection:

a. applies even if the shipment is C.O.D.
b. cannot be waived by the buyer.
c. may affect the buyer's right to sue if the goods are plainly defective.
d. does not prevent the seller from suing for payment.

11.   The seller can stop goods in transit:

       a.   only if the buyer is insolvent.
       b.   only if the buyer has given notice of intent to
            reject.
       c.   only if the contract is a shipment contract.
       d.   only if the carrier is given reasonable notice.

12.   Fine Furniture Co. manufacturers chairs, tables and
       other household items. A fire destroys the warehouse
       and only one-tenth of the goods are salvaged. Fine has
       twenty-five customers to whom it owes furniture.

       a.   Fine can cancel all the contracts.
       b.   Fine can apportion the remaining furniture and the
            buyers must accept the goods if Fine's decision is
            reasonable.
       c.   Fine can apportion the remaining furniture but the
            buyers have the right to accept or reject the
            remaining goods.
       d.   Fine must fulfill all the contracts or be liable for
            breach of contract.

13.   Paul's Produce contracts with Taco Town to deliver fifty
       heads of iceberg lettuce per week. Last week Paul
       accidentally delivered romaine lettuce. Taco purchases
       replacement lettuce for a price of ten cents more per
       head and sells the romaine lettuce to Posh Eatery for
       ten cents less than the contract price.

       a.   Taco can sue Paul for the following damages: the
            extra cost of the iceberg lettuce, the expenses of
            procuring the iceberg lettuce, and the expenses of
            the sale of the iceberg lettuce less the sale price
            of the romaine lettuce.
       b.   Taco can sue Paul for the following damages: the
            extra cost of the iceberg lettuce and the expenses
            in procuring it, but Taco cannot sue for anything
            connected with the sale to Posh Restaurant because
            Taco had no right to sell the romaine lettuce.
       c.   Taco cannot sue Paul because it had no right to sell
            the romaine lettuce but Paul cannot sue Taco because
            it breached the contract.
       d.   Taco cannot sue Paul but Paul can sue Taco for
            wrongfully selling the romaine lettuce.

14.   The duty of good faith applies:

       a.   to both parties, regardless of breach.
       b.   to breaching parties only.
       c.   to merchants only.
       d.   to non-breaching parties only.

15.   Which of the following is <u>not</u> a remedy of the seller:

      a. Cancellation
      b. Withhold delivery
      c. Specific performance
      d. Suit for the contract price

16.   Leather Products, Inc. ships fourteen briefcases to Executive Luggage, a retailer. Although payment is due upon receipt, after two weeks, Leather has received nothing from Executive. Leather:

      a. can assume that Executive has accepted the briefcases and can sue for the contract price.
      b. can assume that Executive has accepted the briefcases but must give Executive a reasonable time to pay.
      c. cannot assume that Executive has accepted the briefcases because Leather must demand that Executive inspect the briefcases.
      d. cannot assume that Executive has accepted the briefcases because Executive must give notice of acceptance.

17.   Patsy orders a ceramic cookie jar from Kitchen Kuties. The order form calls for delivery by OPS overnight service. Kitchen fills Patsy's order but then discovers that due to mechanical failure, OPS will not deliver for two days. Kitchen arranges for transportation by Fast Express Trucking Service.

      a. Patsy can reject the cookie jar if it arrives after the delivery date.
      b. Patsy can reject the cookie jar regardless of the date of delivery because of the perfect tender rule.
      c. Patsy cannot reject the cookie jar becuase Patsy's substitution of carriers was reasonable.
      d. Patsy cannot sue because she received the goods.

18.   AAA Applicance orders fifty autumn gold refrigerators from Kold, Inc. Two weeks before the order is due, AAA cancels wrongfully. Kold, who has not previously filled AAA's order, identified the refrigerators to the contract and sells them to BB's at a slightly lower price and sues AAA for the difference. Is Kold within its rights?

a. Yes, because it had a right to identify the goods to the contract and resell them.
b. No, because it had no right to identify the goods to the contract.
c. No, because it had no right to sell the goods to BB's.
d. No, because although it had a right to sell the refrigerators, it cannot sue AAA for the loss.

19. Same facts as above, but assume BB's is owned by the son-in-law of Kold's president. The sale was not announced to the public.

a. The sale is automatically invalid becuase it was made to an insider.
b. The sale is invalid because it was not announced to the public.
c. The sale is valid if it was made in a commercially reasonable manner.
d. The sale is invalid, because Kold had no right to resell the goods.

20. Peter and Abel had a long-standing agreement. On the first of each month, Peter ships Abel ten boxes of floppy diskettes. Abel pays on delivery. Peter has not received payment for the last four shipments. Peter may:

a. cancel the contract and sue for damages.
b. withhold delivery of further shipments until payment is received.
c. sue for breach of contract.
d. do all of the above.

21. Cindy orders a set of towels from a linen supply store. The store promises to deliver on or before July 13. On July 15, Cindy has not received the towels. The towels arrive on July 16. Cindy:

a. can reject the towels because of the perfect tender rule.
b. cannot reject the towels because the linen supply has substantially performed.
c. cannot reject the towels because late shipments are an exception to the perfect tender rule.
d. can reject the towels only if they do not conform to the contract.

22.   Omega is a manufacturer of television sets. It contracts with X Mart for the delivery of fourty Model 100 sets. Delivery is to occur on the sixteenth of the month. The sets arrive on the due date but X Mart discovers that Omega has shipped the more expensive Model 200 sets with a note that says "we are temporarily out of stock of Model 100, you can have these for the same price". X Mart:

   a.   can cancel the contract immediately because Omega shipped nonconforming goods.
   b.   can cancel the contract because Omega's right to cure expired on the 16th.
   c.   cannot cancel the contract because Omega has substantially performed and X Mart must accept the substitution.
   d.   cannot cancel the contract because Omega retains the right to cure for a reasonable time after the 16th.

23.   The same week, X Mart received a shipment of toothpaste from Dental Products. X Mart discovers that 1 carton of toothpaste is defective. X Mart:

   a.   can accept the defective toothpaste and sue for breach of contract.
   b.   can accept the toothpaste and deduct the cost of the defective toothpaste.
   c.   can choose either remedy.
   d.   must reject the defective goods or pay full price.

24.   Which of the following are exceptions to the perfect tender rule?

   a.   Commercial impracticability
   b.   Destruction of the goods after the risk has passed to the buyer.
   c.   Substantial performance.
   d.   Substitution of merchandise.

25.   Replevin is an appropriate remedy when:

   a.   the seller cannot resell the goods.
   b.   the buyer cannot cover.
   c.   the seller has shipped defective goods.
   d.   the buyer has accepted defective goods.

Answers to Study Questions

Fill-in-the-Blank Questions

Holiday did have the right to cure on November 7th but not on November 15th. The seller has an absolute right to cure before the date performance is due. After the deadline, the seller has the right to cure only if he or she had reason to believe that the substitute goods would be acceptable. Hanukkah cards are not an acceptable substitute for Christmas cards. Sam's purchase of substitute goods is cover; reclamation is a seller's remedy.

True-False Questions

1.   T.

2.   F.   Anticipatory repudiation is a party's notice that he or she does not intend to honor the contract.

3.   F.   It is at the seller's place of business.

4.   T.

5.   F.

6.   T.

7.   T.

8.   F.   Other requirements must be satisfied. This remedy is proper only if the buyer is in possession of the goods or if the risk has passed to the buyer.

9.   T.

10.   F.   The buyer must still pay for the goods.

Multiple-Choice Questions

1.	a	8.	b	15.	c	22.	d
2.	b	9.	b	16.	a	23.	c
3.	d	10.	c	17.	c	24.	a
4.	c	11.	d	18.	a	25.	b
5.	c	12.	c	19.	c		
6.	d	13.	a	20.	d		
7.	a	14.	a	21.	a		

Chapter 14   Warranties and Product Liability

General Principles

A warranty is a promise by a seller. Under the UCC, there are warranties of ownership (title) and warranties of quality. A seller does not have to give a warranty; if the goods are unsuitable, the buyer can sue for breach of contract. Any warranty given may also be disclaimed or cancelled. To determine if the plaintiff has a good cause of action, you should ask yourself the following questions:

    (1)   Was a warrenty made?
    (2)   Was a disclaimer made?
    (3)   Is the disclaimer proper (effective)?
    (4)   Was the warranty breached?

Product liability is the general term for suits by users or consumers against manufacturers and retailers. In addition to suits for breach of warranty, the plaintiff may also have a suit for negligence or strict liability.

Chapter Summary

I.   Warranties of Title--Relates to ownership rights.

      A.   Good Title--This is an implied warranty which attaches automatically to any sale of goods. The seller promises that he or she owns the goods. If the warranty is breached, (i.e. the seller has no title), the true owner can reclaim the goods and the buyer can sue the seller.

B.   No Liens--An implied warranty. Problems may arise
with used goods. The seller promises that no one
else, usually a creditor, has an interest in the
goods. When expensive goods are bought on credit,
the seller-creditor usually retains the right to
repossess the goods if payment is not made. If the
buyer sells the goods to a third party and does not
mention the creditor's lien, the warranty is
breached. If the original seller decides to
repossess, the third party can sue his or her
seller, the original buyer.

C.   No Infringement--The seller promises that any goods
transferred do not violate copyright, trademark, or
patent regulations. If an infringement suit is
brought against the buyer, the seller has a right
to defend it. The buyer must notify the seller and
allow the seller to defend the suit before the
buyer can sue for breach of warranty.

D.   Disclaimer--Can be disclaimed only by specific
words in the contract. Look for phrases like "only
the seller's right, title and interest".

II.   Express Warranty--A warranty of quality.

A.   Elements

(1)   Oral or written statement by the defendant;
model or sample is also sufficient

(2)   Statement must be one of fact; puffing or an
opinion is insufficient unless the seller is
an expert and plaintiff shows reasonable
reliance

(3)   Statement must be an important factor in the
purchase (basis of the bargain)

(4)   Product did not perform as promised (breach)

B.   Disclaimer--If no statements are made by the
seller, no warranty has been made. In addition,
most written contracts contain a disclaimer or oral
promises. Look for phrases like "all warranties
made appear in this writing; no other promises have
been made" or other limiting language.

III. **Implied Warranty of Merchantability - Quality**

   A. **Elements**

      (1) Seller is a merchant

      (2) Product is not fit for the ordinary purpose for which it is used (breach)

      (3) If defects are obvious, there is no breach

      (4) Proximate cause

   B. **Disclaimer**--Can be oral or written, but if written, must be conspicuous. A writing is conspicuous if it is different from the rest of the writing; the difference can be in color, case, type, or size. "As is" and "with all faults" is sufficient; otherwise the disclaimer must mention merchantability.

IV. **Implied Warranty of Fitness for a Particular Purpose - Quality**

   A. **Elements**

      (1) Seller does not have to be a merchant

      (2) Seller has reason to know the buyer's particular reason for the purchase

      (3) Buyer relies on the seller's judgment

      (4) Proximate cause

   B. **Disclaimer**--Must be conspicuously written. "As is" or "with all faults" is sufficient. Need not mention merchantability.

V. **Miscellaneous Warranty Provisions (UCC)**

   A. **Implied Warranty from Commercial Dealings**--A party's course of performance, course of dealing, or trade usage in the industry can give rise to an implied warranty.

   B. **Overlapping Warranties**--Warranties accumulate unless they are inconsistent with each other; a plaintiff may be able to sue under several theories. When warranties do conflict, the most specific prevails. Express warranties and

warranties for a particular purpose override
warranties of merchantability. Samples and
specifications control rather than general
descriptions.

C.   Buyer's Duty to Inspect--If the buyer refuses to
inspect the goods, any defect which would have been
revealed by a reasonable inspection cannot be
raised as a breach of warranty. The seller must
demand that the buyer inspect the goods.

D.   Third-Party Beneficiaries (Who Can Sue?)--A breach
of contract suit can be brought by a party to the
contract. This requirement is "privity of
contract". The UCC gives state legislatures three
choices. Under one option, family members are
covered; in another anyone who would reasonably be
expected to use the product can sue.

VI.   Magnuson-Moss Warranty Act--Consumer protection act
enacted by the Congress. Enforced by the Federal Trade
Commission, an attorney general, or the consumer.
Applies only if a written warranty is given.

A.   Creation--Affects express written warranties where
the purchaser is a consumer. If the cost of the
item is more than $15, the language of the warranty
must be easy to understand and list the name and
address of the manufacturer and the specifics of
the warranty.

B.   Full v. Limited Warranty--When the cost of the item
is more than $10, the warranty must state whether
it is "full" or "limited". A full warranty must
promise to repair or replace any defective part if
it fails and the failure is not the fault of the
consumer. If repair is not possible, the consumer
can choose a refund or replacement. A limit on
consequential damages (which flow from the breach
of warranty) must be printed conspicuously. A full
warranty need not specify a time limit but if it
does it must be stated. A limited warranty lacks
some or all of the provisions of a full warranty.

C.   Effect on UCC Warranties--Although implied
warranties are not covered under the Magnuson-Moss
Act, if an express warranty is made, a seller
cannot disclaim or modify the UCC implied
warranties. Sellers can put a time limit on the
implied warranties but they must be the same as the
time limit of any express warranty.

VII.   Product Liability--Non-Warranty Theories

   A.   Negligence

       (1)   Duty owed by defendant to plaintiff--Assumed
             in product liability cases.

       (2)   Breach of Duty--Plaintiff must show that the
             defendant was careless. Can be proven by
             showing improper testing, warnings, product
             design.

       (3)   Cause in Fact--Breach must have been the
             physical cause of the injury.

       (4)   Proximate Cause--Bystanders and non-purchasers
             can sue if injury to them is foreseeable.
             Privity of contract is not required.

             The advantages of a negligence suit are
             possibly higher damages and non-purchasers can
             sue (no privity of contract). The primary
             disadvantage is the plaintiff must prove that
             the defendant was careless (breach of duty).
             No showing of negligence is necessary under
             breach of warranty.

   B.   Misrepresentation

       (1)   Seller makes factual statement

       (2)   Statement is false

       (3)   Scienter (Guilty Knowledge)--This element is
             not required for innocent misrepresentation.

       (4)   Fact was important (basis of the bargain)

       (5)   Reasonable reliance by the plaintiff

       (6)   Injury related to misrepresentation

   C.   Strict Liability

       (1)   Merchant Seller

       (2)   Product is defective--can be defective due to
             improper manufacturer, improper labeling or
             inadequate warnings

       (3)   Product is unreasonably dangerous

(4) Proximate cause--defect must be related to the injury

(5) Goods must be in the same condition at the time of the sale and at the time of the injury. If a retailer changes the product, manufacturer is not liable. If plaintiff makes changes in the product, neither the manufacturer nor the retailer is liable.

Advantages to this theory are obvious; non-purchasers can sue (bystanders are specifically covered) and the plaintiff need not prove carelessness. The primary disadvantage is that a product may be defective but may not be unreasonably dangerous.

D. Defenses

(1) Assumption of Risk--Plaintiff knows that the product is defective but voluntarily continues to use it.

(2) Product Misuse--Plaintiff uses the product for an unexpected and dangerous use. The misuse must be unforeseeable; if the misuse is fore-seeable, the defendant will be liable.

(3) Contributory/Comparative Negligence--If the plaintiff is careless, recovery in negligence may be defeated in whole or in party. Although this defense usually does not apply to strict liability, some courts apportion the fault between the plaintiff and the defendant.

E. Non-Seller Applications--Manufacturers and re-tailers are the usual defendants in product liability suits. However, manufacturers of parts and lessors may also be found liable.

Study Questions

Fill-in-the-Blank Questions

Rhonda is shopping for a television set. She talks to a salesman at Video World. She tells him that she needs a set that is "cable-ready". The salesman tells her that she needs Model 21-A. The writen sales contract signed by Rhonda describes the set as a Model 21-A and contains the following language in red ink, "This contract contains the only representations by the seller. No other promises have been made." After Rhonda purchases the set, she discovers that the set is not "cable-ready" and that she will have to purchase an expensive adapter from the cable television company.

An express warranty _____ made by the salesman.
(was/was not)

The implied warranty of merchantability _____ breached.
(was/was not)

The implied warranty of fitness for a particular purpose _____
_____ been disclaimed.   (has/
has not)

Rhonda can sue for _____.
(breach of express warranty/misrepresentation)

True-False Questions

1.   The implied warranty of merchantability can be disclaimed. ____

2.   The Magnuson-Moss Warranty act requires a written warranty if the price of the item is more than $15. ____

3.   The warranty of no infringement is a warranty of quality. ____

4.   The implied warranty of fitness for a particular purpose applies to merchants only. ____

5.   Assumption of risk is a defense to negligence but it is not a defense to product liability. ____

6.   In a strict liability case, the plaintiff must prove that the product is unreasonably dangerous. ____

7.   Privity of contract applies to contract cases, but does not apply to negligence suits. ____

8.   An advantage of a negligence suit is that punitive damages may be recovered. ____

9.   A limited warranty is warranty which has an outside time limit of one year. ____

10. An express warranty may be made by showing a representative sample to the buyer. ____

Multiple-Choice Questions

1. Mrs. Curtis purchased a "New Woman" home hair-bleaching kit from Serv-U Drug Stores. The saleswoman told her that it would make her hair look "very nice" and the box described the product as "safe for all types of hair". Mrs. Curtis followed the directions on the package. Her hair and scalp were badly burned. In an action against Serv-U for <u>misrepresentation</u> Mrs. Curtis will:

    a. succeed because the saleswoman told Mrs. Curtis that her hair would look "very nice".
    b. succeed because Mrs. Curtis relied on the saleswoman's opinion.
    c. not succeed because the saleswoman's statement was an opinion.
    d. not succeed because Mrs. Curtis' injury was not related to the salewoman's promise.

2. If Mrs. Curtis sues Serv-U for breach of the implied warranty of merchantability, she will:

    a. succeed because she relied on the saleswoman's statement and Serv-U is a merchant.
    b. succeed because Serv-U is a merchant and the product was not fit for the ordinary purpose of curling hair.
    c. not succeed because Serv-U made no factual representations about the product.
    d. not succeed because Serv-U is not the manufacturer.

3. If Mrs. Curtis sues New Woman for breach of express warranty, she will:

    a. succeed because the writing on the package promised that the product was safe.
    b. succeed because the product was not fit for the ordinary purpose of curling hair.
    c. not succeed because the writing on the package did not substitute an express warranty.
    d. not succeed because there was no breach of the warranty.

4. If Mrs. Curtis sues New Woman on the theory of strict liability, she will:

    a. succeed if she can prove that New Woman was careless in its testing home permanents.
    b. succeed if she can prove that the product was unreasonably dangerous.

c. succeed if she can prove that the statement on the package was a statement of fact.

d. succeed if she can prove that New Woman knew the reason Mrs. Curtis purchased the product.

5. If Mrs. Curtis sues New Woman for negligence, she will:

a. succeed if she can prove that New Woman was careless in its testing home permanents.

b. succeed if she can prove that the product was unreasonably dangerous

c. succeed if she can prove that the statement on the package was a statement of fact.

d. succeed if she can prove that New Woman knew the reason Mrs. Curtis purchased the product.

6. Susan steals Roger's bike and sells it to Sid for $100. When Roger sees Sid with his bike, he demands that Sid return it. Sid refuses. Is Sid within his rights?

a. Yes, because he did not know the bike was stolen.

b. Yes, because Roger must sue Susan.

c. No, because Roger is the true owner and Sid must sue Susan.

d. No, because Roger is the true owner and Sid has no recourse against Susan.

7. Susan:

a. has breached the warranty of good title.

b. has breached the warranty of merchantability.

c. has not breached the warranty of good title because the warranty does not apply to used goods.

d. has not breached the warranty of title because Susan did not tell Sid that the bike was hers.

8. Mrs. Jones purchases a steam iron for $45 from AAA Appliance. The package inserts gave a description of the iron but made no warranties. The iron malfunctions amd Mrs. Jones sues AAA under the Magnuson-Moss Warranty Act. Mrs. Jones will:

a. succeed because a written warranty is required on all products with a price of $15 or more.

b. succeed because the act requires AAA to give a refund or replacement.

c. not succeed because the iron cost less than $50.

d. not succeed because no warranty was made.

9.   If Mrs. Jones sues AAA, under which theories will she succeed?

   a.   Magnuson-Moss Warranty Act and implied warranty of merchantability.
   b.   Magnuson-Moss Warranty Act and express warranty.
   c.   Express warranty and implied warranty of merchantability.
   d.   Implied warranty of merchantability and breach of contract.

10.   Crook & Low, Attorneys at Law, purchase a copier from Reproduction Masters, Inc. The salesman tells Mr. Crook that the copier will make 2,000 copies before a new ink cartridge is needed. The sales contract contains the following language: "THE ENTIRE AGREEMENT OF THE PARTIES IS CONTAINED IN THIS WRITING. NO OTHER PROMISES WRITTEN OR ORAL HAVE BEEN MADE. THE SELLER MAKES NO WARRANTIES AS TO THE MERCHANTABILITY OF THIS PRODUCT OR AS TO ITS FITNESS FOR ANY PARTICULAR PURPOSE." Mr. Crook has to purchase a new ink cartridge after 1,000 copies. Which of the following warranties have been disclaimed properly?

   a.   Implied warranties of merchantability and fitness for a particular purpose
   b.   Express warranty and the implied warranty of merchantability
   c.   Express warranty and the implied warranties of merchantability and fitness for a particular purpose
   d.   None, disclaimers are illegal

11.   If Mr. Crook sues Reproduction Masters, Inc., he will succeed under which of the following theories?

   a.   Misrepresentation
   b.   Breach of express warranty
   c.   Breach of implied warranty of merchantability
   d.   Breach of implied warranty of fitness for a particular purpose.

12.   Tommy is moving to Arizona and holds a garage sale. He sells his refrigerator to Susan. Susan does not know that Tommy has used the refrigerator as security for a loan from E-Z Finance Co. Tommy:

   a.   has breached the warranty of no infringements.
   b.   has breached the warranty of good title.
   c.   has breached the warranty of no liens.
   d.   has breached no warranties.

13.   Which of the following statements correctly describes the difference between a suit for strict liability and a suit for breach of implied warranty of merchantability?

    a.   In a suit for strict liability, the plaintiff need not prove that the seller is a merchant.
    b.   In a suit for strict liability, bystanders are always proper parties to sue but in a warranty case, bystanders may not be able to sue.
    c.   In both suits, the plaintiff must prove that the product is unreasonably dangerous.
    d.   In a suit for breach of implied warranty of merchantability, the plaintiff must prove that the seller is negligent.

14.   Mrs. Green purchases a carving knife by mail from A-1 Products. When she uses the knife for the first time, she notices that the blades are loose. She continues to use the knife and is seriously injured while carving a turkey. The evidence at trial shows that the socket for the blades is too shallow. If Mrs. Green sues A-1 for negligence, A-1's could raise which of the following defenses?

    a.   Product misuse and assumption of risk
    b.   Contributory negligence and assumption of risk
    c.   Product misuse and contributory negligence
    d.   Assumption of risk and no breach of duty

15.   Mrs. Smith is shoppng for a new washing machine. She tells the salesman that she needs a washing machine with a pump guard because her husband is always leaving coins and paper clips in his pockets. The salesman tells her that she needs to purchase the Deluxe Model. Mrs. Smith purchases the washing machine. The first time she uses it, a dime slips into the motor and ruins the machine. Mrs. Smith then discovers that the washer has no pump guard and decides to sue the seller. On which of the following theories will Mrs. Smith succeed?

    a.   Breach of express warranty only
    b.   Breach of express warranty and breach of implied warranty of merchantability
    c.   Breach of express warranty and breach of implied warranty of fitness for a particular purpose
    d.   Breach of express warranty and breach of both implied warranties

16.   Same facts as above but Mrs. Smith purchases the washer from her neighbor, Flo. Assume that Flo made the same statements as the saleman. On which of the following theories will Mrs. Smith succeed?

   a.   Breach of express warranty only
   b.   Breach of express warranty and breach of implied warranty of merchantability
   c.   Breach of express warranty and breach of implied warranty of fitness for a particular purpose
   d.   Breach of express warranty and breach of both implied warranties

17.   Ron purchases a new watch from Clockex, Inc. for $75. The package contains the following statement. "THE SELLER WARRANTS THAT THIS PRODUCT IS FREE FROM DEFECTS. IF THIS PRODUCT FAILS TO FUNCTION PROPERLY, THE MANUFACTURER AGREES TO REPLACE OR REPAIR THE PRODUCT AT NO COST TO THE CONSUMER FOR A PERIOD OF ONE (1) YEAR. THIS WARRANTY DOES NOT APPLY TO MALFUNCTION CAUSED BY ABUSE BY THE PURCHASER."

   a.   The Magnuson-Moss Warranty applies and the warranty is satifactory as written.
   b.   The Magnuson-Moss Warranty does not apply but the warranty must be labeled as "full" or "limited".
   c.   The Magnuson-Moss Warranty applies but the warranty must be labeled as "full" or "limited".
   d.   The Magnuson-Moss Warranty does not apply.

18.   Which of the folowing are proper plaintiffs (can sue) under the Magnuson-Moss Warranty Act?

   a.   Federal Trade Commission only
   b.   Federal Trade Commission and a state's attorney general only
   c.   Federal Trade Commission and the consumer only
   d.   Federal Trade Commission, a state's attorney general and the consumer

19.   Mr. Roberts purchases a stuffed bear manufactured by Unbearably Unique. The bear's eyes are made of small bits of hard plastic. A warning on the package states, "Not suitable for children under six years." Mr. Roberts gives the toy to his three year-old son, who chews on the toy, swallows one of the eyes and is severely injured. Mr. Roberts sues Unbearably on a strict liability theory. Unbearably raises the defense of product misuse.

a. Unbearably will succeed on the product misuse theory only if it can prove that it was unforeseeable that the toy would have been given to a child under six years.

b. Unbearably will succeed on the product misuse theory because a warning was given.

c. Unbearably will succeed because the product was not defective.

d. Unbearably will succeed because the proximate cause element was not satisfied.

20. Cure-All Pharmaceuticals manufacturers "Sneez-Away", a cold remedy. The package insert mentions that the product can cause drowsines but does not mention that it should not be taken with aspirin. Mrs. Miller purchases a bottle of "Sneez-Away" and takes it with aspirin. She breaks out in hives and suffers from blurred vision. If Mrs. Miller sues Cure-All for negligence and strict liability, she will:

a. succeed on the strict liability theory only Cure-All was not negligent.

b. succeed on the negligence theory only because the product was not unreasonably dangerous.

c. succeed on either theory.

d. not succeed on either theory.

21. Ron purchased a new saw from Abe's Hardware. Abe tells Ron that he has used a similar saw but that he can't vouch for its merchantability. Which of the following warranties have been disclaimed properly?

a. Implied warranty of fitness for a particular purpose only

b. Implied warranty of merchantability only

c. Both implied warranties have been disclaimed

d. Neither warranty has been disclaimed

22. Which of the following is not a warranty of quality?

a. Implied warranty of merchantability

b. Implied warranty of fitness for a particular purpose

c. Express warranty

d. Warranty of no infringement

23. Which of the following is not required for a suit in strict liability?

a. Seller is a merchant

b. Proximate cause

c. A promise by the seller

d. Defective product

24.   For which of the following is proximate cause <u>not</u> required?

     a. Negligence
     b. Strict liability
     c. Misrepresentation
     d. Breach of express warranty.

25.   Mary purchases a leash from Pet Emporium. She tells the salesman that she needs a leash which will be suitable for a Great Dane. The salesman, who honestly believes that a metal leash will be sufficient, sells her the top of the line metal leash. Mary's Great Dane snaps the leash on his first walk. On which theories will Mary be successful?

     a. Fraudulent misrepresentation and breach of warranty of fitness for a particular purpose
     b. Breach of implied warranty of merchantability and breach of implied waranty of fitness for a particular purpose
     c. Breach of express warranty and breach of implied warranty of fitness for a particular purpose
     d. Breach of express warranty and fraudulent misrepresentation

Answers to Study Questions

Fill-in-the-Blank Questions

The salesman did make an express warranty when he told Rhonda that she needed to buy Model 21-A because he was stating that Model 21-A was cable-ready. The implied warranty of merchantability has <u>not</u> been breached because the television functions properly. The implied warranty of fitness for a particular purpose has been disclaimed. The writing in red type is conspicuous. Rhonda can sue for misrepresentation. She cannot sue for breach of express warranty because the express warranty made by the salesman was disclaimed.

True-False Questions

  1.   T.

  2.   F. The Magnuson-Moss Act does not require the seller to make a written warranty, but if a written warranty is made, certain disclosures are required.

3.   F. It is a warranty of title.

4.   F. It applies to any seller.

5.   F. It is a defense to both.

6.   T.

7.   T.

8.   T.

9.   F. A limited warranty is one which promises less than free replacement or repair. The time element is irrelevant.

10.   T.

Multiple-Choice Questions

1.	c	11.	a	21.	b
2.	b	12.	c	22.	d
3.	a	13.	b	23.	c
4.	b	14.	b	24.	c
5.	a	15.	c	25.	c
6.	c	16.	c		
7.	a	17.	c		
8.	d	18.	d		
9.	d	19.	a		
10.	c	20.	c		

Chapter 15   Commercial Paper—Basic Concepts

General Principles

Commercial paper is any instrument that operates as a substitute for money. Checks and notes are the most common examples of commercial paper. You may write a check instead of paying cash. In order for commercial paper to be an acceptable substitute for money, its transfer must be relatively risk-free. People who receive a check or note must have some protection against forgery, alteration, and other problems. This concept is essential to an understanding of the subject and is the basis for the rules outlined in the Articles 3 and 4 of the Uniform Commercial Code.

When you read the following chapters, it may help to think of the process of writing and cashing a check. The check may pass through several banks before it is finally paid.

Chapter Summary

I.   <u>Definition</u>--Commercial paper is a written promise or order to pay a sum of money. A promissory note is an example of a promise to pay; a check is an example of an order to pay.

II.   <u>Purpose</u>--Commercial paper is a convenient alternative to cash. A secondary function of commercial paper is to lend money. A ninety-day promissory note allows the borrower to use someone else's money for ninety days. Often the payee of the note cannot wait ninety days for cash. He can sell the note, at a reduced price, to a buyer who can wait ninety days to collect the money.

This transaction, called discounting, is one of the most common uses of commercial paper.

III.   Types of Commercial Paper--There are four basic forms of commercial paper or instruments:

    A.   Draft--A draft is a written order from a drawer to a drawee ordering a sum of money to be paid to a payee. A draft is similar to a check except that the order to pay may occur on a certain date (time draft) or when it is presented to the drawee (sight draft).

        A trade acceptance is a special kind of draft used by a buyer and seller. The seller is both the drawer (who orders payment) and the payee. The order is directed to the buyer, who is the drawee. When the buyer agrees to pay the trade acceptance, he or she signs his or her name. The seller can then discount the trade acceptance to a bank for immediate cash.

    B.   Check--A check is a special type of draft, which is payable on demand. The drawee of a check is always a bank.

    C.   Promissory Note--A note is a written promise made by the borrower or maker to pay a sum of money to the payee.

    D.   Certificate of Deposit (CD)--A CD is a written acknowledgement of receipt of funds and a promise to repay the money. The bank (maker) receives money from a customer (payee) and promises to repay the money with interest at a later date.

    E.   Letter of Credit--A letter of credit is not a type of commercial paper; it is a financing arrangement using a note and a draft. The three parties are the buyer, the seller, and the buyer's bank. The buyer makes a note to his bank; his bank issues a letter of credit, which promises to pay any draft ordered by the buyer. The seller presents the draft and any supporing documents to the buyer's bank for payment. The seller is assured of payment and the buyer can receive his goods immediately.

IV.   Parties to Commercial Paper--All parties to an instrument are either original or secondary. The original parties are those whose names appear on the instrument when it is issued or first used. Drawers,

drawees, makers, and payees are original parties.
Secondary parties are those who come into contact with
an instrument after it has been written or issued.
Secondary parties include banks who process a check for
collection.

The same person can sign an instrument in two places and
can be both an original and a secondary party. For
example, the payee of a check can be an indorser, if he
signs his name on the back of the check.

A.   <u>Maker</u>--The maker of a CD or a note promises to pay
      a sum of money to the payee.

B.   <u>Drawer</u>--The drawer orders payment of a sum of money
      to the payee.

C.   <u>Drawee</u>--The drawee, usually a bank, receives an
      order from drawer of a check or a draft to pay a
      sum of money. The drawee of a check is always a
      bank.

D.   <u>Payee</u>--The payee is the party to whom payment is
      ordered or promised by the drawer or maker.

E.   <u>Indorser</u>--An indorser transfers commercial paper by
      signing the <u>back</u> of an instrument and delivering it
      to another. In most cases, the payee is the first
      indorser.

F.   <u>Indorsee</u>--An indorsee receives an instrument that
      has been indorsed to him or her. An indorser
      transfers an instrument; an indorsee receives it.
      When the indorsee signs the instrument, he or she
      becomes the indorser.

G.   <u>Bearer</u>--A bearer has possession of an instrument
      which is payable to "cash" or to an unspecified
      person. A bearer may also be a person who receives
      an instrument on which no indorsee is named.

H.   <u>Holder</u>--A holder has physical possession of an
      instrument. The instrument must be made payable to
      him or indorsed to him. If the instrument does not
      name a payee or indorsee, anyone in possession of
      the instrument is a holder.

I.   <u>Holder in Due Course (HDC)</u>--A holder in due course
      is a person with possession of an instrument who
      pays value for it and receives it in good faith.
      Good faith means that the holder does not know that
      the instrument is overdue or that it has a defect.

J.   Holder Through a Holder in Due Course (HHDC)--An HHDC is a holder of an instrument who does not meet the requirements of a holder in due course but who receives an instrument sometime after a holder in due course. An example of a holder through a holder in due course may be someone who receives a check as a birthday present. He or she cannot be an HDC because no value was given.

K.   Acceptor--An acceptor is a drawee who promises to pay the instrument by signing it, usually across the front of the instrument. A drawee does not become an acceptor until he signs the instrument indicating his willingness to pay. When a bank agrees to pay a check, it becomes an acceptor.

L.   Accommodation Party--An accommodation party is a person who signs an instrument intending to lend his name and financial support to another party on the instrument. An accommodation party may sign the instrument in any capacity (e.g. payee, drawer) but he is usually the co-signer of a note. The accommodated party is the person who asks the accommodation party for help.

STUDY QUESTIONS

Fill-in-the-Blank Questions

August 1, 1987

60 days from date, pay to the order of B. Law Teacher the sum of $1,000.

C. Student, Jr.

To: C. Student, Sr.

This instrument is a _____.
B. Law Teacher is the _____.
C. Student, Sr. is the _____.
C. Student, Jr. is the _____.

April 2, 1988

On December 2, 1988 I promise to pay B. Law
Teacher the sum of $500.

B. Student

This instrument is a _____.
B. Law Teacher is the _____:
B. Student is the _____.

True-False Questions

1.   The maker of a certificate of deposit is a bank or other financial institution. ____

2.   A draft has two original parties. ____

3.   All checks are drafts but not all drafts are checks.____

4.   The drawee of a check is a bank. ____

5.   The payee of a note, who transfers it to an indorsee for 95% of the amount of the note, has discounted the note. ____

6.   A payee of a check becomes an indorser when he or she signs the back of the instrument. ____

7.   The drawee of a trade acceptance is usually a seller of goods. ____

8.   A letter of credit is a form of commercial paper. ____

9.   Mary finds a signed check for $200. The space for the payee's name is left blank. Mary is a holder of the check. ____

10.   A holder in due course must have possession of the instrument, pay value for it and receive the instrument without notice of any defect in the instrument. ____

Multiple-Choice Questions

1.   Sally Student wants to borrow money in order to buy a
       new car. Sally's banker asks Sally's mother to co-sign
       the note. Sally is:

       a.   the drawee.
       b.   the maker.
       c.   the accommodation party.
       d.   the indorsee.

2.   Sally's mother is:

       a.   the payee.
       b.   the drawer.
       c.   the accommodation party.
       d.   the accommodated party.

3.   Bob writes a check to Gary's Grocery to pay for mushroom
       soup. Gary signs the check on the back naming Will's
       Wholesale as the transferee. Gary is:

       a.   the payee.
       b.   the indorser.
       c.   neither the payee nor the indorser.
       d.   both the payee and the indorser.

4.   Bob is:

       a.   the drawee.
       b.   the drawer.
       c.   the indorser.
       d.   the indorsee.

5.   Will's Wholesale is:

       a.   the payee.
       b.   the indorsee.
       c.   the indorser.
       d.   the drawer.

6.   A bearer is a person in possession of an instrument
       which:

       a.   is payable to "cash".
       b.   is not payable to a specific person.
       c.   is indorsed, but no indorsee is named.
       d.   all of the above.

7.   Sam writes a check for $75.00 to Tom's TV Repair. Tom goes to Sam's bank, indorses the check, and delivers it to the bank. The bank gives Tom $75.00 cash. The bank becomes an acceptor of the check when:

   a.   Sam writes the check.
   b.   Tom accepts the check.
   c.   Tom indorses the check.
   d.   Sam's bank cashes the check.

8.   Sam's bank is:

   a.   the drawee.
   b.   the indorser.
   c.   the drawer.
   d.   the payee.

9.   Connie borrows money from First Bank in order to buy a computer. The instrument Connie will sign is:

   a.   CD.
   b.   note.
   c.   draft.
   d.   trade acceptance.

10.   First Bank is the:

   a.   the maker.
   b.   the payee.
   c.   the drawer.
   d.   the drawee.

Answers to Study Questions

Fill-in-the-Blank Questions

The first instrument is a draft; an order to pay but the drawee is not a bank. B. Law Teacher is the payee. C. Student, Sr. is the drawee. C. Student, Jr. is the drawer.

The second instrument is a note. B. Law Teacher is the payee. B. Student is the maker.

True-False Questions

   1.   T.

   2.   F.   It has three original parties.

3.   T.

4.   T.

5.   T.

6.   T.

7.   F.   The buyer is the drawee; the seller is the payee and drawer.

8.   F.

9.   T.

10.   T.

Multiple-Choice Questions

1. b
2. c
3. d
4. b
5. b

6. d
7. d
8. a
9. b
10. b

Chapter 16   Commercial Paper—
The Negotiable Instrument,
Transferability, and Negotiation

General Principles

This chapter deals with two different but very important topics: the definition of a negotiable instrument and the process of transferring the instrument.

In order for checks and other commercial paper to be an acceptable substitute for money, banks and merchants must be willing to accept them. The law of negotiable instruments outlined in the UCC is designed to lessen the risks associated with commercial paper. As you review, remember that the requirements of negotiability are designed to reduce these risks.

A negotiable instrument is transferred by indorsement and/or delivery. An indorser may incur liability and some forms of indorsement lessen liability and the risk of transfer.

Chapter Summary

I.   Requirements of Negotiability--These rules apply only to the face or front of the instrument.

    A.   Writing--A negotiable instrument must be in writing on a permanent and easily transferable substance.

    B.   Signature--A negotiable instrument must be signed by the maker or the drawer. It does not have to be signed by the drawee or payee. Any writing that is intended as a signature, such as a rubber stamp, is acceptable. The signature may appear anywhere on the document.

An authorized agent may act for the maker or drawer. If an authorized agent signs a negotiable instrument, and his signature clearly indicates that he is an agent, then the drawer or maker, not the agent, will be liable. If the agent did not have the approval or authority from the drawer or maker, the agent will be personally liable.

C.   Promise or Order to Pay--A negotiable instrument must contain an affirmative order or promise to pay. For this reason, an I.O.U., which merely acknowledges a debt, but does not promise to repay it, is insufficient and is not negotiable.

D.   The Promise or Order Must Be Unconditional--A negotiable instrument must promise or order absolute payment. If payment is conditioned on the occurrence of an outside event or on the provisions of another document, this instrument is non-negotiable. A memorandum or reference to an outside document will not destroy negotiability unless payment is conditioned on or made "subject to" the terms of that document. A "memo" line on a check, which shows the reason for payment, is valid.

E.   Sum Certain in Money--A negotiable instrument must specify an exact amount of money to be paid or the amount must be easily calculated from the face of the instrument. An instrument which carries a stated rate of interest or specifies monthly payments is satisfactory. An instrument payable at the prime rate or other variable rate is not negotiable. An instrument which is payable at the "Judgment" or "legal" rate is negotiable.

A negotiable instrument must also be payable in money or currency. If an instrument were payable in goods or services, the value of those goods or services, and the value of the instrument could vary from day to day. Payment in currency of another country is allowed.

F.   Payable on Demand or at a Definite Time--A negotiable instrument must be payable at a definite time, a time that can be calculated from the face of the instrument, or payable when presented to the drawee or maker (payable on demand or on sight).

Many notes contain acceleration or extension clauses. An acceleration clause allows the holder to call the note due if a payment is late. A note with an acceleration clause is negotiable. An extension clause extends time for payment. If the maker or drawer has the option to extend, the extension must be for a stated period of time. If the holder has the option to extend, a definite perid of time need not be specified.

G.   <u>Payable to Order or to Bearer</u>--A negotiable instrument must be payable to the order of a specified person (order paper) or payable to anyone with possession (bearer paper). A check payable to "John Jones" is order paper; a check payable to "cash" is a bearer instrument. An order instrument can name more than one payee or designate the payee by title so long as the payee can be identified with certainty.

II.   <u>Assignment and Negotiation</u>--Assignment and negotiation are special terms used to describe the transfer of commercial paper. Negotiable instruments are negotiated, non-negotiable instruments are assigned.

Proper transfer or negotiation of an order instrument requires delivery from the indorser <u>and</u> the signature or indorsement or the indorsee. Bearer paper requires delivery alone and is therefore much riskier. When these requirements are met, the transferree becomes a holder of the instrument.

III. <u>Indorsements</u>--An indorsement is a signature found on the back of an instrument. In commercial paper, a signature implies liabilty. Some indorsements lessen the risk of transfer by placing conditions on the transfer.

All indorsements have the following characteristics: blank or special, qualified or unqualified, and restrictive or unrestricted.

A.   <u>Blank or Special Indorsement</u>--A blank indorsement is simply the signature of the payee or an indorser.

An indorser can cause the instrument to become order or bearer paper depending on the type of indorsement. A blank indorsement causes the instrument to be bearer paper and anyone with possession of the instrument can transfer it. A special indorsement contains the signature of the indorser and the name of the indorsee. A special indorsement causes the instrument to be order paper and only the indorsee can transfer or cash it.

B. Qualified or Unqualified Indorsement--A qualified indorsement denoted by the words "without recourse", limits to some extent the liability of the signer. An unqualified indorsement does not contain these words.

C. Restrictive or Unrestricted Indorsement--A restrictive indorsement gives directions to the indorsee regarding further transfer of the instrument. The indorsee must follow these instructions. An unrestricted indorsement contains no special instructions.

   1. Conditional Indorsement--An indorsement may condition payment on the happening of a specific event. A holder who receives the instrument after the condition has imposed has no right to payment until the condition is satisfied. (An exception applies to intermediary banks who receive the instrument as it is being processed for collection.) If the condition is on the face of the instrument, the instrument is non-negotiable.

   2. Indorsements for deposit or collection--An indorsement which contains the words "for deposit only" is commonly used when an instrument is transferred from a customer to his bank. This indorsement does not prohibit further transfer but the immediate transferr (usually the payee's bank) must obey the instructions and transfer the money to the depositor's account. "Pay any bank" is a collection indorsement used between banks.

   3. Agency or Trust Indorsement--This indorsement is made by an agent or a trustee acting on behalf of a third person.

IV. UNAUTHORIZED SIGNATURES--An unauthorized signature is one made without the permission of the person whose name was used. A negotiable instrument may pass through several owners or holders and an unauthorized signature may not be detected until the instrument is presented for payment. At that time, if the guilty party cannot be found, someone must absorb the loss. The general rule is that the person who was in the best position to notice or to prevent the wrongdoing is responsible.

A.   Forged Indorsement--Liability usually rests on the
      party who took the instrument directly from the
      forger. Two exceptions to this rule are the
      "fictitious payee" and the "imposter" rules.

B.   "Fictitious Payee"--An employee "pads the payroll"
      with a fake payee. The dishonest employee then
      forges the name of the phony payee, indorses the
      instrument to himself and collects the cash.
      Although the "payee's" indorsement has been forged,
      the drawer was in the best position to spot the
      wrongdoing. The drawer could have supervised his
      employee or determined that the payee did exist.

C.   Imposter--The wrongdoer poses as another and
      induces the maker or drawer to make an instrument
      payable to name used by the imposter. The imposter
      forges the "payee's" indorsement but again, it was
      the drawer or make who could have determined the
      scheme most easily and therefore the maker or
      drawer will be responsible.

Study Questions

Fill-in-the-Blank Questions

July 3, 1987

Thirty days from date, I Wilma Wilson,
promise to pay County Bank the sum of $1,000.
The maker reserves the right to extend the due
date until September 3, 1987. This agreement is
subject to the terms of a sales contract between
the maker and Artie's Antiques.

This instrument is a _____.
                        (draft, note, check, CD)

It is _____.
        (negotiable/non-negotiable)

Wilma's signature is _____.
                        (valid/invalid)

Wilma's promise to pay is _____.
                         (conditional/unconditional)

The maker's right to pay on September 3 is an _____
clause.   (extension/
                                             acceleration)

True-False Questions

1.   A note payable "on the death of my uncle John" is not negotiable. ____

2.   An instrument indorsed "for deposit only" is an example of a conditional indorsement. ____

3.   A note is non-negotiable if it is payable to Bob and Mary Lamb. ____

4.   Order paper is negotiated by delivery and the signature of the indorser. ____

5.   "Pay any bank" is a restrictive indorsement. ____

6.   "Pay to the order of Cindy" is a special, unrestricted, unconditional indorsement. ____

7.   John steals a check payable to bearer. John is a holder of the check. ____

8.   A draft ordering payment of 3,000 French francs is negotiable in the United States. ____

9.   A non-negotiable note can be assigned but is cannot be negotiated. ____

10.   A check written on a paper napkin is non-negotiable.____

Multiple-Choice Questions

Use the following facts to answer questions 1-5.

Edna indorses her paycheck with her name only and gives it to her landlord as payment for her rent. The landlord signs his name on the back of the check and writes "for deposit only, Acme Apartments, by Leonard Landlord, manager."

1.   The landlord:

      a.   is a holder of the check.
      b.   is not a holder of the check.
      c.   is an indorsee.
      d.   is the drawee.

2. The landlord's indorsement:

   a. is unrestricted and blank.
   b. is unrestricted and special.
   c. is restrictive and blank.
   d. is restrictive and special.

3. The check:

   a. is order paper when Edna's employer issues it.
   b. is bearer paper after the landlord indorses it.
   c. is order paper after Edna indorses it.
   d. is bearer paper when Edna's employer issues it.

4. Edna's indorsement:

   a. is blank and restrictive.
   b. is special and restrictive.
   c. is blank and conditional.
   d. is blank and unconditional.

5. The landlord's indorsement:

   a. is an agency indorsement.
   b. is a trust indorsement.
   c. is a blank indorsement.
   d. causes the instrument to be non-negotiable.

6. Paul writes a check for $45.00 payable to the order of
   Ron's Repair service. The face of the check states that
   it is payble only if Paul's TV works properly. The
   check:

   a. is non-negotiable because it is not payable at a
      definite time.
   b. is non-negotiable because it does not state an exact
      sum of money to be paid.
   c. is non-negotiable because it contains a conditional
      order.
   d. is negotiable.

7. Sally receives a birthday check from her aunt Linda.
   Sally signs her name on the back of the check and cashes
   it at her aunt's bank. Sally's indorsement is:

   a. blank, restrictive, and unconditional.
   b. special, restrictive, and unconditional.
   c. special, unrestricted, and unconditional.
   d. blank, unrestricted, and unconditional.

8.   Which of the following is (are) holder(s) of the instrument?

      a.   Sally
      b.   The blank
      c.   Both Sally and the bank
      d.   Sally, Sally's aunt and the bank

9.   On March 23, 1987, Michael makes a note which is payable to First State Bank in forty-eight monthly installments of $100.00. The note contains a clause which allows the bank to collect the entire amount immediately if Michael misses a payment. The note:

      a.   is non-negotiable becuase it is not payable at a definite date.
      b.   is non-negotiable because it fails to state a certain sum of money.
      c.   is non-negotiable because it fails to name a payee.
      d.   is negotiable.

10.   The clause which allows the bank to collect the entire amount immediately is:

      a.   an extension clause.
      b.   an acceleration clause.
      c.   a conditional indorsement.
      d.   a restrictive indorsement.

11.   Ralph, posing as Mr. Brown, a high school bank director, receives a donation check from Mrs. Black, a new teacher. Ralph cashes the check and disappears. When the scheme is discovered, who will be responsible?

      a.   Mr. Brown
      b.   Ms. Black
      c.   The bank which cashed the check
      d.   The high school band

12.   Nancy writes a check to Sam's Supermarket in payment for groceries. She writes "weekly groceries" on the memo line of the check. Sam turns the check over and writes "Payable to Wanda's Wholesalers, if a shipment of oranges is received by next week" and signs his name. Sam's indorsement is:

      a.   special, restrictive and conditional.
      b.   special, unrestricted and conditional.
      c.   special, restrictive and unconditional.
      d.   blank, unrestricted and conditional.

13. The check:

    a. is non-negotiable because of the notation on the memo line.
    b. is non-negotiable because of Sam's indorsement.
    c. is non-negotiable because the check is not payble at a definite time.
    d. is negotiable.

14. Donna writes a check payable to the order of "Cash". The check:

    a. is a negotiable order instrument.
    b. is a negotiable bearer instrument.
    c. is a non-negotiable order instrument.
    d. is a non-negotiable bearer instrument.

15. Anita, a legal secretary, asks her employer to write a check payable to Ozzie's Office Supplies, Inc. as payment for typewriter ribbons. In fact, Anita did not buy ribbons from Ozzie. Anita forges Ozzie's signature and cashes the check at First Bank. If Anita cannot be found, who will be responsible?

    a. Anita's employer
    b. Ozzies's Office Supplies
    c. First Bank
    d. None of the above

16. Harold signs a note payable to Second State Bank to purchase a new car. The note, payable in twenty-four monthly installments of $300.00, states that Harold has also signed a security agreement and if Harold does not pay, the bank has the right to repossess the car. The note:

    a. is non-negotiable because it contains a conditional promise.
    b. is non-negotiable because it fails to state a sum certain.
    c. is non-negotiable because it fails to name a payee.
    d. is negotiable.

17. Cathy issues a draft payable to Felicia. On the back of the draft, Felicia writes "payable to Mona", signs her name, and gives it to Mona. In Mona's possession,

a. the draft is order paper and Mona must indorse it before she can negotiate it.
b. the draft is order paper and Mona can negotiate it by delivery alone.
c. the draft is bearer paper and Mona can negotiate it by delivery alone.
d. the draft is bearer paper and Mona must indorse it before she can negotiate it.

18. Sam makes a check payable to Cindy, who signs her name on the back. On the way to the bank, Cindy loses the check and Tom finds it. Tom cashes the check at his bank. Which of the following are holders of the check?

a. Sam and Cindy
b. Cindy and Tom
c. Cindy and the bank
d. Tom, Cindy and the bank

19. The check:

a. is order paper when Sam issues it and becomes bearer paper when Cindy indorses it.
b. is bearer paper when Sam issues and remains bearer paper when Cindy indorses it.
c. is bearer paper when Sam issues it and becomes order paper when Cindy indorses it.
d. is order paper when Sam issues it and remains bearer paper when Cindy indorses it.

20. Jim makes a note payable to Second National Bank. The note contains the following clause: "The maker or the holder retains the right to extend the time for payment indefinitely. The note:

a. is non-negotiable because Second National Bank has the right to extend payment for an unspecified time.
b. is non-negotiable because Jim has the right to extend payment for an unspecified time.
c. is non-negotiable because a maker never has the right to extend the time for payment.
d. is negotiable.

21. Which of the following clauses in a draft would make it non-negotiable?

a. The draft is payable to Sally and Sid Morrow
b. The draft is payble when delivered to the drawee for payment but no other date is specified
c. The draft is payable in dollars, German marks or diamonds
d. None of the clauses would destroy negotiability

22.   Fine Fashions accepts a check from Harriet Housewife as payment for a dress. Sylvia, the president of Fine Fashions, indorses the check and writes "payable to Rodney's Real Estate, without recourse." Sylvia's indorsement is:

    a. is conditional, qualified and special.
    b. is unconditional, qualified and special.
    c. is conditional, qualified and special.
    d. is unconditional, unqualified and blank.

23.   Roger paints Donna's house and receives a check from Donna in the amount of $2300.00 as payment for his services. Roger writes "Pay to Helen Smith" and signs his name. Roger loses the check and Vinnie finds it. Vinnie forges Helen's name and cashes the check at Helen's bank. Helen's bank transfers the check to Donna's bank, which pays the check and takes the money from Donna's account. Who will be ultimately responsible for payment of the check if Vinnie cannot be found?

    a. Roger
    b. Helen's bank
    c. Donna's bank
    d. Donna

24.   Roger's indorsement:

    a. is special and unqualified.
    b. is blank and unqualified.
    c. is special and restrictive.
    d. is special and conditional.

25.   On January 13, 1988, Valerie borrows $10,000 from County Bank in order to buy a new car. The note states that it is payable in thirty-six monthly installments at an interest rate of thirteen percent per year. The note:

    a. is non-negotiable because the amount of each monthly payment is not specified.
    b. is non-negotiable because the note does not promise to pay an exact sum of money
    c. is non-negotiable because it is not payable at a specific time.
    d. is negotiable.

Answers to Study Questions

Fill-in-the-Blank Questions

The instrument is a note. It is non-negotiable. Wilma's signature is valid; the signature can appear anywhere on the document. Wilma's promise to pay is conditional because it is subject to the terms of the sales contract. The maker's right to pay on September 3 is an extension clause.

True-False Questions

1.   T.

2.   F. It is an example of a restrictive indorsement.

3.   F. A negotiable instrument may be payable to 2 or more payees.

4.   F. The signature of the indorsee is required.

5.   T.

6.   T.

7.   T.

8.   T.

9.   T.

10.   F. It is negotiable because it is in writing on a portable and permanent substance. However, it is probably not very marketable.

Multiple-Choice Questions

1.	a	11.	b	21.	c
2.	d	12.	a	22.	b
3.	a	13.	d	23.	b
4.	d	14.	b	24.	a
5.	a	15.	a	25.	d
6.	c	16.	d		
7.	c	17.	a		
8.	c	18.	d		
9.	d	19.	a		
10.	b	20.	b		

Chapter 17 Commercial Paper—
Holder in Due Course,
Liability and Defenses

General Principles

This chapter discusses the obligations of parties if a dispute arises concerning payment of a negotiable instrument. If payment of the instrument is refused, the holder can sue the maker or drawer of the instrument or he or she can sue the chain of people who transferred the instrument (payee and indorsers). The holder's success depends on four factors:

1. Is the person seeking payment a holder in due course or merely a holder?

2. Has the defendant (indorser) signed the instrument?

3. Has the defendant (indorser) breached warranties made when he or she transferred the instrument or presented it for payment?

4. Does the maker or drawer have a valid defense against payment?

Remember that the lawsuit will focus on the transfer of the instrument and not on the underlying contract. The UCC attempts to shift liability back to the person who was in the best position to prevent the wrongdoing.

Chapter Summary

I.   Holders vs. Holders in Due Course

A.   Holder--A holder is a person in possession of an instrument who is entitled to payment. If the instrument is order paper, a holder is the payee or an indorsee. If the instrument is bearer paper, a holder is anyone with possession of the instrument.

B.   Holder in Due Course (HDC)--A holder in due course is a holder who also meets the following requirements: 1) he or she must have paid value in exchange for the instrument; 2) he or she must have acted honestly with regard to the instrument; and 3) he must receive the instrument without knowledge of a defect in the instrument or its transfer.

C.   Difference in Status--When a maker or drawer refuses to pay or honor an instrument, litigation results. An HDC will be entitled to payment regardless of most problems or defenses claimed by the maker or drawer. A holder does not enjoy the same protection. He or she has to defend against all claims and defenses of other parties. A holder is in the same position as an assignee or a contract; he or she can have no more rights than the person who transferred the instrument.

II.   Requirements for an HDC--An HDC must meet all of the following tests in order to qualify for protected status.

A.   Value--An HDC must give value in exchange for the instrument. Value can be money, services performed or another negotiable instrument. A bank can give value by clearing the instrument. A holder can also give value by taking an instrument in payment of a previous debt owed to him or taking an instrument as collateral for payment of a prior or current debt owed him. A promise to perform in the future is not good value. Partial value is acceptable but the holder is an HDC only to the extent that actual value has been received.

B.   Good Faith--An HDC must act honestly. It does not matter that he received the instrument from a wrongdoer.

C.   Without Notice--An HDC must receive the instrument without notice of any defect in the instrument. Some defects such as crude forgeries, alterations and overdue payments are obvious. The test is whether a reasonable person would have been put on notice and would have investigated the irregularity.

D.   Holder Through a Holder in Due Course (Shelter
     Principle)--A holder who does not qualify as an HDC
     may still receive protected status if a previous
     holder is an HDC. However, a holder cannot receive
     HDC status if he recycles or launders the
     instrument through an HDC.

III. Signature Liability--A holder who indorses an instrument
      impliedly promises to pay the instrument when it comes
      due. This obligation is extremely important because a
      holder seeking payment can sue previous indorsers as
      well as the maker or drawer.

A.   Signature--A signature is any symbol used to
     validate a writing. It need not be handwritten.

B.   Authority to Sign--A party is only responsible for
     a signature if he or she authorizes it or ratifies
     it after the fact. An agent will be personally
     liable for a signature only if it fails to show
     agency status or a named principal. Parol (oral)
     evidence may be admitted to show authorization if
     the signature shows an agency but fails to name a
     principal or if two names are shown but it is
     unclear which party is the principal.

C.   Primary, Secondary or No Liability--A primary party
     is absolutely and immediately liable; a secondary
     party is liable only after a primary party has
     refused to pay.

     1.   An indorser who signs "without recourse" has
          no signature liability although he or she may
          have warranty liability.

     2.   A maker and an acceptor are primarily and
          absolutely liable. The only exception to the
          maker's liability is a real defense (discussed
          below). A drawee has no liability to a
          holder requesting payment until he or she
          accepts the instrument. Some instruments
          require the holder to present the instrument
          to the acceptor before payment is due.

     3.   All other parties to an instrument are
          secondarily liable and will be required to pay
          only if the drawee or maker refuses to do so.
          A drawer of a check must pay unless his bank
          has become insolvent.

Indorsers have more protection against payment. The holder requesting payment must follow the steps listed below. The holder must present the instrument to the primary party usually through the mail or by depositing it in the banking system); the primary party must refuse to pay or dishonor the instrument; and the holder must give notice to the indorsers that the instrument has been dishonored. The notice must be made within specified time limits. Because the holder must follow these rules exactly, many instruments contain a waiver of presentment, dishonor, and notice.

IV.   Warranty Liability--A party to negotiable instrument may also be liable on the basis of implied warranties made by transferring the instrument. A transfer warranty is made by a holder to another holder. A presentment warranty is made by a holder to a party responsible for payment such as a maker, drawer,or drawee.

A.   Transfer Warranties--A holder promises that:

1.   he or she has good title to the instrument.

2.   the signatures are authorized or geniune (no forgeries).

3.   the instrument has not been materially altered.

4.   no party has a defense against payment to the holder (honesty).

5.   if an instrument has been refused, the holder does not know that the maker, drawer or acceptor is bankrupt.

Generally, these warranties operate to protect anyone who takes the instrument after the holder. If the holder has not indorsed the instrument, he or she makes the promises only to the party next in line (his immediate transferree). An indorser who signs "without recourse" changes the forth warranty. The promise is only that the holder has no knowledge of a defense.

B.   Presentment Warranties--A holder presenting the instrument for final payment, as opposed to a simple transfer, promises that:

1. he or she has good title to the instrument.

2. he or she has no knowledge that the signature
    of the maker or drawer is unauthorized.

3. The instrument has not been materially
    altered.

If an HDC is presenting the instrument to the maker
or drawer, he or she does not make the second and
third promises because the maker or drawer should
recognize his own signature and the instrument.

V. Defenses to Payment--If the maker or drawer of the
    instrument is sued, the holder must determine if there
    is a valid defense against payment. At this point, the
    status of the holder becomes very important. A limited
    number of real defenses are good against an HDC. Other
    more common personal defenses are good against a holder
    but not against a holder in due course.

    A. Real Defenses--Forgery, material alteration, fraud
        in the execution, discharge of the debt in
        bankruptcy, minority, extreme duress, illegality,
        or mental incapacity that causes the instrument to
        be void.

    B. Personal Defenses--Breach of contract, payment,
        fraud in the inducement, unauthorized completion of
        the instrument, mental incapacity or illegality
        that causes the instrument to be voidable.

    C. FTC Rule--The FTC Rule is a consumer protection law
        passed by Congress after the UCC went into effect.
        The FTC Rule applies to consumer credit transaction
        only. In these cases, an HDC is not protected
        because anyone who buys a consumer note is subject
        to all defenses (real and personal) of the maker.

VI. Discharge--Discharge is a broad term that covers all
    release of liability on an instrument. Discharge
    normally occurs when the instrument is finaly paid and
    taken out of circulation. Discharge can also occur if
    the instrument has been materially altered. If a party
    reacquires an instrument, everyone in-between the first
    and second possessions is automatically discharged.

Study Questions

Fill-in-the-Blank Questions

Barton Barrister, Attorney at Law, purchases a copier from Once-Owned Office Equipment, Inc. Barrister pays for the copier by making a sixty-day promissory note in the amount of $1,200.00 payable to Once-Owned. Once-Owned is in need of cash to buy more inventory so it sells the note to his bank. The copier does not work and when the bank presents the note to Barrister, he refuses to pay. The bank (holder) sues Barrister (maker-defendant).

The bank _____ an HDC.
      (is/is not)

Barrister has a _____ defense.
       (real/personal)

The bank _____ prevail in the suit.
     (will/will not)

Assume that Barrister is bankrupt and that a court has relieved him of liability for the note. The bank sues Once-Owned for the money. Once-Owned _____ breached the transfer warranty.
       (has/has not)

Once-Owned _____ signature liability.
      (has/has no)

True-False Questions

1. The FTC rules apply to all consumer transactions involving a negotiable instrument. ____

2. A holder who promises to pay a note next week has given good value. ____

3. A rubber stamp can be a valid signature. ____

4. An agent who signs a company check in his own name will always be personally liable for the check. ____

5. Fraud in the execution is a real defense. ____

6. An indorser who signs "without recourse" has no signature liability. ____

7. A holder who transfers a bearer instrument has no warranty liability. _____

8. A presentment warranty is made to an indorser. _____

9. The shelter principle protects holders in due course._____

10. A check may be presented for payment by depositing it in the payee's bank account. _____

Multiple-Choice Questions

1. Alice receives a check from her grandmother as a birthday present.

    a. Alice is holder.
    b. Alice is an HDC.
    c. Alice is a holder through a holder in due course.
    d. Alice is not a holder.

2. Alice indorses the check and deposits it in her bank account. Alice's bank forwards the check to grandmother's bank for payment.

    a. Grandmother is a holder, but not an HDC.
    b. Alice's bank is a holder, but not an HDC.
    c. Alice's bank is an HDC.
    d. Grandmother is an HDC.

3. Tom finds a check payable to Simple Simon. Tom forges Simon's signature and deposits the check in his bank account. Tom's bank stamps "Pay any bank" on the back of the check and forwards it through a clearinghouse to Simon's bank for payment.

    a. Tom's bank has breached the transfer warranty.
    b. Tom's bank has breached the presentment warranty.
    c. Tom's bank is not an HDC.
    d. Tom's bank has no signature liability.

4. Tom:

    a. has breached the transfer warranty.
    b. has not breached the transfer warranty.
    c. is an HDC.
    d. is the payee of the check.

5.   Melinda buys a car from Lemon Limos and signs a four year $12,000 installment note payable to Lemon. Lemon discounts the note to First Bank and receives $10,500 cash. Lemon knows that the car is a bomb. After two months, the car malfunctions and Melinda stos paying on the note.

a.   Melinda is a holder.
b.   Lemon is a holder.
c.   First Bank is a holder but not an HDC.
d.   Lemon is an HDC.

6.   Lemon:

a.   has signature liability only.
b.   has warranty liability only.
c.   has both signature and warranty liability.
d.   has no liability to First Bank.

7.   If First Bank sues Melinda:

a.   Melinda will win because First Bank is not an HDC.
b.   Melinda will win because the FTC rule applies.
c.   First Bank will win because it is an HDC.
d.   First Bank will win because the FTC rule applies.

8.   An indorser who signs "without recourse":

a.   has no signature liability.
b.   has no warranty liability.
c.   has both signature and warranty liability.
d.   has no liability.

9.   Sam Salesman works for Investment Realty, Inc. and is authorized to spend $5,000 without prior approval. He draws a draft in the amount of $1,000 and Investment is named as drawee. Sam signs the draft, "Sam Salesman for Investment Realty, Inc."

a.   Sam is personally liable as a drawer.
b.   Sam is personally liable as a drawee.
c.   Investment Realty is liable as a drawee.
d.   Investment Realty is not liable as a drawer.

10.   If the signer intends to validate a negotiable instrument, which of the following is (are) acceptable as a signature?

a.   Rubber stamp
b.   Typewritten name
c.   Printed name
d.   All of the above are acceptable.

11. Gary's Grocery places a $7,500 order with the Wholesale Fruit Co. and sends them a check for the entire amount. Wholesale cashes the check but sends only half the order. Wholesale promises to send the remainder in two weeks. At the time that Wholesale cashes the check, it is:

   a. a holder but not an HDC.
   b. an HDC for $7,500.
   c. an HDC for $3,750.
   d. not a holder.

12. Wholesale's bank deposits the check in Wholesale's bank account and forwards it to Gary's bank for payment.

   a. Gary's bank is a holder, but not an HDC.
   b. Gary's bank is an HDC for $7,500.
   c. Gary's bank is an HDC for $3,750.
   d. Gary's bank is not a holder.

13. Freddie Forger receives his $1,000 paycheck and skillfully raises the amount of the check to $10,000. He transfers the check to AAA Autos as payment for a car. AAA indorses the check and deposits it in its bank accounts.

   a. AAA has breached the transfer warranty.
   b. AAA has not breached the transfer warranty.
   c. AAA is not an HDC.
   d. AAA has no signature liability.

14. John sells his motorcycle to Tony who is sixteen years old. Tony pays $100 down and promises to pay $25 a month for twelve months. John sells the note to E-Z Finance Co. and receives cash. Tony makes only two payments. E-Z sues Tony.

   a. Tony will lose because he has a personal defense.
   b. Tony will lose because he has a real defense.
   c. Tony will win because he has a personal defense.
   d. Tony will win because he has a real defense.

15. Assume E-Z sues John.

   a. John will win because he is an HDC.
   b. John has no signature liability.
   c. E-Z will win because John has breached the transfer warranty.
   d. John will win because E-Z is not an HDC.

. 16.   Penny sells her dog and receives a check for $200 from
        Cathy. Penny indorses the check to her mother. Which
        of the following persons, if any, have secondary
        liability on the instrument?

        a.   Penny
        b.   Penny and Penny's mother
        c.   Cathy, Penny and Penny's mother
        d.   Cathy's bank

17.   George writes a check payable to "cash" and delivers the
        check to Sally. Sally delivers the check without
        indorsement to Ron. Ron indorses the check and deposits
        it in his bank account. If George and his bank refuse
        to honor the check:

        a.   Ron's bank can sue Ron but not Sally.
        b.   Rons' bank can sue both Ron and Sally.
        c.   Ron's bank can sue Sally only.
        d.   Ron's bank cannot sue.

18.   Sally:

        a.   has signature liability.
        b.   has transfer liability to Ron and his bank.
        c.   has transfer liability to Ron.
        d.   has no liability to Ron or his bank.

19.   Pixie makes a note to Mouse Trailers, Inc. in the amount
        of $500. Pixie signs the note by typing, "Pixie, Dixie"
        on the signature line.

        a.   Pixie is personally liable on the instrument unless
              he can show that he was Dixie's agent.
        b.   Pixie is not personally liable on the instrument
              regardless of proof.
        c.   Dixie is not liable on the instrument regardless of
              proof.
        d.   Neither Pixie nor Dixie is liable because the
              signature is improper.

20.   On August 1, 1987, Rhett makes a sixty-day $400 note
        payable to Scarlett's Souvenir Shop. On October 15,
        1987, the shop discounts the note to the Bank of Georgia
        for $375 cash. The bank:

        a.   is not an HDC because it did not give value.
        b.   is not an HDC because the note is overdue.
        c.   is not an HDC because Eiffel acted in bad faith.
        d.   is an HDC.

21.   Sam owes $300 to Flamingo Factory. Sam receives his
       paycheck and indorses it to Flamingo.

       a.   Flamingo is not an HDC because it did not give
            value.
       b.   Flamingo is not an HDC because it did not take the
            check in good faith.
       c.   Sam is not an HDC because he did not give value.
       d.   Flamingo and Sam are HDC's.

22.   Abel Attorney receives a check for $400 in payment of a
       legal fee. Abel gives the check to his daughter for a
       graduation present. The daughter deposits the check in
       her bank account. Abel's daughter:

       a.   is an HDC.
       b.   is a holder only and cannot claim HDC protection.
       c.   is a holder through a holder in due course and can
            claim HDC protection.
       d.   is a holder through a holder in due course but
            cannot claim HDC protection.

23.   Which of the following is a real defense?

       a.   The instrument has been paid
       b.   Breach of contract
       c.   Fraud in the inducement
       d.   Material alteration of the instrument

24.   Walker Shoes hires Rumpole Roofing to repair the roof of
       its store. Walker gives Rumpole a sixty-day $750 note.
       Rumpole sells the note to Second Bank. Rumpole never
       completes the repairs and is declared bankrupt.

       a.   Second Bank will be successful in a suit against
            Walker because Walker has a personal defense.
       b.   Second Bank will be unsuccessful in a suit against
            Walker because Walker the FTC rule applies.
       c.   Second Bank will be unsuccessful in a suit against
            Walker because Walker has a real defense.
       d.   Second Bank will be unsuccessful in a suit against
            Walker because Second Bank is not an HDC.

25.   Assume that Walker's Bank sues Rumpole.

       a.   Second Bank will be unsuccessful because the FTC
            rule applies.
       b.   Second Bank will be unsuccessful because Rumpole has
            a real defense.

c. Second Bank will be successful because the FTC rule
does not apply.

d. Second Bank will be successful because Rumpole has a
personal defense.

Answers to Study Questions

Fill-in-the-Blank Questions

The Bank is an HDC. It gave value for the instrument by paying
cash to Once-Owned. Did the bank act honestly? Yes. Did the
bank buy the instrument without notice that Barrister's machine
was faulty? Yes, unless Once-Owned told the bank, which is
unlikely.

Barrister has a personal defense. His plea is breach of
contract or possible fraud in the inducement. These are
personal defenses and are not good against an HDC.

The bank wins in a suit against Barrister. Barrister will have
to sue Once-Owned to recoup his losses.

Once-Owned has breached the transfer warranty. It promised
that no defense of any party was good against him. Bankruptcy
is a real defense and is good against Once-Owned. He must pay
the bank. Once-Owned also has signature liability because he
indorsed the note as the payee.

Remember that the bank as an HDC has several options. It can
and should sue Barrister because as the maker he has primary
liability. The bank can also sue Once-Owned by tracing back
the line of transfer. As a transferor of the instrument
Once-Owned incurred signature and warranty liability.

True-False Questions

1. F. The FTC rule applies to consumer credit
    transactions. It does not apply if the consumer uses a
    check to pay for goods or services.

2. F. Value must actually be received; a promise to pay is
    insufficient.

3. T.

4. F. Because the check is on a company account, the agent
    may be able to prove his status by parol evidence.

5.   T.

6.   T.

7.   F. The holder has transfer liability to his immediate tranferree only.

8.   F. It is made to a maker, a drawer or a drawee.

9.   F. It protects holders who do not qualify as HDC's

10.   T. The banking system is a proper method of presentment.

Multiple-Choice Questions

1.	a	11.	c	21.	d
2.	c	12.	b	22.	c
3.	a	13.	a	23.	d
4.	a	14.	d	24.	a
5.	b	15.	c	25.	b
6.	c	16.	c		
7.	b	17.	a		
8.	a	18.	c		
9.	c	19.	a		
10.	d	20.	b		

Chapter 18   Commercial Paper—
Checks and the Banking System

General Principles

This chapter highlights the most common form of commercial paper: the check. There are three parties to a check: the drawer who orders payment, the drawee who pays according to the drawer's orders, and the payee. The rules outlined in previous chapters regarding indorsement, liability and holder in due course apply to checks. It may help to visualize the path of check as it is deposited in the payee's bank and makes its way through the banking system to the drawee bank. The banks are transferees or holders of the check.

Article 4 of the UCC regulates the contractual relationship between a bank and its customer. The bank has a duty to follow the instructions of its customer; the customer has a duty to keep sufficient funds in his account and to examine bank statements for error.

Chapter Summary

I.   Types of Checks

      A.   Cashier's Check--A bank is the drawer and the drawee on a cashier's check. A customer purchases the check from the bank and is named as payee. A cashier's check is more acceptable than an ordinary check because it is presumed that the bank has sufficient funds to insure payment.

B.   Traveler's Check--A traveler's check is misnamed; it is a draft. The drawer and drawee are the same person, usually a financial institution but not necessarily a bank. As protection against forgery, the payee must sign the check twice, once when he or she receives it and again when he or she transfers it.

C.   Certified Check--A certified check is a check that has been formally accepted by the bank. Because the bank has accepted the check, the holder is assured that sufficient funds are available to pay the check. If the drawer requests certification, he or she remains secondarily liable. If a holder requests certification, anyone who has signed the check before certification (drawer and previous indorsers) is discharged from liability.

The bank is liable for the amount of the check at the time of certification. If the check is altered after certification, the bank is not liable for the additional amount.

II.   The Bank-Customer Relationship--The bank acts as its customer's agent is processing checks; it credits and debits the customer's account according to the instruments received.

A.   General Duties--The bank owes a general duty to the customer to follow his or her orders. The bank may be liable to its customer if it does not. The customer owes a duty to keep sufficient funds on hand to pay incoming checks and to act responsibly. The bank may be able to shift liability to the customer if the customer acts negligently.

B.   Honoring Checks--The bank has a duty to honor only those checks which are "properly payable". Altered checks or checks with forged indorsements are not properly payable.

(1)   Overdrafts--A bank may, if it chooses, pay incoming checks even if there are insufficient funds in the customer's account. The bank is then entitled to recoup its losses from the customer. A bank that routinely pays overdrafts may be liable to the customer if it changes policy without notifying the customer.

If the bank chooses not to honor the overdraft, the holder can demand payment from the drawer directly or resubmit the check. A "bounced" check has been dishonored and the holder must notify all previous indorsers or lose the right to collect payment from them.

(2) Stale Checks--An uncertified check presented more than six months after its date is stale and the bank has no obligation to pay it. If the bank pays the check in good faith, it may charge the customer's account.

(3) Missing Indorsements--The bank is the customer's agent and can supply the customer's indorsement unless the instrument requires personal indorsement by the payee (e.g. government checks).

(4) Stop-Payment Orders--If the customer issues a stop-payment order in reasonable manner and within a reasonable time for the bank to act, the bank must follow the customer's instructions. A written stop-payment order is valid for six months; an oral stop-payment order (if permitted) is valid for fourteen days.

The bank will be liable if it fails to follow proper instructions. However, if the customer had no legal right to stop payment, the bank may recoup its losses from the customer. A stop-payment order does not automatically relieve the customer from liability to the holder or payee. That questions must be litigated separately. The outcome will depend on the type of defense presented by the drawer and whether the holder is an HDC.

(5) Forger Drawer's Signature--The bank is responsible for recognizing its customer's signature and will be liable unless it can prove that the customer was negligent. The customer has a duty to examine his or her bank statement and to report forgeries to the bank within fourteen days after the statement is received. If the customer fails to report within the time limit and similar forgeries occur, the customer will be responsible for the forgeries which could have been prevented by reporting promptly.

(6) <u>Forged Indorsement</u>--The bank is liable to its customer for checks paid over a forged indorsement. The bank can then recover from the person who presented the check for payment because the presenter has breached a warranty. The customer must report a forged indorsement within three years in order to hold the bank liable.

(7) <u>Altered Check</u>--The bank is responsible for the difference between the check as written and as altered. The bank will be able to recover the extra amount from the person who presented the check because a presentment warranty has been broken. If the check is presented to someone who should know the original amount (e.g. drawer, maker, acceptor), then that party is responsible. The bank may be able to shift the loss back to its customer if it can prove that he or she was negligent.

C.   <u>Accepting Deposits</u>--The bank's duty is to credit deposits to the customer's account and initiates collection process. A bank may have different responsibilities and liabilities depending on its position in the collection chain.

(1) <u>Definitions</u>--The first bank to receive the check is the depositary bank. The final bank in the chain, the bank which will pay the check, is the drawee or payor bank. An intermediary bank is any bank in the chain except the depositary or payor bank. A collecting bank is one which forwards the instrument for collection and includes the depositary bank and all intermediary banks.

(2) <u>Restrictive Indorsements</u>--A bank in the collection chain is required to follow only the restrictive indorsement from its immediate transferee. The depositary bank must credit the funds to the customer's account if the customer requests. "Pay any bank" is a restrictive indorsement used by banks in the collection process. It specifies that the next holder in the collection chain must be a bank.

(3) Check Collection--The depositary and each collecting bank must forward the check for collection by midnight of the next banking day following its receipt of the check (midnight deadline). As the check travels through the banking system, each bank gives and receives a provisional credit for the amount of the check. When the payor bank receives the check, it must pay or dishonor the check by its midnight deadline. When the depositary bank and the payor bank are the same, the time limit is the opening of the second banking day. This is an "on us" item.

The collection system presumes that payment will be made and unless the payor bank dishonors the check, the provisional credits become final and the payor bank is responsible. If the payor bank and the depositary bank are the same, then the bank has until midnight of the next banking day to pay or dishonor the check.

The time limit for payment or forwarding is so short that the UCC allows a bank receiving a check after a certain time (usually 2 p.m.) to delay formal receipt until the next day. This process is called deferred posting and gives the bank an extra day to forward or pay a check.

III. Electronic Funds Transfer System (EFTS)--This system provides for the transfer of funds without using checks or other written instruments.

A. System Components

(1) Automated Teller Machines--An automated teller machine is connected to the bank by a computer. The customer uses an EFT or debit card and a personal identification number (PIN) to withdraw money, make deposits and complete other banking transactions.

(2) Consumer Terminals--The customer's home computer is linked to the bank's computer and the customer can pay bills and transfer funds without using checks.

(3) Automated Clearinghouses--Federal Reserve Banks and other collecting banks move funds using electronic pulses instead of checks.

(4) <u>Point-of-Sale System</u>--A merchant's store maintains a computer hook-up with the customer's bank. The customer uses his PIN card to make payments instead of writing a check.

B.   <u>Responsibilities and Liabilities</u>

(1) If the customer's EFT card is used without permission, the customer is liable for only $50. However, the customer must inform the bank within two days of the loss or liability increases to $500. The customer can be liable for more than $500 if he or she fails to examine the bank statement and report the loss within 60 days.

(2) If the customer reports an error within sixty days after he or she receives a bank statement, the bank has ten days to investigate. If the investigation exceeds ten days, the bank must recredit the amount to the customer's account until the dispute is resolved.

(3) The bank must provide a receipt for each transaction and each transfer must be reported on the bank statement.

(4) If the customer uses a prepayment system for paying utility bills or insurance premiums, he or she can cancel the transaction three days before the transfer is scheduled.

C.   <u>Advantages and Disadvantages of EFTS</u>

(1) <u>Advantages</u>--The EFTS is more convenient than writing checks because automatic teller machines are located in shopping centers, grocery stores, etc. The customer can order automatic payment of bills. EFTS also reduces the vast amount of paperwork needed to collect checks.

(2) <u>Disadvantages</u>--EFT transactions occur immediately and so it is difficult to issue stop-payment orders. Also, the "float" or the time between writing a check and its payment is eliminated. Although the bank is required to provide a record of EFT transactions, these

records are not as complete as those provided by cancelled checks. Finally, it is easier to tamper with EFT records and the customer's privacy may be reduced.

Study Questions

Fill-in-the-Blank Questions

Aunt Lillie, who lives in New York City, writes a check payable to her niece Beth and mails the check to Beth, who lives in Carmel, California. Beth receives the check and deposits it in her bank account. Beth's bank forwards the check to the Federal Reserve Bank of Los Angeles, who forwards it to the Federal Reserve Bank of New York, which presents the check for payment at Aunt Lillie's bank.

Beth's bank is a(n) _____ bank.
(depositary/intermediary)

Aunt Lillie's bank is a _____ bank.
(payor/collecting)

The Federal Reserve Bank of New York is a _____
_____bank.   (collecting/
depositary)

The Federal Reserve Bank of Los Angeles is a(n) _____
_____ bank.   (intermediary/
payor)

True-False Questions

1. An EFTS transaction is processed more quickly than a written check. ____

2. A check is considered stale if it has not been cashed within 4 months of the date it was issued. ____

3. A cashier's check is a check which has been accepted by the drawee bank. ____

4. A drawee bank is the same as a payor bank. ____

5. A bank which pays a check with a forged indorsement must re-credit its customer's account if the customer discovers and reports the error within 3 years. ____

6.   A traveler's check is a draft and is not a check. ____

7.   An oral stop-payment order is valid in every state. ____

8.   A collecting bank must pay a check or dishonor it before midnight of the next banking day. ____

9.   A bank has the right to pay a customer's overdrafts and charge the amount to the customer's account. ____

10.   When the drawer of a check asks the bank to certify the check and the bank does so, the drawer is no longer liable on the instrument. ____

Multiple-Choice Questions

1.   Mary issues a written stop-payment order to her bank. Four months later, the banks pays the check. In a suit between Mary and her bank:

    a.   Mary will win because the stop-payment order is valid for six months.
    b.   The bank will win because the stop-payment order is valid for fourteen days.
    c.   The bank will win because the check is stale.
    d.   The bank will win because it has the right to refuse payment of any check.

2.   Tony steals his mother's checkbook and writes a check to Ralph's Records for $26. Ralph deposits the check in his bank account. Ralph's bank credits his account and sends the check to mother's bank. In a suit between the two banks:

    a.   Ralph's bank will lose because it violated the transfer warranty.
    b.   Ralph's bank will lose because it violated the presentment warranty.
    c.   Ralph's bank will win because the transfer warranty was not breached.
    d.   Ralph's bank will win because the presentment warranty was not breached.

3.   Ralph's mother receives her bank statement three weeks later. She immediately notifies the bank of the forgery. In a suit between Ralph's mother and the bank:

a. The bank will win because mother waited three weeks to report the forgery.

b. Mother will win because she has three years to report the forgery.

c. Mother would win even without notification because her bank should recognize her signature.

d. Mother will win because she notified the bank of the forgery within two weeks of receiving her bank statement.

4. Linda writes a $500 check to her landlord Mabel. Mabel indorses the check and transfers it to Pete's Plumbing as payment for maintenance. Pete takes the check to Linda's bank and asks the bank to certify it. The bank agrees. When the bank certifies the check:

a. Linda and Mabel are no longer liable.

b. Mabel is no longer liable but Linda is.

c. Linda is no longer liable but Mabel is.

d. Linda and Mabel are liable but Pete cashes the check.

5. Business Law Teacher asks her aide to buy some supplies at Campus Bookstore. She gives the aide a signed check made out to Campus Bookstore but fails to fill in the amount. The aide fills in the check for $100 more than the cost of the supplies and leaves town.

a. Business Law Teacher is only responsible for the lesser amount because she authorized payment for supplies only.

b. Business Law Teacher is responsible for the entire amount because she was negligent in filing out the check.

c. The bank is responsible for the entire amount because is should have been checked with Business Law Teacher before paying the check.

d. The bookstore is responsible because it should have checked with Business Law Teacher before paying the check.

6. Penny writes a check to Sam's Grocery on Tuesday morning. Sam deposits the check in his bank account on Wednesday morning. Assuming that Sam and Penny do not use the same bank, Sam's bank:

a. must forward the check by midnight Wednesday.

b. must forward the check by midnight Thursday.

c. must forward the check by midnight Friday.

d. has no duty to forward the check.

7.   If Sam and Penny use the same bank, the bank:

    a.   must forward the check by midnight Wednesday.
    b.   must forward the check by midnight Thursday.
    c.   must dishonor or pay the check by midnight Wednesday.
    d.   must dishonor or pay the check by midnight Thursday.

8.   Which of the following are parts of an EFT system?

    a.   Automated teller machines
    b.   Point-of-Sale systems
    c.   Automated clearinghouses
    d.   All of the above

9.   Mary has a home computer which is linked to her bank. She pays her bills by transferring funds to the proper accounts. Mary is using:

    a.   an automated teller machine.
    b.   a point-of-sale system.
    c.   an automated clearinghouse.
    d.   a consumer terminal.

10.   Cindy is mugged and the theif takes her wallet. He uses her EFT card to withdraw $1,000 from her bank account. Cindy immediately notifies her bank. Cindy is responsible for:

    a. $0.
    b. $50.
    c. $500.
    d. $1,000.

11.   If Cindy had waited two weeks to report the loss, she would be responsible for:

    a. $0.
    b. $50.
    c. $500.
    d. $1,000.

12.   Susan writes a check to Betty's Boutique. Betty indorses the check and takes it to Susan's bank. Susan's bank refuses to cash the check.

    a.   Betty can sue Susan's bank only if Susan had sufficient funds in the bank to pay the check.
    b.   Betty can sue Susan's bank regardless of the amount of money in Susan's account.

    c. Betty cannot sue Susan's bank because Betty should have deposited the check and let it clear through the banking system.

    d. Betty presented the check in a proper manner but she cannot sue Susan's bank.

13.   Susan:

    a. can sue her bank if she had sufficient funds in her account to pay the check.

    b. can sue her bank regardless of the amount of money in her account because a bank must honor its customer's overdrafts.

    c. cannot sue the bank because Betty did not present the check in a proper manner.

    d. cannot sue her bank because the bank owes no duty to Susan.

14.   On a cashier's check:

    a. the bank is both drawee and payee.

    b. the bank is both drawee and drawer.

    c. the bank is both payee and drawer.

    d. the bank is payee, drawee and payee.

15.   Bill receives a $10,000 check as a down payment for his sports car. Bill asks the buyer's bank to certify the check. Bill then transfers the check to his bank, where a teller skillfully raises the amount to $100,000. Bill's bank presents the altered check to the buyer's bank for payment.

    a. the buyer's bank is responsible for $100,000 because it certified the check.

    b. The buyer's bank is responsible for $10,000 because $10,000 was the amount of the check when the bank certifed it.

    c. The buyer's bank is not responsible for any amount because the check has been altered.

    d. Bill is liable for the additional $90,000.

16.   Cindy deposits her paycheck in the bank but forgets to indorse it.

    a. The bank cannot collect the check because Cindy's indorsement is missing.

    b. The bank can supply Cindy's indorsement if the check does not require her signature.

    c. The bank can supply Cindy's signature on any check because the bank is her agent.

    d. The bank can never supply a customer's indorsement.

17.   Ron buys a microwave oven from AAA Appliance and writes
       a check for $450. Ron changes his mind when he sees the
       same oven on sale for $350 at another store. Ron stops
       payment on the check. When AAA presents the check for
       payment, Ron's bank refuses to pay.

       a.   AAA can sue the bank because it refused to honor the
            check and it can sue Ron for wrongfully issuing a
            stop-payment order.
       b.   AAA can sue the bank but not Ron.
       c.   AAA can sue Ron but not the bank.
       d.   AAA cannot sue Ron or the bank.

18.   Bob steals his employer's checkbook and forges five
       checks on the following dates: March 1, March 8, March
       15, Apri 15, and April 30. Bob takes the money and
       moves to Switzerland. The employer receives his March
       bank statement on April 8 and the checks forged in March
       appear on the statement. The employer notifies the bank
       of the forgeries on April 16.

       a.   Bob's employer is responsible for all the checks.
       b.   The bank is responsible for all the checks.
       c.   Bob's employer is responsible for the March checks
            and the April 15 check.
       d.   Bob's employer is responsible only for the April 30
            check.

19.   Assume that Bob's employer did not report the forgeries:

       a.   Bob's employer is responsible for all the checks.
       b.   The bank is responsible for all the checks.
       c.   Bob's employer is responsible for the March checks
            and the April 15 check.
       d.   Bob's employer is responsible only for the April 30
            check.

20.   Sally gives her EFT card and her PIN number to her
       friend Fred and tells him to withdraw $40 from her bank
       account. Fred withdraws $440 from one automatic teller
       and $100 from another. He returns the card to Sally and
       says nothing about the extra withdrawal. When Sally
       receives the bank statement the following month, she
       discoveres the extra withdrawals and tells the bank she
       will pay only $40.

       a.   Sally is responsible for $40 only because she
            reported the mistake promptly.
       b.   Sally is responsible for $540 ($500 + $40) because
            she did not report the loss within two days.

      c.   Sally is responsible for $90 ($50 + $40) because her liability is limited to $50 for unauthorized use.

      d.   Sally is responsible for $540 ($500 + $40) because she allowed Fred to use her card.

21.   A bank which receives checks after 2 p.m. can postpone recording the transaction until the next day. This process is:

      a.   deferred collection.
      b.   deferred clearing.
      c.   deferred posting.
      d.   deferred payment.

22.   Phil has an account with 1st Bank. Phil is killed in a plane crash on May 30. The bank learns of Phil's death on June 2. The bank pays several checks which were written by Phil before his death. The checks were received by the bank on May 30, June 1, June 2 and June 12. The bank has received no notice from a representative of Phil's estate. The bank has the authority to pay which of the following checks?

      a.   The check received on May 30 only
      b.   The checks received on May 30 and June 1
      c.   None of the checks
      d.   All of the check

23.   Mary has a checking account with State Bank. The bank-customer contract states that the bank will pay overdrafts which total less than $200. The amount of the overdraft and a service fee will be deducted from the customer's account. Mary writes a check for $50 and has only $22 in her account. The bank dishonors or "bounces" the $50 check.

      a.   Mary can sue the bank because a bank must always honor its customer's overdrafts.
      b.   Mary cannot sue the bank because a bank can always choose not to honor an overdraft.
      c.   Mary can sue the bank because the bank promised to honor small overdrafts.
      d.   Mary and the payee of the check can sue the bank because the bank promised to honor small overdrafts.

24.   Sandra receives a check from her brother. She indorses the check "for deposit only" and transfers it to her bank. Sandra's bank forwards the check immediately to her brother's bank.

    a.   Sandra's bank cannot forward the check because it is marked "for deposit only".

    b.   Sandra's bank can forward the check but only if it credits Sandra's account with the money.

    c.   The brother's bank cannot pay the check because it is marked "for deposit only".

    d.   Sandra's bank can cash the check but cannot deposit it in her account.

25.   The brother's bank is:

    a.   a collecting bank and the depository bank.

    b.   a collecting bank and the payor bank.

    c.   an intermediary bank and the payor bank.

    d.   the drawee bank and the payor bank.

Answers to Study Questions

Fill-in-the-Blank Questions

Beth's bank is a depository bank. Aunt Lillie's bank is a payor bank. The Federal Reserve Bank of New York is a collecting bank. The Federal Reserve Bank of Los Angeles is an intermediary bank.

True-False Questions

1.   T.

2.   F. It is considered stale if it has not been cashed within six months of its date.

3.   F. A certified check has been accepted by the drawee bank. On a cashier's check the drawer and the drawee are the same bank.

4.   T.

5.   T.

6.   T.

7.   F.

8.   F. A payor bank must pay or dishonor a check before midnight of the next business day. A collecting bank must forward the check for payment within the deadline.

9.   T.

10.   F. The drawer is relieved only if the drawee bank becomes insolvent.

Multiple-Choice Questions

1.	a	11.	c	21.	c
2.	d	12.	d	22.	d
3.	d	13.	a	23.	c
4.	b	14.	b	24.	b
5.	b	15.	b	25.	d
6.	b	16.	b		
7.	d	17.	c		
8.	d	18.	b		
9.	d	19.	d		
10.	b	20.	d		

Chapter 19   Secured Transactions

General Principles

A secured transaction is a loan where payment is guaranteed by some property of the borrower or debtor. The lender can seize the property if the debtor does not repay the debt. Most car loans are secured transactions. An unsecured loan is not backed by specific property of the debtor; it may be called a "signature loan". Most minor purchases on a credit card are unsecured loans.

A lender, or secured party, has two primary interests: 1) the right to collect the property securing the loan, and; 2) priority if the debtor should be unable to pay several of his or her creditors. The rules attempt to simplify the lending process by granting preferences to lenders and by providing a notice system so that a lender will not advance money to an over-extended debtor. As you review, it may help to think of two types of common secured transactions: the car loan mentioned earlier and the financing of a retail business.

Chapter Summary

I.   A.   <u>Scope and Definitions</u>--Article 9 of the Uniform Commercial Code applies to any transaction where money is loaned and payment is assured by personal property. It does not apply to real estate mortgages, liens by contractors (mechanics) or landlords, or debts arising from litigation.

        B.   <u>Parties</u>--The borrower is the debtor; the lender is the secured party.

C.   Transaction--The lender is given a security interest in the property or collateral. A purchase-money security interest occurs when the buyer receives funds to buy and item. The purchase can be financed by the seller or by a bank. The contract which creates the lender's interest is a security agreement. Attachment gives the lender rights against the debtor. Perfection gives the lender rights against the debtor. Perfection gives the lender rights against other creditors of the debtor who may have an interest in the same property.

D.   Property--The property which secures the debt is called collateral. Collateral is classified according to its use by the debtor. Classification is extremely important because the rules differ depending upon the type of collateral.

(1)   Goods--Tangible items which are movable at the time acquired by the debtor. Goods are further classified into five categories.

(a)   Consumer goods are used for household or personal purposes.

(b)   Inventory consists of goods held for resale or raw materials used in the manufacturing process.

(c)   Fixtures are goods which become attached to real estate.

(d)   Farm products (owned only by a farmer) are crops, livestock and supplies used in farming.

(e)   Equipment consists of goods used to produce goods or carry on a business. This is a catchall category; if the collateral is a good and does not fall into another category, it is classified as equipment.

(2)   Indispensable Paper--Documents which show an ownership or security interest.

(a)   Chattel paper includes documents which show both a loan and a security interest, e.g. a car note.

        (b)   Documents of title are warehouse receipts, bills of landing and any other documents which show a party's right to possession of goods.

        (c)   Instruments includes negotiable instrument, stock certificates and non-negotiable instruments.

    (3)   <u>Intangibles</u>--Accounts are accounts receivable or any contract which promises repayment other than those noted above. General intangibles include all other non-tangible personal property such as a patent or coyright.

II.   <u>Attachment</u>--Creation of a security interest. Establishes rights between the debtor and the secured party; third paties are not affected. The three steps below must occur before the security interest attaches to the collateral (before the creditor has a right to a specific piece of property.)

    A.   A written security agreement signed by the debtor must contain a reasonably definite description of the collateral. The written agreement is unnecessary if the secured party takes physical possession of the collateral.

    B.   The secured party must give value which is usually accomplished by advancing money, promising to do so, or by selling goods on credit. Can apply to loans made in the past (antecedent debt).

    C.   The debtor must have the right to possession or ownership of the collateral.

III.   <u>Perfection</u>--Enforcement of a security interest in collateral against other creditors who also may have any interest in the collateral. Designed to give notice so that creditors will not be misled. The method of perfection depends on the classification of the collateral.

    A.   <u>Physical transfer</u>--Called a pledge. This is the only way to perfect an interest in instruments. Note that if the lender has possession of the document, the debtor cannot show it to another lender to obtain more credit.

B.   Filing--The most common method is to file a financing statement in a public records office. The financing statement must include the signature of the debtor, the addresses of the secured party and the debtor, and a description of the collateral. The statement is filed with the county clerk or the Secretary of State, depending on the type of collateral and state law. In general, financing statements for fixtures, farm products, and consumer goods are filed locally.

C.   Purchase-Money Security Interest in Consumer Goods --Perfects automatically an attachment. This is an exception to the general rule because other creditors are not likely to lend money with consumer goods as collateral and notice is not necessary.

D.   Time Limits--A financing statement is valid for five years. Continuation statements may be filed as many times as necessary. Can file up to six months before expiration. If the collateral is mobile, and the debtor moves it to another state, the original financing statement is valid only for 4 months or the expiration date, whichever is earlier. The secured party can refile in the new state. Perfection can be lost earlier with an automobile if a certificate of title without notation of the security interest is acquired.

IV.   The Floating Lien--When you review these rules, it may help to think of a retail business which has a line of credit with a bank. The bank extends credit so that the retailer can purchase inventory, equipment and pay employees. If the business is successful, the retailer will sell the original inventory, take in cash, checks or accounts receivable. The floating lien allows the original security interest to cover new property acquired by the debtor and to advance funds without making a new agreement if floats over the debtor's assets. The following clauses are often found in such agreements.

A.   After-Acquired Property--The security interest attaches to any property acquired by the debtor after the original agreement is made. This is necessary in inventory financing, otherwise as the retailer sold the goods, the lender's collateral would disappear. Limit on consumer goods: debtor must get rights within ten days of the agreement or a new agreement must be signed.

B.   <u>Future Advances</u>--Used with a line or letter of credit. The lender agrees to advance a sum of money when needed by the debtor. The debtor may not use all the money at once; interest is paid only when the funds are used. A future advance clause allows the lender to give out the funds without creating a new agreement. Each advance of funds dates back to the time of the original agreement.

C.   <u>Proceeds</u>--Covers whatever the debtor receives then he or she sells or disposes of collateral. Necessary in inventory financing or the lender's collateral would evaporate. Because it is difficult to keep track of proceeds, the lender's interest is limited by the following perfection rules.

The lender's interest is automatically perfected for ten days. After that time one of the following must occur:

(1)   the proceeds are identifiable cash (e.g. separate bank account).

(2)   lender perfects an interest in the proceeds.

(3)   original financing statement covers the type of proceeds received (e.g. accounts or chattel paper).

V.   <u>Priorities</u>--Used to resolve disputes between creditors and between creditors and purchasers of collateral.

A.   <u>Disputes Between Secured Creditors</u>--Generally first in time is first in right. A perfected interest always prevails over an unperfected interest. Between perfected parties, the first to file wins. If neither party is perfected, the first to attach wins. The following are exceptions and are designed to prevent one creditor from complete control of the debtor's business.

(1)   <u>Purchase-Money Security Interest</u>--Second in time wins if the following steps are followed:

(a)   <u>Inventory</u>--Lender perfects before or at the time debtor takes possession and written notice is given within twenty-one days to previous creditors on record.

(b) <u>Other</u>--Lender perfects within 10 days after debtor gets possession. No notice.

(2) <u>Crops</u>--Lender who gives new value within three months of planting has priority over a creditor to whom repayment is six months overdue.

B. <u>Disputes Between Secured and Unsecured Creditors</u>-- A perfected secured creditor prevails over all unsecured creditor. (Some states may give priority to contractors under mechanic's and materialmen's liens.) If the secured party is unperfected, he or she loses to anyone with a lien. In order to obtain a lien, a party generally must have established the debt in a court proceeding, received a judgment and filed a lien in the public records.

C. <u>Disputes Between Secured Creditors and Buyers</u>

(1) <u>Buyer in the Ordinary Course</u>--Prevails over a secured party if the purchase was part of the debtor's regular business. Buyer wins even if he or she knows that the property is subject to a security interest. The most common example is a sale to a consumer by a seller who is financed by a bank.

(2) <u>Consumer Goods</u>--Seller sells his or her consumer goods to another consumer. The buyer pays value and has no knowledge of the security interest. The buyer will win <u>unless</u> the secured party has filed a financing statement.

(3) <u>Chattel Paper</u>--Purchaser wins over secured party if the purchaser gives new value, takes possession in the ordinary course of business and had no actual knowledge of secured party's perfection. Can occur if a retailer sells on credit and then sells the buyer's note to a third party.

(4) <u>Purchasers of Other Documents</u>--Purchaser of negotiable instruments, documents of title and securities prevail over secured party. Secured party should have possession of the document and if he or she doesn't, the buyer wins.

VI.   General Rights and Duties of Debtors and Creditors

    A.   Information Requests--The office which keeps
        financing statement records must give creditors
        information on other secured transactions entered
        into by the debtor. A secured party who files is
        entitled to a file-marked copy of the financing
        statement.

        The debtor is entitled to find out the status of
        the debt at any time. The information is free
        every six months; the secured party can charge for
        additional requests. The lender must comploy
        within two weeks or may be liable to the debtor for
        any loss caused by a refusal to give the
        information.

    B.   Assignment, Amendment and Termination--Secured
        party can assign his interest to another; assingee
        is protected if he or she files notice with or on
        the financing statement. Amendments must be signed
        by both the debtor and the secured party.

        When the debt is paid, the lender has the
        obligation to file a termination statement in the
        appropriate public office or send it to the debtor.
        Must be filed within one month for consumer goods
        or ten days after written request by the debtor for
        all collateral including consumer goods. Failure
        to do so will subject the lender to $100 payment
        and any loss caused to the debtor by failure to
        file the termination statement.

    C.   Care of Collateral--The lender has the general duty
        to take reasonable care of the collateral although
        the debtor is responsible for costs of care. If
        the collateral increases in value, the lender can
        keep increase as security unless it is in the form
        of money (e.g. a contract obligation is paid).
        Money must be sent to the debtor or used to reduce
        the debt.

VII.   Default--One advantage of a secured transaction is the
        lender's right to repossess the collateral if the debtor
        fails to repay. The secured party has several options.
        Written notice of the secured party's decisions must be
        given to the debtor unless the debtor waives this right
        after default.

A.   Judgement, Levy and Execution--If the collateral
     has declined in value and the debtor has other
     valuable property, the lender may decide to sue.
     Once judgment is received, a public officer will
     seize propery of the debtor, sell it at a public
     sale and remit the proceeds to the lender. The
     lender may also choose this option if repossession
     would be difficult.

B.   Retention of the Collateral--Secured party may
     decide to keep the collateral as payment of the
     debt. Notice must be sent to the debtor and other
     secured parties who file a written notice of claim.
     If a written objection is filed, the secured party
     must sell the collateral. With consumer goods,
     notice to the debtor is sufficient.

C.   Sale--Public or private sale as long as the sale is
     commercially reasonable. With consumer goods, a
     sale is required if the debtor has paid at least 60
     percent of the purchase price unless the debtor
     waives this right in writing and after default.
     Notification must be sent to other secured parties
     who have filed a written notice of claim.

     When the collateral is sold, the proceeds from the
     sale are applied first to reasonable expenses of
     repossession, storage and sale. Then the secured
     party and other creditors within an interest in the
     property are paid. If any funds remain, they are
     sent to the debtor. Unless otherwise agreed, if
     the sale does not bring enough money to pay the
     debt, the secured party can sue the debtor for the
     remainder (deficiency judgment). The debtor and
     any other secured party with an interest in the
     property have the right to redeem the property
     before sale if the debt and expenses are paid.

D.   Repossession--If the lender keeps the collateral or
     sells it, he or she must first reposses it. the
     lender   can   repossess   the   collateral,   if
     repossession can be acomplished without breaching
     the peace. In general, the lender cannot enter the
     debtor's house or garage without permission. If the
     lender breaches the peace, he or she may be liable
     to th debtor in tort.

Study Questions

Fill-in-the-Blank Questions

Linda purchases a microwave oven for her home from AAA Appliance. She pays $50 down and agrees to pay $25 per month for one year. Linda signs a security agreement but AAA does not file a financing statement. After two months, Linda needs cash and sells the owen to her brother, who does not know of AAA's security interest.

The oven is classified as _____.
                                    (equipment/consumer good/inventory)

AAA _____ a perfected security interest.
            (has/does not have)

If a disputer arises, _____ has priority in the oven.
                              (AAA/Linda's brother)

If Linda had purchased the oven for use in her restaurant, it would have been classified as _____.
                                    (equipment/consumer good/inventory)

True-False Questions

1. If a debtor does not repay a loan, a secured party may repossess the collateral. ____

2. A lender perfects a security interest in a negotiable instrument by filing a financing statement. ____

3. Before a security agreement can attach, the debtor must have physical possession of the collateral. ____

4. A purchase-money security interest is created when a bank lends money and the money is used to purchase a car. ____

5. An unperfected security agreement will always have priority over an unsecured creditor. ____

6. If the debtor makes a written request, the secured party must file a termination statement when the debt is repaid. ____

7. The debtor has the right to request the status of the debt or amount owed at any time and the secured party is obligated to fulfill this request. ____

8.   A "proceeds clause" usually is used in inventory financing. ____

9.   Attachment governs rights between competing creditors. ____

10.   A financing statement must be signed by both the debtor and the creditor. ____

Multiple-Choise Questions

1.   When a secured party repossesses collateral and sells it, the proceeds are applied to debts and expenses. which of the following is the correct order of disposition?

      a.   Expenses of the sale, secured party who conducted the sale, debtor, other secured parties
      b.   Expenses of the sale, all secured parties in a ratio of proceeds to debt, debtor
      c.   Secured party who conducted the sale, expenses of the sale, other secured parties, debtor
      d.   Expenses of the sale, secured party who conducted the sale, other secured parties, debtor

2.   Ronald borrows $200,000 from First Bank to finance his shoe factory. Ronald purchases leather to use in manufacturing the shoes. The leather is classified as:

      a.   equipment.
      b.   inventory.
      c.   general intangible.
      d.   consumer goods.

3.   Connie, who operates a retail card shop, borrows $10,000 from State Bank. She uses the money to purchase birthday cars, candles and other items for sale in the shop. Connie signs a security agreement and State Bank files a financing statement which covers inventory, equipment, fixtures and any property later acquired by Connie. Two months later, Connie borrows $5,000 from her father to purchase a computer for use in her business. A security agreement is signed and a financing statement covering the computer is filed. Connie receives the computer five days later.

      a.   Connie's father and State Bank have security interests in the computer.
      b.   Connie's father only has a security interest in the computer.

    c.   State Bank only has a security interest in the computer.

    d.   Neither State Bank nor Connie's father has a security interest in the computer.

4.   In a priority dispute between Connie's father and State Bank over rights in the computer.

    a.   Connie's father has priority because he has a properly perfected security interest.

    b.   The bank has priority because it did not receive notice of the security interest held by Connie's father.

    c.   The bank has priority because it filed first.

    d.   Connie's father has priority because the computer is a consumer good.

5.   Which of the following are necessary for attachment of a security interest?

    a.   The debtor must have rights in the collateral.

    b.   The lender must file a financing statement.

    c.   The lender must have a floating lien.

    d.   The debtor must have physical possession of the collateral.

6.   In order to perfect a purchase-money interest in consumer goods, which of the following is required?

    a.   A financing statement filed with the Secretary of State

    b.   A financing statement filed with the County Clerk

    c.   A pledge

    d.   None of the above; the interest is perfected when the security interest attaches.

7.   If a secured party repossesses equipment collateral and decides to retain possession, which of the following is required?

    a.   Written notice to the debtor unless the debtor waived this right in the security agreement

    b.   Written notice to the debtor and creditors who send written notice of a claim in the collateral

    c.   Written notice to the debtor, unless the debtor waived this right after default, and to creditors who send written notice of a claim in the collateral

    d.   Written notice to the debtor and all creditors

8.   Second Bank as a perfected floating lien on the inventory, equipment, fixtures and accounts of Tim's Sporting Goods. The security agreement contains an after-acquired property clause and a proceeds clause. John, a customer of Tim's, purchases a snowmobile for his personal use in exchange for a sled, $50 day payment and a note of $300. Tim takes a security interest in the snowmobile. Two weeks after the sale, Second Bank has a perfected security interest in which of the following proceeds of the sale to John?

   a.   The sled only
   b.   The sled and the note signed by John
   c.   The sled, the note and the $50
   d.   The sled, the note and the $50, but the security interest is perfected in the $50 only if it is identifiable as the $50 received from John

9.   Tim sells John's note to City Bank, who knew nothing of Second Bank's floating lien. If a priority dispute arises between Second Bank and City Bank over the note, who will prevail?

   a.   Second Bank because it filed first
   b.   Second Bank because the proceeds clause included the note
   c.   City Bank because Second Bank's interest in the note expired
   d.   City Bank because it bought the note without knowledge of Second Bank's interest

10.   Regina borrows $2,000 from her sister and gives her sister a diamond ring to hold as collateral. The sister takes possession of the ring.

   a.   Regina's sister has a perfected security interest in the ring.
   b.   Regina's sister has a security interest in the ring but it is not perfected because no financing statement was filed.
   c.   Regina's sister does not have a security interest in the ring, because Regina did not sign a security agreement.
   d.   Regina's sister has a purchase-money security interest in the ring.

11.   Which of the following are obligations of a secured party?

       a.   The secured party must file a termination statement when the debt is paid, if the debtor requests in writing.
       b.   The secured party must take reasonable care of collateral in its possession.
       c.   The secured party must sell repossessed comsumer goods if the debtor has paid at least 60% of the purchase price.
       d.   All of the above

12.   Which of the following would be classified as inventory?

       a.   Law books owned by West Publishing
       b.   Law books owned by attorney
       c.   Blender owned by a housewife
       d.   Bicycle owned by delivery service

13.   If the sale of repossessed collateral is less than the debt owed, the secured party generally has the right to sue the debtor for the remaining money owed. This is the right to:

       a.   proceeds.
       b.   after-acquired property.
       c.   deficiency judgment.
       d.   redemption.

14.   Susan, a resident of New Mexico, borrows $4,000 from E-Z Finance Co. in order to buy a cash register for her business. A security-agreement is signed and E-Z files a financing statement on July 1, 1988. Susan moves to Texas on October 1, 1988. Assuming that Susan does not use the collateral for a new loan, when does E-Z's security interest expire?

       a.   October 1, 1988
       b.   November 1, 1988
       c.   October 1, 1993
       d.   February 1, 1989

15.   Edna owns and operates an exotic fashion business. The following events occur. On June 15, 1988, Edna discusses a line of credit for $500,000 with City Bank. The bank files a financing statment covering equipment, inventory, proceeds and after-acquired property on June 16, 1988. On June 17, the bank promises to give Edna her line of credit and Edna signs a security agreement.

On June 18, Edna purchases $5,000 of inventory from Safari Supplies. The security agreement attached to the inventory on:

a.   June 15.
b.   June 16.
c.   June 17.
d.   June 18.

16.   On August 1, 1988, Edna buys $5,000 inventory from African Collectibles on credit. Edna signs a security agreement and African files a financing statement. The new inventory is delivered on August 2, 1988. If a priority dispute arises between African Collectibles and City Bank regarding the inventory purchased from African Collectibles:

a.   African Collectibles and City Bank have interests in the inventory but City Bank's interest has priority because it filed first.
b.   African Collectibles and City Bank have interests in the inventory but African Collectible's interest has priority because it is a purchase-money security interest.
c.   City Bank has no interest in the inventory supplied by African Collectibles.
d.   African Collectibles has no security interest because it failed to notify City Bank of its interest.

17.   On September 8, 1988, Cindy purchases an item of inventory supplied by African Collectibles. Who has priority to the item purchased by Cindy?

a.   City Bank
b.   African Collectibles
c.   Edna
d.   Cindy

18.   Which of the following is not a purchase-money security interest?

a.   Washing machine purchased on credit from retailer
b.   Washing machine purchased using proceeds of bank loan
c.   Equipment owned by retailer to secure loan for remodeling
d.   Equipment owned by retailer and purchased under a line of credit

19.   If the collateral is not moved to another jurisdiction a
        financing statement is valid for:

        a.   four months.
        b.   five months.
        c.   five years.
        d.   indefinitely; there is no expiration date.

20.   Which of the following types of collateral would be
        classified as an account:

        a.   A copyright
        b.   A negotiable promissory note
        c.   A written contract promising to pay for services
             rendered
        d.   All of the above

21.   Which of the following will **not** prevail over an
        unperfected secured party?

        a.   Unsecured creditor
        b.   Judgment creditor without a lien
        c.   Judgment creditor with a lien
        d.   None of the above; all will prevail over an
             unperfected secured creditor

22.   Which of the following are required for proper sale of
        repossessed consumer goods?

        a.   Secured party must sell to the highest bidder at a
             public sale.
        b.   Secured party must give notice of the sale to other
             creditors.
        c.   The debtor must receive notice of the sale.
        d.   Secured party must give notice of the sale to the
             debtor unless this right is waived after default.

23.   Tom purchases a bicycle for his delivery service from
        Wheels Unlimited. He pays $50 down and agrees to pay
        $20 per month for ten months. A security agreement is
        filed but no financing statement is filed. Wheels does
        not know that First Bank has a perfected floating lien
        on all property owned or acquired by Tom.

        a.   Wheels Unlimited's interest in the bicycle has not
             attached and is not perfected.
        b.   Wheels Unlimited's interst in the bicycle has
             attached but it is not perfected.
        c.   Wheels Unlimited's interest in the bicycle has
             attached and is perfected.
        d.   First Bank's interest in the bicycle has attached
             but it is not perfected.

24.   In a priority dispute between Wheels Unlimited and First Bank with regard to the bicycle:

    a. First Bank has priority because it has a perfected security interest in the bank.
    b. Wheels Unlimited has priority because the bike is a consumer good.
    c. Wheels Unlimited has priority because it has a perfected security interest.
    d. First Bank has priority because Wheels Unlimited's security interest did not attach to the bicycle.

25.   Tom also owes money to his attorney, who filed suit against Tom. The attorney prevailed and has levied a lien on Tom's bicycle and other assets of the delivery business. Between Wheels Unlimited and the attorney, who will prevail?

    a. The attorney, because Wheels Unlimited's security interest did not attach to the bicycle
    b. The attorney, because Wheels Unlimited's security interest in the bicycle was not perfected.
    c. Wheels Unlimited because the attorney is an unsecured creditor.
    d. Wheels Unlimited if its interest attached before the attorney's interest attached.

Answers to Study Questions

Fill-in-the-Blank Questions

The oven is classified as a consumer good because Linda is going to use the oven for personal use; the use by the debtor is the deciding factor. AAA does not have a perfected security interest. This is a purchase-money transaction in consumer goods; no filing is necessary. Linda's brother has priority. A consumer-to-consumer transaction in used goods cuts off the interest of the secured party unless a financing statement has been recorded. If Linda has purchased the oven for use in a restaurant, it would have been classified as equipment.

True-False Questions

1.   T.

2.   F.   Perfection can be accomplished only by possession.

3.   F.   The debtor must have rights in the collateral; physical possession is not necessary.

4.   T.

5.   F. A judgment creditor with a lien will prevail over an unperfected secured party.

6.   T.

7.   T.

8.   T.

9.   F. Attachment governs the rights between the debtor and the creditor; perfection governs the rights between third parties.

10.   F. It need only be signed by the debtor.

Multiple-Choice Questions

1.	d	11.	d	21.	b
2.	b	12.	a	22.	d
3.	a	13.	c	23.	b
4.	a	14.	d	24.	a
5.	a	15.	d	25.	b
6.	d	16.	b		
7.	c	17.	d		
8.	d	18.	c		
9.	d	19.	c		
10.	a	20.	c		

Chapter 20   Creditors' Rights and Bankruptcy

General Principles

Not all creditors are secured parties within the scope of Article 9 of the Uniform Commercial Code. However, these creditors are not without remedies. State law outlines the procedures to be followed in collecting a debt. Many states give priority to claims by laborers and contractors. The debtor is also protected by homestead laws; certain assets are exempt from seizure by most creditors. Keep in mind that the law tries to strike a balance between the rights of creditors and protection of debtors.

Bankruptcy is an available form of relief for over-extended debtors. In a typical straight bankruptcy, the assets of the debtor are gathered and distributed to the creditors. Other forms of bankruptcy attempt to establish a plan under which the debtor can continue in business and pay all or part of the money owed. Note that certain debts are given priority in payment and that some debts must be paid regardless of bankruptcy.

Chapter Summary

I.   Laws Assisting Creditors

    A.   Mechanic's Lien on Real Property--Aids creditors who furnish labor and materials used in improving real estate. The typical claimant is a contractor. State law determines the procedure for establishing the lien.

B. <u>Artisan's Lien on Personal Property</u>--Similar to a mechanic's lien but aids creditors who furnish labor and materials used in improving personal property. An auto mechanic would qualify for the lien. The creditor must also prove that the work was to be performed on a cash basis. The creditor must retain possession of the property unless there is an agreement with the debtor to return the property. In most states, the property can be sold to satisfy the debt.

C. <u>Innkeeper's Lien on Personal Property</u>--Similar to an artisan's lien. A hotel or motel operator has a lien on the luggage of the guest to pay for room charges. Also a possessory lien.

D. <u>Writ of Execution</u>--Issued by a court <u>after</u> a creditor has sued the debtor and obtained a judgment against him or her. The writ directs the sheriff to seize property of the debtor and sell it to satisfy the debt. The sale must be public. Certain assets of the debtor are not available to be sold (see Homestead Exemption below).

E. <u>Attachment</u>--A <u>pre-judgment</u> remedy designed to keep the debtor from moving property out of reach of the creditor. The creditor must sign a sworn statement that the debt is owed and must post a bond for the value of the property and any loss to the debtor. The writ directs the sheriff to seize the property and hold it until a judgment is reached. If the creditor prevails, the property may be sold to satisfy the debt.

F. <u>Garnishment</u>--<u>After</u> judgment for the creditor, the court orders a third party in possession of the debtor's assets to pay the creditor. The third party or garnishee is usually the debtor's employer or his bank. State laws vary but usually there is a limit to the amount of wages that can be garnished.

G. <u>Composition of Creditors</u>--A kind of informal bankruptcy where the creditors agree to take less money than is owed and the debt is extinguished. Even though the debtor is not providing consideraton (see Chapter 8), the agreement is enforceable.

H. <u>Suretyship and Guaranty</u>--In both situations, a third party agrees to become responsible for another's debt. The contract is between the creditor and the third party.

(1) <u>Primary v. Secondary Liability</u>--A strict surety is a co-signer and is primarily responsible. The creditor can sue either the debtor or the surety as soon as the debt becomes due. A guarantor is secondarily liable and under the terms of the agreement, the creditor must try to collect the money owed from the debtor before proceeding against the guarantor. The agreement between the guarantor and the creditor must be written unless the guarantor's main purpose in making the agreement was personal gain. Review the discussion in Chapter 10.

(2) <u>Defenses of the Surety and the Guarantor</u>--The surety or guarantor promises to be responsible for the debtor only on the conditions outlined in the original agreement. If the creditor and debtor make significant changes in the original contract, the third party is discharged. Almost all defenses that the debtor could use against the creditor are available to the surety or guarantor. "Personal" defenses of the debtor such as incapacity and bankruptcy cannot be claimed by the surety. If the surety has a personal defense, the promise to pay debt may be cancelled.

(3) <u>Rights of the Surety and Guarantor</u>--These rights come into effect <u>after</u> the surety or guarantor has paid the creditor.

   (a) <u>Subrogation</u>--When the surety pays the creditor, then the surety steps into the creditor's shoes and can sue the debtor. Any rights in the original contract which were given to the creditor can now be enforced by the surety.

   (b) <u>Reimbursement</u>--The surety is allowed to proceed against the debtor for any payment of the debt or expenses in connection with the debt.

   (c) <u>Contribution</u>--Applies only when there is more than one guarantor or surety. If one surety pays more than his or her fair share, suit may be brought against the other guarantors to recover the amount of excess.

I.   <u>Foreclosure</u>--Applies to creditors who have a mortgage on the debtor's property to guarantee repayment. Once the creditor proves that a judgment is owing, the property can be sold (usually at a public sale) to satisfy the debt. If the proceeds of the sale are insufficient to satisfy the debt, the creditor can bring suit to collect the remaining amount (deficiency judgment). If the proceeds of the sale are more than the amount owed, the excess after deduction for expenses is returned to the debtor.

II.   <u>Debtor's Rights and Consumer Protection Laws</u>

A.   <u>State Exemption Laws (Homestead Laws)</u>--As mentioned earlier, certain property of the debtor cannot be seized to satisfy debts. The law varies from state to state but the family home, household furniture, clothing, and a car are usually protected from seizure. The law may also cover a limited number of livestock and pets.

B.   <u>Consumer Credit Protection Act (CCPA)</u>--A federal law which applies to consumer loans. The CCPA requires that credit terms be fully explained.

C.   <u>Uniform Consumer Credit Code (UCCC)</u>--A uniform law which has been proposed for adoption in every state. Only a few states have adopted it. Attempts to establish maximum interest rates and garnishment amounts. The most widely-accepted provision allows consumers to cancel a contract from a door-to-door salesman within three days of the sale.

D.   <u>FTC Rule</u>--Discussed in Chapter 17, this rule applies to consumer credit contracts. Anyone who buys a consumer credit note is subject to all defenses that the consumer could raise against the original seller. In short, there are no holders in due course of a consumer credit note.

III. <u>Bankruptcy - Chapter 7 Liquidations</u>--As stated earlier, bankruptcies fall into two classes: liquidation and reorganization. In a liquidation bankruptcy, the debtor's assets are gathered and distributed to the creditors by a trustee.

A.   <u>Preliminary Procedures</u>--The bankruptcy case begins with the filing of a petition.

(1) Voluntary Bankruptcy--Petition is filed by the debtor. Must file a list of all creditors, their addresses and amounts owed, a list of property owned by the debtor, including property claimed to be exempt, and a list of current income and expenses.

(2) Involuntary Bankruptcy--Creditors can "force" a debtor into bankruptcy only if the following conditions are met. There are penalties for frivilous filings.

  (a) If the debtor has more than twelve unsecured creditors, three or more unsecured creditors with a combined claim of $5,000 may file if (b) is also met. If the debtor has fewer than twelve unsecured creditors, any one creditor who is owed $5,000 may file.

  (b) The creditors must also prove that the debtor is insolvent--not paying debts as they become due or that a receiver has taken possession of part of the debtor's property within 120 days of the petition.

B. Automatic Stay

(1) Voluntary Bankruptcy--If the petition is proper and the required documents are filed, creditors are stayed (prevented) from taking any action to enforce collection of the debt. This includes filing suit, perfecting most liens, and repossession. The time begins to run from the filing of the petition, not from when the creditor learns of the bankruptcy.

(2) Involuntary Bankruptcy--The debtor remains in possession of the property until a hearing is held and it is determined that the filing was proper.

(3) Relief from the Stay--If a secured creditor can prove that the collateral for his debt is declining in value or that he or she is otherwise in danger of losing his security for repayment, the court can order relief. This may be in the form of a monthly payment equal in decline to the value of the property, a lien on other property of the debtor, or a guaranty by a solvent third party.

(4) Appointment of Trustee and Creditors' Meeting--Shortly after the stay is granted (ten to thirty days, unless extended), the creditors meet to examine the debtor and to elect a trustee to take charge of the debtor's affairs.

C. Property of the Estate--All of the assets owned by the debtor at the time the petition is filed are the "property of the estate". The estate also includes income from producing property (e.g. rents), gifts, inheritances and divorce settlements acquired within 180 days after the petition is filed. The debtor can then exempt certain property and the rest is disbursed to the creditors.

Exemptions--The debtor may choose the state or federal exemption laws. This property does not become a part of the estate. Note that if the debtor chooses to exempt property with a lien on it, the debtor must pay off the lien. The federal exemptions include most household items up to a limited dollar amount and equity in cars and the family home.

D. Trustee's Powers--The trustee, whether appointed by the court or elected by the unsecured creditors, has the duty to gather the debtor's assets and to distribute them to the debtors. A creditor's claim stands unless challenged. In order to provide for a fair distribution, the trustee can avoid unfair payments to one creditor.

(1) Lien Creditor Status--The trustee is given the rights of a creditor who has obtained a judgment against the debtor. This gives the trustee the power to collect property for the estate which is subject to an unperfected security interest (review Chapter 19). The trustee also has the powers of a purchaser of real estate and may defeat an unperfected security interest in fixtures.

(2) Debtor Status--The trustee may also step into the debtor's shoes and rescind any contract made on the basis of duress, fraud, incapacity, or other defense available to the debtor. The property recovered is placed in the estate.

(3) <u>Voidable Preferences</u>--Bankruptcy attempts to treat creditors equally and any payment made to one creditor in preference to others may be avoided. However, the following requirements must be met.

    (a) Transfer while debtor was insolvent (ninety days before petition, one year to insider).

    (b) To pay an antecedent (pre-existing) debt.

    (c) Creditor must receive more than he or she would have under Chapter 7 liquidation.

    <u>Exceptions</u>--Debts in the ordinary course of business (e.g., utility bills) and payments by consumer debtors of less than $600.

(4) <u>Fraudulent Transfers</u>--Trustee can rescind transfers made within one year of filing if the purpose of the transfer was to injure creditors. Applies even if some money was paid for the property transferred if the consideration was not reasonably equivalent and the transfer left the debtor insolvent.

(5) <u>Liens</u>--Trustee can avoid some mortgages, mechanic's and landlord's liens. Also any unperfected liens may be avoided and the creditor becomes an unsecured creditor.

E.   <u>Property Distribution</u>--Property is distributed in the order below. Each class must be paid fully before anyone in the next class receives payment. Note the elevated status of a <u>secured</u> creditor.

(1) <u>Secured Creditor</u>--Within a short time after filing, the debtor must tell the trustee how he or she intends to deal with secured collateral. If the debtor decides to claim the property as exempt, the debtor must pay the <u>value</u> of the collateral to the secured party. If the debtor abandons the property, the secured party may accept the property in payment of the debt or sell it and keep the proceeds necessary to satisfy the debt and expenses of the sale. If the proceeds are insufficient to pay the debt, the lender becomes an unsecured creditor for the amount remaining. Any excess proceeds are gathered into the estate.

(2) Expenses--Must be connected with the bankruptcy. Includes court costs, reasonable trustee and attorney's fees.

(3) Interim Creditors in Involuntary Case--When creditors file an involuntary bankruptcy, there is a lapse of time between the filing and the stay. Any creditor who provides services or goods to the debtor in this interval is entitled to priority if the debt was incurred in the ordinary course of the debtor's business.

(4) Employee Claims--Salaries and commissions earned within ninety days of the filing; limited to $2,000 per person. Then contributions to employee benefit plans within 180 days of filing; limited to $2,000 times the number of employees. Excess claims are treated as unsecured debts.

(5) Agricultural Claims--Farmers and fishermen have claims of $2,000 each against debtors who operate storage or processing facilities.

(6) Customers of the Debtor--Customers of the debtor who have deposited money with the debtor for the purchase or lease of property or services can claim priority limited to $900; e.g., a customer who has paid for a year of janitorial service and the service declares bankruptcy.

(7) Taxes and Penalties--Must be owed to the state, local, or federal government. Time limits vary on the type of taxes.

(8) Unsecured Creditors--Includes all creditors without collateral and any excess amounts from priority claims.

Items 2-7 are designated as priority claims.

F. Discharge--A discharge is granted when the distribution by the trustee is approved by the court. Most debts are cancelled at the time of discharge. Some debts are automatically non-dischargeable; bad faith actions on the part of the debtor may void other discharges and the debtor can agree to repay discharged debts.

(1) Exceptions to Discharge

    (a) Back taxes for three years prior to filing

    (b) Claims based on false representations of the debtor

    (c) Unscheduled claims (not listed by the debtor)

    (d) Fraud or misuse of funds by debtor in a position of trust (e.g., trustee), theft

    (e) Alimony and child support

    (f) Damages for intentional torts

    (g) Certain student loans unless hardship is proved

    (h) Luxury goods purchased within forty days of filing, more than $500 to a single creditor

    (i) Consumer credit advances within twenty days of petition if more than $1,000 under an unlimited line of credit

    (j) Judgments or settlements reached in connection

(2) Objections to Discharge--Based primarily on bad conduct of the debtor. The debtor can always execute a written waiver. The assets of the estate are distributed but the debtor remains liable for any existing debts.

    (a) Concealment/destruction of property with intent to harm creditors

    (b) Fraudulent tampering with records, including failure to keep records or explain loss of assets

    (c) Refusal to obey an order of the court

    (d) Previous discharge in bankruptcy within last six years

(3) <u>Revocation</u>--Bankruptcy court can revoke discharge if it finds that debtor was dishonest in the bankruptcy proceedings. One year time limit.

(4) <u>Reaffirmation Agreement</u>--A promise by the debtor to pay a debt that would have been discharged (that need not be paid). A debtor may choose to repay a supplier or someone whose help will be needed in the future.

<u>Requirements</u>--Must be signed before discharge. If the debtor has an attorney, the attorney must file an affidavit stating that the consequences of the agreement have been explained, the agreement is voluntary, and no hardship will result. If the debtor has no attorney, the court must find that the agreement is in the debtor's best interest and that no hardship will result. The debtor has a right to rescind before discharge or within sixty days of the agreement; the right to rescission must be stated in the reaffirmation agreement.

IV.   <u>Reorganizations-Chapter 11</u>--Designed to rehabilitate the debtor's business. Eligibility requirements the same as Chapter 7 except that railroads may also file. Only differences from Chapter 7 are noted here.

A.   <u>Trustee</u>--Debtor stays in possession of the estate unless mismanagement is shown.

B.   <u>Plan</u>--Debtor is given the exclusive right for 120 days to file a workable plan of rehabilitation. After 180 days, the creditors may also submit proposed plans. The creditors form committees to represent their interests. Any order of the court must be with their approval or after a hearing.

<u>Requirements</u>--Must be workable or the creditors can convert it to a Chapter 7. The plan must designate classes of creditors and all creditors <u>within</u> a class must be treated equally. It is <u>not</u> necessary that all classes be treated equally as long as the plan is "fair and equitable" and "in the best interest of the creditors".

<u>Acceptance and Confirmation</u>--The creditors are allowed vote by class on the plan. A class is presumed to accept if the entire debt will be

repaid. In other cases, a class accepts the plan if one-half of the number of the creditors, who hold two-thirds of the amount of the claims, approve.

Cram-Down--The court can confirm the plan as long as <u>one</u> class has accepted the plan if the plan is fair and equitable. Fair and equitable means that each class must be treated the same or better than the classes below it. This is sometimes called the "cram-down" provision. The plan is crammed down the throats of the creditors at the bottom of the line if some class above accepts the plan.

V.   <u>Reorganizations-Chapter 13</u>--Also called "Adjustment of Debts for Wage Earners"

A.   <u>Eligibility</u>--Individuals only. Must have a regular income because payment is expected. Salary, commissions, alimony, pensions, and welfare will qualify. Debt limits of $350,000 secured debts and $100,000 unsecured debts.

B.   <u>Preliminary Procedures</u>--Voluntary petition only. Automatic stay will not apply to co-debtors if creditor requests lift of stay and debtor does not object.

C.   <u>Plan</u>--The debtor must turn over some earnings to the trustee to provide for payment. Must provide for cash payment of all priority claims, even if on deferred basis. Provide for same treatment of creditors within a plan. Three year limit unless extended by the court to five years.

D.   <u>Confirmation</u>--The creditors do not vote. Different tests for secured and unsecured creditors.

(1)   <u>Secured</u>--Will be confirmed if the secured party accepts or the debtor surrenders the property or if secured party retains lien and will receive payment or property equal to the present value of the collateral.

(2)   <u>Unsecured</u>--Will be confirmed if creditor will receive property equal to the value of the claim <u>or</u> all the debtor's disposable income is turned over to the trustee for a period of three years. Disposable income is money in excess of reasonable living expenses of the debtor and reasonable business expenses.

E.   Discharge--Not granted until all payments have been made under the plan or a "hardship" is found. In order to qualify for a hardship discharge, the events preventing repayment must be beyond control of the debtor. Only alimony, child support and priority claims remain after discharge.

VI. Reorganizations-Chapter 12--Designed to rehabilitate farmers whose debts exceeded Chapter 13 limits.

A.   Eligibility--Individual, partnership or closely held corporation if 50 percent of income is made from farming and 80 percent of debts are farm related. Total debt limit $1.5 million.

B.   Plan--Same procedure as Chapter 13.

Study Questions

Fill-in-the-Blank Questions

Kleen Products, Inc. is a vacuum cleaner retailer and repair shop. It has been experiencing financial difficulties and is contemplating filing for bankruptcy. Among other debts, Kleen owes $5,000 to Hoover for inventory under a security agreement, back wages for two employees in the amount of $7,500 and $10,000 to numerous unsecured creditors including the local newspaper and an office supply company.

If Kleen wishes to rehabilitate the business, it should file a Chapter _____ bankruptcy.
        (7/11/13)

If Kleen wishes to liquidate the business, it should file a Chapter _____ bankruptcy.
        (7/11/13)

The _____ is(are) entitled to a priority claim. (newspaper/employees)

In a Chapter 7 proceeding, the office supply company will be paid _____ Hoover is paid.
     (before/after)

True-False Questions

1.   An innkeeper's lien is a possessory lien. ____

2.   A composition of creditors is created during bankruptcy proceedings. ____

3.   The right of one surety to recover against a co-surety is reimbursement. ____

4.   The UCCC is a federal law. ____

5.   In a Chapter 13 bankruptcy, creditors can file an involuntary petition against a debtor. ____

6.   A trustee in bankruptcy can disaffirm any contract made by the debtor. ____

7.   The maximum amount of allowable debt in a Chapter 12 bankruptcy is $350,000. ____

8.   The automatic stay does not apply to secured creditors. ____

9.   Attachment is a creditor's right to sell the debtor's property if a legal judgment is not satisfied. ____

10. In a Chapter 13 bankruptcy, a discharge is granted after a plan is confirmed. ____

Multiple-Choice Questions

1.   Which of the following is a priority claim in bankruptcy?

     a.   Lien creditor
     b.   Child support
     c.   "Gap" creditor
     d.   Unsecured creditor

2.   Jerry the carpenter painted Mr. Jones' house and Mr. Jones now refuses to pay. Which of the following remedies should Jerry seek?

     a.   Artisan's lien
     b.   Mechanic's lien
     c.   Priority lien
     d.   Guarantee

3.   Robert, age sixteen, is buying his first car. The bank has agreed to lend the money to Robert only if his brother co-signs the loan. Robert's brother is a(n):

a.   surety.
b.   guarantor.
c.   artisan.
d.   none of the above.

4.   If Robert does not pay the loan and his brother pays it for him, Robert's brother:

a.   has a right of subrogation and can sue Robert.
b.   has a right of subrogation but cannot sue Robert.
c.   has a right of contribution and can sue Robert.
d.   has a right of contribution but cannot sue Robert.

5.   Which of the following defenses could be raised successfully by Robert's brother?

a.   The bank did not sue Robert before asking for payment from Robert's brother.
b.   Robert is a minor and the contract is voidable.
c.   Robert's brother has received a discharge in bankruptcy.
d.   Robert has received a discharge in bankruptcy.

6.   Which of the following debts would be non-dischargeable in a Chapter 7 bankruptcy proceeding?

a.   Credit card bill from MasterCard
b.   Telephone bill
c.   Mink stole charged one month before declaring bankruptcy
d.   Auto loan where the automobile was declared exempt

7.   Which of the following statements regarding a reaffirmation agreement is <u>false</u>?

a.   The agreement must be signed before a discharge is granted.
b.   The agreement must be approved by the court if the debtor has no attorney.
c.   The agreement can be rescinded by the debtor for up to one year after the discharge.
d.   The right to rescind must be stated in the agreement.

Questions 8-10 are based on the following facts.

Reader's Mecca, a local bookstore owned by Bill Blake, files for Chapter 11 Bankruptcy on March 1, 1988. On February 14, Bill sold the store's computer to his brother for $200. On February 20, Bill transferred $400 to his magazine supplier in payment for magazines delivered in January. Bill's attorney has proposed the following plan: Bill's unsecured creditors are divided into four classes: (1) inventory creditors with debt greater than $5,000; (2) inventory creditors with debt less than $5,000; (3) equipment creditors; and, (4) all other creditors.

8. The sale of the computer to Bill's brother is:

   a. a voidable preference and the trustee can recover the computer.
   b. a voidable preference but the trustee cannot recover the computer.
   c. a fraudulent transfer and the trustee can recover the computer.
   d. a fraudulent transfer and the trustee cannot recover the computer.

9. If the plan is fair and equitable, the plan will be approved if:

   a. all the unsecured creditors accept the plan.
   b. one class of unsecured creditors accepts the plan.
   c. three classes of unsecured creditors accept the plan.
   d. the judge approves the plan and no creditors accept the plan.

10. Assume that all creditors in the magazine supplier's class receive nothing under the plan. The payment of $400 to the magazine supplier is:

    a. a voidable preference and the trustee can recover the $400.
    b. a voidable preference but the trustee cannot recover the $400.
    c. a fraudulent transfer and the trustee can recover the $400.
    d. legitimate and the trustee cannot recover the $400.

11. Which of the following would not be an acceptable payment under the plan:

    a. Class 1 receives payment of 40 percent of its debts paid and Class 2, 3, and 4 get nothing.
    b. Class 1 receives payment of 40 percent of its debts, Class 2 receives 50 percent and Classes 3 and 4 receive nothing.
    c. Class 1 receives 40 percent payment of its debt, Class 2 receives 30 percent and Classes 3 and 4 receive 30 percent.
    d. Classes 1, 2, 3, & 4 receive 40 percent payment.

12.   Rob owes Cindy $300. He refuses to pay although he has
       $4,000 in a savings account. If Cindy wants to satisfy
       her debt from the money in the account, she should file
       an action for:

       a.   attachment.
       b.   execution.
       c.   garnishment.
       d.   subrogation.

13.   Cindy decides to sue Rob. However, she is worried that
       Rob may move his assets to another state. She should
       file an action for:

       a.   attachment.
       b.   execution.
       c.   garnishment.
       d.   subrogation.

14.   In a Chapter 13 bankruptcy, the plan filed by the debtor
       will be accepted if:

       a.   the creditors vote to approve the plan.
       b.   secured creditors receive payment for all debts and
             unsecured creditors receive payment from the
             debtor's disposable income.
       c.   secured creditors receive the value of their
             collateral and unsecured creditors receive payment
             from the debtor's disposable income.
       d.   the secured and the unsecured creditors vote to
             approve the plan.

15.   Which of the following debtors are eligible for a
       Chapter 12 bankruptcy?

       a.   Debtor is an individual, 50 percent of income is
             made from farming and 50 percent of debts are farm
             related
       b.   Debtor is a partnership, 50 percent of income is
             made from farming and 50 percent of debts are farm
             related
       c.   Debtor is a partnership, 50 percent of income is
             made from farming and 80 percent of the debts are
             farm related
       d.   Debtor is a close corporation and 80 percent of
             income is made from farming and 80 percent of debts
             are farm related

16.   The law which protects certain assets from seizure by
        creditors is:

        a.   CCPA.
        b.   FTC Rule.
        c.   execution.
        d.   exemption.

17.   Peter has a $12,000 car loan with First Bank. The bank
        has a perfected security interest in the car. Peter
        declares bankruptcy. At the time of the bankruptcy, he
        owes $8,000 to the bank but the car has a value of
        $4,500. If the bank sells the car for $4,000:

        a.   the debt is extinguished and the bank suffers a
             loss of $4,000.
        b.   the bank remains a secured creditor for $4,000 plus
             the expenses of the sale.
        c.   the bank remains an unsecured creditor for $4,000
             plus the expenses of the sale.
        d.   the bank remains an unsecured creditor for $500
             plus the expenses of the sale.

18.   Which of the following is proper grounds for denying a
        discharge in a Chapter 7 bankruptcy?

        a.   The debtor waived the right to a discharge.
        b.   The debtor disobeyed an order of the bankruptcy
             court.
        c.   The debtor failed to explain adequately a loss of
             $50,000.
        d.   All of the above

19.   Cynthia has two secured creditors (house and car) and 5
        unsecured credit cards (charge accounts). Her total
        debt is $300,000. She owes $8,700 to unsecured
        creditors, including $5,600 to Mastercard. If Cindy is
        behind in her payments:

        a.   Mastercard can file for an involuntary bankruptcy
             under Chapter 7.
        b.   the bank which has a mortgage on Cindy's house can
             file for involuntary bankruptcy under Chapter 7.
        c.   the bank which has a valid security interest in
             Cindy's car can file for involuntary bankruptcy
             under Chapter 7.
        d.   All of the above; any of the creditors can file.

20.   Which of the following would be entitled to an artisan's lien?

a.   Stereo repair shop
b.   Mortgage company
c.   Newspaper carrier
d.   Credit card company

21.   The right of a mortgage company to sell a house held as collateral is:

a.   garnishment.
b.   foreclusure.
c.   execution.
d.   attachment.

22.   Which of the following bankruptcy procedures is in correct chronological order:

a.   Petition, automatic stay, discharge, reaffirmation agreement
b.   Petition, discharge, automatic stay, reaffirmation agreement
c.   Petition, reaffirmation agreement, automatic stay, discharge
d.   Petition, automatic stay, reaffirmation agreement, discharge

23.   Which of the following would not be part of a debtor's estate in Chapter 7 bankruptcy?

a.   Paycheck received the day before filing
b.   Paycheck received the day after filing
c.   Inheritance from an aunt who died the day before filing
d.   Income from debtor's rental property received the day after filing

24.   Which of the following laws are designed to help debtors?

a.   UCCC
b.   FTC rule
c.   Exemption
d.   All of the above

25.   Which of the following is a voidable preference?

        a.   Cash payment for new stereo purchased for cash by
                debtor one month before bankruptcy
        b.   Payment of previous month's electric bill
        c.   Payment of $500 by consumer on MasterCard account
                one month before bankruptcy
        d.   Payment of $500 account payable by corporation one
                month before bankruptcy

Answers to Study Questions

Fill-in-the-Blank Questions

If Kleen, Inc. wishes to rehabilitate the business, it should
file a Chapter 11 bankruptcy.   Chapter 7 is a liquidation
bankruptcy.   Chapter 13 is a reorganization bankruptcy but it
is only available to individuals and Kleen, Inc. does not
qualify.   The employees are entitled to a priority of $2,000
per employee or $4,000.   The newspaper is an unsecured
creditor.   In a Chapter 7 proceeding, Hoover, a secured
creditor, will redeem its collateral before unsecured creditors
are paid.

True-False Questions

1.   T.

2.   F.   A composition of creditors is an informal agreement
        between creditors.   A creditors' committee is formed
        during bankruptcy.

3.   F.   The right of one surety to recover against another
        surety is contribution.   Reimbursement is the surety's
        right to recover against the debtor.

4.   F.   It is a uniform law which has been adopted in a few
        states.

5.   F.   Only the debtor can file for Chapter 13 protection.

6.   F.   The trustee can disaffirm any contract which the
        debtor would have the right to disaffirm, e.g., contract
        based on fraud or undue influence.

7.   F.   It is $1.5 million.

8.   F.

9.   F. Attachment is a pre-judgment remedy.

10.   F. A discharge is granted after the plan is completed
       by the debtor.

Multiple-Choice Questions

1.	c	11.	b	21.	b
2.	b	12.	c	22.	d
3.	a	13.	a	23.	b
4.	c	14.	c	24.	d
5.	c	15.	c	25.	d
6.	c	16.	d		
7.	c	17.	d		
8.	c	18.	d		
9.	b	19.	a		
10.	a	20.	a		

UNIT IV
BUSINESS ORGANIZATIONS

Chapter 21   The Entrepreneur

General Principles

An entrepreneur is one who undertakes to start and manage a new business. The business can take many forms. The four basic forms of business listed from simplest to most complex are the sole proprietorship, the general partnership, the limited partnership, and the corporation. As a general rule, the simpler the business, the greater the risk to the participants. As the form of business becomes more complex, operating costs and regulations increase. These costs are offset by a reduced liability if the business fails.

The forms of business listed above are only the starting point. The business can contract with other businesses to operate under a syndicate, business trust, or joint stock company. In these cases, the form of the business and the agreement will determine the rights and responsibilities of the parties.

Chapter Outline

I.   Types of Business Organizations

    A.   Sole Proprietorship--No formal mechanism required to create. Usually small businesses, owner(s) take all risks but keep all profits. Owner(s) determine management and are personally liable for business debts. Business dissolves if all owners change.

    B.   General Partnership--No formal mechanism required to create but there must be an agreement, express or implied, to carry on business for a profit. Partners share profits, losses and management rights. The personal assets of each partner are liable for partnership debts. Partnership dissolves if a partner changes (death, withdrawal, etc.) If no express agreement, rules of the Uniform Partnership Act (UPA) control operation.

C.   Limited Partnership--Creation according to statute only, usually filing with the Secretary of State is required. Must be at least one limited and one general partner. Limited partner has liability only to the extent of his or her investment. State law controls operation. Most states have adopted either Uniform Limited Partnership Act (ULPA) or its revised edition (RULPA).

D.   Corporation--Formal mechanism, usually filing with the Secretary of State is required to create. Shareholders (owners) have limited liability. General management is performed by a board of directors; officers perform day-to-day operations. Will not dissolve if shareholders die or change (perpetual existence).

E.   Joint Venture--Basically a partnership formed for completion of one project. Participants share profits and losses but in contrast to a partnership, may not have the power to act for each other.

F.   Syndicate--Similar to a joint venture, in that it is usually formed for the completion of one project. Formal ownership may take any form (corporation, partnership, etc.)

G.   Joint Stock Company--No formal mechanism needed to create. Combination of partnership and corporation. Corporate aspects include directors and officers, shareholder's ability to transfer shares and perpetual existence. Members do not have the power to act for the company and each other. Partnership aspects include personal liability of members and property ownership in member's names.

H.   Business Trust--Formal mechanism in the form of a trust agreement where business assets are held in the name of trustee. The owners are beneficiaries. The trustee, not the beneficiaries, has management powers.

I.   Cooperative--Non-profit association designed to provide or receive a service. Can be incorporated (treated as a non-profit corporation) or unincorporated (treated as a partnership). Used primarily to gain greater purchasing or selling power by pooling resources.

II. Comparison of Business Organizations

A.   Liability of Owners--Sole proprietors and general partners are individualy liable for business debts. Corporate shareholders and limited partners are liable only for the amount invested.

B.   Need for Capital--Generally partnerships and corporations are able to raise capital by encouraging investment, but control over the business decreases as the number of owners increases. A sole proprietor retains control but may look only to a lender for funds. A lender may require the shareholders of a small and new corporation to guarantee repayment.

C.   Method of Creation--As noted above, corporations and limited partnerships require formal creation. Sole proprietorships and general partnerships do not.

D.   Legal Entity--A corporation is a separate "legal person" and can sue and be sued in its own name. The owners of the sole proprietorship is the business; no separate legal entity. Most states do not recognize a partnership as a separate entity.

E.   Duration--A partnership and sole proprietorship can be terminated by acts of the members, including death, withdrawal and bankruptcy. A corporation continues in existence regardless of a change in shareholders. In most states, a limited partnership is dissolved only by acts of general partners.

F.   Transferability of Ownership--If a sole proprietor- ship changes hands, the original business ceases to exist. A partner can transfer his or her interest but the assignee does not gain full membership rights. Corporate shareholders can transfer all rights.

G. Management--A sole proprietorship and a general partnership are managed by the owners. A limited partnership is managed by the general partners only. In a corporation, management is separated from ownership. Shareholders (owners) elect directors who provide general management and appoint officers to provide daily administration of the business.

H. Fees and Paperwork--A proprietorship and general partnership pay only fees associated with operation of a business (e.g. license to do business). A general partnership and a corporation pay annual fees and taxes to the state and are required to complete reports.

I. Interstate Business--Because a limited partnership and a corporation are created formally, other states may require a certificate of authority to do business.

J. Taxation--As a general rule, a corporation is a separate legal entity and is treated a such. On the other hand a partnership or sole proprietorship is a channel to the owners and they are taxed directly.

(1) Corporation--Must file a separate federal income tax return. Corporation is taxed on profits when earned and shareholders are taxed when dividends are received. State income tax is also levied against a corporation. Gains, losses and accumulation of earnings are not passed on to the shareholders. Exempt interest received by the corporation is taxed to the shareholders if it is distributed.

Can establish an exempt pension trust for employees; payments are deductible by the corporation. Social security tax applies to employees. Death benefits up to $5,000 tax free to beneficiaries of employees and shareholders.

(2) Partnership--Federal income tax return for information purposes only; the partnership does not pay tax. Partners are taxed on business income even if payment is not distributed. Most states do not levy an income tax against a partnership. Exempt interest flows directly to partner; his or her share is exempt.

Formal pension trust not allowed; partners can file individual retirement plans. Social security tax only for employees who are not partners; partners pay self-employment tax. No exempt death benefits.

III.   Private Franchise--Defined by agreement. The partici-pants may take any form of business organization (e.g. corporation, sole proprietorship). Used generally in national or regional retail businesses.

A.   Parties--The franchisor is a "parent" who owns a trademark, patent or copyright. The franchisor gives the franchisee ("child") a license or permission to use these rights. Legally, the franchisor and the franchisee are separate but the franchise contract may bind the two economically.

B.   Types of Franchises

(1)   Distributorship--The franchisor is a manu-facturer; the franchisee is a retailer or wholesaler. The franchisor gives a license to sell its products to the franchisee.

(2)   Chain-Styles--In addition to the right to sell the franchisor's product, the franchisee generally must maintain standards of operation acceptable to the franchisor. The franchisee may also be required to buy supplies from the franchisor.

(3)   Manufacturing/Plant Agreement--The right to manufacture and to distribute the product is licensed to the franchisee. The franchisee must conduct both aspects of the operation in accordance with the franchisor's standards.

C.   The Franchise Agreement--The primary benefit for the franchisee is name recognition with the parent and an established clientele. The franchisor must be sure that the franchisee conducts business properly. The most common clauses, listed below, are designed to accomplish that purpose.

(1)   Payment--Franchisee usually pays a lump-sum for start-up costs and supplies. Franchisee will also purchase replacement supplies from the franchisor and the franchisor receives a percentage of the profits from the franchisee. Some agreements also require the franchisee to contribute to advertising and administrative costs.

(2) Location and Exclusive Territory--This is determined by the franchisor. The franchisee purchases the right to operate in a particular location; this right may be exclusive or non-exclusive. The franchisor may require the franchisee to purchase or lease a particular location for the business.

(3) Standards of Operation--Varies with each agreement. The franchisor may wish close supervision of employee training, financial management and quality control. As a part of quality control, the franchisor may require that the franchisee purchase supplies from the parent. Price controls are risky because an agreement to set prices is a violation of the antitrust laws; the franchisor may suggest minimum prices.

(4) Termination--Most initial agreements are short-term. Contracts are prepared by the franchisor and usually state that the agreement may be cancelled for any breach of agreement. Courts try to balance the rights of the parties and may imply a reasonable time before cancellation is allowed.

Study Questions

Fill-in-the-Blank Questions

An agreement between two or more persons to carry on a business for profit is a requirement of a _____.
(business trust/partnership)

An incorporated cooperative is treated as a _____
_____ (partnership/
corporation)

In a business trust, the management of the business is conducted by the _____.
(director/trustee/officer/beneficiary)

The owners of a corporation are the _____.
(directors/shareholders)

True-False Questions

1. A corporation must pay federal income tax. ____

2. In order to create a joint venture, the owners must file with the Secretary of State. ____

3. A franchisor may establish the prices at which the franchisee sells its products. ____

4. A limited partner is liable for business debts only up to the amount of his or her investment. ____

5. A corporation is dissolved or terminated when a shareholder sells stock to an outsider. ____

6. Unless otherwise specified, partners share equally in the management of the business. ____

7. A joint stock company is a synonym for a corporation. ____

8. Burger King is an example of a chain-style franchise. ____

9. One disadvantage of a sole proprietorship is the inability to raise capital. ____

10. A limited partnership must have at least one general partner and one limited partner. ____

Multiple-Choice Questions

1. Which of the following forms of business must be created in accordance with a statute?

   a. general partnership
   b. limited partnership
   c. joint venture
   d. sole proprietorship

2. Which of the following are personally liable for the debts of a business organization?

   a. general partner
   b. limited partner
   c. beneficiary
   d. shareholder

3.   Which of the following is <u>not</u> associated with a corporation?

        a. trusteee
        b. director
        c. shareholder
        d. officer

4.   Which of the following forms of a busines is used to complete a single transaction?

        a. joint venture
        b. syndicate
        c. both a & b
        d. neither a nor b

5.   Which of the following is <u>not</u> a characteristic of a general partnership?

        a. creation according to statute
        b. equal management rights of all partners
        c. personal liability for partnership debts
        d. partnership pays separate income tax

6.   Which of the following is an example of a cooperative?

        a. businessmen pooling assets to build a shopping center
        b. consumers pooling assets to buy food at wholesale prices
        c. local outlet of fast-food restaurant
        d. local distributor of farm equipment

7.   Which of the following establishes general management procedures for a corporation?

        a. beneficiaries
        b. officers
        c. shareholders
        d. directors

8.   Which of the following is(are) common clauses in a franchise agreement?

        a. franchisee pays lump-sum for start-up costs.
        b. quality control established by franchisor
        c. supplies purchased from franchisor
        d. all of the above

9. Which of the following is __not__ required to form a partnership?

    a. one or more partners
    b. agreement to share profit and losses
    c. agreement to carry on a business
    d. written partnership agreement

10. Which of the following is __not__ a characteristic of a limited partnership?

    a. at least one limited partner and one general partner
    b. all partners are personally liable for business debts
    c. formal creation according to statute
    d. limited partners cannot participate in management

11. Sam, an entrepreneur, is negotiating a contract with national cosmetics manufacturer, Beautiful You. According to the agreement, Beautiful You will supply the formula and packaging for different products. Sam will purchase a local manufacturing site and will have the right to distribute the cosmetics in a five-state area. Beautiful You will receive 3% of Sam's profits. The agreement between Sam and Beautiful You is a"

    a. manufacturing franchise
    b. chain-style franchise
    c. syndicate
    d. joint venture

12. Beautiful You is a:

    a. director
    b. franchisee
    c. franchisor
    d. beneficiary

13. Sam is a:

    a. general partner
    b. limited partner
    c. franchisor
    d. franchisee

14. Which of the following is a characteristic of a sole proprietorship?

    a. personal liability of the owner for business debts
    b. sole management powers
    c. both a & b
    d. neither a nor b

15.   Which of the following is <u>not</u> a tax characteristic of a corporation?

    a.   corporation pays annual income tax
    b.   shareholders pay taxes on capital gains earned by corporation
    c.   shareholders pay tax when dividends are distributed
    d.   tax-free pension fund may be established

16.   Which of the following forms of busines organizations is most similar to a joint venture?

    a.   corporation
    b.   general partnership
    c.   cooperative
    d.   business trust

17.   Which of the following is a characteristic of a joint stock company?

    a.   equal management rights by all members
    b.   automatically dissolved when members change
    c.   members are personally liable for business debts
    d.   stock is not transferable

18.   Which of the following is a tax aspect of a partnership?

    a.   partners pay tax on profits of a business whether distributed or not
    b.   partnership pays separate income tax
    c.   tax-free pension fund may be established
    d.   partners must pay social security tax

19.   Which of the following is a characteristic of a corporation <u>and</u> of a joint stock company?

    a.   members are personally liable for business debts
    b.   perpetual existence
    c.   all members have equal management rights
    d.   shares are not transferable

20.   In a business trust, management is directed by the:

    a.   director
    b.   beneficiaries
    c.   officers
    d.   trustee

21.   If a general partnership has no formal agreement, which
       of the following will determine the rights of the
       partners?

       a.   RULPA
       b.   ULPA
       c.   UPA
       d.   none of the above, there is no partnership because a
            written agreement is required.

22.   A disadvantage of a sole proprietorship is:

       a.   difficulty in raising capital
       b.   owner determines management
       c.   double taxation
       d.   formal creation by filing required

23.   Which of the following clauses in a franchise agreement
       is most likely to be found illegal?

       a.   franchisor requires franchisee to purchase supplies
            from franchisor
       b.   franchisor requires franchisee to keep minimum
            capital
       c.   franchisor establishes resale price of products
       d.   franchisee given exclusive distributorship

24.   Which of the following forms of business have perpetual
       existence?

       a.   sole proprietorship
       b.   general partnership
       c.   joint stock company
       d.   none of the above

25.   Which of the following is an example of a chain-style
       franchise agreement?

       a.   automobile dealership
       b.   soft-drink bottling plant
       c.   toy manufacturing plant
       d.   fast-food restaurant

Answers to Study Questions

Fill-in-the-Blank Questions

A partnership is an agreement by two or more persons to carry
on a business for a profit. A business trust is a more formal
arrangement where a trustee holds title to assets and manages
the business; the beneficiaries receive the profits.

An incorporated cooperative is treated as a non-profit corporation. An unincorporated cooperative is treated as a partnership.

In a business trust, management is provided by the trustee. Officers and directors manage a corporation. Beneficiaries receive the profits from a business trust but do not participate in management.

True-False Questions

1.   T.

2.   F. Only an implied or express agreement is required.

3.   F. This would be a violation of the antitrust laws. The franchisor may suggest minimum prices.

4.   T.

5.   F. The shares are freely transferable.

6.   T.

7.   F. A joint stock company combines elements of a corporation and a partnership.

8.   T.

9.   T.

10.   T.

Multiple-Choice Questions

1.	b	11.	a	21.	c
2.	a	12.	c	22.	a
3.	a	13.	d	23.	c
4.	c	14.	c	24.	c
5.	a	15.	b	25.	d
6.	b	16.	b		
7.	d	17.	c		
8.	d	18.	a		
9.	d	19.	b		
10.	b	20.	d		

Chapter 22   The Agency

Agency is an agreement between two parties where one person (the agent) agrees to act <u>on behalf of</u> and <u>instead of</u> another (the principal). The relationship between a shop owner and his sales staff is a typical agency relationship. The staff operates on behalf of the owner because all funds received are submitted to the owner. The staff operates instead of the owner when sales are made (i.e. the owner does not have to make all sales in person).

Because the agent works for the principal, there is a trust or <u>fiduciary</u> relationship between the parties. Because the agent deals with third parties in the place of the principal, the principal is held responsible for approved acts of the agent.

Chapter Summary

I.   <u>Types of Agency Relationships</u>--There are three types of agency; the type of agency varies with the amount of control exercised by the principal over the agent. The type of agency may determine the extent of the agent's authority and the principal's responsibility for the agent's acts. It is not the title of the agent that determines his or her status but the nature of the agent's duties.

      A.   <u>Master-Servant</u>--Legal term for employer-employee relationship. Employer has control over details of the employee's work and employee has little or no judgment in manner of work. Employer is responsible for any acts of employee while working. Some duties of an employee may involve agency. EX: restaurant-busboy.

B. Principal-Agent--Employer has less control over details and agent acts in the place of the principal. Principal is responsible for authorized acts of the agent. EX: corporation-officer, manager-sales staff.

C. Employer/Client-Independent Contractor--Employer has little or no control over the details of the contractor's work. Employer is not responsible for acts of the independent contractor. Sometimes difficult to distinguish between an employee and independent contractor; courts will look at factors below. EX: client-attorney; homeowner-contractor

Independent Contractor--A specialist with business apart from client's, uses own tools, paid on a project basis.

Employee--Works only for the employer (second jobs OK), employer provides work space and tools, paid on a salary or commission basis.

II. Formation of Agency Relationships--Voluntary arrangement implied or expressed between the parties. Similar to contract rules with the following exceptions: no formality required, no consideration required, only principal needs contractual capacity.

A. Agency by Agreement--Can be expressed or implied by conduct.

B. Agency by Ratification--Principal consents after the agent has performed. Can be implied if the principal keeps the benefits of the agent's acts.

C. Agency by Estoppel--Representation by the principal that would lead a third party to believe that an agency relationship exists. Acts of the agent alone are insufficient. Principal is prevented or estopped from denying the relationship.

D. Agency by Operation of Law--Exception to the voluntariness standard. The law implies an agency relationship between husband and wife and between partners. Officers are considered agents of a corporation.

III.   Duties of Principal and Agent to Each Other--Based primarily on contractual and fiduciary relationship. Remember that the agent works for the principal.

A.   Duties of the Agent

(1)   Performance--Paid agent has the duty to use ordinary skill based on experience and expertise. Failure to do so is grounds for breach of contract. A non-paid (gratuitous) agent cannot be sued in contract but may be responsible for negligence or misrepresentation.

(2)   Notification--Because the agent acts in the place of the principal, the agent must notify the principal of agency dealings. A third party may assume that notice to the agent is sufficient to notify the principal.

(3)   Loyalty--No self-dealing by agent. Agent cannot represent two principals without the consent of all. Includes confidentiality of agency business.

(4)   Obedience--Agent must obey lawful orders of the principal except in emergency situation. Failure to do so is grounds for breach of contract.

(5)   Accounting--Duty to explain disbursement and receipt of money. No commingling of personal and agency funds. An accounting is also a legal action brought to force agent to explain his or her records.

B.   Duties of Principal to Agent--Based primarily on contract rules.

(1)   Compensation--Unless expressly agreed, the principal has the duty to pay for services rendered by the agent. No duty to gratuitous agent.

(2)   Cooperation--Principal must not interfere with agent's acts if the principal has authorized them. Arises in exclusive dealing arrangements; principal cannot allow competition from other agents in exclusive territory.

(3)   <u>Reimbursement and Indemnification</u>--If agent uses personal funds on authorized agency business, the principal must repay (reimburse) the agent. If the agent is sued by a third party or otherwise suffers a loss in the course of employment, the principal has a duty to stand behind (indemnify) the agent for any loss.

(4)   <u>Safe Working Conditions</u>--Some required by statute, including worker's compensation (employees only). General duty to provide a safe location and equipment.

IV.   <u>Duty to Third Parties</u>--A principal may be responsible for an agent's dealings with third parties. This responsibility is dependent on three factors: the scope of the agent's authority, the cause of action (contract or tort), and disclosure of the agency to the third party.

A.   <u>Scope of Agent's Authority</u>--It may be helpful to look at this problem from a third party's point of view. If the third party can provide authority in <u>any</u> of the ways listed below, the principal will be responsible for the agent's acts. Note also that if the principal is held responsible, he or she may be able to shift the loss to the agent.

(1)   <u>Express Authority</u>--Explicit and stated duties. Can be written or oral. If the agent's duties involve written contracts, then the agent's agreement with the principal must be in writing. This is the equal dignity rule. If the agency agreement is not in writing, the agent has no power to conclude a binding contract and the contract is voidable at the option of the principal. Agent may sue principal for reimbursement.

(2)   <u>Implied Authority</u>--Unstated but customary duties of a person in the agent's position. Includes any power necessary to carry out express duties. Test is whether it is reasonable for the agent to believe that he or she has the authority to do the act. Agent may sue principal for reimbursement.

(3)   <u>Apparent Authority-Estoppel</u>--Similar to rules for creation of an agency discussed above. Based on acts of the <u>principal</u> which would

lead a third party to believe (reasonably) that the agent represented the principal. The acts of the agent do not matter. Usually occurs when the agent has possession of the principal's property. When land is involved, possession alone is not enough, the agent must also have some evidence of ownership such as a deed. Agent may <u>not</u> sue for reimbursement.

(4) <u>Ratification</u>--Occurs after the agent's dealing with a third party (retroactive authority). Although the agent may not have had the express or implied authority to act, the principal accepts the acts of the agent. Third party has the right to withdraw before ratification.

In order for a principal to ratify an act, certain requirements must be met: the principal must know all the facts of the transaction with the third party, the transaction can be ratified completely or not at all (no partial acceptance), principal must have contractural capacity to ratify at the time of the act and at the time of the ratification. In addition, if the equal dignity rule would require a writing, the ratification must be in writing. Agent may sue for reimbursement.

B. <u>Contracts Executed by the Agent</u>--Dependent on disclosure of the agency relationship to third parties.

(1) <u>Disclosed Principal</u>--If the agency relation-ship and the name of the principal are known to the third party, the third party can sue the principal only if the agent's authority is shown. If the third party cannot show that the agent acted with authority, neither the principal nor the agent is responsible.

(2) <u>Partially Disclosed Principal</u>--If the third party has knowledge of the agency relationship but does not know the name of the principal, the same rules apply.

(3)   Undisclosed Principal--If neither the agency relationship nor the name of the principal is known to the third party, the agent is personally responsible. The principal will be liable if the agent acted with authority. The principal, even though unknown to the third party, can hold the third party to the contract unless: (1) contract specifically excludes principal, (2) agent signs a negotiable instrument with agent's name only, or (3) agent's duty is personal and cannot be delegated.

C.   Torts--Agent is always responsible for his or her own torts, but it may be more lucrative to sue the principal. If the principal is held responsible, he or she can sue the agent for indemnification.

(1)   General Rule--The rule of respondeat superior holds that the principal is responsible for acts of the agent performed while the agent was working for the principal (within the scope of the agent's employment). Usually a close question of fact but the courts will look at the following factors: whether the agent is on company or personal business, whether the act (as opposed to the tort) was authorized, whether the agent was using company equipment at the time, whether the employer had reason to know that the agent would do the act, and whether the act had been done before.

(2)   Misrepresentation--Ask if the agent was authorized to make representations (not necessarily misrepresentations). Some courts hold the principal liable if the agent was put in a position to make misrepresentations or if the principal failed to supervise the agent.

(3)   Negligence--Use scope of employment test. A principal is not responsible for the acts of an independent contractor.

(4)   Intentional Torts--Although a principal would never authorize an intentional tort, ask if the act was performed while the agent was within the scope of employment.

(5)   Crimes--Not responsible unless principal is charged under a conspiracy theory.

V.   <u>Termination of the Agency</u>--Distinguish between the power to terminate the agency and the right to do so. Because agency is based on the consent of the parties, either the agent or the principal has the power to terminate at any time. However, if the termination is in breach of the agency agreement, the breaching party has no right to terminate and can be sued for losses sustained by the non-breaching party. The events listed below give a party the <u>right</u> to terminate the agency. Also note the effect of termination on the right of third parties.

A.   <u>Methods of Termination</u>

   (1)   <u>General Rule</u>--If the agency is for a specified period of time, it will lapse if not revived by the parties. The same is true if the agency was designed to accomplish a specific purpose. When the purpose is achieved, the agency ends. The agency agreement can always be rescinded by agreement of the parties.

   (2)   <u>Termination by Operation of Law</u>--Similar to rules for terminating any contract. Death, insanity, or bankruptcy will terminate the agency immediately--notice is not required. (A bank's right to process a customer's checks is an exception to this rule.) The agency can also be terminated by impossibility of performance or commercial impracticability (changed circumstances). If the agent's and principal's countries are at war with each other, the agency is terminated.

   (3)   <u>Irrevocable Agency</u>--An agency created solely for the benefit of the agent normally cannot be revoked if as a part of the agreement, the agent has an interest in the property of the agency. This is an agency coupled with an interest. The most common example is agency property used as collateral for a loan or property transferred to agent for the agent's benefit. Commissions do not suffice; the agent must have some type of ownership interest in the property.

   (4)   <u>Third-Party Notice</u>--None required if the agency terminates by operation of law. If terminated by an act of the parties, the <u>principal</u> has the duty to notify third parties that the agency has terminated. Otherwise, the agent's apparent authority can bind the principal even after the agency has been terminated.

Type of Notice--Any notice to agent is
sufficient unless the agreement was in
writing. If so, must be revoked in writing.
Third parties who have dealt with the agent
are entitled to actual notice. Other third
parties are entitled to "constructive notice",
that is, notice which is likely to reach third
parties. This is usually accomplished by
publication in a newspaper or trade journal.

Study Questions

Fill-in-the-Blank Questions

The Yarn Barn, a needleworks store, is owned by Pearl Cotton.
She hires Cathy Crocket to act as assistant manager. Although
there is no written employment contract, Pearl tells Cathy that
her job is to order inventory, to sell supplies to customers,
and to keep financial and inventory records. While Pearl is
gone to market, the following events occur. Cathy hires
Flossie as a sales clerk. Cathy also orders inventory from
Sewing Supplies and refunds money to a disgruntled customer.

Pearl is the _____.
                    (agent/principal)

Cathy has _____ authority to order inventory.
        (express/implied/apparent)

Cathy has _____ authority to refund a customer's
money.   (express/implied/no)

Cathy has _____ authority to hire Flossie.
                (express/no)

True-False Questions

1.   Agent always has the power to terminate an agency. ____

2.   The equal dignity rule states that an agent has the same
      power to make a contract as the principal does. _____

3.   An agency by estoppel is created by the acts of the
      agent. ____

4.   If an agent makes a contract on behalf of an undisclosed
      principal, only the agent is liable for performance.____

5. When an agency is terminated, the agent must give actual notice to all parties with whom he or she has dealt. ____

6. A principal is generally liable for the torts of an independent contractor. ____

7. A gratuitous agent may not be sued for breach of contract even if he or she fails to perform according to the principal's instructions. ____

8. In an agency by ratification, a third party has the right to withdraw from any contract made by the agent if withdrawal is made before the principal ratifies the agent's acts. ____

9. The relationship between a patient and a doctor is master-servant. ____

10. An agent owes a duty of notification to the principal. ____

Multiple-Choice Questions

1. The authority of a corporate officer to act on behalf of the corporation is an example of an agency formed by:

    a. ratification.
    b. estoppel.
    c. operation of law.
    d. implication.

2. Oliver is hired by Dressman Industries to find and purchase a site for Dressman's new manufacturing plant. Oliver finds a suitable site but purchases it in his brother's name. Oliver has breached:

    a. the duty of obedience.
    b. the duty of loyalty.
    c. the duty of accounting.
    d. no duty.

3. Assuming that Oliver buys the land for Dressman and that he has no written agency agreement with Dressman:

    a. Dressman must honor the contract made by Oliver because Oliver had express authority to make the purchase.
    b. Dressman must honor the contract made by Oliver because Oliver was acting within the scope of his employment.

c.   The contract is voidable at Dressman's option because a principal can always choose whether or not to accept an act of an agent.

d.   The contract is voidable at Dresser's option because of the equal dignity rule.

4.   Bob is a salesman for Microfilm Services, Inc. His territory includes several cities and he drives a company car. Bob is on his way to a customer's office when he causes a car accident with Betty. Betty may sue:

a.   Bob only.
b.   Microfilm Services only.
c.   Bob and Microfilm Service.

5.   Microfilm:

a.   is responsible for Bob's accident because of the doctrine of respondeat superior.

b.   is responsible for Bob's accident because of the doctrine of agency by estoppel.

c.   is not responsible for Bob's accident because of doctrine of respondeat superior.

d.   is not responsible for Bob's accident because of the doctrine of agency by estoppel.

6.   L. Eagle, an attorney, hires Bonnie as his legal assistant. He tells her that her primary duties are to file documents with the clerk's office, to interview witnesses, and to organize documents. L. Eagle also hires Cindy as an assistant for Bonnie. Cindy's job is to make copies of documents and to file incoming mail. The relationship between Eagle and Cindy is:

a.   master-servant.
b.   principal-agent.
c.   employer-independent contractor.
d.   none of the above.

7.   The relationship between Eagle and Bonnie is:

a.   master-servant only.
b.   master-servant and principal-agent depending on which duty Bonnie is performing.
c.   employer-independent contractor only.
d.   principal-agent and employer-independent contractor depending on which duty Bonnie is performing.

8. Bonnie asks Cindy to deliver documents to a client.
    Bonnie has _____ authority to ask Cindy to
    deliver documents.

    a. express
    b. implied
    c. apparent
    d. no

9. When Cindy delivers the documents to the client, the
    client gives Cindy a check made out to Eagle for legal
    services. Cindy cashes the check and moves to Mexico.
    When Eagle discovers what has happended, he demands a
    new check from the client.

    a. Eagle is within his rights because Cindy had no
        actual authority to receive the check.
    b. Eagle is within his rights because Cindy had no
        apparent authority to receive the check.
    c. Eagle is not within his rights because Cindy had
        express authority to receive the check.
    d. Eagle is not within his rights because Cindy had
        apparent authority to receive the check.

10. After working for Eagle for two years, Bonnie takes a
    new job with Abel Advocate, another attorney. While at
    a former client's office, Bonnie picks up a check meant
    for Eagle. Bonnie joins Cindy in Mexico. Eagle again
    demands that the client write a second check.

    a. Eagle is within his rights because Bonnie's
        authority terminated when she went to work for Abel.
    b. Eagle is within his rights because Bonnie should
        have notified the client that she no longer worked
        for Eagle.
    c. Eagle is not within his rights because he should
        have notified the client that Bonnie no longer
        worked for him.
    d. Eagle is not within his rights because Bonnie had
        implied authority to receive the check, even though
        she no longer worked for Abel.

11. Which of the following is most indicative of an
    employer-independent contractor relationship?

    a. Employer's work space provided by employer
    b. Details of employee's work are controlled by
        employer
    c. Employee is paid on a commission basis
    d. Employee is paid on a project basis

12.   Elmer is a delivery person for Gordon's milk. His
        duties are to deliver milk and to take orders. Hannah
        tells Elmer that she no longer wishes to receive
        deliveries from Gordon. Elmer says nothing to Gordon's
        manager. The next day a new route salesman leaves two
        quarts of milk at Hannah's door.

        a. Hannah must pay for the milk because the new
            delivery person had apparent authority to deliver
            milk to Hannah.
        b. Hannah must pay for the milk because she should have
            called Gordon's manager.
        c. Hannah need not pay for the milk because Elmer
            violated his duty of obedience.
        d. Hannah need not pay for the milk because Elmer
            violated his duty of notification.

13.   Belinda is a buyer for local boutique. While at market,
        she uses her credit card to pay for the hotel room and
        meals. The boutique owner's duty to pay Belinda for the
        hotel room and the meals is the duty of:

        a. cooperation.
        b. reimbursement.
        c. indemnification.
        d. compensation.

14.   Although Belinda is told that she can purchase only
        clothes, she orders 25 silver bracelets to sell as
        accessories. The boutique refuses to honor the contract
        with the bracelet merchant.

        a. The boutique is within its rights because Belinda
            has no authority to purchase the bracelets.
        b. The boutique is within its rights because Belinda
            acted outside the scope of her employment.
        c. The boutique is not within its rights because
            Belinda had apparent authority to purchase the
            bracelets.
        d. The boutique is not within its rights because
            Belinda had implied authority to purchase the
            bracelets.

15.   If the boutique pays for the bracelets:

        a. it can seek reimbursement from Belinda, because
            Belinda had no implied authority to order the
            bracelets.
        b. it can seek reimbursement from Belinda because
            Belinda had no apparent authority to order the
            bracelets.

c. it cannot seek reimbursement from Belinda because Belinda had express authority to order the bracelets.

d. it cannot seek reimbursement from Belinda because Belinda had apparent authority to order the bracelets.

16. Without authority, Belinda also orders some pins in the shape of reindeer, thinking that the boutique can sell them during Christmas. Belinda agrees to purchase the pins on consignment. The contract between Belinda and the pinmaker states that after initial sales of twenty pins, any extra unsold pins can be returned. The boutique owner also likes the pins and agrees to honor the contract. However, Belinda neglects to tell her the limits of the consignment

a. The boutique owner is bound to the contract because she ratified it.

b. The boutique owner is not bound to the contract because she did not ratify it.

c. The pin maker has no power to withdraw from the agreement because the the boutique owner has ratified the contract.

d. The pin maker has no power to withdraw from the contract because Belinda had the authority to make the contract.

17. Ann asks Bob, her neighbor, to mail a letter for her. The letter contains an acceptance of employment with an accounting firm. Bob forgets to mail the letter and Ann loses the job.

a. Ann can sue Bob for breach of contract and negligence.

b. Ann can sue Bob for breach of contract but not for negligence.

c. Ann can sue Bob for negligence but not for breach of contract.

d. Ann cannot sue Bob for negligence, nor can she sue him for breach of contract.

18. Ron is a salesman for Mission Motors. He tells Ralph, a customer, that Mission is looking for a new showroom. Ralph offers to sell Ron some land. Ron agrees and signs the contract in the following manner, "Ron, for Mission Motors". When the owner of Mission Motors learns of the contract, he refuses to honor it.

a. Ralph can sue Ron and/or Mission Motors for breach of contract.
b. Ralph can sue Ron, but not Mission Motors for breach of contract.
c. Ralph can sue Mission Motors, but not Ron for breach of contract.
d. Ralph can sue neither Ron nor Mission Motors for breach of contract

19. Which of the following is an example of an irrevocable agency?

a. Homeowner hires real estate salesman to sell house, contract is for a period of six months, salesman will receive 5 percent commission, homeowner breaches after two months.
b. Father gives daughter 50 percent interest in a corporation and authorizes her to sell stock to other investors. Father tries to revoke daughter's right to sell.
c. Barney borrows money from First Bank and uses his vacation home as collateral. The note states that if Barney cannot repay the loan, the bank has the right to sell the property and keep the proceeds to satsify the loan. Barney tries to revoke the bank's power to sell.
d. Door-to-door salesman is hired to sell greeting cards for $4.00 per box. Salesman is allowed to keep $2.50 per box and remits the rest to his employer. Employer fires salesman without cause.

20. Ralph is the manager of a fast-food restaurant. He has worked at the restaurant and has dealt directly with Farmer Brown, who supplies milk to the restaurant, Linen Supply, which furnishes napkins and paper towels, and the bank, where Ralph has the authority to sign checks. Which of the following are entitled to actual notice if Ralph is fired?

a. The bank, Farmer Brown and Linen Supply
b. Farmer Brown and Linen Supply
c. The bank only
d. The bank, Farmer Brown, Linen Supply and customers of the restaurant

21. The agent's duty to return funds collected on behalf of the principal is the duty of:

a. reimbursement.
b. accounting.
c. obedience.
d. indemnification.

22.   If an agent concludes a contract on behalf of an
       undisclosed principal, who is responsible to the third
       party?

       a.   The agent only
       b.   The third party only, but only if the agent acts
            with authority
       c.   The third party and the agent, but the third party
            is liable only if the agent acts with authority
       d.   Neither the agent nor the third party

23.   A cashier is trying to collect payment from a store
       customer. The cashier becomes so exasperated that she
       grabs the customer by the arm. The customer sues the
       store for assault.

       a.   The customer will prevail because the cashier acted
            within the scope of her employment.
       b.   The customer will prevail because a principal is
            always liable for the torts of his or her agent.
       c.   The customer will not prevail because the store did
            not specifically authorize the assault.
       d.   The customer will not prevail because the principal
            is never liable for the intentional torts of his or
            her agent.

24.   Which of the following is **not** a duty owed by an agent to
       a principal?

       a.   Accounting
       b.   Obedience
       c.   Cooperation
       d.   Loyalty

25.   In which of the following cases, is an agent prevented
       from suing a principal for reimbursement?

       a.   Agent had express authority to do the act in
            question
       b.   Agent had implied authority to do the act in
            question
       c.   Agent had apparent authority to do the act in
            question
       d.   Principal ratified the act in question

Answers to Study Questions

Fill-in-the-Blank Questions

Pearl is the principal; Cathy is the agent. Cathy has express authority to order inventory because Pearl specifically listed it as one of her duties. Cathy has implied authority to refund a customer's money. This authority is necessary to carry out her duties as assistant manager. Cathy has no authority to hire employees. It is arguable that she may have apparent authority, but that is not one of the choices listed.

True-False Questions

1.   T.   He or she may not have the right to terminate.

2.   F.   The equal dignity rule states that in order for an agent to have the authority to make written contracts, the agency agreement must also be in writing.

3.   F.   It can be created only by the acts of the principal.

4.   T.

5.   T.

6.   F.   The principal is liable for the torts of an agent or employee but only if the act was done within the scope of employment.

7.   F.   A gratuitous agent has no contract; or she may be sued for negligence.

8.   T.

9.   F.   It is an employer-independent contractor relationship.

10.   T.

Multiple-Choice Questions

1.	c	8.	b	14.	c	20.	a
2.	b	9.	d	15.	b	21.	b
3.	d	10.	c	16.	b	22.	c
4.	c	11.	d	17.	c	23.	a
5.	a	12.	d	18.	d	24.	c
6.	a	13.	b	19.	c	25.	c
7.	b						

Chapter 23   Partnerships—
Creation and Termination

<u>General Principles</u>

A partnership is a voluntary agreement between two or more persons to carry on a continuing business. It can be created informally. It can also be terminated or dissolved easily because the continuation of the business depends on the willingness and financial capability of the partners. A limited partnership is somewhat more formal; it consists of general partners, who operate the business in a manner similar to a partnership, and limited partners, who are treated as investors, and is operated in a manner similar to shareholders of a corporation. A limited partnership must be created according to the rules of a statute. Dissolution is regulated by statute and the limited partnership agreement.

<u>Chapter Outline</u>

I.   <u>Governing Law</u>

   A.   <u>General Partnership</u>--Usually governed by the partnership agreement. The Uniform Partnership Act (UPA) is used as a gap-filler.

   B.   <u>Limited Partnership</u>--Uniform Limited Partnership Act (ULPA) or a revised version (RULPA). These statutes set out some provisions which may be agreed upon by the partners.

II.   <u>General Partnership</u>

A. Definition--"An association of two or more persons
    to carry on as co-owners of a business for profit."
    Each partner must have some ownership interest but
    the interests do not have to be equal. Profits and
    losses must be shared and each partner has a right
    to manage the business. A sharing of profits only
    is not enough if the agreement involves payment of
    a loan, a landlord-tenant relationship, wages on
    commission, payment of an annuity, or a sale of the
    business when the owner retires.

B. Partnership Characteristics--As a general rule, a
    partnership is treated as an entity (rather than a
    collection of individuals) for purposes of lawsuits
    and property ownership. In contrast, individual
    partners pay income tax on their shares of
    partnership profits.

C. Formation

    (1) Formalities--Usually created by an agreement
         called the articles of partnership. Can be
         created orally or by actions as long as
         parties agree. A writing is not necessary
         unless the Statute of Frauds requires one. If
         the partnership is to continue for more than
         one year or if the partnership intends to buy
         and sell land, the agreement must be in
         writing.

    (2) Partnership by Estoppel--May be created if a
         third person reasonably relies on actions of a
         partner or non-partner. A non-partner who
         makes representations will be liable for
         damages caused by his or her actions. If a
         non-partner is held out as a partner, the
         non-partner is treated as an agent of the
         partnership.

    (3) Capacity of Partners--A minor can be a partner
         but because a partnership is an agreement, a
         minor's agreement to be a partner is voidable.
         Some states allow corporations to be partners;
         others do not.

    (4) Mutual Consent--Like an agency, a partnership
         exists only when all partners agree to
         continue the business. Acceptance of a new
         partner must be approved by all partners.
         Each partner has the power to end the
         partnership although he or she may not have
         the right to do so.

D.   <u>Termination</u>--Has   two   parts: dissolution   and
winding up.

    (1)   <u>Dissolution</u>--Can   occur   by   acts   of   the
partners, by operation of law, or by a formal
court proceeding.

        (a)   <u>Acts of the Partners</u>--Admission of a new
partner or withdrawal of a partner. A
new partnership may continue. Sale of
partner's interest to creditors does <u>not</u>
cause dissolution.

        (b)   <u>Operation of Law</u>--Death or bankruptcy of
a partner. Any event which makes the
continuation of the business illegal.

        (c)   <u>Judicial Decree</u>--Must formally petition
the court. Can occur due to insanity,
incapacity, or impropriety of a partner.
May also happen when partners disagree as
to operation of the business and business
is paralyzed.

    (2)   <u>Notice</u>--Actual notice to partners and third
parties with whom the partnership has dealt.
Others are entitled to constructive notice,
usually by publication in the newspaper.

    (3)   <u>Winding Up</u>--Purpose is to pay creditors and to
distribute assets; no new business may be
conducted. Creditors are paid first.
Partnership creditors have first rights to
partnership property but creditors of
individual partners may also sue. After
creditors are paid, partners receive assets in
the following order: repayment of loans made
by partners, return of capital contribution,
distribution of profits.

III.   <u>Limited Partnerships</u>

A.   <u>Definition</u>--Must consist of at least one general
partner and one limited partner. The general
partner is responsible for management of the
business; the limited partner cannot manage the
business

B.   <u>Formation</u>--Must be created in accordance with
statute; a certificate of partnership which
contains the names of the parties and their rights
must be filed with a state official.

314   CHAPTER 23

C.   Termination

   (1) <u>Dissolution</u>--The death, withdrawal, or insanity of a general partner can cause dissolution but the certificate may provide otherwise. Death, bankruptcy, or sale of the interest of a limited partner does not cause dissolution but illegality and bankruptcy of a general partner automatically causes dissolution. Can also be dissolved by judicial decree as a general partnership can.

   (2) <u>Winding Up</u>--Order of payment depends on statute.

      (a) <u>ULPA</u>--Outside creditors and creditors of limited partners. Limited partners profits and capital contributions. Creditors of general partners, profits and capital contributions of general partners.

      (b) <u>RULPA</u>--Creditors of the partnership and creditors of the partners. Repayment of loans. Capital contributions and profits; limited partners always precede general partners.

Study Questions

Fill-in-the-Blank Questions

Pam and Pat agree to open a gift store. They agree that profits and losses will be shared equally. Pam and Pat each contribute $5,000 to the business and borrow $5,000 from Pat's uncle. The business is successful but after two years, Pat decides that she wants to go to law school and she retires from the business.

Pam and Pat have formed a partnership _____.
(at will/for a term)

The agreement between Pat and Pam _____ be in writing.
(must/need not)

Pat has the _____ to retire.
(power but no right/power and the right)

When the partnership is dissolved _____ will receive $5,000 before the others. (Pat/Pam/Pat's uncle)

True-False Questions

1. A limited partnership must consist of at least one general partner and one limited partner. ____

2. The articles of partnership of a general partnership must be filed with the appropriate state official. ____

3. When a partnership is dissolved, each partner is entitled to actual notice of the dissolution. ____

4. The bankruptcy of a limited partner will cause dissolution automatically. ____

5. When a partnership is dissolved, loans made by partners are paid before the partners' capital contributions are returned. ____

6. A partnership can be created only if each partner has an ownership interest in the business. ____

7. Death of a general partner automatically causes dissolution of a limited partnership. ____

8. In all states, a corporation can be a partner. ____

9. A limited partner may not participate in the management of the business. ____

10. A partnership at will may be terminated at any time by any partner. ____

Multiple-Choice Questions

1. Which of the following is grounds for dissolution of a partnership by judicial decree?

    a. Death of a partner
    b. Bankruptcy of a partner
    c. Incapacity of a partner
    d. Illegality of partnership business

2. A general partnership agreement is also known as:

    a. the articles of partnership.
    b. the certificates of partnership.
    c. the estoppel of partnership.
    d. the decree of partnership.

3.   Tom and Susan agree to form a partnership for five years
      for the purpose of manufacturing and marketing false
      teeth. Tom and Susan have a:

      a. partnership at will and their agreement need not be
          in writing.
      b. partnership for a term and their agreement need not
          be in writing.
      c. partnership at will and their agreement must be in
          writing.
      d. partnership for a term and their agreement must be
          in writing.

4.   Which of the following would require a written
      partnership agreement?

      a. Partnership to sell real estate for a term of nine
          months
      b. Partnership to sell ball point pens for a term of
          nine months
      c. Partnership to operate a law practice
      d. All partnership agreements must be in writing

5.   Betty and Sam orally agree to form a partnership to
      operate a dry cleaning business.   Each contributes
      $20,000 to start the business. The profits and losses
      are to be shared equally. Betty is an active partner;
      she works in the shop and keeps the books. Sam provides
      financial backing and handles advertising.

      a. Betty is a general partner; Sam is a limited
          partner.
      b. Betty and Sam are general partners.
      c. Betty and Sam are not partners; Sam is the owner and
          Betty is an agent.
      d. Betty and Sam are not partners; they are co-owners
          of the business.

6.   Sam decides to quit the business and move to Hawaii. He
      tells no one of his decision. Which of the following
      are entitled to actual notice of the dissolution of the
      partnership?

      a. Betty only
      b. Betty and anyone with whom Betty and Sam have done
          business
      c. Betty and the partnership's creditors only
      d. No one; constructive notice is always sufficient

7.   Which of the following are stages of termination of a partnership in order of their occurrence?

a.   Dissolution and winding up
b.   Winding up and distribution
c.   Dissolution and distribution
d.   Winding up and dissolution

8.   Which of the following is **not** a party of winding up of partnership business?

a.   Articles of dissolution
b.   Payment of creditors
c.   Return of capital contribution
d.   Payment of profits to partners

9.   Pages, a bookstore operated as a partnership by Bill Blake and Gordy Byron, is dissolving. The partnership has substantial assets including $20,000 cash and $100,000 in inventory. The partnership owes $1,000 to its supplier. Gordy owes $3,000 to his ex-wife. Which of the following correctly lists the order of payment upon dissolution?

a.   Supplier, Gordy's ex-wife, Bill and Gordy's profits
b.   Gordy's ex-wife, Bill and Gordy's profits, supplier
c.   Supplier, Bill and Gordy's profits, Gordy's ex-wife
d.   Supplier, Bill and Gordy's profits; Gordy's ex-wife is not entitled to partnership assets

10.   Which of the following is not a required element of a partnership?

a.   Agreement
b.   Co-ownership by partners
c.   Management rights of partners
d.   Equal distribution of profits and losses

11.   Which of the following statements about a limited partnership if **false**?

a.   It must consist of at least one general and one limited partner.
b.   All partners, limited and general, have equal management rights.
c.   Illegality of the business will cause dissolution automatically.
d.   It must be created according to statute.

12.   Which of the following is used as a gap-filler when a
       general partnership agreement is incomplete?

       a.   UPA
       b.   ULPA
       c.   RULPA
       d.   Common law

13.   Which of the following can never be a partner?

       a.   Minor
       b.   Corporation
       c.   Corporation and minor
       d.   Person who has been adjudicated insane

14.   John and Jerry form a partnership for the purpose of
       remodeling homes. Jerry's brother Perry tells his bank
       and several friends that he is a member of the
       partnership when, in fact, he is not.

       a.   A partnership by estoppel has been created and Perry
             is a partner.
       b.   A partnership by estoppel has been created and Perry
             is liable for any damages caused as a result of his
             representation.
       c.   A partnership by estoppel has been created; the
             partnership is liable for any damages caused as a
             result of Perry's representation.
       d.   A partnership by estoppel has not been created
             unless John and Jerry agree to the estoppel.

15.   Roger owns a manufacturing business. He tells Marvin,
       his best salesperson, that Marvin will be entitled to 5%
       of all profits over $100,000.

       a.   Roger and Martin are general partners.
       b.   Roger is the owner; Martin is an agent.
       c.   Roger is a general partner; Martin is a limited
             partner.
       d.   Roger and Martin are tenants in common of the
             business.

16.   Rudy, Sandy, and Anne have been partners for several
       years. Anne dies, but Rudy and Sandy agree to continue
       the business.

       a.   Anne's death dissolved the partnership by operation
             of law.
       b.   Anne's death dissolved the partnership unless the
             partnership agreement provided for continuation of
             the business after the death of a partner.

PARTNERSHIPS--CREATION AND TERMINATION 319

    c.   The partnership may be dissolved if a petition is filed with a court.

    d.   Death of a general partner will not dissolve the partnership.

17.   Assume that Rudy, Sandy, and Anne had formed a limited partnership. Rudy is the limited partner; Sandy and Anne are general partners. Anne dies.

    a.   Anne's death dissolved the partnership by operation of law.

    b.   Anne's death dissolved the partnership unless the partnership agreement provided for continuation of the business after the death of a partner.

    c.   The partnership may be dissolved if a petition is filed with a court.

    d.   Death of a general partner will not dissolve the partnership.

18.   Paul, Peter, and Pinky are equal partners in an automobile dealership. When the business started, Paul and Peter contributed $10,000 each; Pinky contributed $5,000. When the partnership needed money, Paul made a loan to the business of $20,000. The partnership has assets of $105,000. When the partnership is dissolved, which of the following is the correct distribution of assets?

    a.   Paul, $50,000; Peter and Pinky $27,000 each

    b.   Paul, Pinky and Peter, $35,000 each

    c.   Paul, $55,000; Peter, $35,000; Pinky, $15,000

    d.   Paul, $50,000; Peter, $30,000; Pinky, $25,000

19.   Which of the following is not required for formation of a limited partnership?

    a.   Agreement of the parties

    b.   Filing of certificate of limited partnership

    c.   Registration with RULPA

    d.   Designation of limited and general partners

20.   Which of the following will never cause dissolution of a limited partnership?

    a.   Bankruptcy of a general partner

    b.   Bankruptcy of limited partner

    c.   Illegality of partnership business

    d.   Death of a general partner

21.   A limited partner:

        a. is not an owner of the limited partnership.
        b. is allowed to manager the limited partnership.
        c. is liable only to the amount of his or her
            contribution to the business.
        d. is entitled to fewer profits than general partners.

22.   Which of the following may be grounds for dissolution of
        a partnership by judicial decree?

        a. Death of a partner
        b. Bankruptcy of a partner
        c. Impropriety of a partner
        d. Illegality of partnership business

23.   In a partnership for a term:

        a. each partner has the right and power to withdraw at
            any time.
        b. there is no right or power to withdraw until the
            term of the partnership has expired.
        c. there is a power to withdraw at any time but the
            right to withdraw does not exist until the term of
            the partnership has expired.
        d. only general partners have the right to withdraw at
            any time; limited partners have the right to
            withdraw only after the term of the partnership has
            expired.

24.   Which of the following correctly describes the
        distribution of assets under RULPA?

        a. Outside creditors of the partnership, limited
            partners' capital contribution, limited partners'
            profits, creditors of all partners
        b. Outside creditors of the partnership, creditors of
            partners, capital contribution of limited and
            general partners, profits of limited and general
            partners
        c. Outside creditors of the partnership, creditors of
            limited partners, limited partners' capital
            contribution and profits, creditors of general
            partners
        d. Outside creditors of limited and general prtners,
            outside creditors of the partnership, capital
            contribution and profits of limited partners,
            capital contributions and profits of general
            partners

25.   Which of the following correctly describes the distribution of assets under ULPA?

    a. Outside creditors of the partnership, limited partners' capital contribution, limited partners' profits, creditors of all partners

    b. Outside creditors of the partnership, creditors of partners, capital contribution of limited and general partners, profits of limited and general partners

    c. Outside creditors of the partnership, creditors of limited partners, limited partners' capital contribution and profits, creditors of general partners

    d. Outside creditors of limited and general partners, outside creditors of the partnership, capital contribution and profits of limited partners, capital contributions and profits of general partners

Answers to Study Questions

Fill-in-the-Blank Questions

Pam and Pat have a partnership at will because the length of the agreement was not specified. The agreement between Pat and Pam need not be in writing because they do not intend to buy real estate and because they did not specify that the agreement was to last for more than one year. Pat has the right and power to leave because it is a partnership at will. Pat's uncle is a creditor and he will receive his money first.

True-False Questions

1. T.

2. F. The certificate of partnership of a **limited** partnership must be filed.

3. T.

4. F. The bankruptcy of a **general** partner will cause dissolution.

5. T.

6. T.

7.   F.   The agreement may provide that the business is to continue.

8.   F.   Only some states allow corporations to be partners.

9.   T.

10.   T.

Multiple-Choice Questions

1.	c	11.	b	21.	c
2.	a	12.	a	22.	c
3.	d	13.	d	23.	c
4.	a	14.	b	24.	c
5.	b	15.	b	25.	b
6.	b	16.	a		
7.	a	17.	b		
8.	a	18.	d		
9.	a	19.	c		
10.	d	20.	b		

Chapter 24   Partnerships—
Operations and Duties

General Principles

As you learned in the last chapter, a partnership implies an equal right of management in each partner. This arrangement may be modified somewhat by agreement. Partners are agents of each other and the rules of agency apply. Partners owe a fiduciary duty to each other. The power of partners to deal with third parties is also governed by agency and the rules of express, implied, and apparent authority. The liability of partners depends on whether recovery is based on tort or on contract. In contrast, limited partners are liable only for the amount of their investment unless they take an active role in management.

Chapter Outline

I.   Management of a Partnership--Each partner has equal rights in management regardless of percentage of ownership. In the absence of agreement, majority rules. Each partner has the right to examine partnership books and the books are to be kept at the place of business.

    A.   Delegation of Management--The partners may agree to delegate management to one partner but this will not affect liability to an outsider unless he or she knows of the arrangement.

    B.   Fundamental Changes--Unanimous consent of the partners is required to admit a new partner, to change the essential nature of the business, to assign partnership property for the benefit of creditors, to dispose of the partnership's good-will, to confess judgment against the partnership, to submit claims to arbitration, or to undertake any act which would cause the business to fail.

II. <u>Property Rights of a Partner</u>

    A. <u>Partnership Interest</u>--Right to profits and losses are divided equally unless otherwise stated. Can be assigned to third parties; creditors of individual partners can attach by a charging order. No right to compensation regardless of time or money spent in the business unless the agreement otherwise provides.

    B. <u>Right to Specific Partnership Property</u>--All property owned as a tenancy in partnership unless otherwise agreed. Property remains in the partnership when a partner dies or retires; this right cannot be assigned. The remaining partners must account for a deceased partner's interest in specific property. Creditors of a partner cannot attach partnership property until dissolution. Partnership property is all property brought into the partnership or otherwise acquired. Record ownership does not determine whether property is considered an asset of the partnership.

III. <u>Powers and Duties of Partners</u>

    A. <u>Agency Powers</u>--Each partner is the agent of every other partner. A partner may bind the partnership if his or her act is within the scope of the partnership. The only exceptions are those listed above, which require the consent of all partners. There is no implied right to make charitable contributions from partnership funds because partnerships by definition exist to make a profit.

    B. <u>Fiduciary Duties</u>--Similar to agency powers. A partner must not compete with partnership business or use partnership funds for private use.

    C. <u>Liability</u>--Partnership can be sued as an entity if state law allows. Otherwise, must sue partners individually.

        (1) <u>Contract</u>--Joint liability. All partners must be sued in the same suit and a judgment against one is a judgment against all. Responsibility for payment of damages depends on partnership interest.

(2) <u>Tort</u>--Joint and several liability. Each partner may be sued individually. If one partner wins, a second partner may be sued and found liable.

(3) <u>Changing Partners</u>--An incoming partner is liable only to the extent of his or her contribution with regards to events occurring before he or she became a partner. Similarly, an outgoing partner is responsible for events occurring before his or her withdrawal. Assuming proper notice of withdrawal, an old partner is not liable for new debts.

IV. <u>Rights and Duties of Limited Partners</u>

A. <u>Property Rights</u>--Same right to profits and losses as general partners. Interest can be assigned; ownership of partnership property cannot.

B. <u>Management Rights</u>--Right to accounting of business and to inspect partnership books. No right to management or limited liability will be cancelled. Under ULPA only, a limited partner's capital contribution cannot be in the form of services as a manager; a limited partner may be an employee. Limited partner's name cannot appear in the firm name unless that name is also the name of a general partner. Under RULPA, a limited partner who participates in management loses limited liability only if a third party actually knows of the limited partner's management.

C. <u>Liability for Defective Formation</u>--A limited partnership does not exist technically until a proper certificate of partnership is recorded in a public office. A limited partner is liable for defective filing if he or she knows of the defect and does not withdraw of correct the mistake. If a false statement is knowingly made, a limited partner is liable as a general partner to a third party who relied on the false statement. Good faith compliance will protect the limited partner and will not affect his or her liability.

Study Questions

Fill-in-the-Blank Questions

Sam, Sid, and Rod form a partnership for the purpose of operating an appliance store. The agreement says nothing about division of profits and losses. Sam and Sid work as salesman; Rod keeps the books and provides the land for location of the store. Betty purchases a steam iron from the store. Sam tells her that the iron is guaranteed for four years and the store will replace any defective iron during that time. Rod is in some financial difficulty and he uses his partnership interest and the entire inventory of the business as collateral for a loan with First Bank.

Sam and Sid are _____ to a salary from the business.   (entitled/not entitled)

Sam's promise to Betty _____ bind the partnership.
                         (did/did not)

Sid and Rod are _____ liable to Betty.   (jointly/jointly and severally/not)

Rod _____ assign his partnership interest to the bank.
      (can/cannot)

Rod _____ assign the store's inventory to the bank.
      (can/cannot)

True-False Questions

1.   Under both ULPA and RULPA a limited partner may contribute personal or real property as part of his or her initial capital contribution. ____

2.   If a limited partnership inadvertantly submits a certificate of partnership containing a false statement, all limited partners are liable as general partners. ____

3.   Unless otherwise stated, management decisions of the partnership are determined by majority vote. ____

4.   A limited partner is treated as an investor and has limited rights to inspect partnership books. ____

5.   A limited partner cannot be hired as an employee of the business. ____

6.   A partnership's liability for a contract made by a partner depends on whether the contract was made within the scope of the partnership. ____

7.   An outgoing partner is not liable for any lawsuit commenced after he or she withdraws, regardless of when the right to sue arose. ____

8.   For purposes of determining powers to bind the partnership, partners are treated as mutual agents. ____

9.   Under RULPA, a limited partner who participates in management is not liable to third parties unless the outsider had actual knowledge of the limited partner's participation in management. ____

10.   If one partner agrees to admit a partnership claim to arbitration, this decision is binding on the partnership. ____

Multiple-Choice Questions

1.   Sarah, Sally, and Beth form a partnership for the purpose of making and selling novelty sweatshirts. They agree that Sarah will receive 60 percent of the profits, because she will perform most of the work. Sally and Beth are to receive 20% each. No provision is made for sharing of losses. Sarah is also given the exclusive power to make all contracts for the partnership if the amount involved is less than $1,000. Because the agreement did not specify the manner in which losses were to be shared:

      a.   Sarah, Sally, and Beth are each liable for one-third of the losses.
      b.   Sarah is responsible for 60 percent of the losses and Beth and Sally are responsible for 20 percent each.
      c.   the agreement is illegal because losses must be apportioned.
      d.   no partnership has been formed because losses must be apportioned.

2.   The decision to make Sarah a managing partner:

      a.   is illegal; all contracts regardless of the amount must have the consent of all partners.
      b.   is unenforceable because all partners have equal management rights.

c. is enforceable between the partners but is not effective against third parties.

d. is enforceable between the partners and between the partnership and any third party who has notice of the arrangement.

3. The partnership of Sarah, Beth, and Sally is sued for breach of contract when one of the sweatshirts is found to be defective. The partnership is sued for $55, the cost of the sweatshirt.

a. Sarah, as the managing partner, has a right to settle the suit because the amount in dispute is less than $1,000.

b. All partners must agree to settle the suit, regardless of the amount.

c. The liability of the partners for damages is joint and several.

d. The plaintiff can sue Sarah or Beth or Sally and recover the full amount.

4. Which of the following does not require the unanimous consent of the partners?

a. Payment of a debt resulting from the action of one partner

b. Submission of a claim to arbitration

c. Sale of the goodwill of the business

d. Admission of a new partner

5. Which of the following is <u>not</u> a right of a limited partner?

a. Inspection of partnership books

b. Filing a legal action to account for partnership funds

c. Working for the partnership as an employee

d. Inclusion of his or her name in the name of the business

6. Bud, Sam, and John form a limited partnership. Bud is the limited partner; Sam and John are general partners. The partnership is sued when Sam, while conducting partnership business, causes an automobile accident.

a. Bud, Sam, and John are jointly liable to the victim of the car accident.

b. Sam and John are jointly liable to the victim of the car accident; Bud is not liable.

c. Bud, Sam, and John are jointly and severally liable to the victim of the car accident.

d. Sam and John are jointly and severally liable to the victim of the car accident; Bud is not liable.

7.   If a judgment is rendered against the partnership:

   a. Bud will be liable to the extent of his
       contribution; Sam and John will be personally
       liable.
   b. All partners will be personally liable without
       limit.
   c. Bud will not be liable but Sam and John will be
       personally liable without limit.
   d. All partners will be liable to the amount of money
       each has contributed to the partnership.

8.   A limited partner who discovers a false statement in the
      certificate of limited liability:

   a. will be treated as a general partner.
   b. will always retain limited partner status if the
       false statement was not made intentionally.
   c. will retain limited partner status even if the false
       statement was made intentionally.
   d. will be protected from liability if he or she
       withdraws from the partnership.

9.   A creditor of a partner can attach which of the
      following to satisfy the debt?

   a. Partner's interest only
   b. Partnership property only
   c. Partner's interest and partnership property
   d. Only personal assets may be attached to satisfy the
       debt.

10.   A suit against a partner's interest is a(n)

   a. order of partnership.
   b. charging order.
   c. secured transaction.
   d. several charge.

11.   A partner's rights include all of the following except:

   a. interest in profits and losses.
   b. rights in specific partnership property.
   c. right of management.
   d. right of assignment of partnership property.

12.   Tom and Lily form a partnership. Lily agrees to
      transfer some land to the partnership in exchange for
      her interest. The partnership business uses the land
      but the land is held in Lily's name. The partnership
      books list the land as an asset.

a. The land is partnership property.
b. The land is Lily's property because she holds title.
c. The land is owned by Tom and Lily as tenants in common.
d. The land is owned by Tom and Lily as joint tenants.

13.   Rudy, Jacob, and Jill form a partnership which lasts for ten years until Rudy's death. The partnership owns several pieces of land, office equipment, and machinery. Rudy's heirs are entitled to:

a. Rudy's partnership interest and Rudy's rights in partnership property.
b. Rudy's partnership interest and the monetary value of Rudy's rights in partnership property.
c. all of Rudy's rights in the partnership, including management.
d. nothing; Rudy's partnership interest and his interest in partnership property pass to the remaining partners.

14.   Sid Salt, Bill Pepper, and Cathy Cayenne form a limited partnership. Sid is the limited partner. All of the following would be proper names for the partnership except:

a. Salt & Pepper.
b. Pepper Manufacturing.
c. Pepper & Cayenne.
d. Spice, Etc.

15.   Cathy agrees to purchase $5,000 of advertising from Good Cooks magazine. The partnership is:

a. bound by Cathy's decision because she is an agent of Salt and Pepper and the contract was within the scope of the partnership business.
b. bound by Cathy's decision only if she is the managing partner.
c. not bound by Cathy's decision because contracts require the unanimous consent of the partners.
d. not bound by Cathy's decision because the contract was not within the scope of the partnership business.

16.   Pepper decides to leave the partnership after Cathy's decision regarding the advertising. Cathy and Sid agree to admit a new partner, Sally Saffron. Which of the following correctly describes liability for the advertising contract?

a. Pepper is personally liable; Sally is not liable.
b. Pepper and Sally are personally liable.
c. Sally is personally liable; Pepper is not liable.
d. Pepper is personally liable; Sally is liable to the extent that she has contributed to the partnership.

17. Which of the following statements about partners' joint liability is <u>false</u>?

a. Each partner may be sued individually.
b. Joint liability applies to suits for breach of contract but not for suits in negligence.
c. Res Judicata will bar more than one suit.
d. All partners are equally exposed to liability.

18. Five brothers in the DeMatto family have operated a restaurant as a partnership for several years. No one has been designated as managing partner. One brother proposes to sell half of the partnership interest to outsiders and to use the proceeds of the sale to open a drive-in grocery. The decision to sell the land:

a. can be carried out by one brother regardless of the consent of the others.
b. requires a majority of the brothers to agree.
c. requires the consent of all brothers.
d. will dissolve the partnership.

19. One of the DeMatto brothers purchases an ice cream parlor across the street from the restaurant. The new store is not in direct competition with the partnership. The purchase of the ice cream parlor:

a. is in violation of the partnership agreement, because a partner cannot operate another business.
b. is a breach of fiduciary duty regardless of the lack of competition between the two businesses.
c. may be a breach of fiduciary duty if the owner of the ice cream parlor neglects partnership responsibilities.
d. is not in violation of the partnership agreement; a partner has the right to enter into business for himself.

20. Res Judicata refers to:

a. the right of partners to demand an accounting of partnership funds.
b. a judgment against one partner which forecloses suits against other partners.

c. the rights of a partner's heirs to his or her rights in the business.

d. the right of a creditor to attach a partner's interest.

21. Which of the following statements regarding partners' rights and duties is <u>false</u>?

a. All partners are agent of each other.
b. Partners owe a fiduciary duty to each other.
c. Admission of a new partner requires unanimous consent of all partners.
d. An incoming partner is not liable for actions occurring before his or her admission to the partnership.

22. Paul, Peter, and Susan form a limited partnership and operate a clothing store. Paul is the limited partner; the others are general partners. Paul is also employed as a salesperson. Paul gives a refund to an angry customer as part of his employment.

a. Paul will be treated as a general partner because a limited partner cannot be an employee of the business.
b. Paul will be treated as a general partner because his decision to give a refund involved a management decision.
c. Paul will retain limited partner status only if he ceases working as an employee.
d. Paul will retain limited partner status because he has not participated in the management of the business.

23. A dispute develops between Peter, Susan, and Paul. Peter and Susan wish to postpone a distribution of profits and remodel the store. Paul disagrees.

a. The store can be remodeled because the vote for remodeling is two to one.
b. The store can be remodeled because Paul is not entitled to vote on this issue.
c. The store cannot be remodeled because this decision requires the unanimous consent of all partners.
d. The store can be remodeled but Paul will not be liable for any damages as a result of the decision.

24.   Paul is dissatisfied with the earnings of the partnership and begins to take an active role in management. The partnership orders $50,000 of clothing from a manufacturer.

   a.   Under ULPA, Paul is liable as a general partner.
   b.   Under ULPA, Paul is liable as a limited partner.
   c.   Under ULPA, Paul is liable only if the clothing manufacturer is aware of his participation in the business.
   d.   Under ULPA, the partnership is dissolved because Paul legally cannot manage the business.

25.   Same facts as question 24, but RULPA applies.

   a.   Under RULPA, Paul is liable as a general partner.
   b.   Under RULPA, Paul is liable as a limited partner.
   c.   Under RULPA, Paul is liable only if the clothing manufacturer is aware of his participation in the business.
   d.   Under RULPA, the partnership is dissolved because Paul legally cannot manage the business.

Answers to Study Questions

Fill-in-the-Blank Questions

Sam and Sid are not entitled to a salary from the business unless the agreement provides; each partner is expected to donate time to the business. The partnership is bound by Sam's promise to Betty; the promise was made within the scope of partnership business. The partners are jointly liable to Betty because Sam's promise creates potential contract liability. Rod can assign his partnership interest (his right to profits) to the bank. He cannot assign the entire inventory of the store; this is an assignment for benefit of Rod's creditor. Rod has no right to bind the entire assets of the partnership.

True-False Questions

1.   T.

2.   F.   A good-faith error will not result in liability.

3.   T.

4.   F.   A limited partner has the same right to inspect books as general partner does; this right is absolute.

5.   F. A limited partner can be hired as an employee; he or she cannot be hired as manager of the business.

6.   T.

7.   F. An outgoing partner is liable for all acts performed while he or she was a partner; the time the suit is filed is irrelevant.

8.   T.

9.   T.

10.   F. A decision to submit a claim to arbitration requires the consent of all partners.

Multiple-Choice Questions

1.	b		11.	a		21.	d
2.	d		12.	b		22.	d
3.	b		13.	b		23.	b
4.	a		14.	a		24.	a
5.	d		15.	a		25.	c
6.	c		16.	d			
7.	a		17.	a			
8.	d		18.	c			
9.	a		19.	c			
10.	d		20.	b			

Chapter 25   Corporations—
Formation and Classification

General Principles

A corporation is an artificial person; it is created only by a statute which allows for formation or incorporation of the business. It possesses some of the same rights as individuals, for example, the right to make contracts, the right to equal protection and due process, and the right to sue. However, some rights are denied to a corporation. Corporations are classified by purpose, by shareholders, and by taxation.

A promoter is the person responsible for forming the corporation. He or she may sell stock in a corporation which is to be formed and can arrange for services and property to be purchased by the corporation. The liability for contracts made by the promoter remains with him or her until the corporation accepts them.

Chapter Summary

I.   Background and Characteristics

      A.   History--The joint stock company was the predecessor of the corporation. Until the nineteenth century, only cities or influential persons could incorporate and the legislature had to pass a special law for each corporation.

      B.   Current Law--All states have incorporation statutes. Most follow the Model Business Corporation Act (MBCA) or its revised version (RMBCA). A few public corporations may be formed under federal law.

C.   Rights and Privileges

(1)   Rights Retained--A corporation has the right
       to equal protection, due process, and freedom
       speech. It is protected against unreasonable
       search and seizures and double jeopardy (being
       tried twice for the same criminal offense.)

(2)   Rights Denied--However, only employees and
       officers retain the privilege against self-
       incrimination. A corporation also does not
       benefit from the privileges and immunities
       clause, which requires all states to treat
       residents of other states equally. A
       corporation can be required to register if it
       does business in a second state.

(3)   Criminal Law--Most states agree that a
       corporation can violate the criminal law and
       be assessed a fine; it obviously cannot be
       imprisoned. If an officer or employee of a
       corporation is responsible for the crime; he
       or she can be sentenced to prison as an
       individual.

D.   Corporate Organization--Shareholders own the
      corporation; it is managed by directors and
      officers. Shareholders generally are not liable
      for the debts of a corporation. Shareholders can
      sue the corporation or on its behalf (derivative
      suit); the corporation can sue the shareholders. A
      corporation is treated as a separate individual for
      tax purposes; it pays taxes on earnings. When the
      corporation pays a dividend, the shareholders are
      taxed on the money they receive.

II.   Classification of Corporations

A.   Residency--A corporation is a resident of the state
      in which it is incorporated. It is a domestic
      corporation in that state; it is a foreign
      corporation in any other state. An alien
      corporation is one incorporated under the laws of
      another country. Before a corporation can do
      business in another state; that state may require a
      certificate of authority; the privileges and
      immunities clause does not apply. As with other
      defendants, a corporation cannot be sued in a state
      unless it does business there or otherwise meets
      the minimum contacts rule.

B.   Purpose--A public corporation is usually formed by a government to meet some public purpose. Private corporations are created by private individuals to benefit themselves. A nonprofit or eleemosynary (charitable) corporation is usually a private corporation; no dividends are paid. Examples of nonprofit corporations include hospitals and private schools.

C.   Size (Close Corporation)--In a close corporation; there are only a few shareholders. It may also be referred to as a family corporation although the shareholders need not be related. Most states limit the number of shareholders and stock cannot be offered for sale to the general public. Management is less rigid than in a larger corporation; shareholders can sign an agreement relating to management of the corporation. The corporation may also require that a shareholder who wishes to sell his or her shares must first offer them to the corporation or to other shareholders; this prevents outsiders from taking control of the corporation.

D.   Tax--An S corporation (Subchapter S of the Internal Revenue Code) is treated as a partnership for tax purposes; the "S" designation relates only to tax law and does not affect state law and other classifications. In order to qualify, the corporation must be a domestic corporation and cannot be associated with other corporations. Shareholders are limited to thirty-five and they must be individuals, estates or certain types of trusts. It may have only one class of voting stock and no more than 25 percent of its income may come from passive activities (e.g. rents and royalties as opposed to fees or sales). "S" corporations are taxed as partnerships; each shareholder accounts for the profits and losses of the business; there is no double taxation. However, it loses some of the benefits of regular or "C" corporations; less money can be sheltered in pension funds.

E.   Shareholders--A professional corporation is one which the shareholders are members of the same profession (e.g. law or medicine). These businesses can only be incorporated as professional corporations (previously, they had to exist as partnerships or sole proprietorships). Some states insist that members are personally liable for malpractice and one shareholder may be liable for the malpractice of another. However, this rule does not apply to other torts.

III. <u>Promoters</u>--A promoter organizes the corporation. This usually involves the purchase of goods and services prior to incorporation and the selling of stock.

    A. <u>Contracts</u>--Promoter remains personally liable even though the act is done on behalf of the corporation. This rule does not apply if the other party to the contract agrees to look only to the corporation or a novation between all three parties occurs. Most states hold that adoption of a contract is insufficient. In addition, a promoter cannot be an agent of the corporation because the corporation did not exist at the time the contract was made and cannot be a principal.

    B. <u>Stock Subscription</u>--Sold by the promoter to potential shareholders. Some states hold that the buyer (subscriber) becomes a shareholder when the corporation is formed (the corporation or promoter is the offeror; the shareholder is the offeree). Others hold that the subscription agreement is an option contract which the corporation can reject or accept. It may also be treated as an agreement between subscribers. Under the MBCA, the subscription is irrevocable for six months.

IV. <u>Incorporations Formalities</u>--In order for a corporation to exist, it must be chartered under state law by submitting documentation to a state official.

    A. <u>Articles of Incorporation</u>--A general document similar to a charter or constitution. It should contain the following information:

        (1) <u>Name</u>--Cannot be too similar to an already existing corporation; name can usually be reserved for a short period of time prior to actual incorporation. The name must include words indicating that it is a corporation--Corp., Inc., or Ltd.

        (2) <u>Purpose</u>--Should set out the general type of business; most now use "any legal purpose". Professional corporations, banks, and insurance companies may be prohibited from using this broad statement of purpose.

        (3) <u>Duration</u>--Must set a specified time or state that its duration is perpetual.

(4)   Capital Structure--A minimum amount of capital (usually $1,000) is required. Must also set out the different types of stock and their par value, if any, and voting rights.

(5)   Internal Organization--Number of officers and directors. Usually general because the bylaws are more specific as to the rights and duties of shareholders, directors, and officers.

(6)   Registered Office and Agent--Must be included for purpose of service of citation if the corporation is sued. The agent must be a specific person and his or her address must be included.

(7)   Incorporators--Submit the articles of incorporation for approval. Usually is a shareholder or promoter, but this is not required. The number of incorporators varies.

B.   Certificate of Incorporation (Charter)--Document received from a public officer (usually secretary of state) that certifies that the articles of incorporation are correct, the fees have been paid, and the corporation has the right to do business.

C.   First Meeting--Required by law. Usually consists of routine initial matters such as issuing of stock, electing directors, and passing bylaws.

V.   Recognizing Corporate Status (Defective Incorporation)

A.   Legal Status--A de jure corporation is one which has substantially complied with all the requirements for incorporation. Usually has received certificate from the state. A de facto corporation occurs when there has been some mistake made in incorporation or the charter has expired. An incorporation statute must exist which the incorporators have tried to follow in good faith and the business must have done business as a corporation. Only the state can challenge the corporate status; other parties cannot sue the shareholders personally. A corporation by estoppel does not actually exist; it occurs when a third party has been led to believe that a corporation exists when it does not.

B.   Piercing the Corporate Veil--Shareholders usually are not personally responsible for the debts of the corporation. However, if the corporation has acted in bad faith or has commingled personal and corporate funds, the courts may look behind the corporation and find the shareholders personally liable.

Study Questions

Fill-in-the-Blank Questions

Paul is helping some friends to form a corporation. He makes a contract with Crook & Low, Attorneys at Law, for their services in drafting the documents necessary to set up the corporation. He also sells thirty shares of stock to his Aunt Millie.

Paul is a(n) _____.
                    (promoter/incorporator)

Before the corporation is formed, _____
is/are responsible for the money   (Paul/the shareholders)
owed to Crook & Low.

When Aunt Millie agrees to purchase the stock she is a
_____.
(shareholder/subscriber)

The document to be drafted by Crook & Low is the
_____.
(articles of incorporation/subscription agreement)

True-False Questions

1.   A de facto corporation is one which has complied with all the requirements for incorporation. ____

2.   A promoter is personally liable for pre-incorporation contracts unless the corporation ratifies the contracts. ____

3.   An eleemosynary corporation is a synonym for a public corporation. ____

4.   An "S" corporation is taxed as a partnership. ____

5.   A joint stock company was an early form of a corporation. ____

6.   An alien corporation is one chartered in another country. ____

7.   A corporation cannot be convicted of a criminal offense. ____

8.   The name of the registered agent of a corporation should be stated in the bylaws. ____

9.   The number of shareholders in a close corporation is limited. ____

10.   A court is likely to pierce the corporate veil if the corporation is undercapitalized. ____

Multiple-Choice Questions

1.   The law which contains a codification of corporation law is the:

      a.   Uniform Corporation and Partnership Code.
      b.   Uniform Business Corporation Act.
      c.   Model Business Corporation Act.
      d.   Model Corporation Code.

2.   Which of the following constitutional rights is held by a corporation?

      a.   Privileges and Immunities Clause
      b.   Right Against Self-Incrimination
      c.   Freedom of Speech
      d.   Right to Travel

3.   Which of the following best describes the application of the right of due process to corporations?

      a.   Corporations enjoy the same right as individuals.
      b.   Corporations have limited due process rights.
      c.   Corporations have no due process rights; only employees and officers have a right to due process.
      d.   Corporations have due process rights in some states but not in others.

4.   Which of the following correctly describes the application of tax law to a "C" corporation?

      a.   It is taxed like a partnership.
      b.   It is taxed on retained earnings but dividends are not taxed.
      c.   It is not taxed on retained earnings; shareholders pay taxes on dividends received.
      d.   It is taxed on retained earnings and shareholders pay taxes on dividends received.

5.   Which of the followng is <u>not</u> part of the articles of incorporation?

    a. Registered agent and business address
    b. Capital structure
    c. Bylaws
    d. Names of incorporators

6.   Which of the following documents governs the internal workings of the corporation?

    a. Articles of incorporation
    b. Bylaws
    c. Charter
    d. Certificate of incorporation

7.   Cathy's Dress Shop is trying to incorporate. Cathy submits the required documents to the proper public officer but neglects to correct a mistake in the address of the registered agent. While waiting to receive authorization from the proper public officer, Cathy does business as a corporation. Cathy's Dress Shop is:

    a. a de jure corporation.
    b. a de facto coproration.
    c. a corporation by estoppel.
    d. is not a corporation.

8.   Which of the following statements about a corporate name is <u>false</u>?

    a. It must not contain the full name of an individual.
    b. It must contain the words "company", "corporation", or other words which show that it is a corporation.
    c. It must not be deceptively similar to the name of another corporation.
    d. It must be included in the articles of incorporation.

9.   Which of the following correctly describes a foreign corporation?

    a. A corporation incorporated in Alabama but doing business in Texas.
    b. A corporation incorporated in Alabama and doing business in Alabama.
    c. A corporation incorporated in Mexico and doing business in Alabama.

10.   Which of the following statements about a professional corporation is true?

    a.   Its shareholders never have personal liability for torts of other shareholders.
    b.   Its shareholders may be liable for the malpractice of other shareholders, but not for other torts.
    c.   Its shareholders may be liable for all torts of other shareholders.
    d.   Its shareholders may be liable for all torts and contracts of other shareholders.

11.   Which of the following most likely would be performed by a promoter?

    a.   Selling share subscriptions
    b.   Purchasing stock in the corporation
    c.   Acting as director of the corporation
    d.   Submitting the articles of incorporation for approval.

12.   In order for a promoter to be released from liability for pre-incorporation contracts, there must be a(n):

    a.   novation.
    b.   ratification.
    c.   adoption.
    d.   amendment.

13.   Which of the following is a synonym for a corporate charter?

    a.   Articles of Incorporation
    b.   Bylaws
    c.   Certificate of Incorporation
    d.   Subscription

14.   Which of the following would probably take place at the first organizational meeting of a corporation?

    a.   Selection of a registered agent
    b.   Selection of a promoter
    c.   Selection of the board of directors
    d.   Selection of a corporate name

15.   Which of the following is not required for a de facto corporation?

a. State statute which allows incorporation of the business
b. Good faith attempt to comply with incorporation statute
c. Business undertaken in the name of a corporation
d. Third party deceived as to fact that no corporation exists

16. Which of the following is an example of an eleemosynary corporation?

   a. Red Cross
   b. Amtrak
   c. Crook & Low, Attorneys at Law
   d. City of Houston, Texas

17. Which of the following statements regarding an "S" corporation is <u>false</u>?

   a. The number of shareholders is restricted.
   b. It enjoys full fringe benefits, including all pension plans.
   c. It is taxed like a corporation.
   d. The types of shareholders are limited.

18. Which of the following terms describes a court's decision to hold a shareholder personally liable for a corporation's debt?

   a. Novation
   b. Piercing the corporate veil
   c. Corporation by estoppel
   d. Adoption

19. Which of the following constitutional rights is denied to a corporation?

   a. Freedom of speech
   b. Due process
   c. Privilage against self-incrimination
   d. Double jeopardy

20. A corporation which has few stockholders, is governed by shareholder agreements, and restricts sale of stock is a description of a(n):

   a. "S" corporation.
   b. close corporation.
   c. nonprofit corporation.
   d. eleemosynary corporation.

21.   With regard to subscription agreements, most courts hold that:

    a.   they are prohibited until the corporations is formed.
    b.   they are continuing offers to the corporation.
    c.   they are acceptances of a corporation's offer to sell stock.
    d.   they are invalid.

22.   Under the Model Business Corporation Act:

    a.   share subscriptions are illegal.
    b.   share subscription are irrevocable for six months.
    c.   share subscriptions are irrevocable until the corporation is formed.
    d.   a promoter is personally liable for all share subscriptions.

23.   Which of the following is not a synonym for a close corporation?

    a.   "S" corporation.
    b.   privately-held corporation.
    c.   closely-held corporation.
    d.   closed corporation.

24.   Which of the following correctly describes a promoter's liability for pre-incorporation contracts?

    a.   The promoter is liable until the corporation ratifies or adopts the contract.
    b.   The promoter remains personally liable until the corporation is formed.
    c.   The promoter is never personally liable but the incorporators are.
    d.   The promoter is personally liable until a novation is concluded.

25.   The duration of most corporations is:

    a.   twenty years.
    b.   fifty years.
    c.   ninety-nine years.
    d.   perpetual.

Answers to Study Questions

Fill-in-the-Blank Questions

Paul is a promoter; an incorporator signs the documents which are submitted to the secretary of state. Paul is personally liable for pre-incorporation contracts unless the corporation, Paul, and the other party sign a novation. Aunt Millie is a subscriber; she does not become a shareholder until the stock is issued. The initial document, which is prepared by the lawyers, is the articles of incorporation; the certificate of incorporation is issued by a public officer.

True-False Questions

1.   F. This is the definition of a de jure corporation; a de facto corporation is one which has failed to comply with incorporation requirements.

2.   F. In most states, ratification is insufficient; a novation is required.

3.   F. It is a synonym for a charitable or nonprofit corporation.

4.   T.

5.   T.

6.   T.

7.   F. It can be convicted but punished only by fine.

8.   F. It should be stated in the articles of incorporation.

9.   T.

10.   T.

Multiple-Choice Questions

1.	c	10.	b	19.	c
2.	c	11.	a	20.	b
3.	a	12.	a	21.	b
4.	d	13.	c	22.	b
5.	c	14.	c	23.	a
6.	b	15.	d	24.	d
7.	b	16.	a	25.	d
8.	a	17.	b		
9.	a	18.	b		

Chapter 26 Corporations—
Corporate Powers and Management

The powers of a corporation are determined by state and federal law, the charter, and the bylaws. It can do no more than is stated in these documents; the bylaws and charter cannot conflict with each other or with higher laws.

Management of a corporation generally rests with the board of directors. They make general decisions and appoint officers to carry out these decisions. Shareholders are the owners of the corporation and have limited management rights. Most of their rights are exercised by electing the board of directors and voting on major changes which will alter the make-up or existence of the corporation.

Chapter Summary

I.   Corporate Powers

    A.   Express Powers--Stated in precise terms. In order of priority, they are: U.S. Constitution, state constitutions, state statutes, charter, bylaws, and resolutions of the board of directors. A lower power cannot conflict with a greater one. Note that the last three are primarily determined by private individuals who form and operate a corporation.

    B.   Implied Powers--Includes powers necessary to carry out express powers and purposes. Usually includes the power to lend and borrow money and to make charitable contributions. Officers have implied power to conduct daily business but not more important changes which require the approval of the board of the directors and major changes which require the approval of shareholders as well.

C.   Ultra Vires Doctrine--Any act that is not expressed or implied. Most charters contain broad purposes and rights to avoid this problem. Most courts allow ultra vires contracts to be voided only if the contract is executory and a shareholder or director objects. If the contract is partially performed, corporation can be released unless the third party would be injured or the corporation would be unjustly enriched. Remedies include derivative suits by shareholders, suing the wrongdoers personally, or dissolution/injunction ordered by the secretary of state.

D.   Torts and Crimes--General rules of agency apply; if agent (director or officer) acts in the scope of employment, the corporation is liable. As stated earlier, most states hold a corporation liable for criminal acts if the act can be punished by a fine.

II.   Corporate Management--Shareholder's Rights--Shareholders are the owners of the corporation and have no specific rights in management. They act by electing the board of directors and voting on fundamental changes. The officers owe no fiduciary duty to the shareholders, but a director may.

A.   Express Powers--Right to vote on merger, dissolution, sale of most of business assets, and amendment to the articles of incorporation. Power to remove directors for cause by majority vote. Some charters allow for removal at any time if a majority of the shareholders approve. Can sue on behalf of the corporation (derivative suit) if the board of directors is abusing power or fails to correct an ultra vires act.

B.   Shareholders' Forum (Meeting)--Must be held annually and shareholders receive written notice within a reasonable time. Special meetings may be called on emergency matters and regular notice must state the purpose of the meetings, which is limited to votes on this issue.

C.   Voting Rights

(1)   <u>Quorum</u>--In order for a vote to be taken, a certain number of shareholders must be present in person or represented. It is usually 50 percent although the articles of incorporation can set a higher number. Shareholders present vote on resolutions; a majority must approve most resolutions but fundamental changes may require a higher vote. The right to vote is determined by the voting list which states the record (legal) owner and the number of shares.

(2)   <u>Voting Techniques</u>--Number of votes is determined by number of shares held; some shares may be non-voting.

    (a)   <u>Cumulative Voting</u>--Used to help minority shareholders gain a seat on the board of directors. Each shareholder is entitled to vote the number of shares multiplied by the number of directors to be elected. Minority shareholders cast all their votes for one director; majority shareholders must split their votes in order to elect the rest of the board.

    (b)   <u>Shareholder Agreements, Proxies, and Voting Trusts</u>--All are approved techniques for providing that votes are cast in a certain way. A shareholder agreement obligates shareholders to vote in a particular way. A proxy is a formal written document giving another the right to vote for the shareholder; the holder of the proxy can generally vote as he or she sees fit. Management often solicits proxies. In a voting trust, shareholders transfer legal title to their shares to a trustee, who also holds the stock certificates. The shareholders receive a voting trust certificate. It is more formal than a proxy.

III.   <u>Corporate Management--Directors' Rights and Duties</u>

A.   <u>General Rules</u>--Most states have no qualification requirements. Compensation, if any, must be stated in the bylaws or charter.

B.   <u>Election and Removal</u>--Initial board is named in the charter or appointed by the incorporators. Shareholders then elect at the annual meeting. The number of directors is set in the charter. Can be elected annually or for longer terms, if the terms are staggered. (E.g. There are nine directors who serve for three years; three directors are elected each year.) Director can be removed for cause as specified in the bylaws or by shareholder vote. Vacancies are filled by the shareholders or current board members, depending on state law and the bylaws.

C.   <u>Rights</u>--Direct policy of the corporation, including decisions outside the regular course of business. Declare and pay dividends, appoint and remove corporate officers, and issue stocks and bonds. Can delegate some functions to the officers but still have the right and duty to oversee officers. An executive committee may also be appointed.

D.   <u>Voting</u>--Meeting dates are set in the bylaws, but special meetings can be called. No notice is required for regular meetings and notice can be waived. Voting is proper only in person (no proxies) and each director has only one vote. Quorum is 50 percent or set in the bylaw; majority vote required for most resolutions.

E.   <u>Liabilities</u>--Because of fiduciary duty to the corporation, can be liable for improper use of corporate funds, lax supervision of officers, and ultra vires acts. Business judgment rules protects honest mistakes; due care and compliance with charter and bylaws is the test.

F.   <u>Officers</u>--Serve at the will of the board of directors; can be removed at any time but the corporation may be liable for breach of contract. They are agents of the corporation; directors are not. Qualifications are set by the board. The number and title of officers are set by state law, charter, and bylaws. Usually one person can serve in more than one office.

<u>Study Questions</u>

Fill-in-the-Blank Questions

Alpha Corporation's bylaws provide for the election of directors in the following manner. There are nine directors; their term of office is three years and three directors are elected every year. Furthermore, each shareholder is entitled to split his or her voting among the directors to be elected. Most of the stock is owned by Beta Corporation, however, Ralph owns fifty shares.

At each annual meeting, Ralph is entitled to cast _____
votes.   (1/50/150/450)

The directors are elected for _____ terms.
                                    (regular/staggered)

Alpha Corporation _____ cumulative voting.
                            (has/does not have)

Ralph is entitled to vote on _____.
                                    (policy decisions/fundamental
                                                    changes/both)

True-False Questions

1.   Corporate directors have a fiduciary duty to the corporation. ____

2.   Directors may vote by proxy. ____

3.   A shareholder vote may remove a director for cause. ____

4.   The business judgment rule protects officers from liability for negligent acts. ____

5.   A director must be a shareholder of the corporation.____

6.   A shareholder can bring a derivative suit to enjoin an ultra vires act. ____

7.   Cumulative voting is designed to help management retain control of the corporation. ____

8.   Shareholders are entitled to written notice of special meetings only. ____

9.   In a voting trust, the trustee holds legal title to the shares of stock. ____

10. Shareholders are entitled to written notice of special meetings only. ____

Multiple-Choice Questions

1.   The board of directors can delegate:

    a.   all of its power to an executive committee, but it must oversee officers.
    b.   all of its power to officers, but it must supervise them.
    c.   some of its power to either an executive committee or to officers, but both are limited to ordinary business acts. ____
    d.   some of its power to an executive committee, but it cannot delegate board duties to officers.

2.   Which of the following incorrectly describes the difference between shareholders' and directors' meetings?

    a.   Shareholders must receive notice of all meetings; directors need receive notice of only special meetings.
    b.   Shareholders may only meet once per year at an annual forum; directors may meet more often for regular and special meetings.
    c.   A shareholder's vote is based on the number of shares he or she owns; each director is entitled to only one vote.
    d.   Shareholders can vote by proxy; directors cannot.

3.   Which of the following is true?

    a.   A corporation has only the powers listed in its articles of incorporation and bylaws; it has no implied powers.
    b.   A corporation has express powers which are noted in its articles of incorporation and it has implied powers to carry out express powers.
    c.   The express powers of a corporation usually include the right to give money to charity.
    d.   The bylaws of a corporation are superior to its charter.

4.   "Ultra vires" means:

    a.   illegal.
    b.   unauthorized.
    c.   beyond the powers of.
    d.   limited.

5. Which of the following would most likely be an ultra
    vires act of a corporation formed for the purpose of
    manufacturing and selling toys?

    a. A resolution by the board of directors to borrow
        money for the purpose of creating a new product
        line.
    b. A resolution by the board of directors to give
        employees the right to a profit sharing plan.
    c. A resolution by the board of directors to order
        supplies from a plastics company.
    d. A resolution by the board of directors to forego
        dividends for one year.

6. Audiotronics, Inc. has 100,000 shares which are issued
    and held by shareholders. In the absence of special
    bylaws, how many votes are needed to pass a resolution?

    a. 25,001
    b. 17,001
    c. 50,001
    d. 75,000

7. A shareholder gives written consent to another to cast
    his or her vote at the annual shareholders' meeting.
    The shareholder retains the stock certificate. This
    voting technique is a:

    a. shareholder agreement.
    b. voting trust.
    c. shareholder resolution.
    d. proxy.

8. Which of the following correctly describes the
    management rights of directors?

    a. They have an absolute right to examine corporate
        books.
    b. They have an implied right to compensation.
    c. They have the right to vote by proxy.
    d. They have the right to be notified of all meetings.

9. Which of the following is most likely to result in
    personal liability of a director?

    a. An expensive mistake of judgment even if fraud is
        not involved
    b. Failure to attend meetings or supervise employees
    c. Reliance on bad advice of professionals hired by the
        corporation
    d. Voting for an ultra vires contract which has been
        executed by both sides

10.   Which of the following correctly lists the order of priority rules governing a corporation?

    a.   State statute, state constitution, resolution
    b.   State constitution, state statute, charter
    c.   State statute, bylaws, charter
    d.   State constitution, resolution, bylaws

11.   Which of the following correctly describes the MBCA position on an ultra vires contract of a corporation?

    a.   The contract can be voided on principles of agency.
    b.   The contract is valid between the parties to the contract.
    c.   The contract cannot be voided if unfairness would result.
    d.   The corporation can avoid the contract, if it has not yet performed.

12.   Which of the following is not a remedy for correction of an ultra vires act?

    a.   Shareholder ratification of the act
    b.   Derivative suit brought by the board of directors
    c.   Suit against the board of directors
    d.   Dissolution by a public official

13.   In the absence of special provision in the bylaws:

    a.   shareholders can remove directors for cause by a majority vote at any time.
    b.   shareholders can remove directors at any time for any reason by majority vote.
    c.   shareholders can remove directors at any time only if the director has committed a criminal act.
    d.   shareholders can remove directors for cause but a two-thirds vote is necessary.

14.   Dumont Corporation has six directors who are elected annually.   There are 20,000 outstanding shares of which majority shareholders hold 6,000.

    a.   The minority shareholders will be able to elect a director if straight voting is used.
    b.   The minority shareholders will be able to elect a director if cumulative voting is used.
    c.   The minority shareholders will be able to elect a director regardless of the voting method.
    d.   The minority shareholders will not be able to elect a director regardless of the voting method.

15.   Which of the following is true?

    a.   Directors may serve for a term of one year and this cannot be altered by corporate bylaws.
    b.   Directors may serve for a term of more than one year if state law permits.
    c.   Cumulative voting is not allowed in most states.
    d.   All directors must be elected at the same time.

16.   Which of the following statements about a voting trust is _false_?

    a.   The shareholder gives his or her right to vote to a trustee, but the shareholder retains the stock certificate.
    b.   The shareholder gives his or her right to vote and legal title to the stock to the trustee.
    c.   A voting trust is more difficult to revoke than a proxy.
    d.   A shareholder retains equitable title to the stock and the right to receive dividends.

17.   Which of the following responsibilities of the board of directors normally requires shareholder approval?

    a.   Major policy decisions
    b.   Hiring of officers
    c.   Declaration of dividends
    d.   Amendment of the corporate charter

18.   Ken is president of Mammoth Corporation. He feels that he has been wrongfully dismissed by the board of directors. Which of the following would be a proper remedy for Ken?

    a.   Suit against each director personally
    b.   Suit against the corporation
    c.   Shareholder vote to reinstate Ken
    d.   Derivative suit against the board of directors as a whole

19.   Which of the following correctly describes a corporation's liability for wrongful acts of its employees and officers?

    a.   The corporation is never liable for their torts; the officers and employees are personally liable.
    b.   The corporation is liable for torts committed in the officers' and employees' scope of employment.

c. The directors may be liable personally if they failed to supervise the employee but the corporation is not liable.

d. Both the corporation and the directors are protected by the business judgment rule.

20. Which of the following owe a legally recognized duty to the other?

a. Officers to shareholders
b. Officers to corporation
c. Shareholders to creditors
d. Shareholders to officers

21. Which of the following is correct?

a. Shareholders are entitled to reasonable notice of annual and special meetings.
b. The agenda of annual and special meetings must be included in notice to the shareholders.
c. Special meetings may be called only if two-thirds of the shareholders agree.
d. A quorum is not required at special meetings.

22. The number of directors required to take action at a meeting is a:

a. proxy
b. quorum.
c. quotient.
d. resolution.

23. Which of the following correctly describes a proper vote of directors on ordinary business matters?

a. A majority of the directors must approve the action.
b. A quorum must be present and all present must approve the action.
c. A quorum must be present and a majority of those present must approve the action.
d. A quorum must be present and a majority of the total directors must approve the action.

24. A voting list:

a. records the votes of shareholders at annual meetings.
b. records the votes of directors at annual meetings.
c. lists the name, address, and number of shares for each shareholder.
d. lists the directors present at each meeting.

25.   In a voting trust:

   a.   the trustee always has discretion to vote as he or
         she wishes.
   b.   the trustee may be told how to vote or have
         discretion.
   c.   the shareholder gives a trust certificate to the
         trustee.
   d.   the shareholder gives a proxy to the trustee.

Answers to Study Questions

Fill-in-the-Blank Questions

Ralph is entitled to cast 150 shares (fifty shares X three
directors). The directors are elected for staggered terms,
three per year. Alpha does use cumulative voting because it
allows Ralph to split his shares. Ralph, as a shareholder, is
entitled to vote on fundamental changes; directors vote on
policy decisions.

True-False Questions

1.   T.

2.   F. They must vote in person; shareholders may vote by
      proxy.

3.   T.

4.   F. It protects directors from mistakes of honest
      judgment.

5.   T.

6.   T.

7.   F. It is designed to allow minority shareholders to
      elect a director.

8.   F. Only the board of directors cna declare a dividend.

9.   T.

10.   F. They are entitled to written notice of all meetings.

Multiple-Choice Questions

1.	c	11.	b	21.	a
2.	a	12.	b	22.	b
3.	b	13.	a	23.	c
4.	c	14.	b	24.	c
5.	b	15.	b	25.	c
6.	a	16.	b		
7.	d	17.	d		
8.	a	18.	b		
9.	b	19.	b		
10.	b	20.	b		

Chapter 27 Corporations—
Rights and Duties of Directors,
Managers, and Shareholders

General Principles

Directors and officers are fiduciaries of the corporation and they owe a duty to act honestly and with loyalty to the corporation. In some situations, major shareholders may have a fiduciary duty to minority shareholders.

Directors have the right to participate in management, to inspect corporate books, and to have the corporation stand behind them if they suffer loss because of proper corporate action. In addition to the fiduciary duties outlined above, directors have the duty to attend meetings, to supervise officers, and to act in the best interest of the corporation.

Most shareholders rights are connected with voting but in certain circumstances they have the right to inspect corporate books, to retain relative power within the corporation (pre-emptive rights), and to sue on behalf of the corporation. A shareholder is not liable for the actions of the corporation unless he or she accepts watered stock or abuses the privileges of corporate ownership and a court decides to pierce the corporate veil.

Chapter Summary

I.   **Rights and Duties of Directors and Officers**--Most come from fiduciary duties. A director differs from an agent because he or she can control the corporation-principal; a director differs from a trustee because shareholders do not transfer ownership of the corporation to the directors.

A. Duties

    (1) **Duty of Care**--Standard is reasonably prudent judgment in business affairs and the business judgment rule controls. Duty to reasonably supervise officers. Permissible to rely reasonably on the opinions of experts. The duty of care also includes the duty to attend meetings and to vote. A director who disagreees or who is absent should record a dissent in order to avoid liability.

    (2) **Duty of Loyalty**--Allegiance to the corporation first. Director must disclose conflicts of interest. Cannot compete with the corporation, steal a corporate opportunity, or use inside information to profit personally. No self-dealing.

    (3) **Conflict of Interest**--Occurs when the corporation and the director personally have competing interests. Disclosure is always required. Contracts between a director and the corporation are allowed if disclosure of self-interest is revealed, the contract is reasonable and, the other directors approve it by a majority. Interlocking directorates (one director sitting on the board of competing corporations) is prohibited by the Clayton Act if either corporation has capital surplus and retained profits of more than $1 million.

B. Rights

    (1) **Participation and Voting**--Includes right to participate in meetings and to vote. Absolute right to corporate books (compare shareholders).

    (2) **Indemnification**--Most states and the MBCA give a corporation the right to pay directors for cost incurred if a director is sued in connection with his or her appointment with the corporation. This right of indemnification is allowed even if a judgment is made against the corporation as long as the director acted in good faith and the business judgment rule was used. Corporations can purchase insurance specifically tailored for officers and directors.

(3) <u>Compensation</u>--Not granted automatically, although most bylaws provide for it.

C. <u>Officers' Rights and Duties</u>--Fiduciary duty to the corporation; must follow proper resolutions passed by the directors. Rights are defined in the employment contract.

II. <u>Rights and Duties of Shareholders</u>

A. <u>Duties</u>--Shareholder is usually not liable for corporate actions except when a majority shareholder acts for personal benefit and to the detriment of minority shareholders or creditors. Other liabilities stem from actions with the corporation. Contract liability to pay for stock subscriptions or purchase agreement. If a shareholder purchases par value stock for less than par value or if an inflated value is placed on property transferred in exchange for no par value stock, he or she can be held liable for the difference (watered stock).

B. <u>Rights</u>

(1) <u>Stock Rights</u>--Right to stock certificate and to vote his or her shares. Some classes of stock, usually preferred, may be denied voting rights.

(2) <u>Preemptive Rights</u>--The number of shares owned by a stockholder is a measure of his or her voting strength because it is a percentage of the whole. (An owner of ten shares in a corporation with fifty shares owns one-fifth of the corporation.) Preemptive rights allow a stockholder to purchase stock whenever a new offering is made; this allows the stockholder to keep his or her vote from being diluted. (If the corporation above issues fifty more shares, the stockholder would own ten out of 100 or one-tenth; his strength has been cut in half.)

In most states, corporations can deny these mrights. In general, the rights apply only when new stock is issued (not authorized). The stockholder receives a stock warrant, which is an option to buy stock for a stated period of time.

(3) <u>Dividends</u>--Board of directors decides when to declare; shareholders cannot challenge unless an abuse of discretion is shown. Responsible for return of dividends which would make the corporation insolvent; dividends paid from illegal funds must be returned only if the shareholders knew the dividend was illegal. However, directors who voted for the decision can be personally liable.

(4) <u>Inspection Rights</u>--More restricted than those of directors. Has right to minutes of meetings and tax return for proper purpose. MBCA and most states allow the shareholder to inspect books if he or she has been the owner for six months or owns 5 percent of the total shares. Written demand must be made. There are penalties for denial. Limited because shareholders could use information wrongfully or for harassment. List of shareholders must be kept open for inspection at the annual meeting.

(5) <u>Sale of Shares</u>--General right to sell because shares are personal property. Most close corporations limit transfer; corporation may have the first right to buy (first refusal). Ownership determined by the corporate records; notification is the duty of the shareholders.

(6) <u>Dissolution</u>--Right to vote on this issue and to receive pro rata share of any remaining assets. Preferred shareholders may be given the right to come first. Can sue for dissolution on behalf of the corporation if the directors are deadlocked, the shareholders cannot break it, and the corporation is suffering irreparable injury. Can also sue if the directors are acting illegally, fraudulently, wastefully, or against the interest of minority shareholders.

Study Questions

Fill-in-the-Blank Questions

Bubba owns 20 percent (200 shares) of a corporation which manufactures football equipment. The par value of the shares is $1, for which Bubba paid $100 dollars. The corporation decides to issue an additional 1,000 shares. It sends a notice to Bubba telling him that he has the right to buy 200 more shares if he returns the enclosed document.

Bubba _____ the owner of watered stock.
    (is/is not)

Bubba has _____ rights.
    (preferred/preemptive)

Bubba purchased his initial stock two months ago. Under the
MBCA, he _____ have the right to look at the corporate
books.   (does/does not)

The document which allows Bubba to purchase more shares is a
_____.
(subscription option/stock warrant)

True-False Questions

1. At common law, shareholders had no right to inspect
    corporate books. ____

2. A director's right to be reimbursed for losses in
    connection with corporate business is the right of
    participation. ____

3. If a director does not attend a meeting, he or she will
    be presumed to have approved any resolutions passed at
    the meeting. ____

4. Certain rights of officers are automatic, e.g. the right
    to hire and fire subordinate employees. ____

5. A contract between a director and a corporation is
    prohibited unless the other directors unanimously vote
    to approve the contract. ____

6. Directors owe a fiduciary duty to the corporations;
    officers do not. ____

7. A shareholder can be held personally liable for the
    amount of any dividend which causes the corporation to
    be insolvent. ____

8. Dividends are declared by a majority vote of
    shareholders at the annual meeting. ____

9. Usurping of a corporation opportunity occurs when a
    director sits on the board of more than one corporation.
    ____

10. A director can operate a business which competes with
    the corporation if the other directors and the
    stockholders approve. ____

Multiple-Choice Questions

1.   The rule against interlocking directorates is found in:

   a.   MBCA.
   b.   Securities and Exchange Act.
   c.   Clayton Act.
   d.   court decisions.

2.   A contract between a director and a corporation:

   a.   is always valid.
   b.   is always void.
   c.   is always voidable.
   d.   is valid, if certain requirements are met.

3.   The power of a corporation to purchase insurance for its directors and officers is:

   a.   proper only if the charter so permits.
   b.   proper only if the bylaws so permit.
   c.   part of a corporation's implied powers.
   d.   improper; directors and officers must purchase their own insurance.

4.   Which of the following correctly describes the right of access to corporate books?

   a.   Directors and shareholders have an abolsute right to inspect the books.
   b.   Directors have an absolute right to inspect the books; shareholders have no right to inspect the books.
   c.   Directors have an absolute right to inspect the books; shareholders have limited rights.
   d.   Directors and shareholders have limited rights.

5.   In which of the following situations would indemnification of a corporate director be improper?

   a.   Director is sued as part of a products liability suit against the corporation.
   b.   Director is sued for fraud in a shareholder's derivative suit.
   c.   Director pleads guilty to fraud.
   d.   Director is sued but the case is settled out of court.

6. Betty, a shareholder of Mega Corporation, loses her stock certificate. Which of the following is correct?

   a. She cannot vote or receive dividends.
   b. Betty remains the record owner of the stock, but she cannot vote.
   c. Betty can vote and receive dividends.
   d. Betty must present her certificate in order to receive a dividend.

7. Preemptive rights:

   a. give the shareholder the right to remove directors without cause.
   b. give the shareholder the right to transfer his or her stock.
   c. gives the corporation the right of first refusal if a shareholder decides to sell his or her stock.
   d. gives the shareholder the right to purchase more stock when the corporation issues it.

8. Mary receives a notice that Alpha Corporation has declared a dividend which will be paid in one month. Mary's right to a dividend:

   a. became final when the board of directors declared the dividend.
   b. becomes final when the dividend is paid.
   c. is not absolute; the board of directors can revoke the declaration.
   d. is absolute; she is entitled to be paid a dividend every year but the board of directors can set the amount.

9. The authority to preemptive rights is contained in a:

   a. stock dividend.
   b. stock rights.
   c. stock warrant.
   d. dividend right.

10. The transfer (sale or gift) of stock certificates:

    a. is an absolute right of the shareholder.
    b. may be banned totally in a close corporation.
    c. may be subject to reasonable restrictions.
    d. may not be limited except in a close corporation.

11.   Which of the following statements about watered stock is incorrect?

    a.   A shareholder who receives watered stock is liable to the corporation for the difference between the value paid and the true value.
    b.   It cannot occur if the stock has no par value.
    c.   In some states, a shareholder who receives watered stock may be liable to the creditors of the corporation.
    d.   It occurs if stock is issued in exchange for services rendered by the shareholder.

12.   Allan owns 90 percent of the stock in Beta Corporation. He decides to sell his shares to Chris. Allan owes a fiduciary duty to:

    a.   Chris only.
    b.   the minority shareholders only.
    c.   the minority shareholders and the corporation.
    d.   no none.

13.   Which of the following correctly describes the relationship of a director to a corporation?

    a.   The director is a trustee of the corporation.
    b.   The director is an agent of the corporation.
    c.   The director is both an agent and trustee of the corporation.
    d.   The director is a fiduciary, but is neither a trustee nor an agent.

14.   Bob is a director of Gamma Corporation. While Bob is on vacation, the other directors vote to issue a stock dividend from improper funds. Bob:

    a.   is personally liable because a majority of the directors approved the dividend.
    b.   is personally liable unless he recorded his dissent.
    c.   is not personally liable because he did not attend the meeting.
    d.   is not personally liable if he did not know that the directors were going to authorize the dividend.

15.   Meg is a director of Lambda Corporation, which manufactures household appliances. She hears that Price, an inventor, has created a new portable dishwasher. Meg buys the patent rights from Price.

    a.   Meg has breached her fiduciary duty to Lambda Corp.

    b.   Meg has not breached her fiduciary duty to Lambda Corp.

    c.   Meg has breached her fiduciary duty unless she discloses her interest to Lambda Corp.

    d.   Meg has breached her fiduciary duty unless she receives the consent of the other directors.

16.   Sam is a director of two corporations. Mega Corporation manufactures auto parts; Minor Corporation is a retail clothing store.

    a.   Sam has violated the duty of loyalty to both corporations.

    b.   Sam has not violated the duty of loyalty to either corporation.

    c.   Sam is in violation of the Clayton Act.

    d.   Sam is in violation of the Clayton Act only if one of the corporation has assets of $1 million and 500,000 shareholders.

17.   The right to declare a dividend:

    a.   belongs to the board of directors and the shareholder cannot force payment.

    b.   belongs to the board of directors but the shareholders may override its decision by a unanimous vote.

    c.   belongs to the board of directors but the shareholders may override its decision if a court finds that the board is abusing its descretion.

    d.   belongs to the shareholders and directors jointly.

18.   All states allow dividends to be paid from which of the following fund(s)?

    a.   Retained earnings only

    b.   Capital surplus only

    c.   Retained earnings and capital surplus

    d.   Retained earnings and net profits

19.   Which of the following correctly describes a shareholder's right to inspect corporate books under the MBCA?

    a.   The shareholder must hold at least 5 percent of the stock, owned the shares for six months, and have a proper purpose.

    b.   The shareholder must hold at least 5 percent of the stock or owned shares for six months, and purpose is irrelevant.

c.   The shareholder must hold at least 5 percent of the stock or owned shares for six months and his or her reason for inspection must be proper.

d.   The shareholder must hold at least 5 percent of the stock or owned shares for six months and receive the permission of the board of directors.

20.   Which of the following correctly describes the personal liability of shareholders?

a.   Watered stock, illegal dividends, and dividends which make the corporation insolvent

b.   Watered stock, stock subscriptions, and dividends which make the corporation insolvent

c.   Stock subscriptions, illegal dividends, and dividends which make the corporation insolvent

d.   Illegal dividends and watered stock

21.   Alice is a shareholder in Gamma Corporation. She has evidence that the board of directors is wasting corporate assets. Alice:

a.   cannot sue the corporation but she can sell her stock.

b.   can sue in a derivative suit and force the directors to reimburse the corporation or she can sue to dissolve the corporation.

c.   can sue in a derivative suit but cannot sue for dissolution.

d.   cannot sue the directors because they are protected by the business judgment rule.

22.   Anne is a director of Mina Corporation. She is an attorney and the corporation wants to hire her to amend the articles of incorporation and the bylaws.

a.   The contract, if approved by the board, will be void.

b.   The contract, if reasonable and if approved by a majority of disinterested directors, will be valid.

c.   The contracts, if approved by a majority of the shareholders, will be valid.

d.   The contract, if reasonable, will be valid.

23.   Which of the following correctly describes the voting rights of stockholders?

a.   All stockholders have the right to vote.

b.   The charter may limit the right to vote to certain classes of stock.

c.   Treasury stock is voted by the board of directors.

d.   Stockholders with preemptive rights are denied the right to vote.

24. Which of the following is not an automatic right of a shareholder?

    a. Right to stock certificate
    b. Right to sell stock, although may be limited
    c. Right to receive dividends annually
    d. Right to attend annual and special meetings

25. Bill is a director of Beta Corporation. He is wrongfully refused entrance to a director's meeting. Bill has been denied his right of:

    a. indemnification.
    b. preemption.
    c. participation.
    d. inspection.

Answers to Study Questions

Fill-in-the-Blank Questions

Bubba is the owner of watered stock; the stock is valued at $200 and Bubba paid only $100. Bubba has preemptive rights; preferred rights refer to payment of dividends. He does have the right if he has a proper purpose because he owns more than 5 percent of the stock. The stock warrant gives Bubba the right to purchase more stock; a stock subscription is a shareholder's promise to buy stock.

True-False Questions

1. F. They always have the right for a proper purpose.

2. F. It is the right of indemnification.

3. T.

4. F. Their rights are defined in the employment contract.

5. F. A majority vote is needed if the contract is reasonable.

6. F. Both owe a fiduciary duty to the corporation.

7. T.

8. F. Dividends are declared by the board of directors.

9.   F.   This   is   a   description   of   an   interlocking
      directorate; usurping of a corporate opportunity occurs
      when a director competes with a corporation.

10.   F.

Multiple-Choice Questions

1.	a	11.	b	21.	b
2.	d	12.	c	22.	b
3.	c	13.	d	23.	b
4.	c	14.	b	24.	c
5.	c	15.	a	25.	c
6.	c	16.	b		
7.	d	17.	c		
8.	a	18.	a		
9.	c	19.	c		
10.	c	20.	b		

Chapter 28 Corporations— Merger, Consolidation, and Termination

General Principles

This chapter deals with fundamental changes within corporations. These changes include merger, consolidation, sale of assets, and dissolutions. The proper procedure may involve approval by one or two boards of directors, passage of resolution by shareholders, and approval of the Department of Justice. Shareholders' rights after the change is completed may include buy-out agreements, stock swaps, or nothing at all.

Chapter Summary

I.   Merger, Consolidation, and Sale of Assets

   A.   Definitions

      (1) Merger--Two corporations combine asset and liabilities and only one corporation remains. Articles of merger are filed with the secretary of state. A short-form merger occurs when one corporation (parent), which holds 90 to 95 percent of another corporation (subsidiary), decides to merge. Procedures are different as noted below.

      (2) Consolidation--Two corporations combine assets and liabilities and a new corporation is formed. Articles of consolidation are filed with the secretary of state and are the articles of incorporation for the new corporation.

(3)   Purchase of Assets--One corporation purchases virtually all the assets of another corporation; the legal status of the corporations is not changed. Liabilities are not transferred. Justice Department regulates because it could be a merger in disguise.

(4)   Purchase of Stock (Takeover Bid)--Offer made directly to shareholder (compare procedures below). The federal government regulates offers to the public (tender offers).

B.   Procedures

(1)   Mergers and Consolidations--Boards of directors of both corporations must approve. Shareholders of both corporations must approve, usually by a two-thirds vote, although may be higher. Articles of merger of consolidation are filed; secretary of state issues a certificate of merger or consolidation. Short-form mergers can occur without shareholder approval because it would happen even if a vote were taken.

(2)   Sale of Assets--Purchasing corporation needs only the vote of the directors. The selling (acquired) corporation requires a shareholder vote.

(3)   Sale of Stock--Purchasing corporation makes the offer directly to the shareholders of the selling or target corporation. No formal approval is required but federal securities law regulates public or tender offers.

C.   Appraisal Rights and Results of Sale or Merger

(1)   Stock--In a merger or consolidation, the shareholders of the old or merged corporation receive shares of the surviving or new corporation. When shareholders sell their stock in a tender offer, they may receive cash, property, or stock in the acquiring corporation.

(2)   Appraisal Rights--Used when the shareholder disagrees with the fundamental change; the dissenting shareholder is paid for his or her shares.

(a) <u>Persons Entitled</u>--Always permitted in mergers and consolidations. In most states, the purchase of assets is treated as a merger and the shareholders of the selling corporation receive appraisal rights. Some states give these rights when the articles of incorporation are amended and a shareholder suffers from the decision. There are no such rights in a tender offer since each stockholder makes the decision whether or not to sell.

(b) <u>Procedure</u>--Must be followed strictly. Shareholders must file written notice of intent to dissent and written demand for payment after the change has occurred. Usually cannot back out. Entitled to the fair market value of the stock on the day before the vote was taken. If the value is not readily determined, the parties can agree or the court can decide.

II. <u>Termination</u>--Includes dissolution and liquidation or winding up.

   A. <u>Dissolution</u>

      (1) <u>Voluntary</u>--The board of directors and the shareholders (two-thirds majority) can vote; a unanimous vote of the shareholders will override the board of directors.

      (2) <u>Involuntary</u>--Legislature passes law which forces dissolution. Court can order dissolution if the corporation does not comply with state requirements, incorporation occurred due to fraud, the directors abuse the ultra vires doctrine, the corporation never does business or ceases to do so. Remember that shareholders can petition for dissolution if the board of directors is deadlocked and the corporation cannot be saved.

   B. <u>Liquidation</u>--Sale of assets and payment of liabilities; the remainder, if any, is distributed to the shareholders. Usually carried out by the board of directors (as trustees). The court can appoint a receiver if the directors refuse to liquidate, there is reason to believe that the board would not act properly, or when a court dissolves the corporation due to deadlock or mismanagement.

Study Questions

Fill-in-the-Blank Questions

Ruth is a shareholder in Profitable Corporation. The directors of the corporation have voted to combine with Mediocre Corporation. After the combination, only Profitable Corporation will exist.

This is an example of a _____.
                    (merger/consolidation/purchase of assets)

Ruth _____ entitled to vote on the combination.
       (is/is not)

The shareholders of Mediocre Corporation _____ entitled to vote.   (are/are not)

Ruth _____ entitled to appraisal rights.
       (is/is not)

The shareholders of Mediocre Corporation _____ entitled to appraisal rights.   (are/are not)

True-False Questions

1. The two parts of termination are dissolution and abandonment. ____

2. In a purchase of assets, the shareholders of the purchasing corporation are entitled to vote. ____

3. A tender offer is a synonym for a purchase of assets. ____

4. In a consolidation, the new corporation must file new articles of corporation. ____

5. Appraisal rights will be awarded only if a dissenting shareholder gives written notice of dissent before the merger. ____

6. A corporation cannot be terminated voluntarily without the consent of a majority of the board of directors.____

7. The value of stock for appraisal purposes is determined as of the day before the vote was taken. ____

8. If a corporation is dissolved involuntarily, a receiver will be appointed to carry out liquidation.

9.   In a merger, the surviving corporation absorbs the assets and losses of the merged corporation. ____

10.   A short-form merger can occur only when a parent and subsidiary merge. ____

Multiple-Choice Questions

1.   "The sale of assets of a business or an individual for cash and the distribution of cash to creditors with the balance going to the owners" is a description of:

   a.   preemptive rights.
   b.   termination.
   c.   dissolution.
   d.   liquidation.

2.   The right of a shareholder to force the corporation to buy his or her stock after a merger is:

   a.   appropriation rights.
   b.   appraisal rights.
   c.   preemptive rights.
   d.   preferred rights.

3.   "A right which can be enforced in a court to recover a debt or damages" is a definition of:

   a.   appraisal right.
   b.   preemptive right.
   c.   chose in action.
   d.   equity.

4.   Which of the following would be least likely to receive appraisal rights?

   a.   Shareholders of a surviving corporation after merger
   b.   Shareholders of a corporation which has been consolidated
   c.   Shareholders of a corporation which has sold its assets to another corporation
   d.   Shareholders who are the subject of a tender offer

5.   Which of the following is least likely to require a shareholder vote?

   a.   Merger
   b.   Consolidation
   c.   Amendment to the charter
   d.   Amendment of the bylaws

6. Gamma Corporation and Beta Corporation are planning to merge. Which of the following parties are entitled to vote on the proposal?

   a. Directors of both corporations only
   b. Shareholders of both corporations only
   c. Directors and shareholders of both corporations
   d. Directors of the surviving corporation; directors and shareholders of the merged corporation

7. In order for the merger in Question 6 to occur:

   a. the merged corporation must dissolve and the surviving corporation must file an amendment to its charter.
   b. the merged corporation must sell its assets and liabilities to the surviving corporation and the merged corporation must dissolve.
   c. the surviving corporation must file an amendment to its charter.
   d. the surviving corporation must file articles of merger.

8. After the merge in Question 6 occurs, which of the following have appraisal rights?

   a. The directors and shareholders of the merged corporation
   b. The directors and shareholders of both corporation
   c. The shareholders of the merged corporation
   d. The shareholders of both corporations

9. In order to enforce appraisal rights:

   a. notice must be given before and after the vote.
   b. notice must be given before the vote.
   c. notice must be given after the vote.
   d. the parties must agree on a value of the stock.

10. X Corporation and Y Corporation are consolidating. Paul, a shareholder of X Corporation, wants to enforce his appraisal rights. The board of directors of both corporations vote to approve the merger on March 10. The shareholders of both corporations vote on May 10. The articles of merger are filed on May 15; the certificate of merger is approved on May 30. For purposes of appraisal rights, Paul's shares will be valued on:

    a. March 10.
    b. May 9.
    c. May 10.
    d. May 30.

11.   The merger officially occurs on:

        a. March 10.
        b. May 9.
        c. May 10.
        d. May 30.

12.   Mega Corporation is purchasing the assets of Minor Corporation. In most states, which of the following have the right to vote on the purchase?

        a. Board of directors of both corporations only
        b. Board of directors of both corporations and the shareholders of Mega Corporation
        c. Board of directors of both corporations and shareholders of Minor Corporation
        d. Board of directors and shareholders of both corporations

13.   Which of the following laws restricts the purchase of assets described in Question 12?

        a. Justice Department only
        b. Clayton Act and the Justice Department
        c. Clayton Act
        d. Robinson-Patman Act

14.   In most states, approval of fundamental changes requires the approval of:

        a. a majority of the shareholders with voting stock.
        b. two-thirds of the shareholders with voting stock.
        c. a majority of the shareholders in each class.
        d. two-thirds of the shareholders in each class.

15.   Which of the following will **not** cause termination of a corporation?

        a. Unanimous vote of the board of directors
        b. Unanimous vote of the shareholders
        c. Two-thirds vote of the board of directors and shareholders
        d. Expiration of the time provided in the charter

16.   Which of the following cannot bring about the dissolution of a corporation without the approval of another party?

        a. The legislature
        b. The shareholders
        c. A court
        d. The board of directors

17.   When a corporation terminates voluntarily, which of the following cannot occur?

        a.   A receiver will be appointed if the board refuses to liquidate.
        b.   Shareholders will receive assets remaining after liquidation.
        c.   The trustees will be personally liable for any breach of duty committed during liquidation.
        d.   Shareholders will be personally liable for any fraud committed during liquidation.

18.   Gamma and Rho Corporations are combining their assets and liabilities in order to form Tau Corporation. This is a description of a:

        a.   merger.
        b.   consolidation.
        c.   purchase of stock.
        d.   tender offer.

19.   When the combination is complete, the secretary of state will issue:

        a.   articles of merger.
        b.   articles of consolidation.
        c.   certificate of consolidation.
        d.   certificate of completion.

20.   The stock of Beta Corporation is valued at $10 per share. Alpha Corporation is planning a takeover bid. The takeover bid will involve:

        a.   tender offers to the shareholders of Beta Corporation.
        b.   tender offers to the shareholders of Alpha Corporation.
        c.   purchase of the assets of Beta Corporation.
        d.   filing of articles of merger.

21.   Sally is a shareholder in Beta Corporation. Alpha Corporation will most likely:

        a.   give Sally appraisal rights of $10 per share.
        b.   give Sally appraisal rights of $12 per share.
        c.   offer Sally $8 per share for the purchase of her stock.
        d.   offer Sally $12 per share for the purchase of her stock.

22.   Gamma, Inc. owns 85 percent of the stock of Lambda, Inc. The merger of Gamma and Lambda will require the approval of:

    a.   the board of directors of both corporations, but not the approval of the shareholders.
    b.   the board of directors and shareholders of both corporations.
    c.   the board of directors and shareholders of Gamma Inc., and the board of directors of Lambda, Inc.
    d.   the board of directors and shareholders of Lambda, Inc. and the board of directors of Gamma, Inc.

23.   Tender offers are regulated by:

    a.   federal law.
    b.   the charter of the acquiring corporation.
    c.   state law.
    d.   the charter of the target corporation.

24.   A target corporation is:

    a.   the corporation which ceases to exist after a merger.
    b.   the corporation which is created after a consolidation.
    c.   the corporation which is the subject of a takeover bid.
    d.   the corporation which is conducting a takeover bid.

25.   Which of the following would not require filing a document with the secretary of state?

    a.   Regular Merger
    b.   Short-form Merger
    c.   Consolidation
    d.   Purchase of assets

Answers to Study Questions

Fill-in-the-Blank Questions

This is an example of a merger; a consolidation causes both corporations to dissolve and a purchase of assets has no effect on legal status. Ruth and the shareholders of Mediocre Corporation are entitled to vote and both are entitled to appraisal rights.

True-False Questions

1.   F.   They are dissolution and liquidation.

2.   F.   Only the shareholders of the selling corporation are entitled to vote.

3.   F.   It is a synonym for a public offering for purchase of stock.

4.   F.   The articles of consolidation become the articles of incorporation.

5.   T.

6.   F.   The shareholders can terminate by unanimous vote.

7.   T.

8.   T.

9.   T.

10.   T.

Multiple-Choice Questions

1.	d	11.	d	21.	d
2.	b	12.	c	22.	b
3.	c	13.	b	23.	a
4.	d	14.	d	24.	c
5.	d	15.	a	25.	d
6.	c	16.	d		
7.	d	17.	d		
8.	d	18.	b		
9.	a	19.	c		
10.	b	20.	a		

Chapter 29 Corporations—
Financing, Financial Regulation,
and Investor Protection

General Principles

Corporations are financed by selling stock and borrowing money.
Bonds are a form of borrowing money from investors. Investors
are protected from fraud and bad faith by state (blue sky) and
federal laws. The federal laws require large public
corporations to disclose financial statements and regulate the
sale of stock. These laws also prevent fraud on the part of
insiders and others in connection with the sale of stock.

Chapter Summary

I. Corporate Financing--Stocks and bonds are collectively
referred to as securities. Stocks (equity securities)
represent ownership in the corporation and purchasers
are shareholders. Bonds (debt securities) are essen-
tially loans made from bondholders to the corporation
and usually are for long periods of time. They must be
paid by the corporation; a stockholder receives payment
only when and if a dividend is declared. Stockholders
vote; bondholders do not. Stockholders may receive
assets on dissolution; bondholder receives nothing once
the bond has been paid.

   A. Bonds--(Bond is $1,000; others are debentures)

      (1) Bond indenture--The agreement between the
          bondholders and the corporation. It usually
          provides that the bond will be paid back at a
          stated rate of interest and payment dates.
          Most bonds are paid in installments semi-
          annually based on the rate of interest on
          $1,000.

(2) <u>Payment</u>--A bond has a face (issued) value of $1,000. The corporation promises to pay back this amount and a stated rate of interest. When interest rates change, the relative value (but not the face value) can change. If the bonds are sold below the face value (discount), then the buyer will receive more money (yield) when the bond is paid off. If the bonds are sold above face value (premium), the buyer will receive less money when the bond is paid off.

EX: Paul purchases a bond at face value of $1,000. Before the bond is repaid, he sells his remaining rights to Sharon, who pays the equivalent of $998. When the corporation pays Sharon, she will receive the same amount of money (principal and interest) as if she had paid $1,000.

(3) <u>Classification</u>

   (a) <u>Debentures v. Mortgage</u>--The latter use the property of the corporation as security for payment; the former does not.

   (b) <u>Convertible v. Non-Convertible</u>--The former can be converted into stock at a stated rate. This option remains with the shareholders who will probably choose to do so if the corporation is doing well.

   (c) <u>Callable v. Non-Callable</u>--The former allows the corporation to pay off the bonds (call) early and under conditions specified in the indenture.

B. <u>Stocks</u>

   (1) <u>Common Stock</u>--Owners of the corporation with voting rights and the right to receive dividends. Preferred stock usually receives a dividend first.

   (2) <u>Preferred Stock</u>--May or may not be allowed to vote. Usually generates a fixed-amount dividend. This is more secure but may not receive as much if the corporation is doing well and is paying high dividends. Preferred

stockholders are paid dividends before common
stockholders receive theirs and come before
common stockholders upon distribution of
assets at dissolution.

Preferred cumulative stock is entitled to the
same rights as a preferred stockholder but if
the corporation does not pay a dividend as
promised, the right to a dividend accumulates
and the owner may be paid two dividends before
a common stockholder receives any. Participating preferred stock allows the owner to
share in dividends with common stockholders
after both classes have been paid one
dividend. Preferred convertible stock can be
exchanged for common stock; callable preferred
stock can be repurchased by the corporation.

(3) Stock "Owned" by the Corporation--The articles
of incorporation states the authorized shares
or the number of shares that the corporation
can sell. Issued shares are those which have
been sold. Treasury shares are issued shares
which have been repurchased by the
corporation. Outstanding shares are those
which have been issued and have not been
repurchased.

(4) Value of Shares--Par value is the value given
to the stock by the corporation. No par value
stock is not assigned a value. Watered stock
has been purchased for less than its true
value.

II. Securities Regulation

A. Securities Act of 1933--A disclosure statute which
requires most large, publicly-held corporations to
inform prospective buyers about the corporation.

(1) Exemptions--Private offerings, offerings to
institutions, to small numbers of investors,
offerings to the residents of the incorporated
states, and sales not generally advertised if
the investor is sophisticated. In general
offerings under $500,000 made in one year are
exempt and offerings of up to $5,000,000 if
made to less than thirty-five investors,
without general advertising. Stock dividends
and stock splits are exempt as are securities

of a reorganized or charitable corporation. There are other minor exemptions, most of which occur in industries which are tightly regulated by other laws. Note that the exemptions above are usually relatively small in amount or are made to sophisticated investors.

(2) Requirements

    (a) Registration Statement--Must be filed with the SEC before any offering using mail or interstate commerce is made. Investors must be given a prospectus or description of the company and the offer. The registration statement must include a financial statement prepared by a CPA, notice of pending lawsuits, a description of management and its holdings or interests in the corporation, a description of properties and business and facts about the sale.

    (b) Sale--Before the registration statement is filed, the corporation may hire an underwriter who will oversee the distribution. No written advertising until twenty days after the registration statement is filed. An interim prospectus (red-herring) may be distributed. After the waiting period, the securities can be bought and sold but the only written advertising allowed is a tombstone ad which simply tells investors where they can get a copy of the prospectus.

B. Securities Act of 1934--An anti-fraud statute.

(1) General Provisions--Applies to all corporations listed on stock exchanges, and any corporation with assets in excess of $1 million and at least 500 shareholders (Section 12 companies). SEC regulates all aspects including proxy solicitation, brokers, dealers, and operations of the stock exchanges.

(2) Insider Trading--Occurs when a person who has knowledge before the general public receives it. An insider can make money by buying or selling the stock before information is released to the general public.

(a) Rule 10b-5--Applies when an insider sells or purchases stock and misrepresents or omits to state a material fact to the other party. An insider can be a director, officer, controlling stock-holder, or someone who has learned information before it is released to the general public. Intent to deceive is required and there are criminal and civil penalties.

(b) Section 16(b)--Applies to sale or purchase made within six months of each other. The profits must be returned to the corporation; intent is irrelevant. Applies to officers, directors, and some major shareholders. There are some exemptions. Only the corporation or a shareholder can bring suit.

(c) Proxy Statements--A disclosure and anti-fraud statute which regulates the content of proxy statements issued by management. Remedies include damages and injunction.

C. Miscellaneous Regulations

(1) Investment Companies--Companies which manage portfolios made up of smaller investors must register with the SEC and its activities are regulated.

(2) Mutual Funds--A type of investment company which offers the public shares of ownership in a portfolio on a continuing basis. Annual reports must be filed with the SEC and either a bank or a member of the securities exchange must hold the securities. Investment activities and payment of dividends are also restricted.

(3) Foreign Corrupt Practices Act--An amendment to the act prohibits bribes to foreign officials in exchange for favors. Only payments to lower-level employees, who have little authority, are allowed. Criminal fines of up to $1 million and officers and employees can also be fined or imprisoned.

III.   State Laws (Blue Sky Laws)--Anti-fraud statutes which usually require registration before the stock can be offered for sale. Filed with corporations commissioner. Some states have absolute requirements; others use good faith standard.

Study Questions

Fill-in-the-Blank Questions

Bill and Sally have purchased securities from Mega Corporation. Bill paid $5,000 and every six months he receives a stated payment for twenty years. The money is paid regardless of whether the corporation makes a profit. Sally also paid $5,000. She received the right to elect directors of Mega Corporation and she will receive money only if the corporation makes money. However, the corporation promises her that if for some reason they cannot pay her every year, she will receive a payment for each year, when payments are finally made.

Bill is a _____.
    (stockholder/bondholder)

Sally is a _____.
    (stockholder/bondholder)

Sally's rights are _____.
    (cumulative/convertible)

The agreement between Bill and the corporation is a(n):

_____.
(subscription/prospectus/indenture)

Sally owns _____ securities.
    (equity/debt)

True-False Questions

1.   Rule 10b-5 applies only to corporations who trade stock on a securities exchange. ____

2.   Authorized shares include treasury shares, issued shares, and unissued shares. ____

3.   A debenture is any bond with a value of more than $1,000. ____

4.   State securities laws are called red-herring laws. ____

5.   Rule 10b-5 applies to short-swing profits only. ____

6.   A mutual fund is a type of investment security. ____

7.   Proxy statments are regulated in order to prevent non-stockholders from lobbying stockholders. ____

8.   A callable bond may be paid off early by the corporation. ____

9.   The Securities and Exchange Act of 1934 regulates the manner in which corporations can offer stock for sale. ____

10.   Majority shareholders are considered insiders. ____

Multiple-Choice Questions

1.   A bond is classified as a:

       a.   short-term equity security.
       b.   long-term equity security.
       c.   short-term debt security.
       d.   long-term debt security.

2.   Which of the following is not required in the registration statement under the Securities Act of 1933?

       a.   Financial statement certified by a CPA
       b.   Red-herring prospectus
       c.   Description of the corporation's management and its fringe benefits
       d.   List of pending lawsuits

3.   The Securities Act of 1933 is a(n):

       a.   disclosure statute.
       b.   anti-fraud statute.
       c.   blue sky law.
       d.   federal law.

4.   Which of the following is not allowed while approval of a registration statement is pending?

       a.   Selection of an underwriter
       b.   Sale to certain institutional investors
       c.   Issuance of red-herring prospectus
       d.   Oral offers between the corporation and investors

5.   Which of the following is automatically exempted from the registration requirements of the Securities Act of 1933?

a.   Stock dividends
b.   Sale of stock in public corporations
c.   Sale of all commercial paper
d.   Sale of unadvertised stock to any investor

6.   Rose and Stan own stock in Mina Corporation. Rose receives a dividend of 8% per year if and when a dividend is paid. If a dividend is not paid, Rose receives no rights. Rose does not vote. Stan is also promised an 8% return on investment but he may also share in extra dividends after all stockholders have been paid. Rose owns:

a.   common, non-voting, non-cumulative stock.
b.   common, non-participating stock.
c.   preferred, non-cumulative stock.
d.   preferred, participating stock.

7.   Stan owns:

a.   common, participating stock.
b.   common, cumulative stock.
c.   preferred, participating stock.
d.   preferred, cumulative stock.

8.   Bob purchased ten $1,000 bonds from Tau Corporation, but he paid only $990 per bond. He is promised a return on investment of 12 percent for a period of fifteen years. Bob purchased the stock:

a.   at face value.
b.   at a discount.
c.   at a premium.

9.   Bob will receive:

a. $9,990 at 12 percent interest.
b. $10,000 at 12 percent interest.
c. $10,200 at 12 percent interest.

10.   A bond which is backed by the personal and real property of the corporation is a(n):

a.   indenture.
b.   debenture.
c.   mortgage bond.
d.   preferred bond.

11.   Which   of   the   following   federal   laws   regulates
       short-swing profits?

       a.   Blue Sky laws
       b.   Securities Act of 1933
       c.   Rule 10b-5
       d.   Securities Act of 1934

12.   The short-swing profits rule applies to:

       a.   directors and officers only.
       b.   directors, officers, and majority shareholders.
       c.   the general public.
       d.   tippees, officers, and directors.

13.   The time limit applicable to short-swing profits is:

       a.   one year.
       b.   one month.
       c.   six months.
       d.   sixty days.

14.   a person who is not affiliated with a corporation but
       who receives non-public information and uses the
       information to make a profit is best described as a(n):

       a.   insider.
       b.   red herring.
       c.   tippee.
       d.   underwriter.

15.   The state official with whom a sale of securities must
       be registered is the:

       a.   underwriter.
       b.   registrar.
       c.   corporations commissioner.
       d.   stock commissioner.

16.   Which   of   the   following   correctly   describes   the
       difference between Rule 10b-5 and Section 16?

       a.   The former applies to insiders only; the latter
            applies to the general public.
       b.   The former requires proof of fraud; the latter does
            not.
       c.   The former is part of the Securities Act of 1933;
            the latter is part of the Securities Act of 1934.
       d.   The former contains numerous exceptions; the latter
            does not.

17.   Under its articles of incorporation Alpha corporation
        can issue 100,000 shares of stock. 50,000 shares are
        currently held by shareholders; 10,000 shares were
        recently purchased from Samuel, a shareholder. The
        number of authorized shares is:

        a.   10,000.
        b.   50,000.
        c.   90,000.
        d.   100,000.

18.   The number of treasury shares is:

        a.   10,000.
        b.   50,000.
        c.   90,000.
        c.   100,000.

19.   The number of outstanding shares is:

        a.   50,000.
        b.   60,000.
        c.   90,000.
        d.   100,000.

20.   John purchased a bond from Mega Corporation. The bond
        agreement states that John may trade his bond in for
        five shares of common stock. The agreement also gives
        Mega the right to pay the bond earlier than is stated in
        the agreement. John's bond is:

        a.   preferred and convertible.
        b.   callable and convertible.
        c.   preferred and callable.
        d.   cumulative and convertible.

21.   Participating preferred stock gives the shareholder the
        right to:

        a.   trade in the stock for a bond.
        b.   stated dividends every year.
        c.   stated dividends and the right to surplus dividends
             after common stockholders have been paid.
        d.   receive dividends for every year in which dividends
             were not paid.

22.   Outstanding shares equal:

        a.   authorized shares less treasury shares.
        b.   authorized shares less issued shares.
        c.   issued shares less treasury shares.
        d.   issued shares plus treasury shares.

23.   The purpose of the Securities Act of 1933 is to:

        a.   give unsophisticated investors information.
        b.   prevent short-swing profits.
        c.   prevent watered stock.
        d.   regulate proxy statements.

24.   "A type of investment company which continually sells
        and buys to investors of ownership in a portfolio" is
        a(n):

        a.   underwriting company.
        b.   Section 12 company.
        c.   blue sky fund.
        d.   mutual fund.

25.   The information which can be released before a
        registration statement is approved includes which of the
        following?

        a.   Red-herring prospectus only
        b.   Tombstone ad only
        c.   Red-herring prospectus and tombstone ad
        d.   Portfolio

Answers to Study Questions

Fill-in-the-Blank Questions

Bill is a bondholder; Sally is a stockholder. Sally's rights
are cumulative. The agreement between Bill and the corporation
is an indenture; a prospectus is used in connection with a
stock sale; a stock subscription is an agreement to buy stock.
Sally owns equity securities; Bill owns debt securities.

True-False Questions

1.   F.

2.   T.

3.   F.   A debenture is an unsecured bond.

4.   F.   They are called blue sky laws.

5.   F.   It applies to any fraudulent statement or omission.

6.   T.

7.   F.   They   are   designed   to   regulate   management
      solicitation of shareholder votes.

8.   T.

9.   F.   The Securities Act of 1933 does this.

10.   T.

Multiple-Choice Questions

1.	d	11.	d	21.	c
2.	b	12.	b	22.	c
3.	a	13.	c	23.	a
4.	b	14.	c	24.	d
5.	a	15.	c	25.	a
6.	c	16.	b		
7.	c	17.	d		
8.	b	18.	a		
9.	b	19.	a		
10.	c	20.	b		

UNIT V
GOVERNMENT REGULATION

Chapter 30   Antitrust

The purpose of antitrust laws is to protect the consumer against practices by businesses which would monopolize the economy. When a monopoly occurs, a few sellers can set the price of goods which consumers will be forced to pay. A business may obtain a monopoly through price-fixing agreements, distribution practices, and mergers. In some cases, concentration of manufacturing and distribution may cut costs and only unreasonable market power is prohibited. Some practices have no purpose except to maintain monopoly power and these actions are absolutely prohibited (violations per se). As in the textbook, this chapter will briefly review the antitrust statutes and will focus on behavior that is prohibited.

Chapter Summary

I.   Antitrust Statutes

    A.   Sherman Act--Section 1 applies to agreements between two or more persons which restrain trade (cartel). Section 2 applies to monopolies, which can be created by one person. Actions must have a significant effect on interstate commerce.

        (1)   Enforcement--Justice Department may sue to enforce criminal provisions: fines, dissolution, or divestiture (forcing a company to give up one of its operations). Private persons who have been injured may sue for treble (triple) damages and attorney's fees.

(2) <u>Legal Test</u>--Most cases apply to <u>rule of reason</u>, which asks about the motives and results. Price-fixing arrangements are absolutely prohibited (<u>per se</u> violation).

B. <u>Clayton Act</u>--Prohibits price discrimination unless based on economic factors such as transportation and distribution costs. Also prohibits exclusive dealing arrangements, mergers, and directors who sit on the boards of more than one powerful company.

C. <u>FTC Act</u>--Gives general power to the agency to investigate antitrust violations and to define unfair competition and deceptive business practices. FTC can issue cease-and-desist orders which order business to stop prohibited action. Violators can be fined; no action for treble damages.

D. <u>Robinson-Patman Act</u>--Outlaws predatory price-cutting and price discrimination unless based on transportation, production, or distribution costs.

II. <u>Enforcement of Antitrust Acts</u>--Listed below are actions by business which are prohibited. The definition of each action includes the source of law which prohibits the action and the level of enforcement (per se or rule of reason). Horizontal activities occur between business at the same level of production (e.g. two manufacturers); vertical activities occur between businesses at different levels of production (e.g. manufacturer and distributor).

A. <u>Horizontal Activities</u>--Must look at the effect of the activity and the intent of the actors.

(1) <u>Joint Refusals to Deal</u>--Two or more sellers agree to refuse to sell to a buyer. Per se violation. (Sherman Act and Clayton Act)

(2) <u>Territorial/Customer Restrictions</u>--Two or more sellers divide market into exclusive territories or sell only to one type of customer. Per se violation (Sherman Act).

(3) <u>Monopolization</u>--One or more persons hold a monopoly power over a defined market. Monopoly power is presumed at 75 percent; no monopoly is presumed if market share is less

than 25 percent. Rule of reason applies. Must show that the defendant acted willfully. Monopoly based on superior product, business practices, historical accident is not outlawed. (Sherman Act)

B. Vertical Activities

   (1) Resale Price Maintenance--Occurs when the manufacturer forces the retailer to sell at a maximum or minimum price; only suggested prices are allowed. Per se violation. (Robinson-Patman Act)

   (2) Territorial/Customer Restrictions--Manufacturer gives retailer or wholesaler exclusive territory or customer list. Rule of reason applies; lawful unless there is an unreasonable restriction of trade. (Sherman Act)

   (3) Refusals to Deal--An individual seller may refuse to sell to an individual buyer. Rule of reason applies. (Sherman Act)

   (4) Tying Arrangements--Occurs when seller ties the sale of two products together. Usually the seller will refuse to sell a popular or patented (tying) product unless the buyer also purchases a related, less popular, unpatented (tied) product. Rule of reason applies and tying will be unlawful only if the seller holds significant market power in markets for both the tying and the tied product or unlawful purpose is discovered. Rule of reason applies. (Sherman Act)

   (5) Exclusive Dealing--Seller tries to prevent buyer from carrying products of other sellers. Modified rule of reason applies; outlawed only if competition is substantially restricted. (Clayton Act)

III. Mergers--Rule of reason applied under the Clayton Act.

   A. Horizontal--Competitors on same level of production. Allowed as long as it does not increase the possibility of monopoly or illegal agreements between competitors. Generally allowed if will increase efficiency of operations.

B. Vertical--Company at one level of production acquires a company at a different level. If a manufacturer acquires a retailer, a forward integration exists; if a manufacturer acquires a parts supplier, a backward integration exists. Rule of reason applies; outlawed if competition in either market is substantially restricted.

C. Conglomerate--Companies making different products merge. Usually occurs when one company wants to diversify or broaden its product line. Rule of reason applies; usually lawful because market structure (percentage of market) will not change.

IV. Exemptions from Antitrust Laws

A. Labor Unions--Allows collective bargaining agreements and strikes. Union collaboration with nonlabor may be prohibited. (Clayton Act)

B. Farming/Fishing Operations--Allows sellers to act as a cooperative in order to reduce costs. Price-setting is allowed as long as it is done for a proper purpose. Cannot be used to exclude competitors. (Clayton Act and Capper-Volstead Act).

C. Insurance--Exempted whenever state law governs operation of these companies. States usually have extensive regulation. Does not apply to boycotts, coercion, and other wrongful practices. (McCarren-Ferguson Act)

D. Foreign Trade--Allows exporters to form cooperatives to share costs and to compete with foreign sellers. Outlawed if trade within the United States is restricted or other exporters are injured. (Webb-Pomrene Act)

E. Baseball--Court decision rules that baseball is not part of interstate commerce; although theory has changed, sport is still exempt. Other sports are not.

F. Oil Marketing--Producers can set quotas for oil to be sold in interstate commerce. (Interstate Oil Compact)

Study Questions

Fill-in-the-Blank Questions

Widget Manufacturing and Thingamabob Creations are manufacturers of small tools used by carpenters. Widget and
Thingamabob secretly agree not to sell to Henry's Hardware.

The agreement between Widget and Thingamabob is an example of
_____ .
(joint refusal to deal, customer restriction)

Their action is an example of a _____ activity.
(horizontal/vertical)

If Henry sues the court will apply _____ .
(rule of reason/per se rule)

The _____ will apply.
(Clayton Act/Sherman Act)

True-False Questions

1.   The Sherman Act was the first antitrust act to be passed
      by United States Congress. ____

2.   All activities of fishing and agricultural cooperatives
      are exempt from the antitrust laws. ____

3.   A tying agreement is an example of a horizontal
      activity. ____

4.   The Sherman Act contains both criminal and civil
      penalties. ____

5.   In order to find a violation under the Sherman Act, the
      Justice Department need only find a restriction of
      trade; the intent of the actor is irrelevant. ____

6.   Price discrimination is legal if a difference in prices
      is caused by distribution or transportation costs. ____

7.   Section 1 of the Sherman Act deals with monopolies. ____

8.   The FTC has the power to issue guidelines for mergers
      and other possibly restrictive activities. ____

9.   If a restaurant chain merges with a meat-packing plant,
      a conglomerate merger has occurred. ____

10.   An agreement between manufacturers to sell only in certain parts of the country is per se illegal. ____

Multiple-Choice Questions

1.   Which of the following would be issued if sellers were unlawfully agreeing to set prices?

    a. Divestiture
    b. Dissolution
    c. Cease-and-desist order
    d. Treble damages

2.   Which of the following statements about the Sherman Act is false?

    a. It applies only to monopolies.
    b. Private parties may sue for treble damages.
    c. A rule of reason is applied to monopolies.
    d. It was the first antitrust statute.

3.   Cutlery, Inc., a manufacture of silverware, sells to thousands of retail outlets. Cutlery and its retailers agree that the forty-piece set of silverware will not sell for more than $200.

    a. Cutlery is guilty of a tying agreement.
    b. Cutlery is guilty of resale price maintenance.
    c. Cutlery is guilty of a horizontal price agreement.
    d. Cutlery has not violated any antitrust statute.

4.   Which of the following statutes provides an exemption from the antitrust laws to exporters?

    a. Sherman Act
    b. Volstead Act
    c. Webb-Pomrene Act
    d. FTC Act

5.   Which of the following actions by a labor union is not exempt from the antitrust statutes?

    a. Collective bargaining
    b. Agreements covering nonlabor activities
    c. Strikes
    d. All union activities are exempt

6.   Photo, Inc. produces an automatic camera which is in
     great demand. It requires retailers who sell the camera
     to sell only Photo, Inc. film with its cameras. The
     agreement between Photo, Inc. and its retailers is a:

     a.   retail price maintenance.
     b.   vertical customer restriction.
     c.   horizontal customer restriction.
     d.   tying agreement.

7.   The agreement in Question 6 is:

     a.   a per se violation of the Sherman Act.
     b.   a per se violation of the Robinson-Patman Act.
     c.   a possible violation of the Sherman Act (rule of
          reason)
     d.   exempt under the Clayton Act.

8.   Yard Products, a manufacturer of gardening tools and
     supplies, distributes its products in all fifty states.
     As an incentive to retailers, Yard Products agrees to
     license only one authorized distributor within each
     town. The promise by Yard Products is:

     a.   an example of vertical territorial restriction and
          the rule of reason applies.
     b.   an example of horizontal territorial restriction and
          the per se rule applies.
     c.   an example of vertical territorial restriction and
          the per se rule applies.
     d.   an example of horizontal territorial restriction and
          the rule of reason applies.

9.   Yannon Yogurt, a manufacturer and distributor of yogurt
     products, acquires Dan's Dairy Farm. This is an example
     of a:

     a.   conglomerate merger.
     b.   horizontal merger.
     c.   backward vertical merger.
     d.   forward vertical merger.

10. The Justice Department will outlaw the merger:

     a.   automatically; this type of merger is always
          prohibited.
     b.   if Yannon has a substantial share of the yogurt and
          milk market.
     c.   if Yannon has a substantial share of either the
          yogurt market or the milk market.
     d.   unless Yannon can prove that the merger will lower
          prices and benefit the consumer.

11.   If the Justice Department determines that the merger is illegal, the most likely remedy will be a(n):

       a.   dissolution.
       b.   divestiture.
       c.   award of treble damages.
       d.   cease-and-desist order.

12.   Which of the following activities is per se illegal?

       a.   Tying agreement
       b.   Monopoly
       c.   Price-fixing agreement
       d.   Vertical territorial restriction

13.   A monopoly will be presumed if a business has _____ percent of the market.

       a.   51
       b.   60
       c.   75
       d.   90

14.   Which of the following is <u>not</u> exempt from the antitrust laws?

       a.   Insurance
       b.   Fisheries
       c.   Oil Marketing
       d.   Trucking

15.   Which of the following is an example of a horizontal merger?

       a.   Bicycle manufacturer acquires retail outlet
       b.   Bicycle manufacturer acquires title manufacturer
       c.   Tire manufacturer acquired tire manufacturer
       d.   Tire manufacturer acquires chemical company

16.   Discount Pharmacy writes to Medi-All a drug manufacturer requesting permission to carry its product line. Medi-All refuses because it thinks that the personnel at Discount Pharmacy are not trained properly.

       a.   Discount Pharmacy can sue Medi-All for violation of the Sherman Act.
       b.   Discount Pharmacy cannot sue, but Medi-All can be fined for a criminal violation of the Sherman Act.
       c.   Medi-All cannot be sued only if the personnel at Discount Pharmacy are trained properly.
       d.   Medi-All has not violated an antitrust statute; individual refusals to deal are usually upheld.

17.   Excess Corporation manufactures over 75 percent of the robots in the country and is charged with a violation of the Sherman Act. Excess will be found not guilty if:

   a. it has a monopoly but keeps its prices low.
   b. the monopoly resulted from superior business practices.
   c. the monopoly resulted from mergers.
   d. it has less than 90 percent of the robot market.

18.   Mojo, a manufacturer of motorcycles, distributes its products to several hundred retailers. The retailers must agree not to sell competing motorcycles, although several sell cars. This is an example of:

   a. resale price maintenance.
   b. exclusive dealing.
   c. vertical refusal to deal.
   d. tying agreement.

19.   Mojo's practice is:

   a. a per se violation of the Sherman Act.
   b. a per se violation of the Clayton Act.
   c. a per se violation of the Robinson-Patman Act.
   d. not a per se violation; the rule of reason applies.

20.   Video Manufacturing, a manufacturer of televisions and related products agrees to sell 1,000 sets to X-Mart for $100 each. It agrees to sell ten sets to Y-Mart at $110 each. Video Visions:

   a. has committed a per se violation of the Robinson-Patman Act.
   b. has committed a per se violation of the Sherman Act.
   c. probably has not committed a violation of the Robinson-Patman Act because it probably costs less per set to deal with X-Mart.
   d. has not committed a violation of any antitrust act; price discrimination is never forbidden.

21.   Which of the following has been exempted from the antitrust laws by court rulings?

   a. Baseball
   b. Insurance
   c. Oil marketers
   d. Trucking

22.   Which of the following is a horizontal activity?

       a. Joint refusal to deal
       b. Price discrimination
       c. Resale price maintenance
       d. Tying agreement

23.   Which of the following is subject to a _modified_ rule of reason?

       a. Joint refusal to deal
       b. Price discrimination
       c. Resale price maintenance
       d. Tying agreement

24.   Ula's Unmentionables, a manufacturer of lingerie, acquires New West, a jeans manufacturer. This is an example of a:

       a. forward vertical merger.
       b. backward vertical merger.
       c. horizontal merger.
       d. conglomerate merger.

25.   A product-extension merger is a form of a:

       a. forward vertical merger
       b. backward vertical merger
       c. horizontal merger.
       d. conglomerate merger.

Answers to Study Questions

Fill-in-the-Blank Questions

The agreement between Widget and Thingamabob is a joint refusal to deal. A customer restriction is a division of customers between two sellers. This is a horizontal activity because Widget and Thingamabob are at the same level of production. This is a per se violation under the Sherman Act.

True-False Questions

1.   T.

2.   F. Cannot be used to restrict trade unreasonably or to injure competitors.

3.   F. It is a vertical activity involving a seller and a buyer.

4.   T.

5.   F. The Justice Department must also prove intent.

6.   T.

7.   T.

8.   T.

9.   F. This is an example of a backward vertical merger.

10.   T. It is a horizontal territorial restriction.

Multiple-Choice Questions

1.	a	11.	b	21.	a
2.	a	12.	c	22.	a
3.	b	13.	c	23.	d
4.	c	14.	d	24.	d
5.	b	15.	c	25.	d
6.	d	16.	d		
7.	c	17.	b		
8.	a	18.	b		
9.	c	19.	d		
10.	c	20.	c		

Chapter 31   Consumer and Environmental Law

General Principles

Consumer protection laws protect buyers from false advertising, usury, discrimination, and dangerous products. Consumer protection legislation developed in the 1960's; court opinions also created common law remedies. Today many of the consumer protection laws are created by administrative agencies. Environmental law also emerged in the 1960's. Federal statutes and administrative regulations provide protection against pollution and hazardous waste. In contrast to the chapters on contracts and sales, this section provides an overview of the law.

Chapter Summary

I.   Sources of Consumer Protection

    A.   Legislation--Uniform Commercial Code, Consumer Credit Protection Act, Magnuson-Moss. Covers advertising, packaging, warranties, product safety, credit. State and federal laws.

    B.   Administrative Law--Enforcement through rulings of the Federal Trade Commission, Consumer Product Safety Commission, and state agencies.

    C.   Private Organizations and Consumers--Better Business Bureau, small-claims courts, and class-action suits where one suit is brought on behalf of numerous consumers who have been injured by the same product.

II.   Advertising--Common law fraud protects from deceptive advertising but a violation is easier to prove under statutes and the FTC Section 5 because the intent of the seller is irrelevant.

A.   Deceptive Advertising--FTC defines as an ad which has more than one meaning. Can be caused by claims about quality, effects, price, origin, or availability. Omissions or incomplete statements may also be misleading.

B.   Bait and Switch--Seller advertises low price on one item (bait) which is usually unavailable and salesperson encourages the buyer to purchase another more expensive item (switch). Can occur if seller doesn't have adequate supply, refuses to supply within a reasonable time, or tells salespersons to sell other products.

C.   Labeling and Packaging--Fur, wool, flammable fabrics, food, and drugs are protected under special statutes. The Fair Labeling and Packaging Act requires labels to be accurate. Consumer goods must list name and address of manufacturer and distributor, net quantity and quantity of servings if number of servings is indicated. Enforced by FTC and Department of Health and Human Services.

III.   Sales and Credit

A.   Sales

(1)   Door to Door--FTC regulation gives consumers three days to cancel any sale. Also notification must be given in Spanish if the sale was made in Spanish. State law may also regulate; remedies are cumulative.

(2)   Mail-Order--Federal mail fraud statutes prohibit false sales. Post Office regulations allow consumers to keep unsolicited merchandise and sellers who send it are subject to prosecution (free samples are excepted). States may also regulate.

B.   Credit

(1)   Truth in Lending Act (TILA)--Also known as Consumer Credit Protection Act. (Federal)

(a) Disclosure of all credit terms required by the Federal Reserve Board. Advertisement of credit terms must include all information. Retail and installment sales, loans for the purchase of personal property or small amounts of real estate are covered. Applies to those who lend money as a regular part of business; individuals only, not corporations are protected.

(b) Prevents dicrimination in granting credit if denial is based on race, religion, age, marital status, and type of income. Questionnaires cannot ask.

(c) Liability for lost credit cards is limited to $50 per card for unauthorized charges made before credit card company is notified. Consumers are given procedure to follow for disputing errors on credit card bill.

(2) **Fair Credit Reporting Act**--Applies to credit bureaus, collection agencies, and anyone conducting an investigation. Consumer has the right to be notified of an investigation and has access to files. Procedures for correction of erroneous information are provided. (Federal)

(3) **Uniform Consumer Credit Code**--Comprehensive law including all of the above. Has been passed by only a few states.

IV. Health and Safety

A. **Health**--Food and Drug Act and Food, Drug and Cosmetic Act provide for product testing, regulate food additives and marketing of drugs, and protect against dangerous food or medicine. Also includes warning against dangers caused by tobacco. Special Act covers smokeless tobacco. Warnings must appear on packages and advertising (except billboards).

B. **Product Safety**--Acts involving individual products now combined under the Consumer Product Safety Act which created the Consumer Product Safety Commission. The agency develops safety standards, investigates product-related injuries, and publishes findings so that consumers can comparison shop. Can remove dangerous products from the marketplace and ban the sale of dangerous products.

V.   Environmental Protection

   A.   Sources of Law

      (1)   Common law--Allowed individual who was injured
             (apart from general public) to sue for a
             private nuisance; only a public authority
             could sue on behalf or more than one person
             (public nuisance).   Early cases limited the
             right to join more than one defendant.

   B.   Administrative Law--In 1970, Congress passed the
         National Environmental Protection Act. Council on
         Environmental Quality was created to study effects
         of pollution and every federal action that affected
         the environment was required to complete an
         environmental impact statement or a statement
         showing why a report is not needed.   The
         Environmental Protection Agency (EPA) is the
         coordinator of smaller agencies.

   C.   Types of Pollution

      (1)   Air--Clean Air Act passed on 1963 regulates
             pollution by automobiles.   Timetable
             established for ban of lead in gasoline and
             emission of carbon monoxide and hydrocarbons.

      (2)   Water--River and Harbor Act regulated
             discharging waste in public streams.   The
             Water Pollution Control Act gave enforcement
             powers to the EPA.   Regulations make water
             safe for swimming, protect fish and wildlife,
             and prevent discharge of polluting substances.
             The Clean Water Act sets up timetables for
             installation of pollution prevention devices
             by industry.

      (3)   Waste Disposal--Materials Policy Act regulates
             solid waste disposal and encourages recycling.
             Provides funding for research and pilot
             projects.   Resource Conservation and Recovery
             Act regulates disposal of hazardous waste.
             Hazardous waste must be disposed of properly
             and labeled when transported. New amendments
             tighten standards.

      (4)   Toxic Substances--Toxic Substances Control Act
             requires manufacturers and users to test
             chemicals for their effect on humans and on
             the environment. Also regulates use of known
             toxins.

Study Questions

Fill-in-the-Blank Questions

Today modern pollution control is governed mainly by _____ _____. (common law/administrative law)

Most consumer protection legislation was passed in the _____ _____. (1960's/1980's)

Truth in advertising is enforced by the _____. (FTC/CEQ/CPSC)

Testing of new consumer products is regulated by the _____ _____. (FTC/EPA/CPSC)

True-False Questions

1. Before Congress passed legislation, suits against seller for deceptive advertising were brought on the basis of nuisance. _____

2. Under the Equal Credit Opportunity Act, an applicant for credit can be asked to state the amount of alimony received annually. _____

3. The Truth-in-Lending Act regulates disputes between a credit card issuer and a consumer. _____

4. Smokeless tobacco ads do not have to include health warnings. _____

5. Postal regulations prohibit the mailing of unsolicited merchandise. _____

6. The Consumer Product Safety Commission can require manufacturers to test products, but it cannot force manufacturers to recall products which have passed safety tests. _____

7. The UCCC is a federal law. _____

8. The Better Business Bureau is an example of a federal agency which deals with consumer protection. _____

9.   The federal government and most states regulate door-to-door sales by allowing the buyer to cancel within a few days of purchase. ____

10.   The Council on Environmental Quality coordinates all federal agencies which set pollution standards. ____

Multiple-Choice

1.   A postal regulation provides that unrequested merchandise which is sent to a consumer:

   a. may be kept by the consumer at no charge and the seller may have committed an unfair trade practice.
   b. may be kept by the consumer if the consumer wishes to pay the cost and the seller may have committed an unfair trade practice.
   c. may not be kept by the consumer and the seller has not committed an unfair trade practice.
   d. may not be kept by the consumer even though the seller has not committed an unfair trade practice.

2.   Which of the following statements about door-to-door sales is _false_?

   a. They are regulated by the federal government.
   b. They are regulated by state government.
   c. The sellers must register with the Federal Trade Commission.
   d. Most laws provide that the buyer can cancel within three days of the sale.

3.   Which of the following type(s) of tobacco need not post a Surgeon General's warning?

   a. Cigarettes only
   b. Smokeless tobacco only
   c. Small cigars and smokeless tobacco
   d. All of the above must post warnings.

4.   Which of the following is not a duty of the Consumer Product Safety Commission?

   a. Research product-related injuries and deaths
   b. Grant approval for sale of new drugs
   c. Assist consumers in evaluating the safety of products
   d. Issue recalls of dangerous consumer products

5.   Another name for the TILA (Truth-in-Lending Act) is:

    a. CCPA.
    b. UCCC.
    c. CPSA.
    d. FCRA.

6.   Which of the following types of discrimination is __not__ prohibited by the Truth-in-Lending Act?

    a. Race
    b. Type of Income
    c. Amount of Income
    d. Marital Status

7.   Which of the following is __not__ part of the Clean Air Act?

    a. Ruling to decrease carbon monoxide emitted by cars
    b. Ruling to eliminate lead from gasoline
    c. Provide assistance to states in regulating air pollution
    d. Ruling to decrease the number of cars on national highways

8.   At common law, legal action against factories which polluted the air of an entire town:

    a. could be brought by private citizens as a public nuisance suit.
    b. could be brought by private citizens as a private nuisance suit.
    c. could be brought by city government as a private nuisance suit.
    d. could be brought by city government as a public nuisance suit.

9.   Which of the following agency(ies) was (were) created to regulate environmental protection?

    a. NEQ and EPA
    b. NEPA and NEQ
    c. EPA and CPSC
    d. NEQ and FDA

10.   Which of the following was the first federal statute to regulate water pollution?

    a. Water Pollution Control Act
    b. Clean Water Act
    c. River and Harbor Act
    d. Federal Highway Regulation Act

11. Which of the following is <u>not</u> concerned with waste disposal?

    a. RCRA
    b. Materials Policy Act
    c. EPA
    d. CPSC

12. Which of the following is the definition of "deceptive advertising" as adopted by the FTC?

    a. Advertising which the seller intends to induce the buyer to purchase the product
    b. Advertising which is capable of more than one meaning
    c. Advertising which contains a false statement about the quality of a product
    d. Advertising which offers low prices on a product which is not available.

13. Which of the following is a definition of "bait and switch"?

    a. Advertising which the seller intends to induce the buyer to purchase the product
    b. Advertising which is capable of more than one meaning
    c. Advertising which contains a false statement about the quality of a product
    d. Advertising which offers low prices on a product which is not available

14. Which of the following statements about the Federal Trade Commission is <u>false</u>?

    a. Rulings of the FTC cannot be appealed to the courts.
    b. The FTC has the power to define deceptive advertising.
    c. The FTC has the power to issue cease-and-desist orders.
    d. The FTC has the power to issue decisions on anti-trust cases.

15. Which of the following agency(ies) enforce(s) the Fair Packaging and Labeling Act?

    a. FTC only
    b. FTC and CPSC
    c. FTC and Department of Health and Human Services
    d. FTC and EPA

16.   Which of the following is not a part of the Truth-in-Lending Act?

       a.   Fair debt collection practices
       b.   Disclosure of interest rates
       c.   Outlaws discrimination in granting of credit
       d.   Regulates credit bureaus

17.   Which of the following statements about the UCCC is false?

       a.   It is a federal law.
       b.   It has been adopted by a few states.
       c.   It tries to regulate all aspects of consumer credit.
       d.   It regulates fine print in contracts.

18.   The difference between a case for fraud based on advertising and a case based on deceptive advertising is:

       a.   fraud is based on a statute; deceptive advertising is based on a statute and administrative regulations.
       b.   private persons may sue for fraud; only a government agency may sue for deceptive advertising.
       c.   fraud requires proof of the seller's intent; deceptive advertising does not.
       d.   fraud cases are heard in courts; deceptive advertising cases are heard by administrative agencies and are never heard by courts.

19.   Which of the following is not part of "bait and switch" advertising?

       a.   Seller advertises one product at a low price.
       b.   Salesperson discourages buyer from purchasing advertised item.
       c.   Salesperson refuses to negotiate with buyer for purchase of any item.
       d.   Seller fails to have sufficient quantities of the advertised item in stock.

20.   An environemntal impact statement:

       a.   must be issued when a federal project or law will affect the environment.
       b.   must be issued by the EPA for any governmental project.
       c.   is required by the Materials Policy Act.
       d.   is required only on federal projects involving more than $1 million.

21.   The CPSC:

    a.   regulates advertising of consumer products.
    b.   regulates safety of consumer products.
    c.   regulates pollution of consumer vehicles.
    d.   regulates hazardous waste disposal.

22.   Which of the following is <u>not</u> part of the Clean Water Act or Water Pollution Control Act?

    a.   Make water safe for swimming
    b.   Regulate traffic on navigable rivers
    c.   Regulate pollution of public waters
    d.   Issue guidelines for protection of fish in public waters

23.   Environmental law is:

    a.   any law which protects the consumer from health hazards.
    b.   any law which pertains to health and preservation.
    c.   any law which pertains to water, air, or land use.
    d.   any law which regulates buisness use of water, air, or land.

24.   Which of the following is a consumer right under the Fair Credit Reporting Act?

    a.   Equal opportunity for credit
    b.   Right to see credit reports issued by credit bureau
    c.   Right to procedure for settling billing disputes
    d.   Right to be free from harassment from creditors

25.   Which of the following statements about the Truth-in-Lending Act is <u>false</u>?

    a.   It applies to small real estate loans.
    b.   It applies to anyone who arranges for credit as part of a business.
    c.   It is a disclosure law.
    d.   It protects corporations and individual consumers.

Answers to Study Questions

Fill-in-the-Blank Questions

Modern pollution control is governed by administrative law. Most consumer protection legislation was passed in the 1960's. Truth in advertising is enforced by the FTC (Federal Trade

Commission). Testing of new consumer products is regulated by the CPSC (Consumer Product Safety Commission). The CEQ and EPA are concerned with environmental law.

True-False Questions

1.   F.   They were brought on the basis of fraud.

2.   T.

3.   T.

4.   F.

5.   T.   Unless the merchandise is a free sample.

6.   F.   THE CPSC has the power to recall dangerous products.

7.   F.   It is a uniform law adopted by a few states.

8.   F.   It is a private organization.

9.   T.

10.   F.   This is the job of the EPA.

Multiple-Choice Questions

1. a	11. d	21. b
2. c	12. b	22. b
3. d	13. d	23. b
4. b	14. a	24. b
5. a	15. c	25. d
6. c	16. a	
7. d	17. a	
8. d	18. c	
9. a	19. c	
10. c	20. a	

Chapter 32   Employee and Labor Law

General Principles

At common law, the employer controlled all aspects of
employment. Beginning in the 1930's labor unions were given
power to strike and to negotiate with management. Almost all
aspects of employment are now regulated by the federal
government including employment discrimination, job safety,
retirement programs, and other protection for workers.

Chapter Summary

I.   Unions and Collective Bargaining--Initially workers had
      no rights; then legislation was passed which favored the
      workers. Corrective legislation was then passed.

      A.   Norris-LeGuardia Act (1932)--First statute gave
            workers the right to peaceful strikes, picketing
            and boycotts.

      B.   National Labor Relations Act (1935)--Also known as
            the Wagner Act. Provided for collective bargaining
            and prevented owners from interfering in labor
            activities by influencing workers. Contributing to
            union funds, discrimination against union members,
            and refusal to bargain collectively. National
            Relations Labor Board was created to investigate
            violations and issue complaints. Pro-labor.

      C.   Labor-Management Relations Act (1947)--Also known
            as the Taft-Hartley Act. Swing back pro-management.
            allowed employers to lobby before union election.
            Prohibited business which hired only union members

(closed shop). Union shops, which require workers
to join union some time after beginning work, are
allowed but states may pass right-to-work laws
which outlaw union ships. President can obtain
injunction against strikes for eighty days if a
national emergency would otherwise exist.

D.   Labor-Management Reporting and Disclosure Act
(1959)--Also known as the Landrum-Griffin Act.
Regulates internal union procedures; requires
regular and open elections at which no communists
or convicts can be elected. Officials are
responsible for union funds. Also prohibited
hot-cargo contracts under which an employer is
induced to boycott non-union products of another.
This is a secondary boycott. Under the Taft-
Hartley Act a union cannot induce employees to
engage in secondary boycotts.

II.   Civil Rights Legislation and Employment--The Civil
Rights Act of 1964 was a comprehensive anti-
discrimination law; TItle VII relates to employment.

A.   Employers--Applies to local, state, and federal
governments. Also applies to unions with more than
fifteen members or which operate a hiring hall
which rations jobs. Private employers with more
than fifteen employees are also covered.

B.   Discrimination Methods--Affects not only hiring but
benefits and promotions. Job testing and minimal
education requirements must be related to duties
performed. Polygraph tests have been outlawed by
some states and collective bargaining agreements;
courts are split on employer's right to demand
lie-detector tests.

C.   Protected Workers--No discrimination on account of
race, color, or sex unless it is a bona fide
requirement of the job. No advertising separated
by sex. In contrast, an employer need only make
reasonable accommodation to a worker's religion.
Employee cannot force shift or job change or
violate union agreement. Some states have passed
laws which allow employees to declare a religious
day of the week on which they are not required to
work.

III.   Injury, Compensation, and Safety

A.   <u>Worker's Compensation</u>--State law which protects workers from injuries received on the job. Strict liability standard; accidental injuries and injuries resulting from negligence are covered, but intentional injuries are not. Some states allow recovery for injuries resulting from medical problems.

B.   <u>Occupational Health and Safety Act (1970)</u>--Federal law designed to regulate working conditions. Covers all employers who have at least one employee.

     (1) <u>Agencies</u>--Created administrative agency as part of the department of labor (OSHA). Has the power to issue standards, make inspections, and enforce rules by fining or giving cease-and-desist orders to violators. National Institute for Occupational Safety and Health is part of the Department of Health and Human Services and conducts research on health and safety issues. There is a review commission to hear appeals from action by OSHA employers.

     (2) <u>Reporting Requirements</u>--Employers with more than ten employees must keep records of job-related illnesses and injury and report them to the agency. Deaths and accidents involving more than five employees must be reported within two days and an inspection is required. Under recent court rulings, the agency cannot search an employer's premises without a search warrant.

C.   <u>Retirement and Security Income</u>--Social Security Act of 1935.

     (1) <u>OASDI</u>--Employers and employees contribute to a fund which pays for loss of income after a worker retires.

     (2) <u>Medicare</u>--Health insurance administered by the Social Security Administration. Applies to people over sixty-five and disabled persons of any age. Covers hospital and outpatient treatment; can buy additional coverage from the government.

     (3) <u>Unemployment Compensation</u>--Employers submit taxes to state governments which forwards them to the federal government. Funds are used to pay qualified individuals who lose their jobs.

(4) Private Retirement--Federal legislation governs activity of persons who administer private pension funds under the Employee Retirement Income Security Act (ERISA).

IV.   Fair Labor Standards Act (1938)

A. Child Labor--Children under sixteen cannot be employed full-time except for some family businesses. Children between sixteen and eighteen cannot be employed in jobs that would be hazardous to health. Some states require work permits of children under sixteen.

B. Maximum Hours and Minimum Wages--Most employees must be paid at one and one-half times the usual rate for more than forty hours in more than one week. Professional and union members covered by collective bargaining agreements are exempt. Also sets lowest wage which employer can pay to full-time employees.

C. Government Contracts--Davis-Bacon Act and Walsh-Healy Public Contract Act regulates wages to employers of contractors and subcontractors on federal projects. Also requires overtime and minimum wage to employees of federal suppliers.

Study Questions

Fill-in-the-Blank Questions

The federal agency which regulates employee safety is
_____.
(NLRB/OSHA/OASDI)

Most worker's compensation laws are _____ law.
(federal/state)

The _____ Act was the first labor law.
(Taft-Hartley/Norris-LaGuardia)

Private pension funds are regulated by _____.
(FUTA/ERISA/OASDI)

True-False Questions

1. Hot cargo contracts apply to coercion of employees only.
____

2.   Child labor laws prohibit any child under age sixteen from working. ____

3.   Title VII establishes the national minimum wage. ____

4.   The Occupational Health and Safety Act applies only to employers with more than fifteen employees. ____

5.   Governmental agencies are not prohibited from discriminating against employees on the basis of sex. ____

6.   The National Labor Relations Board has the power to investigate charges of unfair labor practices. ____

7.   Union shops are illegal in all states. ____

8.   The right-to-work law was passed by the United States Congress. ____

9.   Worker's compensation covers injuries received on the job regardless of the negligence of the injured employee. ____

10.   Management is prohibited from lobbying against unions prior to an election. ____

Multiple-Choice Questions

1.   Which of the following facts about a right-to-work law is true?

      a.   It outlaws union shops.
      b.   It is a part of federal labor law.
      c.   It provides disability payment for injured workers.
      d.   It prevents discrimination on the basis of an employee's sex.

2.   Which of the following acts outlawed hot-cargo contracts?

      a.   Taft-Hartley
      b.   Norris-LaGuardia
      c.   Wagner
      d.   Landrum-Griffin

3.   Which of the following is a duty of the National Labor Relations Board?

      a.   Regulate closed shops
      b.   Investigate unfair labor practices
      c.   Provide unemployment insurance for displaced members
      d.   Represent the employer in worker's compensation suit

4.   A secondary boycott occurs when:

    a.   union members strike against their own company.
    b.   union members induce other workers to strike against
          their company.
    c.   union members boycott another company.
    d.   non-union members boycott union products.

5.   Which of the following statements is _false_?

    a.   Collective bargaining is the right to enter into
          negotiations with management.
    b.   Collective bargaining was the subject of the first
          labor laws.
    c.   Right-to-work laws are designed to protect union
          workers.
    d.   Closed shops are illegal in all states.

6.   Which of the following is in correct chronological
      order?

    a.   Norris-LaGuardia Act, Wagner Act, Taft-Hartley Act,
          Landrum Griffin Act
    b.   Landrum-Griffin Act, Norris-LaGuardia Act, Wagner
          Act, Taft-Hartley Act
    c.   Taft-Hartley Act, Wagner Act, Norris-LaGuardia Act,
          Landrum-Griffin Act
    d.   Wagner Act, Taft-Hartley Act, Norris-LaGuardia Act,
          Landrum-Griffin Act

7.   Which of the following is not an unfair labor practice
      under the National Labor Relations Act?

    a.   Refusal to bargain with union representatives
    b.   Management's lobbying against a union
    c.   Management's contribution to a labor union
    d.   Discrimination against whistleblowers

8.   Which of the following is _not_ a provision of the
      Taft-Hartley Act?

    a.   Cooling-off period if ordered by a federal court
    b.   Right of president to request an injunction against
          strikes for eighty days
    c.   Closed shops made illegal
    d.   Hot-cargo contracts made illegal

9.   Which of the following does not deal with a public
      retirement fund?

a. OASDI
b. ERISA
c. Medicare
d. FICA

10. The Fair Labor Standards Act:

a. established a provision for a national minimum wage.
b. prohibits children under age sixteen from working in government jobs.
c. outlawed discrimination against women in the workplace.
d. established a fund for unemployment compensation.

11. Title VII of the Civil Rights Act:

a. banned all religious descrimination in the workplace.
b. banned sex discrimination in the workplace unless a bona fide job qualification is shown.
c. applies to all employers who use an instrumentality of interstate commerce.
d. applies to state, local, and federal governments.

12. Which of the following correctly describes the standard for an employee's right to religious freedom?

a. The federal law prohibits an employer from forcing an employee to work on his or her religious holiday.
b. An employer cannot force a worker to perform jobs against his or her religion.
c. An employer must make reasonable accommodations to an employee's religious practice.
d. An employer must grant a shift change to an employee who claims a religious right.

13. Which of the following describes the federal law relating to job testing?

a. An employer must show a relationship between the test and the job duties.
b. An employer may require a high school diploma for any job.
c. An employer may never require a polygraph test.
d. An employer may never require that an employee speak English.

14. Which of the following correctly describes an employer's responsibility under worker's compensation laws?

a.   The employer must pay if the injury was caused by an accident regardless of the time or location.
b.   The employer must pay only if the employee was not negligent.
c.   The employer must pay only if the employee did not commit an intentional tort.
d.   The employer must pay regardless of the employee's intent if the accident occurred on the job.

15.   Which of the following regulates worker safety?

a.   NLRB
b.   Right-to-work law
c.   OSHA
d.   OASDI

16.   Which of the following facts about the OSHA is _false_?

a.   It creates three agencies which deal with worker safety.
b.   It gives administrators the right to investigate job-related injuries and deaths.
c.   It allows administrators to inspect a plant without a warrant.
d.   It requires most businesses to keep records of on-the-job injuries.

17.   Warrantless searches by OSHA administrators:

a.   violate the Fair Labor Standards Act.
b.   violate the Fourth Amendment.
c.   violate Title VII of the Civil Rights Act.
d.   are legal if locations are not selected at random.

18.   Which of the following facts about FUTA is _false_?

a.   Employers and employees contribute to the fund.
b.   Funds collected by employers are remitted to state goverments.
c.   It is a federal law.
d.   It provides for a tax to fund unemployment compensation.

19.   Which of the following correctly describes regulation of child labor?

a.   Children under age sixteen cannot work.
b.   Children under age eighteen cannot work in dangerous jobs.
c.   States may require work permits for children.
d.   Children need not be paid for overtime.

20. The standard overtime wage is:

    a. twice normal wage.
    b. the same as normal wage.
    c. applied only to companies which receive federal funds.
    d. required when an employee works more than forty hours.

21. Medicare is administered by:

    a. OASDI.
    b. Social Security Administration.
    c. NLRB.
    d. OSHA.

22. Which of the following are subject to state laws?

    a. Right-to-work law
    b. Worker's compensation
    b. Right-to-work law and worker's compensation
    d. Minimum wage and right-to-work law

23. If a state has adopted a right-to-work law:

    a. closed shops only are illegal.
    b. union shops only are illegal.
    c. closed shops and union shops are illegal.
    d. employer's may refuse to hire non-union employees.

24. Which of the following correctly describes the use of lie detector tests in employment?

    a. Some courts have held that they are illegal.
    b. They are illegal unless the employer can show that the job requires honesty.
    c. They have been banned by federal law.
    d. They have been shown to be unreliable in most cases.

25. Which of the following deals with unemployment compensation?

    a. ERISA
    b. FICA
    c. OSHA
    d. FUTA

Answers to Study Questions

Fill-in-the-Blank Questions

OSHA (Occupational Safety and Health Administration) regulates employee safety. Worker's compensation is state law. The Norris-LaGuardia Act was first. Private pension funds are regulated by ERISA.

True-False Questions

1.   F. They also apply to employers.

2.   F. They cannot work full-time except in certain circumstances.

3.   F. Title VII regulates employment discrimination.

4.   F. Only one employee is requried.

5.   F.

6.   T.

7.   F. Closed shops are illegal; union shops are illegal in states with right-to-work law.

8.   F. It is state law.

9.   T.

10.   F. This is allowed under the Taft-Hartley Act.

Multiple-Choice Questions

1. a	11. d	21. b
2. a	12. c	22. c
3. b	13. a	23. c
4. c	14. c	24. a
5. c	15. c	25. d
6. a	16. c	
7. b	17. c	
8. c	18. b	
9. b	19. a	
10. a	20. b	

Chapter 33   Personal Property and Bailments

General Principles

Personal property includes all property except real estate (land) and items permanently attached to the land (fixtures). It includes chattels (touchable items), rights under a contract, and the use of services. Ownership of property includes the right to use the property and to transfer it. Transfer may occur by gift, by sale, or the owner may choose to abandon the property.

A bailment is a transfer of possession of property without transfer of ownership (title). Typical bailments include rental or repair contracts. It may help to think of taking a suit to the dry cleaners or renting a car. In most bailments, the owner of the property (bailor) agrees to pay the transferee (bailee) for the bailee's repair or storage charges. The bailee agrees to take care of the property and to return it to the bailor.

Chapter Summary

I.   <u>Nature of Personal Property</u>--Personal property includes all property except land (realty or real estate) and items permanently attached to the land (fixtures).

     A.   <u>Tangible</u>--Anything that can be touched, for example a car. A chattel is a good or livestock.

     B.   <u>Intangible</u>--Anything that cannot be touched, for example, a patent. It includes ownership in a corporation, rights under a contract, or the right to receive services. Although a corporate stock certificate or a contract may be written on paper and "touchable"; the documents only represent ownership. A stock certificate shows the right to vote on corporate policy and to receive dividends; a contract shows the right to sue if the other party does not live up to the agreement.

II.   Methods of Ownership--Property may be owned by more than one person at a time.

   A.   Fee Simple--Complete ownership by one or more persons. The owner has the right to use and dispose of the property as he or she wishes.

   B.   Tenancy in Common--Ownership by one or more persons. Each person has an undivided interest in the entire property and may only dispose of his or her portion. When a tenant in common dies, his or her share is determined by the tenant's will or it goes to the heirs. The shares do not have to be equal.

   C.   Joint Tenancy with Right of Survivorship--Ownership by two or more persons in equal shares. When one joint tenant dies, his or her share is split between the remaining joint tenents. If a joint tenant transfers his or her interest before death, the joint tenancy is destroyed and the new owners become tenants in common.

   D.   Ownership by Husband and Wife--A tenancy by the entirety is a joint tenancy between husband and wife. In a few states, husband and wife own community property, which includes only property acquired during the marriage.

III.   Methods of Acquiring Ownership

   A.   Sale, Purchase, or Production--A sale or purchase is the transfer of ownership for a price. Production occurs when the property is created by owner.

   B.   Possession--Applies mainly to capture of wild animals. The person who captures the animal retains ownership unless the capture was made by a trespasser on another's land (the landowner also owns the animal) or unless the capture is in violation of law (the states owns the animal).

C. Accession--Usually occurs when a non-owner makes changes, additions, or improvements to another's property. The original owner will retain the property unless the person making the improvements acted in good faith and the value of the improved item is substantially higher as a result of the improvement.

D. Confusion--Occurs when the property of several people is mixed and it is impossible to determine who owns what. If the goods are mixed wrongfully and intentionally, the innocent parties receive title to all of the property. Otherwise, the parties own the goods as tenants in common.

E. Gifts--Voluntary transfer of ownership without consideration. The donor gives the property to the donee. An inter vivos gift is made while the donor is alive; a gift causa mortis or deathbed gift must be made by the donor when the possibility of death is imminent. The gift is valid only if the donor dies. All three requirements listed below must be met in order for a valid gift to occur.

   (1) Donative Intent--The donor must intend to give, rather than sell, the property to another. A gift usually will be presumed if the donee is a relative or friend of the donor and if the gift is not most of the donor's assets.

   (2) Delivery--The donor must give control and possession of the property to the donee. The donor may hand the property to the donee (actual delivery) or give the donee access to the property (constructive delivery). For example, a car could be delivered by giving the keys to the donee. If a third party or agent is used, delivery is complete if the property is transferred to the donee's agent. If the agent is more closely associated with the donor, the agent must transfer the property to the donee.

   (3) Acceptance--The donee must agree to take the property.

IV. Rights of Finders--A person who finds property may acquire title to (ownership) it depending on the status of the property and the intent of the original owner.

A.   Mislaid Property--The owner deliberately leaves the property but forgets where it is. The finder acquires no rights because the owner will come looking for it. The finder is a bailee of the property.

B.   Lost Property--The owner involuntarily leaves the property. The finder acquires ownership rights which are good against everyone except the true owner. A finder who knows the owner but does not return the property is liable for conversion. Estray statutes give rewards to finders who turn the property into a governmental agency.

C.   Abandoned Property--The owner deliberately leaves the property with no intention of recovering it. The finder becomes the owner.

V.   Bailments--Transfer of possession of property; title is retained by the owner. The owner is the bailor; the party with possession is the bailee. The bailor must give the bailee exclusive rights to use and possess the property and the bailee must knowingly accept the property. (Hidden property cannot be the subject of a bailment.) The agreement between the parties may be express or implied.

A.   Ordinary Bailments

(1)   Types--Most bailments are for the mutual benefit of both parties; the bailor transfers the property for repair and the bailee receives compensation. A bailment for the sole benefit of the bailor occurs when the bailee agrees to act without compensation, e.g. storing goods in a friend's garage. A bailment for the sole benefit of the bailee occurs when the bailor lends the property at no charge.

(2)   Rights and Duties of the Bailee--The bailee has the right to possession of the property for the time of the bailment. The bailee also has the right to make reasonable use of the property and to be compensated for expenses incurred while using the property. Unless otherwise stated, the bailee is entitled to compensation for his or her services. A bailee may normally limit liability if the limitation is known by the bailor. Exculpatory clauses, which try to relieve a

bailee of liability for negligence, are usually not valid. The bailee has the duty to take care of the property or risks being sued for negligence. The bailee must also return the property at the end of the bailment; if the bailee does not return the property as promised, he or she will be liable for breach of contract or conversion. The bailee is not liable if a third party with better title takes the property or if the bailee uses due care.

(3) Rights and Duties of the Bailor--The bailor has the right to the return of the property in the same or better condition than when it was delivered to the bailee. The bailor has the duty to compensate the bailee, unless otherwise agreed. The bailor must notify the bailee of any known defects in the property. In a bailment for mutual benefit, the bailor must also inform the bailee of any defects which could be discovered by a reasonable inspection.

(4) Termination--By agreement, completion of the purpose of the bailment, demand by either party, operation of law, or an act by the bailee that is not a part of the bailment agreement.

B.   Special Bailments--Includes bailments by persons who move or store another's property as a part of their business. The standards of liability depend on the type of bailment.

(1) Common Carriers--Anyone who is publicly licensed to transport goods and persons. Includes airlines, train companies, and bus lines. The bailee is strictly liable for the bailed property unless he or she can show that loss or damage occurred due to an act of God, of the shipper-bailor, of a public authority, or of a public enemy. The bailee will not be strictly liable if the goods are fragile or easily destroyed. Subject to governmental rules, a common carrier can limit liability if the bailor is made aware of the limitation.

(2) Warehouse Companies--Liability for negligence and regulated by Article 7 of the UCC. A warehouseman-bailee has the power to issue a

negotiable   or   non-negotiable   warehouse
receipt. The warehouse receipt is a document
of title and can be used to transfer ownership
of the property without moving it. A
warehouse company can limit liability if the
bailor is given the option of paying extra for
more coverage.

(3) <u>Innkeepers</u>--Includes only those who offer
lodging to the public for transportation. At
common law, an innkeeper was strictly liable
for the property of guests but in most states
they are only liable for negligence if a safe
is provided for the guest's valuables.

Study Questions

Fill-in-the-Blank Questions

Uncle Paul decides to give a car to his favorite niece,
Stephanie. He gives the keys to the car to Stephanie's
husband, Brad, because Stephanie is out of town on business.
When Stephanie returns, Brad hands her the keys.

Uncle Paul is the _____.
                        (donor/donee)

Stephanie is the _____.
                        (donor/donee)

Delivery of the car occurs when _____ receives the
_____.   (Stephanie/Brad)
 (car/keys)

Giving the keys to Stephanie is an example of _____
delivery of the car.   (constructive/actual)

The gift of the car is an example of a(n) _____
gift.   (causa mortis/inter vivos)

True-False Questions

1. A stock certificate is an example of tangible personal
    property. ____

2. Sid writes a play; his ownership of the play is an
    example of production. ____

3.   A stereo installed in a car is an example of an accession. ____

4.   Estray statutes apply to lost property only. ____

5.   If confusion of goods is caused by the negligence of one party, the innocent party will obtain ownership of all the goods. ____

6.   A finder of mislaid property obtains title against everyone except the true owner. ____

7.   In a gratuitous bailment, the bailor has the duty to warn the bailee of all hidden defects including defects which would be found by a reasonable inspection. ____

8.   As a general rule, warehousemen are strictly liable for the loss of bailed property, although some exceptions exist. ____

9.   Valet parking is an example of a lease; it is not a bailment. ____

10.   An innkeeper is an example of a special bailee. ____

Multiple-Choice Questions

1.   Alice, Beth, and Cecil are co-owners of a horse. Alice owns 60 percent. Beth and Cecil own 20 percent each. When one of the owners dies, his or her share is to be divided equally between the remaining owners. This is an example of a:

      a.   tenancy by the entirety.
      b.   community property.
      c.   tenancy in common.
      d.   joint tenancy.

2.   Which of the following is not required for a gift?

      a.   Delivery to the donee or the donee's agent
      b.   Acceptance by the donee
      c.   Donative intent by the donor
      d.   Donative intent by the donee

3.   Which of the following statements about a gift causa mortis is false?

a. The donor must die in order for the gift to be valid.
b. Donative intent is not required.
c. The donor must make the gift thinking that he or she is about to die.
d. The gift is automatically revoked if the donor lives.

4. Cynthia delivers her dog to the Cozy Canine Kennels. She pays the kennel $15 for three nights. The dog is wearing an expensive leather collar. When Cynthia returns, she discovers that the collar is missing and that the dog is sick. The agreement between Cynthia and the kennel is an example of a(n):

a. involuntary bailment.
b. bailment for mutual benefit.
c. bailment for sole benefit of the bailor.
d. bailment for sole benefit of the bailee.

5. Cynthia decides to sue the kennel for the vet bills she incurred in curing the dog. If Cynthia can prove that the kennel did not take reasonable care of the dog, she can sue for:

a. breach of contract only.
b. negligence only.
c. breach of contract and negligence.
d. breach of contract and conversion.

6. The Cozy Canine Kennel is:

a. responsible for the loss of the leather collar.
b. not responsible for the loss of the collar because the kennel did not knowingly accept possession of the collar.
c. not responsible for the loss of the collar because it is an involuntary bailee.
d. not responsible for the loss of the collar because it is an involuntary bailor.

7. Which of the following is true?

a. An ordinary bailee may not limit liability; a special bailee can.
b. An ordinary bailee is liable only for negligence; a special bailee is strictly liable.
c. An ordinary bailment is one for mutual benefit; a special bailment benefits only one party.
d. A special bailee is one who stores or transports goods as part of his or her business; an ordinary bailee is not.

8.   A chattel is a synonym for:

   a.   real estate.
   b.   personalty.
   c.   goods.
   d.   intangible property.

9.   Ann and Mike own a car as joint tenants. Ann sells her
        share of the car to Pat.

   a.   Pat and Mike are joint tenants.
   b.   Pat and Mike are tenants in common.
   c.   Pat does not own a share in the car; Ann cannot
        transfer her interest.
   d.   Mike owns the car in fee simple.

10.   Sam is preparing to undergo open-heart surgery. He
        tells Paula that she may have his dog if he dies. Sam
        recovers.

   a.   The gift is valid unless Sam tells Pauls he wants to
        keep his dog.
   b.   The gift is valid; Sam cannot revoke the gift.
   c.   The gift is invalid; Sam recovered.
   d.   The gift is invalid; it was not in writing.

11.   Lucy finds a large tree branch on John's land. Lucy
        varnishes the branch and attaches felt mushrooms and
        leaves to the log. She sells it to her mother for $200.
        Lucy:

   a.   acquired title to the log, but she must pay John for
        this value.
   b.   acquired title to the log and owes nothing to John.
   c.   did not acquire title to the log because she found
        it on John's land.
   d.   did not acquire title to the log because John did
        not give her permission to use the log.

12.   Lucy's act of taking the log and improving it is an
        example of:

   a.   ownership by protection.
   b.   ownership by accession.
   c.   ownership by bailment.
   d.   ownership by gift.

13.   Paul lends his bicycle to Renee. Paul does not know
        that the chain is loose. The chain falls off while
        Renee is riding to the bank and she suffers minor
        injuries.

a.   Paul is responsible for Renee's injuries because Paul and Renee had a bailment for mutual benefit and Paul was obliged to warn Renee of any discoverable defects.

b.   Paul is responsible for Renee's injuries because Paul and Renee had a bailment for the sole benefit of the bailee and Paul had an obligation to warn Renee of any discoverable defects.

c.   Paul is not responsible for Renee's injuries because Paul and Renee had a bailment for mutual benefit and he had a duty to warn her of obvious defects only.

d.   Paul is not responsible for Renee's injuries because Paul and Renee had a bailment for the sole benefit of the bailor and he had a duty to warn her of known defects only.

14.   Which of the following is not a right of the bailee?

a.   Right to compensation
b.   Right to exclusive possession of the property during the bailment
c.   Right to any use of the property during the bailment
d.   Right to limit liability within reason

15.   Susan is moving from Georgia to Texas. She packs her china in a box with proper padding and marks "fragile" on the outside of the box. She ships the china by bus. When the china arrives, several pieces are broken.

a.   The bus company is responsible for the china on the basis of strict liability.
b.   The bus company will be responsible only if it was negligent in moving the china.
c.   The bus company is not responsible because china is inherently fragile.
d.   The bus company is not responsible if it offered Susan more protection in exchange for a higher transportation charge.

16.   Mike attends class in the Fine Arts Auditorium. He places his coat on the chair next to him but forgets to pick it up at the end of class. Barney, the janitor, finds the coat. The coat is:

a.   mislaid property.
b.   lost property.
c.   abandoned property.
d.   bailed property.

17. Barney:

   a. is an involuntary bailee and has no right to the property.
   b. is an involuntary bailee and has a right to the coat that is good against anyone except Mike.
   c. is a finder and has a right to the coat that is good against anyone except Mike.
   d. is a finder and has absolute right to the coat.

18. An estray statute:

   a. allows common carriers to limit their liability.
   b. allows warehousemen to issue documents of title.
   c. allows finders of lost property to claim a reward.
   d. allows donors to make gifts after death.

19. Which of the following is an example of a gratuitous bailment for the sole benefit of the bailor?

   a. Lending a car to a friend
   b. Storing a car in a friend's garage
   c. Renting a car from an agency
   d. Parking a car in a parking place at the airport

20. Which of the following is not a bailment?

   a. Lending a car to a friend
   b. Storing a car in a friend's garage
   c. Renting a car from an agency
   d. Parking a car in a parking place at the airport

21. Which of the following is not personalty?

   a. Fixture
   b. Chattel
   c. Good
   d. Intangible Copyright

22. Which of the following is not an element of a bailment?

   a. Transfer of possession
   b. Transfer of title
   c. Bailment agreement
   d. Personal property

23. Martin operates a car repair shop. Cindy leaves her car with Martin for repairs. Martin uses Cindy's car to pick up a package in a nearby town. The car is repaired and returned to Cindy. Martin:

    a. has breached the bailment agreement and is liable in
        tort or contract.
    b. has breached the bailment agreement and is liable in
        contract only.
    c. has not breached the bailment agreement because he
        has the exclusive right to use the car during the
        bailment.
    d. has not breached the bailment agreement because the
        car was not damaged.

24. Which of the following is <u>false</u>?

    a. At common law, innkeepers were strictly liable for
        the possessions of their guests.
    b. An innkeeper is an ordinary bailee.
    c. In most states, an innkeeper is liable only for
        negligence if the guest has an opportunity to store
        valuables in a safe.
    d. Many statutes have allowed innkeepers to limit
        liability for items which cannot be stored in a
        safe.

25. Which of the following is true?

    a. A warehouseman is an extraordinary bailee.
    b. A warehouseman is not allowed to limit liability.
    c. A warehouseman is strictly liable for goods stored.
    d. A warehouse may issued only non-negotiable documents
        of title.

Answers to Study Questions

Fill-in-the-Blank Questions

Uncle Paul is the donor; Stephanie is the donee. Delivery of
the car occurs when the keys are given to Brad, who is
Stephanie's agent. Transfer of the keys is sufficient because
it gives Stephanie access to the car. This is an example of
constructive delivery. The gift is inter vivos; a gift causa
mortis occurs only when the donor dies.

True-False Questions

1.   F. It is an example of intangible personal proeprty; a
         stock certificate represents ownership in the
         corporation.

2.   T.

3.   T.

4.   T.

5.   F.   The innocent party acquires title to the whole only
       if the goods are wrongfully and intentionally mixed.

6.   F.   A finder of mislaid property acquires no title; he
       or she is an involuntary bailee.

7.   F.   In a gratuitous bailment, the owner need only warn
       of known defects.

8.   F.   A warehouseman is liable under a negligence
       standard; this sentence describes the liability of a
       common carrier.

9.   F.   The valet keeps the keys, so it is a bailment.

10.   T.

Multiple-Choice Questions

1.	d	11.	a	21.	a
2.	d	12.	b	22.	b
3.	b	13.	d	23.	b
4.	b	14.	c	24.	b
5.	b	15.	c	25.	a
6.	a	16.	a		
7.	d	17.	a		
8.	b	18.	c		
9.	b	19.	b		
10.	c	20.	d		

Chapter 34   Real Property

You have seen that ownership of property includes not only the right to possess the property, but the right to use it or dispose of it. Ownership of real property includes the right to live on the land, the right to use it for production of minerals or crops, and the right to sell it or give it away.

One or more persons can own land at the same time and one person can own it in the present and another person can own it in the future. Non-owners, including tenants, neighbors, and the government may also have rights. Rights in land may be transferred by deed, by will, or by use without permission of the owner.

Chapter Summary

I.   The Nature of Real Property--Ownership includes rights to surface, the subsurface, items attached to the land, and to a limited extent, space above the land (air rights).

    A.   Air and Subsurface Rights--Air rights are not absolute, but the owner has the right to be free from low flying planes and other uses which destroy the enjoyment of the property. The subsurface includes water, oil, gas, and other minerals. The subsurface and the surface may be owned by different people.

B.   Crops and Fixtures--As a general rule, the land also includes items attached to the land such as growing crops or fixtures. A fixture is an item of personal property that has been attached to the land more or less permanently; the intent of the owner to treat it as real or personal property is the test. The more firmly attached, the more likely the property is a fixture.

II.   Freehold Estates in Land (Present and Future)--Ownership of land is called an estate. A freehold estate is one where the person on the land has ownership rights in contrast to a tenant who has the right to use the land but does not own it. Ownership in land may also be divided along a time span; some people may own the land for a limited period of time. Remember that the land always has to belong to someone.

A.   Fee Simple Absolute--Owner has all present and future rights, can dispose of the land as he or she wishes.

B.   Life Estate--Owner has the land only until he or she dies. At that time, the land may go back to the original owner (reversion) or to a third party (remainder). The rights of a life tenant are restricted because another has a future right to the land. As a general rule, the life tenant can receive income from the land but cannot injure it. If the land is injured, the life tenant may be liable for waste.

C.   Fee Simple Defeasible--The current owner has the right to the land as long as a specified condition exists. If the condition fails to exist, the property may go back to the original owner (possibility of reverter) or to a third person (executory interest).

III.   Non-Freehold Estates (Tenancies)--The possessor of the land (the tenant) and the owner of the land (landlord) are different people. The tenant has a non-freehold estate because he or she does not own the property.

A.   Types of Tenancies

(1)   Tenancy for Years--Has a definite termination date; it need not be in multiples of a year. The tenancy survives the death of either party.

(2) <u>Tenancy from Period to Period</u>--Has no definite termination date but the tenant pays rent on a regular basis. Either party must give notice before terminating the lease.

(3) <u>Tenancy at Will</u>--Exists when the landlord consents to the tenants occupancy. If no definite termination date is specified, the lease can be ended without notice. If rent is paid on a regular basis, the tenancy at will may become a tenancy from period to period.

(4) <u>Tenancy by Sufferance</u>--Exists without permission of the landlord and usually exists when a tenant wrongfully stays after the expiration of a lease.

B.   <u>Rights and Duties of the Parties</u>

(1) <u>Duties of the Tenant</u>--Must pay rent as it comes due. If the tenant wrongfully leaves, he or she still owes the rent. At common law, the landlord had no duty to try to find another tenant; statutes in many states have changed this. Also at common law, destruction of the premises had no effect on the tenant's duty to pay rent; this has also been changed by statute. Other duties of the tenant are spelled out in the lease which usually includes a clause requiring the tenant to take reasonable care of the premises.

(2) <u>Duties of the Landlord</u>--Must promise that the premises have been rented to only one party (covenant of possession) and that a tenant's lawful possession will not be disturbed (convenant of quiet enjoyment). In many states, the landlord also promises that the premises will be livable (warranty of habitability). Breach of the last two clauses may result in constructive eviction of the tenant and the tenant may sue. In addition, a landlord is required to keep the structure and all common areas in good repair.

(3) <u>Assignment and Subleasing</u>--An assignment is the transfer of <u>all</u> of the tenant's interest to a third party. A subleasing transfers <u>part</u> of the tenant's interest (usually for less time than the entire lease). In either case, the original tenant remains liable for the

rent. Under most leases, the tenant cannot transfer possession without the consent of the landlord although the landlord may waive this right if he or she accepts rent from the tenant's assignee.

IV.   Transfer of Ownership

A.   By Will or Inheritance

B.   Eminent Domain--The government takes private property for a valid public purpose. The Constitution requires that the owner by paid just compensation which is usually the market value of the land.

C.   Adverse Possession--A non-owner may obtain title by living on and using the land for a long period of time (usually three to thirty years). If the true owner checks the land with reasonable frequency, the adverse possessor can be evicted. Therefore, an adverse possessor must meet the following four requirements in order to gain ownership of the land.

   (1)   Actual and Exclusive--Must live on the land and prevent others from occupying it.

   (2)   Open and Notorious--Cannot hide when the true owner checks on the land.

   (3)   Continuous and Peaceable--If the owner evicts the adverse possessor, the time required must begin again.

   (4)   Hostile and Adverse--Must claim the property as an owner and not as a tenant; must be adverse to the claims of the true owner.

D.   Deed--Most common way of transferring land.

   (1)   Requirements--The deed must be in writing, contain the names of the transferor (grantor) and the transferee (grantee), show an intent to transfer the land, contain a description of the land, and be signed by the grantor.

   (2)   Types of Deeds--A general warranty deed is most common and contains the most protection for the grantee. A quit-claim deed promises only to transfer the interest of the grantor

which may be full rights or no rights at all. In most states, a deed must be recorded in order to prevent an assertion of right to the land by third parties.

V.   Non-Possessory Interests--Rights to use the land that belong to outsiders (not owners or tenants).

A.   Types--A profit is a right to come on another's land. It is revocable by the owner of the land. An easement is a right to use the property but not to take anything from it; it is not revocable. A profit is a right to take items from the land such as soil or minerals. It is not revocable. An easement appurtenant is one which benefits neighboring land; an easement in gross may benefit anyone. The following requirements relate only to easements and profits.

B.   Creation and Termination

(1) Creation--Expressly by deed or by implication. Also may be created by necessity between two adjacent parcels of land (e.g. a landlocked owner has the right to use a road that goes through another's property). Uninterrupted use may create an easement by prescription (similar to adverse possession but the user does not acquire title).

(2) Termination--The easement owner may deed the easement back to the landowner; the easement owner abandons use of the easement; or the easement owner buys the property of the landowner and the rights are merged.

(3) Sale of Property with an Easement Appurtenant --If the easement owner sells his or her land, the easement is transferred to the new owner. If the landowner whose property is burdened by the easement sells his or her land, the new owner must recognize the easement if the easement is publicly recorded or if the new owner knows or should have known that the easement exists.

Study Questions

Oscar owns some land in Georgia. He gives the land to his old high school. The deed contains the following language: "Old High School owns the land as long as it is used for educational purposes. If the land ceases to be used for educational purposes, then the land shall pass to my grandchildren."

Old High School has a _____.
                    (fee simple absolute/fee simple defeasible)

Oscar's grandchildren have a(n) _____.
                               (remainder/executory interest)

The deed _____ be recorded in order to transfer the land.   (must/need not)

Old High School's estate is _____.
                               (freehold/non-freehold)

Oscar's grandchildren have a _____ interest.
                                 (present/future)

True-False Questions

1. The surface and subsurface of land may be owned by different people. ____

2. An easement appurtenant can exist only on adjoining land. ____

3. At common law, a tenant was obliged to pay rent even if the leased premises had been destroyed. ____

4. A tenancy at will exists with the consent of the landlord. ____

5. A tenancy for years has a definite termination date.____

6. A tenancy is a freehold estate. _____

7. An adverse possessor must live openly on the land. ____

8. An easement by prescription is created by deed. ____

9. A deed requires the signatures of the grantor and the grantee. ____

10. When land is taken by eminent domain, the Constitution guarantees just compensation for the property owner.____

Multiple-Choice Questions

1. Susan rents an apartment from Larry Landlord. The lease states only that Susan must pay rent on the first day of every month but does not state when the lease expires. Susan has a:

   a. tenancy for years
   b. tenancy from period to period
   c. tenancy at will
   d. tenancy at sufferance

2. Susan discovers that the heating in the building does not work and that the pipes are rusty. Her bathroom floods whenever she uses the sink. Larry:

   a. has breached the covenant of quiet enjoyment and Susan has been evicted constructively.
   b. has breached the warranty of possession and Susan has been evicted constructively.
   c. has breached the covenant of quiet enjoyment but there is no constructive eviction.
   d. has not breached any warranty or covenant.

3. Which of the following is least likely to be considered a fixture?

   a. Kitchen cabinets
   b. Drapes
   c. Bed
   d. Ceiling fan

4. Which of the following is the highest and most complete form of land ownership and includes present and future rights?

   a. Fee simple defeasible
   b. Possibility reverter
   c. Fee simple absolute
   d. Executory interest

5. Randy rents a house from Mrs. Jones for a period of two years. At the end of the first year, Randy decides to move and transfers his interest to Cathy. Randy:

   a. has assigned his rights but is still liable for the rent.
   b. has subleased his rights but is still liable for the rent.
   c. has assigned his rights and is not liable for the rent.
   d. has subleased his rights and is not liable for the rent.

6.   Which of the following is <u>not</u> required for adverse possession?

    a.   Visible occupancy of the premises
    b.   Cultivation or building on the land
    c.   Possession over a required period of time
    d.   Exclusive possession of the land

7.   Which of the following is <u>not</u> required for a deed?

    a.   Name of the grantee
    b.   Signature of the grantee
    c.   Description of the land
    d.   Words of conveyance

8.   John owns a house near the beach. Every weekend for the last ten years, John's neighbors have crossed John's land to get to the beach. John has never given them permission to do so. The neighbors have:

    a.   an easement by prescription.
    b.   an easement by implication.
    c.   a profit by prescription.
    d.   a profit by necessity

9.   If John does not stop the neighbors from crossing his land, the neighbors will acquire:

    a.   adverse possession of the walkway to the beach.
    b.   an easement of the walkway to the beach.
    c.   a license to use the walkway to the beach.
    d.   fee simple absolute of the walkway to the beach.

10.   Which of the following occurs when a tenant holds over without permission of the landlord?

    a.   Tenancy by the entirety
    b.   Tenancy from period to period
    c.   Tenancy at will
    d.   Tenancy by sufferance

11.   Which of the following is revocable by the action of the landowner?

    a.   Profit in gross
    b.   Easement appurtenant
    c.   License
    d.   Life estate

12.   Bob owns some land. He deeds it to Mary. The deed contains the following words, "To Mary for life, then to my cousin Cora." Mary has a (n):

       a. life estate.
       b. executory interest.
       c. fee simple defeasible.
       d. possibility of reverter.

13.   Cora has a(n):

       a. executory interest.
       b. fee simple defeasible.
       c. remainder.
       d. possibility of reverter.

14.   If Mary damages the land, Cora may sue Mary for:

       a. breach of covenant of quiet enjoyment.
       b. breach of warranty for habitability.
       c. breach of warranty of possession.
       d. waste.

15.   Beth rents an apartment from Cecil. They agree that Beth can stay as long as she likes. Beth pays rent on the fifth of the month for eight months. When the tenancy was created, Beth and Cecil had a:

       a. tenancy for years.
       b. tenancy from period to period.
       c. tenancy at will.
       d. tenancy at sufferance.

16.   Which of the following cannot be terminated without notice by either party?

       a. Tenancy for years
       b. Tenancy from period to period
       c. Tenancy at will
       d. Tenancy at sufferance

17.   Paul deeds Cindy the right to come onto his land and mine for gold. Cindy has a(n):

       a. easement appurtenant.
       b. profit in gross.
       c. license.
       d. easement in gross.

18.   Which of the following correctly describes the difference between an easement and adverse possesion?

a.   An adverse possessor may obtain title to the land; an easement owner will not.
b.   An easement owner may obtain title to the land; an adverse possessor will not.
c.   An easement owner must live next door to the burdened property; an adverse possessor need not.
d.   An easement owner must use the land; an adverse possessor need not use the land.

19.   Which of the following will not terminate an easement?

a.   Merger
b.   Abandonment
c.   Deed from easement owner to landowner
d.   Eviction

20.   Which of the following gives the grantee only the rights possessed by the grantor?

a.   Warranty deed
b.   Covenant of quiet enjoyment
c.   Quit-claim deed
d.   Deed of possession

21.   Which of the following describes a joint tenancy by husband and wife?

a.   Tenancy by the whole
b.   Tenancy by the entirety
c.   Tenancy in common
d.   Tenancy in marriage

22.   Which of the following is not a future estate?

a.   Possibility of reverter
b.   Reversion
c.   Remainder
d.   Fee simple defeasible

23.   Which of the following describes a future estate held by the original owner of the property?

a.   Remainder
b.   Executory Interest
c.   Possibility of reverter
d.   Fee simple defeasible

24.   Which of the following is <u>not</u> made by a landlord?

    a.   Warranty of habitability
    b.   Warranty against waste
    c.   Covenant of quiet enjoyment
    d.   Warranty of possession

25.   The government's right to take private property for public use is called:

    a.   adverse possession.
    b.   eminent domain.
    c.   adverse domain.
    d.   constructive eviction.

Answers to Study Questions

Fill-in-the-Blank Questions

Old High School has a fee simple defeasible because it can lose the right to the land if it is not used for educational purposes. A fee simple absolute has no strings attached to ownership. Oscar's grandchildren have an executory interest; a remainder can only follow a life estate. Old High School has a freehold estate; a non-freehold estate is a tenancy. Oscar's grandchildren have a future interest.

True-False Questions

1.   T.

2.   T.

3.   T.

4.   T.

5.   T.

6.   F. A tenancy of any kind is a non-freehold estate.

7.   T.

8.   F. It is created by use against the wishes of the landowner.

9.   F. It requires only the signature of the grantor.

10.   T.

Multiple-Choice Questions

1.	b	11.	c	21.	b
2.	a	12.	a	22.	d
3.	c	13.	c	23.	c
4.	c	14.	d	24.	b
5.	a	15.	c	25.	b
6.	b	16.	b		
7.	b	17.	b		
8.	a	18.	a		
9.	b	19.	d		
10.	d	20.	c		

Chapter 35   Insurance, Wills, and Trusts

Insurance is a contract in which one party receives protection against risk in exchange for payment of money. The general rules of contract law apply to insurance policies. This chapter focuses on unique provisions of insurance policies.

Wills and trusts involve transfer of property. A will takes effect at death and transfers the deceased's property to persons named as beneficiaries. Certain formalities are required as protection against fraud. A trust also transfers ownership of property and may take effect during the life of the owner or at his or her death. A trust splits ownership; a trustee holds legal title to the property and manages it for the beneficiaries, who hold equitable title and are entitled to income from the trust property.

Chapter Outline

I.   Insurance--The purpose of insurance is to distribute or allocate risk.

    A.   Contract Terminology and Parties--An insurance contract is a policy. The person covered by the contract (the insured) pays money (premium) to the insurer. The insurance company (insurer or underwriter) promises to pay a beneficiary if certain contingencies occur. An insured may use a broker or agent to complete the contract.

    B.   Special Provisions

(1) <u>Insurable Interest</u>--In order to obtain an insurance policy, the insured must have a monetary interest or relationship to the subject of the policy. The owners and lienholders of property have a property interest at the time the property is destroyed. Life insurance may be purchased by relatives or by co-owners of a business (key-man insurance); the insured's interest must exist at the time the contract is made. The insurable interest differentiates an insurance contract from gambling.

(2) <u>Indemnity</u>--An indemnity policy (used in fire insurance) pays the replacement cost of the property destroyed <u>less</u> depreciation. Once the insurer pays, the insurer takes over any rights the insured may have had against third parties who caused the loss (subrogation).

(3) <u>Brokers and Agents</u>--A broker is an independent contractor and "works for" the insured. An insurance agent "works for" the insurance company.

(4) <u>Timing</u>--If a broker is used, no contract exists until the insurer accepts the policy. If an agent is used, the insured is covered when the application is made. A binder is written to insure coverage. Some contracts require payment of a premium or a physical examination before coverage takes effect.

C. <u>Defenses Against Payment</u>--The insurer can take advantage of any defense available for breach of contract.

II. <u>Wills</u>

A. <u>Terminology</u>--The maker of a will is called a testator (male) or testatrix (female). A probate court distributes the decedent's property according to the terms of the document; an executor(ix) may be named in the will to pay the debts of the estate and to arrange for the transfer of property. A gift of real estate is a devise; its recipient is a devisee. A gift of personal property is a bequest or legacy; its recipient is a legatee. The Uniform Probate Code (UPC) has been adopted in fourteen states.

B.   <u>Will Provisions</u>

   (1)   <u>General and Specific Bequests</u>--A specific
         bequest is an identifiable piece of property.
         A general bequest usually consists of money.

   (2)   <u>Abatement and Lapsed Legacy</u>--If the estate is
         insufficient to pay all the general bequests,
         each legatee takes a reduced share through
         abatement. If a legatee dies before the
         testator, the legacy may lapse. The property
         may then pass with the remainder of the estate
         or may pass to the heirs of the legatee (if
         the legatee is a family member of the
         deceased).

   (3)   <u>Residuary Clause</u>--All property of the estate
         not mentioned in the will passes to a residual
         legatee. This is usually the last clause in a
         will.

C.   <u>Requirements of a Valid Will</u>

   (1)   <u>Writing</u>--A formal will must be in writing and
         signed by the testator. A will can make
         reference to another written document which
         will be incorporated into the provisions of
         the will. A holographic will is written
         entirely in the testator's handwriting; it is
         valid in some states.

   (2)   <u>Witnessing</u>--A formal will must be witnessed.
         State law varies on the requirements of
         witnesses. Usually two or three mentally
         competent witnesses must watch the
         testator(ix) and they must sign the will in
         the presence of each other. Some states
         require that the witnesses be a certain age
         and/or disinterested (not receiving a benefit
         from the will). A witness does not have to
         read the will.

   (3)   <u>Publication</u>--Some states require the testator
         tell the witnesses that the document is his or
         her will.

   (4)   <u>Testamentary Capacity</u>--The testator must be of
         sound mind and of legal age when the will is
         made.

D. Revocation of a Will--A will does not take effect until the testator(ix) dies, so it may be revoked.

   (1) Acts of the Testator(ix)--The maker can revoke it by tearing, cutting, or obliterating it. A single provision cannot be crossed out or an additional term added without the formalities stated above.

   (2) Later Instrument--A codicil, or an amendment to the will, can revoke it in whole or in part if it is executed formally. A new will can also revoke a previous will. An intent to revoke previous wills, usually the first item in a will, is necessary or both wills will be read together although the second will control in the case of conflict.

   (3) Operation of Law--Can occur if the testator(ix) marries or has children after the will is executed. Unless it appears that the new spouse or child was intentionally omitted, they will be entitled to a share of the estate they would have received if the deceased had died without a will.

E. Will Substitutes and Probate Substitutes--A testator can avoid the expense of probate by giving his or her property away before death or by placing it in a trust or joint tenancy with right of survivorship. When a will is probated, the executor pays the deceased's creditors and distributes the remaining assets. Some states allow family settlement agreements where the legatees and devisees agree to divide the estate after the deceased's creditors have been paid. Other states allow property to be transferred by filling out forms or making a sworn statement (affidavit).

F. Intestacy

   (1) Procedure--If a person dies without a will, state law govern the distribution of the estate. An administrator(ix) is appointed to pay debts and distribute the property.

   (2) Order of Distribution

      (a) Wife and children (or grandchildren)--Wife receives one-half if there is one child; one third if there is more than one.

      (b)   <u>Wife and no descendants</u>--Wife takes all.

      (c)   <u>Lineal descendants</u>--If no wife or direct descendants, parents and siblings.

      (d)   <u>Collatertal heirs</u>--If no lineal descendants, nieces, nephews, aunts, uncles.

      (e)   <u>Next of kin of collateral heirs</u>--Adopted children may take; stepchildren may not.

      (f)   <u>Escheat</u>--If none of the above can be located, the property passes to the state.

  (3) <u>Method of Distribution</u>--Problems may arise if a testator(ix)'s child dies first and leaves grandchildren. The estate may be distributed per stirpes (along family lines) or per capita (an equal share to each survivor, regardless of family lines).

III. <u>Trusts</u>

A.   <u>Parties</u>--The owner of the property, who creates the trust, is the settlor. Legal title and management of the property is given to the trustee, who may receive a fee for services rendered. The beneficiaries acquire equitable title to the property and receive income from the property. Eventually the entire title may pass to the beneficiaries.

B.   <u>Types of Trusts</u>

  (1) <u>Express</u>--Usually set out in writing and intended to take effect by the settlor.

      (a)   <u>Inter vivos</u>--Created during the life of the settlor.

      (b)   <u>Testamentary</u>--Takes effect at the settlor's death.

      (c)   <u>Charitable</u>--Created for the benefit of the public and is made for educational, religious, or charitable purposes.

(d) <u>Spendthrift</u>--Created to protect an imprudent person from creditors; a small amount of the property is distributed at a time and creditors cannot attach the trust.

(e) <u>Totten</u>--The settlor is the trustee. Revocable until the settlor dies when the entire property passes to the beneficiary.

(2) <u>Implied</u>

(a) <u>Constructive</u>--Imposed by the court to prevent wrongdoing. A person wrongfully holding funds will be made into a trustee for the benefit of the rightful owner.

(b) <u>Resulting</u>--Occurs when one person holds property for another; it must be clear that a gift was not intended.

Study Questions

<u>Fill-in-the-Blank Questions</u>

Randall is the president of a small engineering firm. The other officers of the corporation are worried that the business may fail if anything happens to Randall. They convince him to buy life insurance which will pay the company if Randall dies. Randall submits an application to Bob, a broker, who forwards the application to Corporate Life Insurance.

Randall is the _____.
            (underwriter/insured/beneficiary)

The engineering firm is the _____.
                        (underwriter/insured/beneficiary)

The engineering firm _____ have an insurable interest.
                  (does/does not)

Bob is an agent of _____.
            (Randall/Corporate Life Insurance)

The memorandum which Bob will write to cover Randall while the contract is being transmitted is a(n) _____.
                                    (indemnity/binder/policy)

True-False Questions

1. The person who creates a trust is the testator. ____

2. A formal will must be witnessed. ____

3. A will may be revoked by burning or tearing it. ____

4. The Uniform Probate Code has been adopted by all fifty states. ____

5. A totten trust is a form of express trust. ____

6. A constructive trust must be in writing. ____

7. Collateral heirs are brothers and sisters of the deceased. ____

8. A gift of real property made in a will is a legacy. ____

9. If a person dies without a will, an executor(ix) will be appointed to distribute the estate. ____

10. An indemnity policy is a life insurance policy. ____

Multiple-Choice Questions

1. Which of the following is <u>not</u> a party to a trust?

   a. Beneficiary
   b. Trustee
   c. Testator
   d. Settlor

2. Mrs. Adams had her lawyer draft a formal will. After she had signed it in the presence of witnesses, she decided to leave her silverware to her cousin rather than to her daughter. She crossed out her daughter's name and substituted that of her cousin. Who will receive the silverware?

   a. Mrs. Adams' daughter
   b. Mrs. Adams' cousin
   c. Mrs. Adams' heirs because the will is invalid
   d. The state because the will is invalid

3. An oral will is called a _____ will.

   a. holographic
   b. formal
   c. codicil
   d. nuncupative

4.   Which of the following requirements of a formal will is
      not used in most states?

      a.   Writing
      b.   Witnessing
      c.   Publication
      d.   Escheat

5.   Which of the following is <u>not</u> a will substitute?

      a.   Inter vivos trust
      b.   Joint tenancy with right of survivorship
      c.   Totten trust
      d.   Constructive trust

6.   Aunt Mary has just died. In her will she left her ranch
      to her granddaughter Sally, her diamond ring to her
      sister Helen, $6,000 to the SPCA, and the remainder of
      her estate to her grandson, Bob. Bob was also named as
      the person to distribute the estate. Bob is an:

      a.   executor and a residuary legatee.
      b.   administrator and a residuary devisee.
      c.   administrator and specific devisee.
      d.   executor and specific legatee.

7.   Sally is a(n):

      a.   executrix.
      b.   legatee.
      c.   devisee.
      d.   testatrix.

8.   The SPCA will receive a:

      a.   specific bequest.
      b.   specific devise.
      c.   general devise.
      d.   general bequest.

9.   Helen predeceased Aunt Mary. Helen's gift is an example
      of a(n):

      a.   abatement.
      b.   escheat.
      c.   lapsed legacy.
      d.   intestate gift.

10.   Bob and Bill are partners. Bob suspects that Bill has
        been hiding business funds and placing them in a
        separate bank account. Bob should ask the court for a:

        a. constructive trust.
        b. resulting trust.
        c. testamentary trust.
        d. spendthrift trust.

11.   Tom creates a trust for his daughter. He is the settlor
        and the trustee. Tom has created a:

        a. testamentary trust.
        b. totten trust.
        c. resulting trust.
        d. no trust; Tom cannot be the settlor and the trustee.

12.   In the absence of express agreement, an insurance policy
        which is obtained through an agent of the insurance
        company, is:

        a. binding when the application is submitted because
            the agent works for the company.
        b. binding when accepted by the company because the
            agent is an independent contractor.
        c. binding when accepted by the company because the
            agent is an underwriter.
        d. binding when returned to the insured.

13.   Which of the following statements regarding a holograhic
        will is false?

        a. It is entirely in the handwriting of the testator.
        b. It must be witnessed.
        c. It is valid in only some states.
        d. It may dispose of real and personal property.

14.   Which of the following may cause a revocation of a will
        by operation of law?

        a. Tearing the will
        b. Executing a codicil
        c. Marriage after the will has been executed
        d. Marking through the will

15.   The duties of an executor include all of the following
        except:

        a. Paying the debts of the estate
        b. Overseeing the distribution of the estate
        c. Submitting the will to probate
        d. Acting as guardian for the testator's children

16.   Which of the following trusts would be used if you asked your roommate to keep your car for you while you went on vacation?

    a.   Resulting trust
    b.   Constructive trust
    c.   Totton trust
    d.   Inter vivos trust

17.   Although requirements for witnesses to a will vary; which of the following is is not required in most states?

    a.   Witnesses must see the testatrix sign the will.
    b.   Witnesses must see each other sign the will.
    c.   Witnesses must be of sound mind.
    d.   Witnesses must read and verify the will.

18.   Martha dies without a will; she is survived by her husband and two small children. In most states, the distribution will be:

    a.   one-third to Martha's husband; one-third to each child.
    b.   one-half to Martha's husband; one-quarter to each child.
    c.   one-half to each child.
    d.   all to Martha's husband.

19.   Which of the following are collateral heirs?

    a.   Spouse
    b.   Uncles and aunts
    c.   Children
    d.   Grandchildren

20.   Sam executes a simple will which states, "All of my property except for the money in my savings account is left to my wife, Bettina. The money in my savings account is to be apportioned to several charitable agencies as set out by a list in the possession of my attorney." The money in the savings accmount will go to:

    a.   Bettina, because the gift to the charities is a lapsed legacy.
    b.   Bettina, because the gift to the charities is an abatement.
    c.   The charities; this is an example of incorporation by reference.
    d.   The state; this is an example of an escheat.

21.   When an intestate person has no relatives, his or her
      property passes to the state. This is an example of
      a(n):

      a. abatement.
      b. escheat.
      c. lapsed legacy.
      d. devise.

22.   Sarah executes one will in which she leaves her land to
      Bud and her personal property to Meg. Sarah has second
      thoughts and executes a new will in which Bud receives
      the land, but Meg and Adrienne divide the personal
      property. Sarah's second will has no revocation clause.
      How will the estate be divided?

      a. Bud will receive the land; Meg and Adrienne will
          receive one-half of the personal property each.
      b. Meg will receive the personal property and Bud will
          receive the land.
      c. Sarah's heirs will receive all the property because
          the will is invalid.
      d. The state will receive all the property because the
          will is invalid.

23.   Which of the following documents must be witnessed?

      a. Holographic will
      b. Formal will
      c. Inter vivos trust
      d. Charitable trust

24.   Cindy, who has three children, dies intestate. One
      child, Mike, has died previously. He left two children
      (Cindy's grandchildren, Jay and Lonnie). Cindy's other
      children, Bob and Tom, survived her. Which of the
      following is the correct distribution of the estate if
      the distribution is to be made per capita?

      a. Bob, Tom, Jay, and Lonnie will receive one-fourth
          each.
      b. Bob and Tom will receive one-half; Jay and Lonnie
          will receive nothing.
      c. Bob and Tom will receive one-third each; Jay and
          Lonnie will split one-third.
      d. Bob and Tom will split one-third; Jay and Lonnie
          will receive one-third each.

25.   Which of the following is a synonym for insurer?

    a. Broker
    b. Underwriter
    c. Administrator
    d. Indemnitor

Answers to Study Questions

Fill-in-the-Blank Questions

Randall is the insured; the engineering firm is the
beneficiary. The engineering firm does have a monetary and
insurable interest. This is an example of key-man insurance.
Bob is a broker and is Randall's agent. Bob's memorandum is a
binder.

True-False Questions

1.   F. It is the settlor; a testator makes a will.

2.   T.

3.   T.

4.   F. It has been adopted by fourteen states.

5.   T.

6.   F. It is implied by the court and is never in writing.

7.   F. Collateral heirs are aunts and uncles; siblings are
          lineal descendants.

8.   F. It is a devise; a legacy is a gift of personal
          property.

9.   F. An administrator will be appointed.

10.   F. It is a policy that pays only for the value of the
          lost property.

Multiple-Choice Questions

1.	c	11.	b	21.	b
2.	c	12.	a	22.	a
3.	d	13.	b	23.	b
4.	c	14.	c	24.	a
5.	d	15.	d	25.	b
6.	a	16.	a		
7.	c	17.	d		
8.	d	18.	a		
9.	c	19.	b		
10.	a	20.	c		

Chapter 36   International Law In a Global Economy

General Principles

International law is the set of rules followed in business which crosses borders of countries. It is created primarily by treaties, and unlike national law, compliance is completely voluntarily. International law has developed rules to follow when laws of different countries conflict. In general an act of a foreign government undertaken for a legitimate public purpose will not be questioned by courts of other countries. The last part of this chapter focuses on the process of an international sale of goods and the application of American antitrust laws to transnational business.

Chapter Summary

I.   <u>Principles and Sources of International Law</u>--A nation can choose whether or not to follow international law; there is no way to force a nation to comply other than the threat of war.

    A.   <u>Treaties</u>--Contract agreed between nations. In the United States, the president negotiates the treaty which must be approved by a two-thirds majority of the Senate.

    B.   <u>International Organizations</u>--The United Nations issues declarations and resolutions agreed on by its members.

    C.   <u>International Court of Justice</u>--A branch of the United Nations, which hears cases involving U.N. resolutions. The parties must agree to allow the court to hear the case (voluntary jurisdiction).

II.   <u>Conflicts Between National and International Law</u>--When
        the laws of two nations contradict, the following
        principles are used to settle disputes.

        A.   <u>Act of State Doctrine</u>--The courts of one country
             will not interfere with the decision of a foreign
             government. This principle applies only if the
             government is formally recognized and if the action
             complained of occurs within one nation's borders.
             Used when private industry is taken for
             governmental use (expropriation). The private
             party must be compensated. If not, a confiscation
             occurs.

        B.   <u>Comity</u>--Used when the Act of State doctrine does
             not apply, that is when a government's actions have
             effects beyond its borders (extraterritorial). A
             United States court will recognize the decision of
             a foreign court or government only if that decision
             is consistent with American policy.

        C.   <u>Sovereign Immunity</u>--As a general rule most states
             (sovereigns) are immune from suit. The Foreign
             Sovereign Immunity Act determines when a foreign
             country can be sued in an American court. A
             country gives up its right to immunity if it waives
             it or if it conducts commercial activity in the
             United States. The act also governs the right of
             attachment of a country's funds kept in the United
             States.

III.   <u>International Business Transactions</u>

        A.   <u>Letters of Credit</u>--A buyer and seller use a bank(s)
             as an intermediary in a sales transaction. The
             buyer (account party) places an order with the
             seller (beneficiary) and arranges for a loan from
             the bank (issuer). When the seller ships the goods
             and shows the bank the bill of lading, the bank
             pays the buyer. A bank in the seller's country may
             help speed the transaction (advising bank). The
             seller must comply with the terms of the letter of
             credit in order to receive payment; courts are
             becoming more lenient and now only require
             substantial compliance. There are three contracts
             involved:

             1)   contract between buyer and seller
             2)   contract between buyer and issuer (loan)
             3)   contract between seller and issuer

B.   Sales Contracts--In addition to contract terms
      discussed   in   other   chapters,   international
      contracts should also include the language of the
      contract, the currency of payment, and which
      country's law is to be applied (choice-of-law
      clause). Many also contain arbitration clauses.
      In case of arbitration, the International Chamber
      of Commerce or other third party may be designated.
      The United Nations rules on arbitration have been
      adopted by fifty countries.

C.   Investment Protection--Used as a hedge against
      expropriation. May be contained in a national law
      or treaty. Some countries provide insurance for
      overseas   investors.   OPIC   (Overseas   Private
      Investment   Corporation)   insures   American
      businesses.

D.   Antitrust Laws--Sherman Act and other antitrust
      laws apply to international law whenever a per se
      violation exists or whenever the effect on American
      commerce is substantial. Plaintiffs and defendants
      can be Americans or foreign persons.

Study Questions

Fill-in-the-Blank Questions

Arnold Fabrics, an American manufacturer, is importing jute
from India. Arnold arranges with First Bank for a loan and
payment to Indian Industries, the jute supplier. First Bank
agrees to pay Indian Industries when it has proof that the jute
has been shipped to the United States.

This three-party transaction is a _____.
                                   (bill of lading/letter of credit)

Arnold Fabrics is the _____.
                       (issuer/account party/beneficiary)

First Bank is the _____.
                   (issuer/account party/beneficiary)

Indian Industries will receive payment when it presents a bill
of lading to _____.
              (Arnold Fabrics/First Bank)

True-False Questions

1. The International Court of Justice hears cases only if the parties agree to allow the court to hear the case. ____

2. Foreigners cannot sue as plaintiffs under American antitrust acts. ____

3. Expropriation occurs when a government takes private property for public use. ____

4. Comity is applied only when one country's laws are inconsistent with the laws of the United States. ____

5. OPIC is an international agency which drafts rules for arbitration between countries. ____

6. Municipal law is a synonym for foreign law. ____

7. A government's actions which involve commercial activity are protected by the Act of State doctrine. ____

8. Sovereign immunity applies only to individuals. ____

9. All treaties entered into by the United States must be approved by both houses of Congress. ____

10. A choice-of-law clause determines where a case involvng two countries will be heard if a dispute develops. ____

Multiple-Choice Questions

1. Which of the following does not apply to the acts of a foreign government which have extraterritorial effects?

    a. Act of State doctrine
    b. Sovereign Immunity
    c. Comity
    d. Antitrust laws

2. United States antitrust laws will apply to international transactions if:

    a. the act complained of has an effect on interstate commerce and the defendants are residents of the United States.
    b. the act complained of has a substantial effect on interstate
    c. the act complained of has an effect of foreign commerce.

    d.   the act complained of has a substantial effect on interstate commerce and the defendants may be residents of any country.

3.   The International Court of Justice is a branch of:

    a.   the United Nations.
    b.   the United States Department of Justice.
    c.   the International Chamber of Commerce.
    d.   OPIC.

4.   A treaty is ratified by:

    a.   the president.
    b.   Congress.
    c.   the Senate.
    d.   the House of Representatives.

5.   Municipal law is a synonym for:

    a.   international law.
    b.   national law.
    c.   antitrust law.
    d.   sovereign immunity.

6.   Which of the following is an international commission on trade law?

    a.   U.N. General Assembly
    b.   UNCITRAL
    c.   FSIA
    d.   OPIC

7.   The judicial rule that a court will not review acts of government which take place within its borders is a description of:

    a.   comity.
    b.   Act of State doctrine.
    c.   extraterritoriality.
    d.   sovereign immunity.

8.   Sovereign immunity is not a defense if:

    a.   a foreign state conducts a governmental act which affects United States commerce.
    b.   a foreign state takes private property for a proper public purpose.
    c.   a foreign state conducts commercial business in the United States.
    d.   the United States government takes private property for public use.

9.   Comity:

    a. states that a government cannot be sued for actions
        taken which have an effect only within its borders.
    b. allows the courts of one country to recognize the
        laws of another country.
    c. states that a government is always immune from suit.
    d. is a mandatory provision of international law.

10.   Which of the following statements is <u>false</u>?

    a. A letter of credit usually involves at least three
        parties.
    b. A letter of credit is used in sales agreements.
    c. A letter of credit is issued by a buyer to a seller.
    d. The beneficiary of a letter of credit is usually a
        seller of goods.

11.   Which of the following is not a contract under a letter
      of credit?

    a. Bank's promise to pay account party
    b. Bank's promise to pay beneficiary
    c. Beneficiary's promise to ship goods
    d. Beneficiary's promise to pay account party

12.   Which of the following would present a bill of lading in
      order to receive payment under a letter of credit?

    a. Issuer
    b. Buyer
    c. Account Party
    d. Seller

13.   FSIA is an abbreviation for:

    a. Foreign Services Immunity Act.
    b. Foreign State and International Arbitration.
    c. Foreign Sovereign Immunity Act.
    d. Foreign State Immunity Act.

14.   United States antitrust laws apply only if a court
      determines that:

    a. a per se violation has occurred or an act has a
        substantial effect on United States commerce.
    b. a per se violation has occurred.
    c. an act has an extenuating effect on intrastate
        commerce.
    d. an act has a substantial effect on international
        commerce.

15.   Which of the following is most likely to be involved in
        international arbitration?

        a. UNCITRAL
        b. International Chamber of Commerce
        c. OPIC
        d. FSIA

16.   A force majeure clause in an international sales
        contract:

        a. specifices that enforcement of the contract will be
            implemented by the International Court of Justice.
        b. designates the currency of payment.
        c. names the beneficiary of a letter of credit.
        d. protects the parties against acts of God or events
            beyond their control.

17.   The difference between expropriation and confiscation
        is:

        a. expropriation is committed by a government;
            confiscation is committed by an individual.
        b. expropriation refers to acts of a goverment within
            its borders; confiscation refers to extraterritorial
            acts.
        c. expropriation is a public taking of private property
            with compensation; confiscation is a taking without
            compensation.
        d. expropriation disputes are submitted to arbitration;
            confiscation disputes are not.

18.   Which of the following correctly describes the
        jurisdiction of the International Court of Justice?

        a. Jurisdiction is compulsory and the court interprets
            national laws.
        b. Jurisdiction is compulsory and the court interprets
            resolution of the United Nations.
        c. Jurisdiction is voluntary and the court interprets
            national laws.
        d. Jurisdiction is voluntary and the court interprets
            resolutions of the United Nations.

19.   Which of the following is a United States agency which
        provides protection for overseas investors?

        a. FSIA
        b. OPIC
        c. International Chamber of Commerce
        d. United Nations General Assembly

20.   Which of the following statements regarding sovereign
         immunity is true?

         a.   It can be waived if the defendant conducts
              commercial activity in another country.
         b.   It cannot be waived except by treaty.
         c.   It applies to individuals and governments.
         d.   It applies to extraterritorial acts.

21.   Which of the following statements about comity is _true_?

         a.   It applies only if actions by a foreign government
              are consistent with United States law.
         b.   It applies only if a foreign government acts within
              its own borders.
         c.   Its application is mandatory; it must be granted by
              American courts.
         d.   It is a synonym for the Act of State doctrine.

22.   Which of the following is an example of extra-
         territoriality?

         a.   Foreign country appropriates the land of an American
              investor in its country.
         b.   Foreign country sells goods below cost in the United
              States.
         c.   Foreign government declares martial law.
         d.   Foreign individual sues his or her government.

23.   Under a letter of credit, an advising bank is:

         a.   usually the seller's bank.
         b.   usually the buyer's bank.
         c.   one who issues a bill of lading.
         d.   one who lends money to the account party.

24.   Which of the following is not used in a letter of
         credit?

         a.   Note (loan)
         b.   Sales contract
         c.   Bill of lading
         d.   Treaty

25.   Which of the following correctly describes the courts'
         attitudes toward enforcement of a letter of credit?

         a.   All courts demand strict compliance.
         b.   All courts demand reasonable compliance.
         c.   The courts are split; some courts demand strict
              compliance and others demand reasonable compliance.

Answers to Study Questions

Fill-in-the-Blank Questions

The transaction is a letter of credit; a bill of lading is a shipping document which is presented by the buyer to the bank. Arnold Fabrics is the buyer and account party. First Bank is the issuer. Indian Industries will present the bill of lading to First Bank.

True-False Questions

1.   T.

2.   F. Foreign residents and residents of the United States are protected by the act.

3.   T.

4.   F. It is applied only when the laws of another country are consistent with the laws of the United States.

5.   F. It is a United States agency which provides insurance for overseas investors.

6.   F. It is a synonym for national law.

7.   F. Only governmental functions are protected.

8.   F. It applies only to countries or a subdivision of a country.

9.   F. A treaty must be ratified by a two-thirds vote in the Senate.

10.   T.

Multiple-Choice Questions

1.	b	11.	a	21.	a
2.	d	12.	d	22.	b
3.	a	13.	c	23.	a
4.	c	14.	a	24.	d
5.	b	15.	b	25.	c
6.	b	16.	d		
7.	b	17.	c		
8.	c	18.	d		
9.	b	19.	b		
10.	c	20.	a		

UNIT VII
ETHICS AND SOCIAL RESPONSIBILITY

Chapter 37   Ethics and Social Responsibility

General Principles

Criminal law defines the minimum ethical values that a society will accept; anyone who breaks these standards is subject to punishment. Ethics is a higher standard which asks what is fair, not necessarily what is legal. Ethics in the workplace may involve discrimination between employee's or an employee's decision to reveal an employer's "unethical" practice. A corporation often must choose between its legal duty to benefit its shareholders and an ethical duty to its customers.

Chapter Summary

I.   Ethics and Its Relation to Law--Ethics is a set of values or morals shared by members of society; it determines what is fair. Positive law (black-letter law) defines the lowest standards that a society will accept. As ethics change, the law will change also although it takes longer for the law to change.

II.   Ethics in the Workplace

    A.   Employment Discrimination--Under Title VII of the Civil Rights Act, employment discrimination of the basis of sex, religion, race, age, or national origin is illegal.

        (1)   Affirmative Action--Hiring policies which favor or compensate victims of past discrimination. Quotas or absolute numbers may not be used to reserve jobs for minorities, but the factors listed above may be used in choosing

applicants.   True (bona fide)   seniority systems   are   protected   even   though   its application may have a discriminatory effect.

(2) Reverse Discrimination--Response to affirm-ative action by majority groups. The majority now claims that it is being treated unfairly.

(3) Procedure--Affirmative action usually occurs where the defendant has shown a pattern or practice of discrimination. Parties can enter into a consent decree in which the defendant admits no fault but agrees to a settlement.

B.   Whistleblowing--An employee publicizes illegal or unethical actions of the employer.

(1) Disruption of Work--Whistleblowers can disrupt the   smooth   operation   of   business   and   an employee's sense of fairness may not coincide with   that   of   the   employer.   Only   some whistleblowing is protected.

(2) Legal Protection--Under common law and in some states today, the employer has the right to hire   and   fire   employees   at   will   unless   a statute   forbids   it.   Some   states   and   the federal   government   have   enacted   laws   which protect whistleblowers.   Other courts use a public policy exception or an implied contract between   the   employer   and   employee   which prevents the firing of an employee except when the action is reasonable.

III.   Ethics and the Corporation

A.   Social Responsibility--One view says that the corporation owes a duty only to its shareholders (owners) and that is the duty to make a profit and to help the company expand.   Others say that a corporation owes a duty to society as a whole to produce safe products.   Note that the product safety laws studied earlier provide minimum standards only.

B.   Social Responsiveness--At common law, a corporation could not donate to charity because it would injure the shareholders by diminishing profits.   Public policy or specific statutes allow a corporation to do this. Some corporations also may refuse to do business with countries or companies who have been accused of unethical practices.

C.   Social Investing--Decision to invest in a company
     based on the company's ethical or moral practices
     and not on the basis of profit alone. Ethical
     funds are invested by money managers on this basis
     although these companies have shown a lower rate of
     return. Some financial investors may be liable for
     investing in a socially responsible firm if the
     return on investment is imprudent or unwise.

D.   Shareholders v. Consumers--Shareholders have a
     limited right to bring suit on behalf of the
     corporation if they consider that the board of
     directors is taking action which may injure the
     corporation (derivative suit). Severely limited by
     the business judgment rule which protects reason-
     able decisions by directors. Safety procedures or
     provisions for a pleasant working place which may
     benefit employees may raise prices or lower profits
     to shareholders.

E.   Environmental Ethics--Government regulations sets
     the minimum standards. Anti-pollution devices raise
     prices and/or lower profits. If only one company
     decides to install the devices, then it will fail
     because its prices will be higher than those of its
     competitors who do not install costly equipment.

IV. Contracts, Bankruptcy, and Insurance

A.   Consumer Credit--Many stores which offer credit to
     people with bad or no credit records, may charge
     higher interest or use add-on clauses which
     provides for repossession of all goods purchased
     from a seller if the buyer defaults. Although the
     clause may seem unfair, without it many firms would
     be unwilling to lend money.

B.   Insurance--Extensive coverage may "encourage" the
     insured to act less responsibly and perhaps,
     negligently. This is a "moral hazard"; there is no
     incentive or encouragement for the insured to act
     responsibly.

C.   Bankruptcy--May create the moral hazard of encour-
     aging people to be careless with money and may
     allow solvent debtors to file in order to avoid
     certain debts. The new bankruptcy act allows a
     company to discharge collective bargaining
     agreements if the company has proposed a good-faith
     alternative which is rejected by the union. The
     rise in bankruptcy filings causes interest rates to
     rise and lenders to lend money more cautiously.

Study Questions

Fill-in-the-Blank Questions

The basis of shared social ethics is represented by
_____.
(social responsibility/positive law)

Title VII of the Civil Rights Act of 1964 governs
_____.
whistleblowing/employment discrimination)

Under current law, corporations _____ give money to
charity.   (can/cannot)

True-False Questions

1.   Ethics and the law reflecting ethical decisions change
      at the same time. _____

2.   A consent decree is a settlement in which the defendant
      admits no guilt. _____

3.   Add-on clauses operate to keep the overall cost of
      credit down. _____

4.   The Supreme Court has decided that race, sex, religion,
      and age may not be used as factors in hiring employees.
      _____

5.   Bona fide seniority plans are allowed under employment
      discrimination even if the plan causes more minority
      employees to be dismissed. _____

6.   A moral hazard is an inexpensive but unsafe product
      created by manufacturers. _____

7.   At common law, employers could dismiss employees with or
      without proper reason. _____

8.   A decision to ban the sale of products to South Africa
      is an example of corporate responsiveness. _____

9.   Lenient bankruptcy laws may cause a moral hazard by
      allowing a debtor to avoid creditors. _____

10.   A collective bargaining agreement cannot be discharged
      in bankruptcy. _____

Multiple-Choice Questions

1. Which of the following may result from a corporation's decision to take responsibility for producing products above minimum safety standards?

    a. The price of the product will rise and profits will increase.
    b. The price of the product will decrease and profits will increase.
    c. The price of the product will rise and profits will decrease.
    d. The price of the product will decrease and profits will decrease.

2. Which of the following is an example of a moral hazard?

    a. A decision to create unsafe but legal products
    b. A decision to invest funds in a company which follows unethical practices.
    c. A decision to use bankruptcy laws to avoid creditors when the debtor is not insolvent.
    d. A decision to employ an affirmative action plan at the risk of reverse discrimination.

3. Which of the following is not protected by the employment discrimination laws?

    a. Race
    b. Sex
    c. Religion
    d. All of the above are protected

4. Discrimination against majority groups is:

    a. at-will employment.
    b. affirmative action.
    c. reverse discrimination.
    d. a violation of Title VII of the Civil Rights Act of 1964.

5. Which of the following is least likely to result from whistleblowing?

    a. Disruption of the employer's business
    b. Dismissal of the employee
    c. Frivolous and annoying lawsuits
    d. Proof of discrimination in violation of Title VII

6.   Which of the following is an example of a legal but ethically questionable act of corporation?

    a. Donating corporate funds to charity
    b. Producing products abroad to avoid high labor costs
    c. Producing products abroad to avoid safety regulations
    d. Hiring males only for factory jobs

7.   Which of the following is the most likely remedy for disgruntled shareholders?

    a. Social investing
    b. Derivative suit
    c. Punitive damages
    d. Whistleblowing

8.   An add-on clause:

    a. is used in making loans to middle-class debtors.
    b. keeps down the cost of borrowing.
    c. is part of an insurance contract which provides for a higher deductible.
    d. is a way to insure socially responsible investing.

9.   Ethical funds are:

    a. money set aside by a corporation for donation to charity.
    b. money set aside by a corporation to defend product liability suits.
    c. money invested in a socially responsible corporation.
    d. money invested in compliance with the business judgment rule.

10.   Which of the following is least likely to result from lenient bankruptcy laws?

    a. Higher credit costs
    b. Demand by lenders for increased collateral
    c. Fewer debtors will file for bankruptcy
    d. Fewer loans to needy debtors

11.   Which of the following is a synonym for positive law?

    a. Moral law
    b. Affirmative action
    c. Legislation
    d. Black-letter law

12.   A pattern-or-practice suit is most likely brought by:

a.   minority job applicants.
b.   disgruntled shareholders.
c.   whistleblowers.
d.   angry consumers.

13.   Ethics is most closely related to:

a.   civil law.
b.   criminal law.
c.   social standards.
d.   legislation.

14.   In which of the following is a moral hazard likely to occur?

a.   Insurance
b.   Shareholder's rights
c.   Affirmative action
d.   Environmental regulation

15.   Actions of corporate directors are protected by:

a.   derivative suits.
b.   business judgment rule.
c.   Chapter 11 filings.
d.   ethical funds.

16.   Which of the following has been banned by the court in employment discrimination cases?

a.   Affirmative action
b.   Reverse discrimination
c.   Quotas
d.   Consideration of sex, race, or religion in hiring practices

17.   A violation of positive law will result in:

a.   civil or criminal penalties.
b.   no legal penalties but may be considered unethical.
c.   affirmative action under court order.
d.   derivative suit.

18.   Which of the following may not benefit from improved factory procedures?

a.   Shareholders in the corporate factory
b.   Consumers purchasing the product
c.   Both of the above
d.   None of the above

19.   Which of the following is not an example of corporate responsiveness?

    a. Donating corporate funds to charity
    b. Refusing to deal with the South African government
    c. Complying with rules of the Environmental Protection Agency
    d. Creating   job-training   programs   for   minority employees

20.   Which of the following statements about whistleblowing is _false_?

    a. At common law, the employer could dismiss employees at will.
    b. Some courts have created a public policy exception to protect whistleblowers.
    c. A federal law protects whistleblowers in all businesses.
    d. Some courts create an implied contract between employer and employee which is breached when an employer dismisses an employee for justified whistleblowing.

Answers to Study Questions

Fill-in-the-Blank Questions

Positive law is the description of basic ethics; it is the least common denominator. Title VII regulates employment discrimination. Under common law, corporations could not donate money to charity. Now specific statutes or public policy allow charitable donations.

True-False Questions

1.   F. Changes in ethics occur first; the law lags behind.

2.   T.

3.   T. It helps the creditor recoup losses.

4.   F. They may be used as factors but absolute quotas are forbidden.

5.   T.

6.   F.   A moral hazard is a practice or protection which causes a person to be careless, for example, medical insurance.

7.   T.

8.   T.

9.   T.

10.   F.   Under recent amendments, it can be discharged if the employer proposes a reasonable plan and the union refuses in bad faith to accept it.

Multiple-Choice Questions

1.	c	8.	b	15.	b
2.	c	9.	c	16.	c
3.	d	10.	c	17.	a
4.	c	11.	d	18.	b
5.	d	12.	a	19.	c
6.	c	13.	c	20.	c
7.	b	14.	a		